METHUEN'S
MANUALS OF MODERN PSYCHOLOGY

(Founder Editor C. A.
General Ed

Readings in Human Intelligence

Readings in Human Intelligence

Edited by

H. J. BUTCHER and D. E. LOMAX

METHUEN & CO LTD
11 New Fetter Lane London EC4

First published 1972
by Methuen & Co Ltd,
11 New Fetter Lane, London EC4.
© *1972 H. J. Butcher and D. E. Lomax*
Printed in Great Britain by

Printed in England by
Richard Clay (The Chaucer Press) Ltd.
Bungay, Suffolk

SBN hardbound 416 60250 9
SBN paperback 416 60260 6

Distributed in the U.S.A.
by HARPER & ROW PUBLISHERS, INC.
BARNES & NOBLE IMPORT DIVISION

Contents

Contents

Acknowledgements

The editors and publishers thank the following for their permission to reprint material from the sources listed below.

Academic Press Inc. and the author for Chapter 7 by A. R. Jensen, from *Analyses of Concept Learning* by A. R. Jensen (1966). American Educational Research Association for Chapter 12 by D. E. Broadbent, from *American Educational Research Journal*, 3 (1966), 281–95 (© by American Educational Research Association, Washington, D.C.). American Psychological Association for Chapter 3 by Q. McNemar, from *American Psychologist*, 19 (1964), 871–82, Chapter 5 by L. G. Humphreys, from *American Psychologist*, 17 (1962), 475–83, Chapter 6 by J. L. Horn, from *Psychological Review*, 75 (1968), 242–59, and Chapter 17 by N. Bayley, from *American Psychologist*, 23 (1968), 1–17. The Bobbs-Merrill Company Inc. for Chapter 11 by R. B. Cattell and H. J. Butcher, from *The Prediction of Achievement and Creativity* by R. B. Cattell and H. J. Butcher (© 1968 by the Bobbs-Merrill Company Inc.). The British Psychological Society and the author for Chapter 14 by C. Burt, from *British Journal of Psychology*, 57 (1966), 137–53. The Eugenics Society and the author for Chapter 22 by S. Wiseman, from *Genetic and Environmental Factors in Human Ability*, edited by J. E. Meade and A. S. Parkes (Oliver & Boyd, 1966). W. H. Freeman & Company, Publishers, for Chapter 13 by M. Minsky, from *Scientific American*, 215 (1966), 246–60 (© September 1966 by Scientific American Inc. All rights reserved). Holt, Rinehart & Winston Inc. for Chapter 9 by M. A. Wallach and N. Kogan, from *Modes of Thinking in Young Children* by M. A. Wallach and N. Kogan (© 1965 by Holt, Rinehart & Winston Inc., New York), and for Chapter 20 by J. McV. Hunt, from *Social Class, Race and Psychological Development*, edited by M. Deutsch, I. Katz and A. R. Jensen (© 1968 by Holt, Rinehart & Winston Inc., New York). McGraw-Hill Book Company for Chapter 10 by J. P.

Guilford, from *The Nature of Human Intelligence* by J. P. Guilford (©
1967 by McGraw-Hill Inc.). Charles E. Merrill Publishing Company
for Chapter 8 by D. Zeaman and B. J. House, from *Learning and Individual Differences*, edited by R. M. Gagné (1967). Oxford University Press
for Chapter 18 by J. McV. Hunt, from *Studies in Cognitive Development:
Essays in Honour of Jean Piaget*, edited by D. Elkind and J. H. Flavell
(© 1969 by Oxford University Press Inc.). The University of Chicago
Press for Chapter 16 by C. J. Bajema, from *Eugenics Quarterly*, 10
(1963), 175–87. University of Illinois Press for Chapter 1 by C. E.
Spearman, from *American Journal of Psychology*, 15 (1904), 206–21.
University of London Press Ltd for Chapter 4 by C. Burt from *The
Factors of the Mind* by C. Burt (1940).

Introduction

This collection of readings is designed as a companion volume to *Human Intelligence* (Butcher, 1968). The three main aims of that book were to treat 'intelligence' as a fundamental topic in psychology, to restore to the concept some of its waning respectability, and to provide an up-to-date guide to the very considerable variety of literature that is relevant in one way or another.

The aims of the present book are the same, but with particular emphasis on the last. Our intention has been to collect between two covers a representative selection of the most important recent articles and then let the writers speak for themselves. But first, a few words about the need for such a collection and about the principles of selection adopted.

Most lecturers would agree that a student trying to master a particular area of psychology finds a textbook on that area welcome, but capable only of providing a framework on which to hang more detailed study. It is just at that point – of advancing from the ingestion of a processed diet to the much stiffer task of coping with original articles – that many students encounter their greatest difficulties, material and psychological. Getting hold of the journals is often hard enough. Even people with access to university libraries may find that it is weeks or months before a particular issue is available; and the more seminal the article, the more common it is to find that the volume containing it has gone missing from the library and has not been replaced. The average position in polytechnics and colleges of education is probably worse, and to someone working on his own the difficulty of obtaining a bare minimum of essential research reports must be even more severe.

As already suggested, there are likely to be psychological as well as material difficulties in obtaining knowledge from scientific journals. The way in which articles are presented, the rigid structure imposed on them, the formal statement of hypotheses, the obscure and unexplained abbreviations, and most of all the unusual language employed, with its often contorted syntax and rough neologisms – all these factors may readily combine to set up a resistance to the whole mode of communication, especially in students whose previous education has been on the arts side. For these and other reasons, books of readings have been found increasingly useful in the last few years. They may be thought of not only as labour-saving devices to reduce mileage to and from the library, but also as forming an intermediate stage in the student's self-education, one at which he is ready to read something more specialized and technical than an introductory textbook, but at which he still requires help in selecting and evaluating this more specialized material. It is, therefore, desirable that articles reprinted should appear in a fairly intact state and also that some quite technical accounts should be included. The educative value of a book of readings will be reduced if it becomes a digest.

Apart from these general considerations, there is a special case for presenting a collection of readings about human intelligence. The parent book ranged widely and was based on the view that findings from half a dozen fields needed to be considered, including for instance, genetics, sociology and the new science of computer simulation. If the student is expected to familiarize himself with such a widely scattered literature, his difficulties as just described must be increased. Nor has there been available, before the present volume, any alternative collection of readings about intelligence broadly conceived.

All this said, it is by no means easy to provide a collection that will adequately meet the obvious need. The literature is very extensive and the number of papers to be included limited by the space available; the result has been that our first list of essential articles had to be cut right back and a stricter selection imposed. We became conscious of a number of criteria for such selection, which often conflicted, and had to impose our own ideas about their relative importance. Such ideas are always better made explicit; these are the main principles we tried to bear in mind:

1 Where possible to present whole papers or long and continuous sections from them, even though this necessitated a smaller number than could have been included by ruthless work with scissors and paste. The student should surely be encouraged to read and evaluate as far as possible what the writer thought worth putting in – not a bowdlerized version imposed by an editor at a later date.

2 To include for the most part only articles written at a high level of generality or reporting experiments with far-reaching implications. A selection of papers as specific as the typical research report would either have to be quite arbitrary, leaving a majority of topics uncovered, or would fill a dozen volumes. A large proportion of our readings are therefore review articles which direct the reader to more detailed and specific accounts.

3 To represent recent and current theorists and to sample mainly recent literature, rather than to provide a full historical background or reprint classic articles. At the time of writing, all but two of the twenty-two contributions were published during the last decade and the majority within the last five or six years.

4 To provide a balanced and synoptic view and to avoid the propagation of ideological prejudice. An example of such prejudice would be, for instance, to exclude papers emphasizing the importance of genetic (or equally of environmental) factors.

5 To emphasize, however, and to discuss more fully in much the same degree as in *Human Intelligence*, theories of intelligence or theories in which the concept of intelligence is implicit, rather than theories of abilities such as Guilford's, from which it is (despite the title of his 1967 book) virtually excluded. In this sense our selection will not be an unbiased sample of all work on abilities, especially when one takes into account the volume of recent work in the U.S.A. investigating very narrow and specific cognitive skills (see the forceful comments by Eysenck in our second reading, page 22).

6 In general to parallel the structure and order of topics in *Human Intelligence*, with two or three readings relating to each chapter. We soon found, however, that any such parallel would have to be quite rough, as many of the most useful articles cut across the division into chapters. Again, reasons of space made it impossible fully to carry through this plan, and we chose, rather than spread the butter too thinly, to omit readings corresponding to two of the chapters and to supply one only in the case of a third. These chapters were chosen as being the least theoretical and the most 'applied' or psychometric, being concerned respectively with principles of test evaluation, with the prediction of achievement, and with tests currently available.

The two older papers we have chosen, those of Spearman (1904) and Burt (1940) have been included for special reasons. The importance of the former – and particularly of the 'review of the literature' section (all we have reprinted) – is primarily historical; it is highly desirable when studying such topics as intelligence to be conscious of how rapidly psychological concepts (including 'intelligence') have emerged which, although familiar and over-learned at the present day, were then quite novel and suspect. Spearman's review is of great interest in this respect. Apart from the researches (in the last decade of the nineteenth century) of such forgotten figures as Oehrn, Boas and Gilbert, we hear his reactions to the work of Galton, J. McK. Cattell, Bagley, Wiersma, Binet, Simon, Kraepelin, Woodworth, Titchener, Thorndike, Ebbinghaus, Wundt. We notice also, perhaps rather smugly, that technical and statistical skills have developed since 1904. We should probably be wary about publishing a finding based on seven subjects in all that 'the average fencer is not quicker in simple reaction time than a trained scientist, and neither class shows an excessive rapidity'.

Apart from such incidental points of interest, our main reason for reprinting this extensive review of what may now seem somewhat archaic and primitive experiments is this: it is impossible fully to appreciate the revolution in thinking achieved by the joint influence of Spearman and Binet without a direct perception (as is provided by this paper) of the state of affairs in which they were working. In so far as the views described now sound naïve and the approach to the study of individual differences generally crude, this impression is a vivid indicator of the advances made (very largely by Spearman himself) during the first decade of this century.

The reason for including the paper by Burt was quite different, indeed opposite. So far from being a description of a climate of opinion that has now been superseded, it provides a more penetrating and profound account of the epistemology of correlational psychology than we have been able to find in the literature of the subsequent thirty years. Incidentally it also demolishes the recent stereotype of Burt as a whole-hogging and simple-minded hereditarian; he writes here, for instance (on page 61), 'The overt mental types, which are all that the psychologist can detect with his tests and rating scales, are related only in a very remote and indirect fashion to inherited types or tendencies. . . . Indeed, if there were any likelihood of establishing mental genotypes, factor analysis, I imagine, would hardly be the main line of approach which the genetic psychologist would adopt in his endeavours to discover them.'

The first modern article in our collection, that of Eysenck, is in that position as a consequence of the ordering principles we have already outlined, but it might well be the first in terms of lucidity, of concentration on fundamentals, and of the deceptive ease with which Eysenck relates and reconciles previously unrelated findings, including, for instance, the early work on reaction times (as surveyed in the Spearman paper we have already discussed), the research of Woodrow, the recent work of Jensen, information theory, and Eysenck's own experiments done in collaboration with Furneaux. In particular, Eysenck makes an overwhelming case for a rapprochement between intelligence testers and experimental psychologists and accounts plausibly for the development of the gulf that has existed between them for the last thirty or forty years at least. He ascribes this polarization in part to the apparent refutation by experiment of two hypotheses: (*a*) the relation of intelligence to reaction time, (*b*) its relation to performance of learning tasks; and he suggests convincingly that in both cases the supposed negative result was based on an over-simple approach. (The second of these relationships is also discussed and analysed in considerable detail in Paper 8 by Zeaman and House.)

The next four papers (excluding Burt's, already discussed) are by American psychologists who form an atypical and biased sample from their population in that they are all in varying degrees neo-Spearmanians or neo-Burtians. That is to say, they are all conscious of the conceptual advantages of a system that allows for a superordinate and coordinating kind of ability, although their views differ markedly in other respects. McNemar, Horn, Humphreys and Jensen (and, of course, R. B. Cattell, with whom Horn worked as a graduate student and associate) are perhaps the most eminent American theorists of individual differences who are not committed to the primacy of specific abilities.

Papers 7–13 follow approximately the content of Chapters 3–5 in *Human Intelligence* and provide a fuller account of some of the research discussed in those chapters. Although concerned with somewhat more circumscribed aspects of human intelligence than were the earlier readings, they still deal with large and primary topics, namely the relationship between intelligence and learning (8), the extent to which originality or creativity can be distinguished from intelligence (9), the relation of creative thinking to problem solving (10), how originality in thinking may be cultivated (11), current hypotheses about how information is stored in the brain (12), the characteristics and potentialities of machine intelligence (13).

At about this point, we suspect, the papers tend on the average to appear rather more technical, especially perhaps the three that are directly concerned with human genetics, the effect on subsequent behaviour of the uterine environment, and the complex factors affecting trends in national intelligence, i.e. the papers by Burt, by Stott and by Bajema. All these deal with subtle and controversial points and repay repeated reading. The Bajema paper may appear rather formidable at first sight, since it makes use of concepts and formulas unfamiliar to most psychologists. But it is in fact very clear in terms of logic, and suggests a plausible explanation of phenomena about which psychologists have long disputed.

Similarly, the paper by Nancy Bayley (on a thirty-year follow-up forming part of the Berkeley Growth Study) introduces one or two concepts that may not be very familiar, such as the circumplex pattern of correlations first defined by Louis Guttman. Again, once this idea is grasped, the paper is very lucid. The circumplex pattern of personality traits (p. 269), and the two axes imposed upon it, strongly recall the familiar Eysenckian taxonomy. It is also interesting to compare Bayley's account of empirical findings in the Berkeley Study with the theoretical account by Hunt in a later paper of hypothesized major factors in early infancy that affect subsequent cognitive development. Some of the Berkeley findings about the average course of development have recently been paralleled in long-term surveys in this country, such as the conclusion that girls' mental abilities stabilize at an earlier age (cf. Hindley, 1971) than those of boys.

The account by the late Frank Warburton and his associates of the construction of the British Intelligence Scale stands on its own. It remains the fullest account in many respects of this important work, although other aspects have subsequently been described by Warburton (1970) and Ward and Fitzpatrick (1970). The development of the Scale is continuing at the time of writing, with the main task of test development almost complete, but with standardization not yet attempted.

The three final readings combine to give a good idea of bridgeheads achieved in the struggle to isolate crucial environmental factors. Progress is being made quite fast in this area, as is illustrated by a comment Made by J. McV. Hunt). He points out that in the first version of his paper, written in 1962, he had emphasized the very broad and undifferentiated nature of the concept 'cultural deprivation' and consequently the lack of specificity in hypotheses about its effects. By the time he came to revise the paper some six years later, the scene had considerably changed and ideas about cultural deprivation had been greatly clarified.

Finally, it is our hope that this volume will convey to the student some idea of the ways in which psychological inquiry moves forward, and perhaps of the excitement that a confrontation with its raw facts can generate.

I

C. E. Spearman (1904)

'General intelligence' objectively determined and measured

American Journal of Psychology, 15, pp. 206–21

I HISTORY OF PREVIOUS RESEARCHES

Though mental correlation has in general met with great neglect, yet a certain number of psychologists, including several of the best known, have from time to time turned their attention that way also. It therefore seems advisable briefly to survey the results of these previous researches; they will be found on the whole to indicate some very remarkable conclusions.

Only those correspondences will be taken into account in which both terms compared are of a psychical nature; many investigators, after determining the chief measurements of their subject's mind, proceed to make their record still more complete by also noting his most prominent bodily characteristics and external relations, such as his height and weight, the shape of his head, the colour of his eyes and hair, the birthplace of his mother, etc. Such considerations, however interesting, do not quite fall within the scope of the present inquiry.

Galton. The first hint appears to have come from that suggestive writer, Francis Galton. As early as 1883, the latter stated that he had found men of marked ability to possess on the whole an unusually fine discrimination of minute differences in weight.[1] The pregnancy of this idea is unmistakable. But Galton appears to have been diverted from the point by other interests, and to have contented himself with the above general impression, without clinching the matter in systematic investigation. In 1890, however, on Cattell publishing an article about 'Mental Tests and Measurements',[2] a remark was appended by Galton suggesting the desirability of comparing such laboratory values with 'an independent estimate of the man's powers. . . . The sort I would suggest is something of this kind – "mobile, eager, energetic; well

[1] 'Inquiries into the Human Faculty'.   [2] *Mind*, 1890, p. 380.

shaped; successful at games requiring good eye and hand; sensitive; good at music and drawing". ' It will be seen that subsequent investigators have unanimously preferred a much less lively programme.

Oehrn. The earliest actual experiments in mental correlation seem to have been those of Oehrn,[1] in 1889, which at the same time furnished the starting point for that special branch termed by him, and now popular as 'Individual Psychology'. The latter must, however, be fundamentally distinguished from the 'Correlational Psychology' here advocated. For the former deliberately bases itself upon introspectively determined faculties and upon mental tests; whereas the latter *begins* by empirically ascertaining both the faculties and the precise value of the tests. The former endeavours to discover those small deviations from general law which constitute 'individuality';[2] while the latter, on the contrary, proposes methodically to eliminate individualities as an obstacle to further progress, being itself, no less than General Psychology, in search of laws and uniformities.

Oehrn tested ten subjects in Perception (*Wahrnehmungsvorgang*),[3] Memory, Association and Motor Functions. In accordance with his standpoint of *a priori* assumed faculties, he does not correlate the results with any independent estimate of his subjects' intellectual powers, but only the tests with one another. He eventually comes to the conclusion that Perception, Memory and the Motor Functions are 'proportional to one another', but that Association is rather inverse to all the others!

Boas. The comparison desired by Galton between these laboratory tests and on the other hand the psychics of practical life was, as far as I am aware, first undertaken seriously by Boas. In 1891, the latter examined no less than 1500 school children as to their Sight, Hearing and Memory; and then – following the example of the semi-anthropometrical correlations of Porter and others – he proceeded to compare their performances in the above respects with their 'Intellectual Acuteness' (as estimated by their teachers). On the first two heads, unfortunately, the results have never been published. But as regards Memory, wherein his method of procedure in the main resembled that of Oehrn,

[1] 'Experimentelle Studien zur Individual-Psychologie', Dorpater Dissertation, 1889.
[2] Oehrn and Krapelin propose to study 'the fine deviations from the great fundamental features of psychical conformity to law'; or again, 'to determine the essential differences between minds'.
[3] Even the term 'individual' does not seem very happy, since it chiefly awakens the impression of dealing with individuals as contrasted with masses. In this latter and much more appropriate sense, Wundt uses 'Individual Psychology' in opposition to his 'Folk Psychology' (*Grundriss der Psychologie*, p. 28).

the facts elicited were elaborated by Bolton,[1] who comes to the following conclusions:

The Memory Span increases with Age rather than with the growth of Intelligence.

The Memory Span measures the power of concentrated and prolonged Attention.

Intellectual Acuteness, while more often connected with concentrated Attention, does not require it, and it cannot be said that those pupils who are bright intellectually are more distinguished on account of their good memories.[2]

It will be observed that these results are in sharp antagonism with the view of many modern psychologists, notably Wundt, who would make Attention the very essence of intellectual power.

Gilbert. In 1893, at New Haven, another series of experiments was carried out upon an almost equally extensive scale, and is still among the most important contributions to the subject. J. Gilbert applied several mental tests to about 1200 children of both sexes, and then compared the results with their 'general ability' (again as estimated by their respective schoolmasters).[3]

On this occasion, the original assertion of Galton was to some extent practically corroborated. For Gilbert believes himself to find a real correspondence of Intelligence with Sensory Discrimination both of weights and of shades. He also, like Bolton, discovers a slight correspondence with Memory; in Gilbert's experiments the child, instead of learning by heart a row of figures, had to give his judgement as to when a musical tone had lasted just as long as a previously sounded standard one.

But the correspondence deemed most positive and conspicuous was that between Intelligence and 'Reaction-time'. This is particularly suggestive, on reflecting how especially this Reaction-time depends upon concentration of the Attention. The indication would therefore accord rather with Wundt's view than with that of Boas. Curiously enough, when the Reaction-time is made more obviously intellectual by further complications (Discrimination and Choice), then the above correspondence becomes reduced in amount.

Scripture. In the same little volume appears an account of an interesting experiment by Scripture, as to the correspondence between shortness

---

[1] *Amer. J. Psychol.*, 4, 362.
[2] *Amer. J. Psychol.*, 4, 379, 365, 366.
[3] *Stud. Yale Psych. Lab.*, 2, 40.

of Reaction-time and swiftness in lunging with foils. Unfortunately, his subjects are only seven in number. He feels himself, however, 'fully justified' in coming to the conclusion that 'the average fencer is not quicker in simple reaction than a trained scientist, and neither class shows an excessive rapidity'.[1]

The first part of the above sentence would well harmonize with the intellectuality found also by Gilbert to be connected with speed in pressing a button; but the latter part is difficult to reconcile therewith, at any rate without painfully lowering the credit of 'trained scientists'.

Binet and Henri. In France, towards the end of 1895, there appeared an important article of similar tendency, bearing the well-known signatures of Binet and Henri[2] and setting forth the urgent need of 'studying the relations that exist between different psychical processes'. They propose the following ten tests: Memory, Mental Images, Imagination, Attention, Faculty of Comprehending, Suggestibility, Aesthetic Sentiment, Moral Sentiments, Muscular Force and Force of Will, Cleverness and *Coup d'oeil.* By these means, they hope to measure off 'a personality' in a fairly exhaustive manner within one to one and a half hours.

In the tests themselves, there is a new feature to be noticed. Hitherto, these had been of the most elementary and unequivocal nature possible, as befits the rigour of scientific work. But this very simplicity had much increased the difficulty of making the test truly representative of any more complex psychosis. Binet and Henri appear now to seek tests of a more intermediate character, sacrificing much of the elementariness, but gaining greatly in approximation to the events of ordinary life. The result would seem likely to have more practical than theoretical value.

Next year Binet begins to put his interesting programme into execution.[3] He examines about eighty children and six adults as to powers of describing a picture shown to them, and by this means discovers the existence of five fundamental types of character, the 'describer', 'the observer', 'the erudite', 'the emotional' and 'the idealist'. 'It is perhaps the first result,' Binet remarks, 'that has hitherto been produced by the experimental study of the higher intellectual faculties.'

Binet then compares these new types with 'the notes and comments which the professors wrote about their pupils and which the Director of the school has carefully checked'. But as to the result of this comparison, unfortunately, only the following brief remark is made public:

[1] *Stud. Yale Psych. Lab.*, 2, 122.
[2] *L'année psychologique*, 2, 411.
[3] *L'année psychologique*, 3, 296.

'Of five pupils whom I had put into the "emotional" group, four had a cold temperament, a dry nature, and a little sensitiveness; the fourth alone seemed sensitive.'

Sharp and Titchener. The above work of Binet and Henri found a speedy re-echo from the other side of the Atlantic. Some experiments with the avowed object of examining this new class of test are now recorded as taking place at Cornell University under the direction of Dr Sharp and with the aid of Professor Titchener.[1] These were expressly intended to depart from the older 'German procedure' of dealing solely with the 'elementary mental processes', and instead were to subject to trial the 'French procedure' of directly handling the 'complex' ones.

The following classification was adopted: Memory, Mental Images, Imagination, Attention, Observation, Discrimination and Taste. The subjects consisted of three male and four female advanced students. No independent information was obtained concerning the subjects' respective mental powers, it being only attempted to ascertain whether the tests were consistent among themselves.

The results are not very encouraging:

> The lack of correspondences in the individual differences observed in the various tests was quite as noticeable as their presence.

> But little result for morphological psychology can be obtained from studies of the nature of the above investigation.

> In the present investigation the positive results have been wholly incommensurate with the labour required for the devising of tests and evaluation of results.

In conclusion, Sharp suggests the advisability of judiciously combining the characteristics of both the French and German procedures with one another.

Wagner. Almost simultaneously, the idea of collating mental tests with more practical methods of appraisement begins to take root in Germany also. In 1896, a series of experiments for the purpose of inquiring into the question of fatigue of school children was carried out at Darmstadt under the direction of Dr Wagner.[2] The children were from the new Gymnasium there and seem to have amounted in all to forty-four (though the information on this point is not very definite). The test investigated was the old one of Weber which had recently again been brought to the notice of pedagogical circles by Griesbach. As is well known, it consists in ascertaining how near together two points can

[1] *Amer. J. Psychol.*, 10, 348.
[2] Sammlung von Abhandlungen a. d. Gebiete der päd. *Psych.*, 1.

still be distinguished from one another by touch. On this occasion, care was taken to obtain an estimate of every child's Natural Talent (*Begabung*), Industry, Attentiveness, Nervousness and sometimes Temperament.

Unfortunately for our present purpose, the intention of the experiment was not so much to correlate these psychical qualities with the children's absolute sensitivity, as with the reduction in such sensitivity produced by the fatigue of lessons. This reduction is stated to correspond closely with the amount of Attention paid by the child, but to be almost independent of his Natural Talent. Once more, therefore, Attention and Ability are contrasted instead of being identified.

As far as concerns the children's unfatigued condition, our real present topic, we only learn that the nervous and indisposed have a less fine tactual sensitivity than the others.

Ebbinghaus. About the same time, another and much more extensive investigation was officially instituted in Silesia for the same purpose. Two entire upper schools, a boys' Gymnasium and a girls' High School, were before and after work subjected to three tests: the two old ones of Oehrn for Memory and Association (memorizing and adding numbers respectively), and the new 'Combination Method'[1] of Ebbinghaus. The latter observer in discussing the results devotes no less than one entire section out of four to considering the relations shown between these tests and the children's general intellect.[2]

He comes to the conclusion that the school order shows an appreciable correspondence with all three tests, but least so with Memory and most with his own new Combination Method. He particularly points out that in the last mentioned this correspondence applies, not only to difference of class, but also to position within each class; whereas in the case of Memory, he thinks that if anything the least intelligent succeed the best!

The Combination Method would appear to resemble the new type of test recommended by Binet and Henri, to the extent of presenting a rather intermediate character between the elementariness of normal laboratory work and the complexity of practical activities.

Wiersma. To depart for a moment from the chronological to the logical order of events, this favourable verdict of Ebbinghaus concerning his own new method was in 1902 strongly corroborated by some experiments of Wiersma.[3] This time, three schools were brought into service.

[1] In this, a purposely defective text is given to the subject, and the latter has conjecturally to fill in the missing parts.
[2] *Zeitschrift für Psychologie und Physiologie*, **13**, 401.
[3] *Zeitschrift für Psychologie und Physiologie*, **30**, 196.

Two of them were special training establishments for male and female teachers respectively, from 14 to 19 years old. The third was a 'Nach-bildungs' School, namely, one for those of both sexes who had already gone through the six classes of the elementary school; they consequently aged from 11 to 14. The total number came to about 300.

Following closely in the steps of Ebbinghaus himself, Wiersma finds his average results to improve regularly with the higher classes and with the higher sections of each class. He takes great pains to analyse the factors upon which such school position depends, and arrives at dis-tinguishing Age, Educational Development (*Entwickelung*) and Natural Talent (*Begabung*). In many complicated tables and graphs, he marshals evidence that the observed correspondence is most of all due to the last named factor.

Binet and Vaschide. In 1897, the question is again attacked by Binet, now in partnership with Vaschide.[1] But there is a remarkable return, as far as psychics are concerned, to the old less aspiring forms of tests. For he once more examines children in Reaction-time, Reaction-time with Choice, and Memory of Numbers. In addition thereto, he devises the ingenious test of motor ability called Dots (*petits points*); this consists in seeing how often the subject can tap with a pen on a piece of paper in five seconds. The intellectual order of the children was again obtained from their respective ranks in class. The subjects numbered forty-five and averaged about 12 years of age. The results are exactly opposite to those of Gilbert, for Binet sums up as follows: The Intel-lectual Order harmonizes badly with Reaction-times and harmonizes well with the Memory of Numbers.' But better than either appears the correspondence with his own 'Dots'.

This work was quickly followed by similar tests upon older subjects. For such purpose, Binet and Vaschide turned to the Normal School of Teachers at Versailles and there examined forty-three youths ranging from 16 to 20 years of age.[2] This time, the scanty positive results of the former experiments are still further reduced; for even the correlation with Memory is somewhat less in evidence. The relation with the 'Dots' again presents an unbroken regularity, but this time it seems to have become *inverse*, the stupidest tapping with the greatest speed!

Thorndike and Woodworth. Hitherto, we have only seen attempts to ascertain what I may, perhaps, be allowed to call 'statical correlation'. But in 1901, Thorndike and Woodworth make a vigorous onslaught upon the still more important and difficult 'dynamical correlation'. It is useful enough to know whether any child that 'taps', etc., with

[1] *L'année psychologique*, 4. [2] *L'année psychologique*, 4.

unusual slowness may thereupon straightway be considered as 'dull'; but it would be even more to the point to learn that daily practice with the tapping machine could make him any brighter.

Various previous researches had been distinctly encouraging in this matter. Stumpf declares: 'The power of mental concentration upon certain points, in whatever region acquired, will show itself effectual in all others also.'[1] Gilbert and Fracker had found that practice in one form of discrimination or reaction-time brought with it improvement in the other forms.[2] Scripture writes, intending apparently to include intellective activities: 'Development of will power in connection with any activity is accompanied by a development of will power as a whole.'[3] And again, Davis comes to the conclusion that 'practice in any special act' develops ability 'for all other acts'.[4]

The experiments of Thorndike and Woodworth, however, give once more a flat negation. The indications are rather that the effect of training in any one mental achievement is of little or no use for other intellectual performances, even very closely akin. The persons tested were carefully exercised until they had acquired considerable proficiency in judging the relative sizes of some pieces of paper of a particular shape. But this so obtained talent seemed completely to depart as soon as new tests were made with papers of a different shape, or even of a somewhat different size. Similar experiments in other sorts of feats led to the same result.

Binet. About the same time, we have another interesting and long contribution from Binet.[5] His subjects numbered eleven and were specially selected as being the five cleverest and the six most stupid out of a class of thirty-two. These two groups, the 'intelligent' and the 'unintelligent', were in all the tests opposed and compared.

Binet again confirms, and more positively than ever, that Reaction-time, either with or without the complication of 'Choice', has no correspondence with Intelligence. He also contradicts the correlation found by Griffing with the *extensive* dimension of Attention, in the form of simultaneously reading a large number of letters exposed to view for a small fraction of a second; though, curiously enough, Binet finds a certain amount of correspondence when he quite similarly exposes some arabesque designs. And finally, he finds no correlation with a new test of his own devising, namely: a trial how small a change in the rate of the beats of a metronome can be accurately detected.

---

[1] *Tonpsychologie*, 1883, part I, p. 83.
[2] *Univ. Iowa Stud. Psych.*, 1.   [3] *Psych. Rev.*, 6, 165.
[4] *Stud. Yale Psych. Lab.*, 6.   [5] *L'année psych.*, 6, 248.

But, on the other hand, his formerly successful method of Memory of Numbers now once more showed a marked correspondence with Intelligence. So also, and to a similar amount, is a correlation shown by Erasure of Letters (like that of Oehrn and Bourdon) and by Arithmetical Addition (more complicated than that of Ebbinghaus). So, again, do his new tests of Accuracy in Counting Metronome Taps and in Counting Dots. And so does his other new test, that of Copying: the subject is to copy a certain amount of writing, and then note is taken as to how many syllables he writes from each glance at the original; the more intelligent, the more words per glance.

But the fullest correspondence of all was presented by the very old test of Tactile Discrimination, which we have already seen successfully assayed by Wagner in 1896.

Binet is further strongly of opinion that all these correlations with Intelligence are most marked upon first trial, and that they continually diminish in proportion as the intelligent and unintelligent are both alike given more and more practice in the tests.

Simon. Directly inspired, apparently, by the last research, the correspondence there discovered between intelligence and the Copying test was now corroborated under new conditions. M. Simon conceived the idea that any such correlation should be manifested in especially prominent relief at the Vaucluse colony for backward children. He therefore tries seventeen of them, and finds in fact that, with one exception, all those classed medically as *Idiot* or *Imbécile* can copy fewer syllables at a time than do those merely termed *Dégénéré* or *Débile*.[1] He concludes enthusiastically as follows: 'Convenient, short, and exact, this copying of phrases at once constitutes a good method of diagnosing a child's intellectual development at the very moment of the experiment.'

Kraepelin, Cron. Other observers, however, would appear to have been less fortunate in this region. Their application of experimental tests, even to such trenchant opposition as intellectual health and disease, has not led them to results that they have felt able to pronounce entirely unequivocal. The careful work of Kraepelin and Cron[2] comes to the following close: 'At the end of these considerations, we will not hide from ourselves that the obtained results have fallen far short of what one is accustomed to expect from collective experiments with the simplest "mental tests".'

Reis. When the above investigation was renewed on a more extensive scale by Reis, the latter finds indeed that these tests perfectly well admit

[1] *L'année psych.*, 7, 490.   [2] *Psych. Arbeiten*, 2, 324.

of being executed upon the patients in the asylum; but the success would appear almost *too* great to fulfil the desired purpose, for often the patients prove the better performers of the two; a man, for instance, medically diagnosed as suffering from Dementia Paralytica with marked mental incapacity (*deutliche geistige Schwäche*) more than once comes out top of all fifteen subjects, sane and insane alike.

Cattell, Farrand, Wissler. Now we come to about the latest and in many respects far the most important of all these attempts to correlate laboratory work with the psychics of real life. For amplitude of design, special experience of the directors, and lucid collation of the results, nothing up to the present has approached the researches which for about the last ten years have been progressing at Columbia University under the guidance of Cattell.

In 1896, the latter, together with Farrand, allowed a brief insight into the nature and extent of the proceeding being carried on. But not till 1901 was the total upshot of all this labour carefully put together and published by Wissler.[1] By that time, 250 freshmen and some 35 seniors of the university, besides about 40 young women in Barnard College, had undergone the following elaborate series of tests (in addition to others not belonging to the present topic, such as anthropometrical, etc.):

Perception of Size	Reaction-time
Strength of Hand	Rate of Perception
Fatigue	Naming Colours
Eyesight	Rate of Movement
Colour-vision	Rhythm and Perception of Time
Hearing	Association
Perception of Pitch	Imagery
Perception of Weight	Auditory Memory
Sensation Areas	Visual Memory
Sensitiveness to Pain	Logical Memory
Colour-preference	Retrospective Memory

The general intelligence of each student was settled by his average grading in all the different university courses; an amalgamation of these separate gradings resulted in forming eleven classes.

This class standing and all the above laboratory tests are now, for the first time in the history of the problem, correlated together with some mathematical precision. The final conclusions are about as blankly negative as could well be imagined. We are summarily informed that

[1] *Psych. Rev. Monograph Supplement*, June, 1901.

The laboratory mental tests show little intercorrelation. The markings of students in college classes correlate with themselves to a considerable degree, but not with the tests made in the laboratory.

And on inspecting the actual figures representing the faint correlations in question, it is mathematically evident that not one of them is more than would be expected to occur by mere accidental coincidence.

Aiken, Thorndike and Hubbell. Finally, in 1902, there appears an interesting contribution to the subject from Aiken, Thorndike and Hubbell. Here 'the functions in question were much more alike than were those examined by Wissler.[1] We have examined the relationships between functions in an extremely favourable case.' Nevertheless, on the whole the previous negative results are once more strongly corroborated; when some mental functions usually regarded as most purely typical of the associative process are compared together, their correlation turns out to be 'none or slight'.

2 CONCLUSIONS TO BE DRAWN FROM THESE PREVIOUS RESEARCHES

Thus far, it must be confessed, the outlook is anything but cheerful for Experimental Psychology in general. There is scarcely one positive conclusion concerning the correlation between mental tests and independent practical estimates that has not been with equal force flatly contradicted; and amid this discordance, there is a continually waxing inclination – especially noticeable among the most capable workers and exact results – absolutely to deny any such correlation at all.

Here, then, is a strange enough answer to our question. When Laboratory and Life, the Token and the Betokened, are at last objectively and positively compared as regards one of the most important Functional Uniformities, they would seem to present no correspondence whatever with one another. Either we must conclude that there is no such thing as general intelligence, but only a number of mental activities perfectly independent of one another except for this common word to designate them, or else our scientific 'tests' would appear to have been all so unhappily invented as to lie outside the widest limits of those very faculties of which they are supposed to form a concentrated essence.

It is true that Functional Uniformities might conceivably exist of other kinds; but for any such there is even less evidence; nor would

[1] *Psychol. Rev.*, 9, 374.

they appear at all *a priori* probable, in view of the complete and surprising absence of that important one constituted by community of organism. Failing all Functional Uniformities, any connection between the experimental procedure and practical intelligence can then be no more than 'Conceptual'. But this is a position scarcely tenable for those whose chief claim is finally to have escaped from the endless tangle of purely introspective argument; moreover, such an admission would shear every experimental research of almost its whole worth and deprive the systems built thereon of their essential base.

Further, if thus the only correspondences hitherto positively tested, those between Intelligence and its variously supposed Quintessences, have totally failed to reveal any real existence, what shall we say of all the other by no means so apparently self-evident correspondences postulated throughout experimental psychology and forming its present backbone? To take one of the most extensive and painstaking of them, Dr Schuyten, from 1893 to 1897, continuously amassed evidence to prove a close relation of the middle European temperature with the faculty of 'voluntary attention' and even more generally with 'the intensity of cerebral activity'; he seems to have repeated his observations on about 500 different days, upon each occasion indefatigably proceeding round Antwerp from one school to another, visiting most of the time as many as eight. Now, his actual test of 'voluntary attention' and 'cerebral activity' consisted entirely in noting how many children kept their eyes on their lesson books for five consecutive minutes; but, as far as I am aware, there has not yet been any positive proof that this posture sufficiently coincides with all the other activities coming under this general term of 'voluntary attention', and in view of the universal breakdown of evidence for much more plausible correlations, Schuyten's *a priori* assumption can hardly be admitted as an adequate basis for his wide-reaching theoretical and practical conclusions. To try another example, we have seen that a favourite test, sucessively adopted by Oehrn, Bourdon and Binet,[1] is that of erasing from a printed page certain given letters of the alphabet; but sceptics are still able to contend that because any person can dash a stroke through a's and i's with unusual speed, he need not therefore be summarily assumed to possess an abnormally large capacity for discrimination generally speaking, say, for telling a fresh from an overnight deer's trail, or distinguishing sound financial investments from unsound. Precisely similar criticism may be extended to almost the whole mass of laborious attempts to establish

[1] The last named seems to have been the first to inquire into, rather than assume the range of function involved in this test.

practical applications of Experimental Psychology, whether for pedagogical, medical or other purposes.

Nor is the case much otherwise even with those stricter and more
theoretical researchers who are rather inclined to regard as superficial
any experiments involving large numbers of subjects. For, however
modest and precise may seem the conduct of their own actual investigation, it nearly always terminates with and justifies itself by a number
of sweeping conclusions; and these latter will be found to essentially
imply some assumed general function or process such as 'memory',
'association', 'attention', 'fatigue', 'practice', 'will', etc., and at the same
time that this function is adequately represented by the laboratory test.
To take for instance the speed of mental association, there is hardly a
psychologist of note who has not at some time or other made wide-
reaching assertions on this point, often indeed finding herein one of
the pillar stones of his philosophy; the more practically minded, as
Kraepelin and his school, content themselves with demonstrating the
details of its actual conduct, showing us how the rate will rise with
practice or on imbibing tea, how it sinks in proportion to fatigue or
mental disorder, how under the influence of alcohol it for a brief moment
slightly ascends and then becomes permanently and profoundly depressed. But all these conclusions are derived from observation of one or
two supposed typical forms of this 'association', while the extensive
experiments of Aiken, Thorndike and Hubbell reveal that every form
of association, however closely similar on introspection, must, nevertheless, always be considered separately on its own merits, and that
'quickness of association as an ability determining the speed of all one's
associations is a myth'.[1] The most curious part of the general failure to
find any correspondence between the psychics of the Laboratory and
those of Life is that experimental psychologists on the whole do not
seem in any way disturbed by it. But sooner than impute to them – the
avowed champions of positive evidence – such a logical crime as to
prefer their own *a priori* convictions to this mass of testifying facts, it
it perhaps pardonable to suspect that many of them do not realize the
full significance of the situation!

[1] *Psychol. Rev.*, 9, 375.

2

H. J. Eysenck (1967)

Intelligence assessment: a theoretical and experimental approach

British Journal of Educational Psychology, 37, pp. 81–98

I DEVELOPMENT OF A CONCEPT

Attempts to measure intelligence have passed through several stages since Galton tried to use the measurement of sensory processes to arrive at an estimate of the subject's intellectual level (1883), and McKeen Cattell (1890) employed tests of muscular strength, speed of movement, sensitivity to pain, reaction-time and the like for a similar purpose. These largely abortive efforts were followed by the first stage of intelligence measurement properly so called; it may with truth be labelled the *g* phase because both Spearman (1904) and Binet and Simon (1905) stressed the importance of a *general factor of intellectual ability*, Binet contributing mainly by the construction of test items and the invention of the concept of mental age, Spearman contributing mainly by the application of correlational methods and the invention of factor analysis.

The second stage was concerned with the proper definition of intelligence, and theories regarding its nature. Several books concerned themselves with this problem (Thurstone, 1926; Spearman, 1923), and a number of symposia were held (*Brit. J. Psychol.*, 1910; *J. Educ. Psychol.*, 1921; *Internat. Congress of Psychol.*, 1923). Among the theories canvassed were 'mental speed' hypotheses which placed the burden of intellectual attainment on speed of mental functioning, and 'learning' hypotheses which protested that the ability to learn new material was fundamental. Both hypotheses faced difficulties; the fact that reaction times showed no relation to ability tended to discourage believers in the 'speed' hypothesis, and the negative results of the large-scale work of Woodrow (1946) on the relation between different learning tasks and intelligence discouraged believers in the 'learning' hypothesis. Psychologists learned to agree to disagree, and to present their work with the dictum that 'intelligence is what intelligence tests measure' – a saying less circular than it sounds, but only acceptable if all intelligence tests did, in fact, measure the same thing, which they quite emphatically did not.

We thus reach the third stage, which is essentially a continuation of the early factor analytic approach, but now fortified by recourse to multiple factors and matrix algebra. This phase owes most to Thurstone, but Thomson, Burt, Holzinger and many others made valiant contributions. In this factorial phase, investigators went back to Binet's idea of different mental faculties making up the complex concept of intelli-

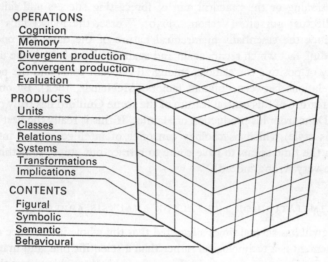

OPERATIONS
Cognition
Memory
Divergent production
Convergent production
Evaluation

PRODUCTS
Units
Classes
Relations
Systems
Transformations
Implications

CONTENTS
Figural
Symbolic
Semantic
Behavioural

Fig. 2.1 Model of the structure of intellect (Guilford, 1966).

gence, and used factor analysis to sort out these alleged faculties; they emerged with verbal, numerical, perceptual, memory, visuo-spatial and many other factors. At first, Thurstone and his followers believed that these 'primary factors' put paid altogether to the notion of intelligence, but when they found the primary factors to be themselves correlated they resurrected the concept of intelligence as a second-order factor, a solution already implicit in the earlier methods and theories of Burt (Eysenck, 1939).

The fourth stage constitutes essentially an extension of the third, and is associated specifically with J. P. Guilford (1966), whose publication of his '1965 model of intelligence' provided some of the motivation for this paper. This model, which shows some similarities to one I published in *Uses and Abuses of Psychology* (1953, p. 38), is illustrated in Fig. 2.1. Guilford classifies the intellect into *operations* which it can perform, different *contents* of these operations, and different *products*; by taking all possible interactions we obtain 120 cells corresponding to different mental abilities. Of these Guilford claims to have evidence in actual factorial studies for eighty; he is optimistic about discovering the remainder. To some critics, this factorial extension of Thurstone's work has appeared almost as a *reductio ad absurdum* of the whole approach. There is a possibility of infinite subdivision inherent in the statistical method employed, and evidence is lacking that further and further subfactors add anything either to the experimental analysis of intellectual functioning or the practical aim of forecasting success and failure in intellectual pursuits (Vernon, 1965b). Worse, the model fails to reproduce the essentially hierarchical nature of the data; the one outstanding fact which recurs again and again in all analyses is the universality of positive correlations among all relevant tests, and the positive correlations between different factors (McNemar, 1964). By omitting any feature of this central feature of the scene Guilford has truly cut out the Dane from his production of Hamlet. If this is really the best model (1965 style) which psychology can offer of intelligence and intellect, then the time seems to have come to retrace our steps; something has gone very wrong indeed!

II LIMITATION OF THE FACTOR ANALYSIS APPROACH

Zangwill has several times suggested that the whole intelligence testing movement is a technological rather than a scientific one, and in essence my own diagnosis is not too different from his. I would suggest that the psychometric approach has become almost completely divorced from both psychological theory and experiment, and that factor analysis, while an extremely useful tool, cannot by itself bear the whole burden which has been placed upon it. It is the purpose of this paper to raise certain questions in this connection rather than to give definitive answers; a few empirical results from some of our work will be presented more in order to illustrate an approach than because we believe that these results settle the questions the experiments were designed to investigate.

Our work started out with a fundamental criticism of the whole testing movement, directed at the unit of analysis chosen. Nearly all factor analysts and psychometrists correlate test scores and then proceed to work with these correlations; they thus assume that equal scores are equivalent. Such an assumption is unwarranted in the absence of proof, and consideration of typical intelligence test papers shows that it is, in fact, mistaken. Consider Table 2.1 which shows the results of giving an imaginary five-item test to five candidates. Let R stand for an item correctly solved, W for an item incorrectly solved, A for an item abandoned, and N for an item not attempted. Let us also assume that the items increase in difficulty. It will be seen that all five children obtain an identical mark of 2; but it will also be seen that no two children obtain this mark in the same way. Jones gets the easiest two right, but uses up all his time and does not attempt any more; he works slowly and carefully. Charles gets some easy items wrong and some difficult ones right;

TABLE 2.1. *Five-item intelligence test, administered to five children all having a score of 2.*

	1	*2*	*3*	*4*	*5*	*Total score*
Jones	R	R	N	N	N	2
Charles	W	R	W	R	N	2
Smith	R	A	A	R	A	2
Lucy	R	A	N	N	N	2
Mary	R	W	R	W	W	2

R – Right answer.   W – Wrong answer.   A – Abandoned item.   N – Item not attempted. (In most tests A and N cannot be distinguished.)

he works quickly but carelessly. Smith gives up on three items; had he been more persistent, he might have solved some of them. Lucy is rather selective in the choice of item to be tackled, and Mary fails to check her answers, getting three of them wrong. Can it really be maintained that the mental processes and abilities of these five children are identical, merely because they all obtained the same final mark? This is the implicit assumption underlying the factor analysis of test scores, and it may be suggested that this assumption requires careful investigation before we can regard it as acceptable. Such investigations are notable by their absence, and factor analysts proceed throughout as if the problem did not exist. This, it may be suggested, is not a proper scientific procedure.

III THE FURNEAUX MODEL

Our own approach had been to emphasize the point that the fundamental unit of analysis must be the individual test item, and that in addition to determining the category (R, W, A, N) into which it falls for each candidate, it is important to determine the *speed* with which each R item is solved, the length of time devoted to each A item (persistence or continuance), and the number of W items together with the time spent on each. Furneaux (1960) has given a detailed analysis of scores obtained in this fashion, and has suggested on the basis of this evidence that the solution of mental test problems has three main parameters: (1) Mental Speed, i.e. speed of solution of R items; (2) Continuance, or persistence in efforts to solve problems the solution to which is not immediately apparent; and (3) Error-Checking Mechanism, i.e. a mental set predisposing the individual to check his solution against the problem instead of writing it down immediately. Two interesting and important consequences follow from this analysis. In the first instance, Furneaux reinstates the mental speed factor to its theoretical

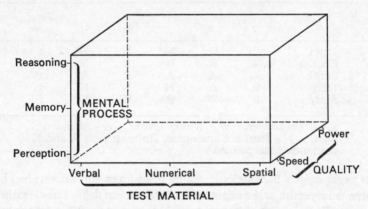

Fig. 2.2 Model of the structure of intellect (Eysenck, 1953).

pre-eminence as the main cognitive determinant of mental test solving ability, and in the second instance he emphasizes the importance of non-cognitive (personality) factors in determining mental test performance – both persistence and carefulness in checking are personality attributes rather than cognitive abilities. I have attempted to incorporate some elements of this analysis into my own model of intellect (Eysenck, 1953), which is shown in Fig. 2.2 and which may be compared with Guilford's. What I call 'mental processes' he calls 'operations'; what I call 'test material' he calls 'contents'; so far there is close agreement. But instead of having a third dimension concerned with 'products' (which seems to me a weak and not very important principle of division) I have suggested a dimension rather vaguely labelled 'quality' into which I wanted to incorporate concepts of mental speed and power, somewhat after the fashion of Thorndike's fundamental contribution (1926). The suggestion is that mental speed and power are fundamental aspects of all mental work, but that they are to some extent qualified by the mental processes involved and the materials used. This seems to me a more realistic concept than Guilford's, as well as having the advantage of retaining the central *g* concept in a hierarchical structure in which the major source of variation is mental speed, averaged over all processes and materials. 'Primary mental abilities', so called, would then emerge at a lower level of generality, and be related to different processes and different materials used.

Furneaux has demonstrated the fundamental nature of the mental

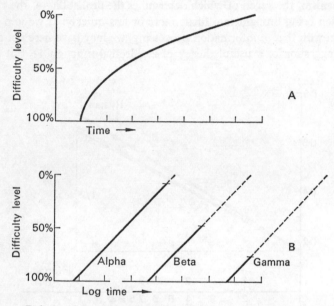

Fig. 2.3 Relation between difficulty level of test items and time (A) and log time (B) needed for solution. Alpha, Beta and Gamma are three imaginary subjects of high, medium and low mental ability respectively (Eysenck, 1953).

speed function by showing that when an individual's R latencies are plotted against the difficulty level of the items concerned, a negatively accelerated curve is obtained (Fig. 2.3A); when the time units are then logarithmically transformed *all plots become linear and parallel* (Fig. 2.3B). This may be interpreted to mean that the only source of difference in intellectual ability between individuals (in relation to the particular set of test items chosen at least) is the intercept on the abscissa. The increase in log latency with increase in item difficulty turns out to have the same slope for all individuals tested, and is thus a *constant*, one of the few which exist in psychology. It seems to me that the scientific study of intelligence would gain much by following up the important leads given by Furneaux in this extremely original and path-breaking work.

IV MENTAL SPEED AND INTELLIGENCE

On the theoretical side Furneaux has suggested that what may be involved in problem solving activity may be some kind of scanning mechanism, the speed of which determines the probability of the right solution being brought into focus more or less quickly. If we join this notion with that of information processing, we may have here not only the suggestion of a useful theory of intellectual functioning, but also

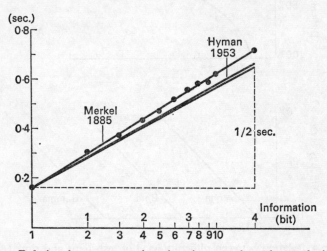

Fig. 2.4 Relation between reaction time in seconds and complexity of task, in bits. Data from Merker (1885) and Hyman (1953) (the Hyman data show results before and after practice). After Frank (1963).

an argument against those who abandoned the whole theory of 'speed' as underlying intelligence because of the failure of reaction time experiments to correlate with intelligence tests. Let us consider the amount of information conveyed by flashing a light and requiring the subject to press a button located underneath the light flashed. When there is only one light/button combination, no information is, in fact, conveyed. As the number of combinations increases, the amount of information conveyed increases logarithmically, so that one bit of information is conveyed with two combinations, two bits with four combinations and three bits with eight combinations. Response speed has been shown by Hick (1952), Hyman (1953) and Schmidtke (1961) to increase linearly with increasing number of bits of information, as shown in Fig. 2.4 (Frank, 1963). We have two separate items of information for each subject: one is the raw reaction time, as shown by the intercept on the ordinate, the other is the slope of the regression line, i.e. the rate of increase in reaction time with increasing amount of information processed. If intelligence is conceived of as speed of information processing, then simple reaction time, involving o bits of information, should not correlate with intelligence, but the slope of the regression line, showing increase of reaction time with amount of information processed, should correlate (negatively) with intelligence; in other words, intelligent subjects would show less increase in reaction time with increase in number of light/button combinations than would dull ones (this is a slightly more precise way of phrasing Spearman's first noegenetic law). Experimentally, the prediction has been tested by Roth (1964) who demonstrated that while as expected simple reaction time was independent of IQ, speed of information processing (slope) correlated significantly with IQ, in the predicted direction. Reaction time experiments, properly interpreted, do not appear to contradict a theory of intellectual functioning based on the motion of mental *speed*.

V LEARNING AND INTELLIGENCE

The theory that *learning* is basic to intellectual functioning is not necessarily antagonistic to a theory stressing speed; within the more general speed theory we might expect that speedy learning would be characteristic of the bright, slow learning of the dull. In other words, learning would be one of the 'mental processes' subdivisions in Fig. 2.2. The early work of Woodrow (1946) was often considered to have disproved such an hypothesis, but his experiments were too simple altogether to throw much light on the problem; it is not adequate to take subjects who are at different stages of mastery and practice on various types of tasks, who are differentially motivated towards these tasks, and who vary considerably with respect to the abilities involved in these tasks, and then to correlate speed of learning on these tasks with each other and with IQ. Improved experimental and statistical methods have given more positive results regarding the relationship between IQ and learning (Stake, 1961; Duncanson, 1964).

Another argument has often been presented, e.g. by Wechsler; he has pointed out that a learning task such as 'memory span' correlates poorly with the other tests in the WAIS and does not predict final total score well. Jensen (1964) has argued that this view is based on a neglect of the low reliability of the test as described by Wechsler; this, in turn, can be raised to any height by simply lengthening the (very short) test, or by improving its design, or both. When correlations are corrected for attenuation, Jensen shows that digit span correlates 0·75 with total IQ, has a factor loading of 0·8 on a general factor extracted from the Wechsler tests, is more culture free than other tests, and can be shown to obey the Spearman–Brown prophecy formula, thus making it possible to increase its reliability to any desired degree. The test can be made more predictive of IQ by measuring forward and backward span separately, rather than by throwing them together into one score; apparently these two measures are not, in fact, highly correlated and should not be averaged but combined in some multiple correlation formula, if at all.

Jensen has used Digit Span and serial learning experiments of the traditional laboratory kind in an extensive investigation into personality determinants of individual differences in these tests; we shall return to this study later. Here it is relevant to mention that he found a multiple correlation of +0·76 between learning ability as so measured and college Grade Point Average, a measure of academic standing. When it is considered that this value was obtained in a relatively homogeneous group of persons from the point of view of IQ, and that this correlation is considerably higher than those usually reported with highly regarded IQ tests, then it may became apparent why I am suggesting here that we should take seriously the theory relating the concept of 'intelligence' to learning efficiency and speed, and attempt, by means of laboratory studies such as those of Jensen and Roth, to investigate deductions from such an hypothesis. It seems reasonable to expect that such investigations are more likely to help in the elucidation of the nature of intellectual functioning than is the continued construction of IQ tests of a kind that has not materially altered in fifty years. And it is also possible that from the practical point of view, this method of procedure may result in tests and devices which enable us to give better predictions of school and university success than do existing tests.

As an example of the much increased possibility of psychological analysis opened by the use of laboratory methods in this field, consider Schonfield's (1965) study of memory changes with age. The general loss of ability of the aged to do IQ tests well has been known for a long time, as has their failure to acquire new skills and information, or to retain acquired material. These defects may be due either to a loss of ability to retrieve memories from storage, or to a deficiency in the storage system itself. By comparing recall and recognition scores on a learning task, Schonfield showed that recall was impaired in aged subjects, but recognition was not; he concluded that it was retrieval from memory storage which was at fault, rather than storage itself, thus suggesting that learning itself might be unimpaired with age. This experiment is cited, not because the results are definitive in any way, but because they illustrate well the approach suggested here; simple IQ testing cannot in the nature of things do any more than reveal the existence of a deficit, but in order to reveal the precise psychological nature of the intellectual deficit in question more experimental methods are required.

VI LEARNING AND PERSONALITY

In our discussion of Furneaux's contribution, we found that of his three components of intellectual functioning, only one (speed) was cognitive, while two (persistence and the error-checking mechanism) seemed more orectic in origin, and likely to be related to personality. Most workers in the field of intelligence testing disregard personality factors altogether, but this is almost certainly a mistake. There are several experiments which bring out fairly clearly the importance of personality factors such as neuroticism and extraversion/introversion in the measurement of intelligence, and much of our work has centred on this aspect. Consider first of all the simple learning experiments which we have just discussed; here one can perhaps expect personality to play little if any role. This, however, is not so, and it may be interesting to speculate about the kind of relation which one might expect to find. We may with advantage begin by considering the well-known experiments of Kleinsmith and Kaplan (1963). These authors argued, briefly, that learning is mediated by a *consolidation process* which takes place after the learned material has been registered, but before it is transferred into permanent memory storage. Consolidation is a function of the state of arousal of the organism; the greater the arousal, the longer and more efficient the consolidation, so that higher arousal leads to better memory in the long run. However, while consolidation is proceeding, it interferes with recall, so that while the consolidation process is going on the highly aroused organism is at a disadvantage. Kleinsmith and Kaplan tested their theory by measuring the amount of arousal (GSR reaction) produced by different paired stimuli; for each subject they then picked the most arousing and the least arousing stimulus

pairs and had the subject remember the paired stimulus after presentation of the original stimulus. Recall was arranged at different times
after original learning for different groups of subjects, and Fig 2.5 shows
the results; it will be seen that as expected high arousal words are
poorly remembered immediately after learning, but show very marked
reminiscence effects, while low arousal words are well remembered

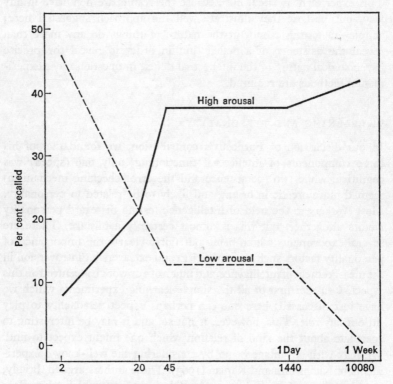

Fig. 2.5 Differential recall of paired associates as a function of
arousal level (Kleinsmith and Kaplan, 1963).

immediately after learning, but fade out quickly. There is little doubt
of the reality of this phenomenon, which has since been demonstrated
several times.

In this experiment stimuli were measured and grouped according to
their arousing qualities. It is equally possible to group subjects
according to their arousability, and I have argued that introverts are
characterized by high arousal, extraverts by poor arousal (Eysenck,
1963, 1967a). If this theory is along the right lines, we would expect

extraverts to behave in the manner of the low arousal words in Fig. 2.5, and introverts in the manner of the high arousal words. In other words, for short recall times, extraverts should be superior, while for long recall times introverts should be superior. There are about half-a-dozen experiments in the literature demonstrating the superiority of extraverts over short-term intervals, including the work of Jensen already mentioned; these have been summarized elsewhere (Eysenck, 1967a), and all that need be said here is that results are in good agreement with prediction. Some unpublished work on pursuit rotor reminiscence also supports the prediction of better learning for introverts after long rest intervals.

A specially designed experiment by McLaughlin and Eysenck was undertaken to test, in addition to the hypothesis stated above, a further one relating to the personality dimension of neuroticism, which we may regard as associated with drive (Spence, 1964). Subjects were tested on either an easy list of seven pairs of nonsense syllables, or on a difficult list, difficulty being manipulated through degree of response similarity. It was predicted that in accordance with the Yerkes–Dodson law the optimum drive level for the easy list would be higher than that for the difficult list, and it was further assumed that N subjects (high scorers on the N scale of the EPI) would be characterized by higher drive than S subjects (stable, low scorers on the N scale of the EPI). Extraverts, as already explained, were regarded as low in arousal, introverts as high. There are thus four groups of subjects, which, in order of drive, would be (from low to high): stable extraverts; neurotic extraverts and stable introverts; neurotic introverts (no prediction could be made about the position of the two intermediate groups relative to each other). The results of the experiment are shown in Fig. 2.6; extraverts, as predicted, are significantly superior to introverts, and the optimum performance level of drive is shifted towards the low end as we go from the easy to the difficult list, thus shifting the SE group up and the NE group down (the figures in the diagram refer to number of errors to criterion).

If introverts, as hypothesized, are characterized by a more efficient consolidation process, due to their greater cortical arousal, then we should be able to predict that they should be superior to extraverts with respect to aquired knowledge. As an example, we may take vocabulary scores, which are clearly the product of learning, and which usually correlate very highly with other IQ tests. Eysenck (1947) has reported personality differences between 250 neurotic male soldiers whose Matrices scores were much superior to their Mill Hill Vocabulary scores, and 290 male soldiers whose scores showed a similar difference in the

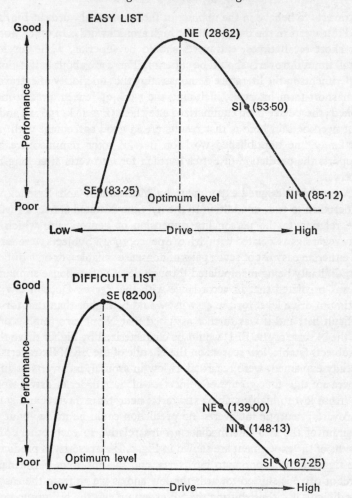

Fig. 2.6 Performance of stable extraverts, neurotic extraverts, stable introverts and neurotic introverts on easy and difficult paired associate learning tasks (R. J. McLaughlin and H. J. Eysenck, unpublished data).

opposite direction; he also studied 200 and 140 neurotic women soldiers showing similar differences. In both sex groups those subjects whose vocabulary was relatively good showed dysthmic (introverted) symptoms, while those whose vocabulary was relatively poor showed hysteric (extraverted) symptoms. Farley (unpublished) has carried out a study of forty-seven normal subjects in which he found a substantial positive correlation ($r = +0.48$) between introversion and vocabulary.

This is of course in line with the alleged 'bookish' character of the typical introvert. There was no such correlation between Introversion and Raven's Matrices.

It is possible to go further than this and argue that introverts should do rather better at school and university because of this superiority in consolidation of learned material; there is much evidence to indicate that such a prediction may be along the right lines (Furneaux, 1962; Lynn and Gordon, 1961; Savage, 1962; Bendig, 1958, 1960; Otto, 1965; Otto and Fredricks, 1963; Child, 1964; Ranking, 1963a, 1963b). Not all the results are favourable, but the overall impression is certainly in accordance with expectation. It might be suggested that some form of zone analysis (Eysenck, 1966) which included the N variable as well as the E variable would throw much needed light on these relationships. It should be added that the results do not so much support the hypothesis, as rather fail to disprove it. There are so many alternative hypotheses to account for the finding that not too much should be read into the data.

VII INTELLIGENCE AND PERSONALITY

It will be clear from this discussion that personality features such as neuroticism and extraversion/introversion interact with learning in complex though meaningful ways, and that great care has to be taken in the design of experiment not to fall foul of the complex laws relating performance to personality. It might be objected that such relations only obtain when laboratory learning tasks are used, but that they fail to appear when orthodox intelligence tests are employed. This is not so. One of the earliest findings relating to extraversion/introversion was that extraverts opt for speed, introverts for accuracy, when there is the possibility of a choice in the carrying out of an experimental task (Eysenck, 1947), and we would expect this difference to appear in relation to intelligence tests also. Jensen (1964) correlated extraversion scores on the EPI with time spent on the Progressive Matrices test and found a signficant correlation of -0.46; in other words, extraverts carried out the task more quickly. They also made more errors, but this trend was not significant. Farley (1966) applied the Nufferno test individually to thirty Ss, divided on the basis of their EPI scores into ten extraverts, ten ambiverts and ten introverts. The mean log speed scores on all problems correctly solved for the groups were respectively: 0.78, 0.88 and 0.93. This monotonic increase in solution time with introversion was fully significant by analysis of variance. Other examples of this relation between speed and extraversion are given elsewhere (Eysenck, 1967a); there seems little doubt about its reality.

Farley (1966) also discovered a significant relation with neuroticism, but as might have been expected (Payne, 1961) this showed a non-linear trend, subjects with average scores being superior to those with high or low N scores. Lynn and Gordon (1961) have also published a study showing a similar trend; they used the Progressive Matrices test. The rationale underlying the prediction of a curvilinear relationship in this context derives, of course, from the Yerkes—Dodson law; it is believed that the optimum drive level for complex and difficult tasks like those involved in an intelligence test lies below the high level reached by high N subjects, and above that reached by low N subjects. The general drive level of the group tested is, of course, quite critical in this connection, and it must be emphasized that unless this can be specified or measured, predictions will not always be fulfilled. Changes in difficulty level of the items, changes in the importance the result of the test assumes in the eyes of the subjects, and changes in the motivational value of the instructions, may all lead to a general shift in the drive level of the subjects which may displace the optimum level in either direction. It would seem useful in tests of this prediction to have separate measures of drive, or of arousal, against which performance could be plotted (Eysenck, 1967a): without such direct measures the subjects' N score may often be difficult to interpret, giving us essentially merely a measure of their *probability* of responding with autonomic activation to an anxiety-producing situation. If the situation is not perceived as anxiety-producing by the subjects, then differences in N cease to matter. This line of argument has led to a better understanding of the conditions under which N correlates with eyeblink conditioning (Eysenck, 1967a), and it may be used to design experiments explicitly aimed at increasing the correlation posited.

This dependence of results on precise control of parameter values can also be illustrated by some recent unpublished experiments undertaken by M. Berger. We have noted that extraverts are faster and make more errors when conditions are such that the test is administered without stress on speed; in other words, when no explicit instructions are given emphasizing speed, extraverts opt for speed and neglect accuracy, while introverts opt for accuracy and go slow. These are response styles well familiar from other types of activity (Eysenck, 1960). What would we expect to happen when stress was placed, explicitly and implicitly, on speed of problem solving activity? Let us return to Fig. 2.6, in which we postulated that stable extraverts would have low drive level, neurotic introverts high drive level, with the other two groups (stable introverts and neurotic extraverts) intermediate. Given the specific stress on *speed* as the proper index of performance, we would expect the low drive stable extraverts to have the slowest speed, and the neurotic introverts the highest, with the other two groups intermediate; we might also expect that the neurotic introverts would produce more errors in order to make up for the excessive speed shown.

Berger tested twenty-one 13-year-old schoolchildren in each of the four personality groups; the groups were equated for age, sex and intelligence, using their 11+ records for this purpose. Fifty problems were presented for solution individually, followed by a rest, and finally by another set of thirty problems. Each problem was shown to the child on a screen, with numbered alternative solutions; having selected the correct solution, the child pressed a numbered button, which activated a time switch, thus recording solution latency, and also caused the projector to project the next problem on to the screen. Instructions emphasized speed of working, and the whole experimental set-up added to this impression; furthermore, the disappearance of the problem after the button had been pressed eliminated the possibility of checking the correctness of the answer. Fig. 2.7 shows the results of the first fifty items; the next thirty showed similar results. Fig. 2.7 is arranged in the form of a cumulative time record, with time arranged along the ordinate and the problems, 1 to 50, along the abscissa. It will be clear that the stable extraverts are much the slowest, the neurotic introverts much the fastest, with the other two groups intermediate; these differences are highly significant. It was also found, at a high level of significance, that neurotic introverts compensated for their speed by making more errors than the other groups. Thus, the Yerkes—Dodson law appears to be working here very much as it did in the case of the McLaughlin-Eysenck experiment: the low drive SE group does poorly because it is so slow, the high drive NI group does poorly because it makes too many errors, and the intermediate NE and SI groups do best because they work at an optimum level of motivation.

VIII FLUENCY AND INHIBITION

This study illustrates the value of applying theories and laws from general and experimental psychology to intelligence testing. Another example may serve the same function. From the point of view of the experimental psychologist, a typical intelligence test is a good example

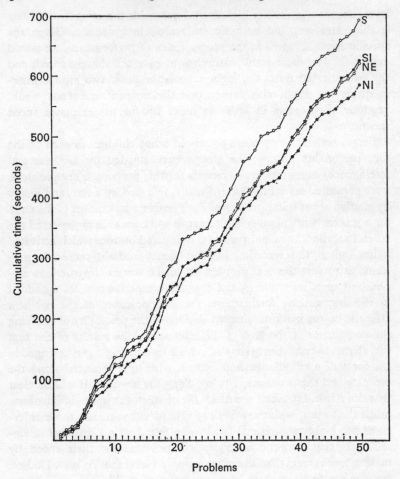

Fig. 2.7 Solution times of stable extraverts, neurotic extraverts, stable introverts and neurotic introverts on fifty intelligence problems, timed separately and cumulated (M. Berger, unpublished data).

of a task undertaken in the condition of massed practice; we would, therefore, expect it to generate reactive inhibition. Extraverts generate such inhibition more strongly and more quickly than do introverts (Eysenck, 1957, 1967a), and consequently we would expect that when groups of extraverts and introverts are matched for performance during the earlier part of an intelligence test, then they will diverge towards the latter part, with the introverts superior in performance. Another way of saying the same thing would be to regard an intelligence test as a vigilance test, and use the well-known fact that introverts preserve vigilance better than extraverts to predict their better performance towards the end. Eysenck (1959) has reported such an experiment, in which he used sixty items from the Morrisby Compound Series test, individually but unobtrusively timed. Using speed of correct solutions, it was found that on the first forty-five problems introverts were slower than extraverts, but on the last fifteen items, the two groups reversed position and the extraverts were now the slower. On the last fifteen items, it was also found that the extraverts gave up more easily. It would thus seem true to say that extraverts do show the predicted decline in performance during the latter part of their performance on a typical test of intelligence, administered as far as the subjects were concerned in the usual manner, and without any special stress on speed. This experiment, taken in connection with the others already quoted, leaves little doubt that personality plays an important part in intelligence test performance, and that its influence has hitherto been very much underestimated.

Personality factors interact with intelligence test performance in many ways, and neglect of these factors may easily lead to quite incorrect conclusions. As an example, we may, perhaps, take the large body of work recently done on convergent and divergent types of tests (Hudson, 1966). In studies of this kind, candidates good on divergent tests are often called 'creative', and the argument is sometimes extended to other desirable qualities of intellect, such as 'originality' (Barron, 1963; Taylor and Barron, 1963). In fact, divergent tests are by no means new; under the title of 'fluency' tests they were among the early discoveries of the London school, and a typical set of such tests is reprinted in Cattell's (1936) *Guide to Mental Testing*. Tests of this kind were found to be correlated with extraversion (Eysenck, 1960) and Spearman (1927) already pointed out that this particular factor 'has proved to be the main ground on which persons become reputed for "quickness" or for "originality".' Hudson's work supports some such interpretation quite strongly; 'divergent' schoolboys, as compared with 'convergent' ones, are more fluent, make more errors on orthodox tests, are emotionally more forthcoming, are more sociable, and prefer 'arts' to 'science' subjects – all characteristics of extraverts as compared with introverts. There is, in fact (as Hudson acknowledges) no evidence to show that 'divergent' boys are more creative than 'convergent' ones; as he points out, one can be 'creative' in different ways. All that we seem to be dealing with in this distinction would seem to be a kind of response set or 'style'; it is, perhaps, unusual to apply this concept in relation to intelligence tests, but it applies here probably more than in relation to personality inventories.

IX THE LIMITATION OF PSYCHOMETRY

These various ways in which personality and intelligence testing interact do not by any means exhaust the available evidence. Factor analysts usually assume, without proof, that groups which do not differ in performance on a group of tests will also not differ in factorial solution. Lienert (1963) showed that this assumption is, in fact, erroneous; children high and low on N, respectively, do not produce identical correlation matrices or factors, when administered sets of intelligence tests, nor do the two groups even agree in the number of factors produced. As Eysenck and White (1964) have shown in a reanalysis of the data, 'the stable group has a more clearly marked structure in the cognitive test field than has the labile group'. (It has also been found that students differing in intelligence do not have identical factor patterns on personality questionnaires; the evidence is presented by Shure and Rogers, 1963.) It is not unlikely that some of the observed differences in factor structure are connected with the intellectual response styles which we have found to be characteristic of different personality groups, but at present there is no evidence to indicate precisely how this may have come about. Much further work is clearly required before we can be sure of our facts in this complex field.

All that has been said in this paper is only suggestive, and I do not in any way believe that the hypotheses stated, and sometimes supported by experimental data, are at the moment anything but guideposts pointing in the direction of interesting and important factors which will almost certainly have a bearing on the proper measurement of intelligence. We have noted four stages in the development of intelligence tests; it is the main purpose of this paper to suggest the importance of starting out on a fifth stage of intelligence assessment, a new stage based on theoretical and experimental work, and not divorced from the main body of academic psychology. Psychometrics and factor analysis have important contributions to make, but they can do so only in conjunction with other disciplines, not by 'going it alone'. What is required is clearly an integration of intelligence testing with the main stream of academic psychology, and a more determined experimental and laboratory approach to the problems raised by the various theories of intellectual functioning. Some obvious suggestions emerge from the inevitably somewhat rambling and uncoordinated discussion of this paper. (1) Analysis of performance should always take into account individual items, rather than tests, i.e. averages taken over what may be, and usually are, non-homogeneous sets of items. Such analysis should be made in terms of latencies, i.e. speed of individual item solution, as well as of errors, persistence before abandoning items, and other similar differential indicators of response style. (2) Investigators should pay more attention to laboratory studies of learning and memory functions, of speed of information processing, and other experimental measures in the testing of specific hypotheses regarding the nature of intellectual functioning. Analysis of intelligence tests of the orthodox kind raises problems, but cannot in the nature of things go very far towards answering them. (3) Investigators should experiment with variations in experimental parameters, such as rest pauses, time from end of learning to recall, rate of presentation, degree of motivation, etc., in an effort to support or disprove specific theoretical predictions regarding the process of learning and problem solving. (4) Personality variables, such as stability/neuroticism and extraversion/introversion, should always be included in experimental studies of intellectual functioning, because of their proven value in mediating predictions and their interaction potential in all types of learning and performance tasks. Vigorous research along these lines carries with it the promise that notions such as intelligence, IQ, ability and factor will cease to be regarded as poor relations, and will return to the eminent and successful status they held before the war; it also furnishes the only means of making these concepts scientifically meaningful, academically respectable, and practically more useful.

3

Q. McNemar (1964)

Lost: our intelligence? Why?

American Psychologist, 19, pp. 871–82

The Greeks had a word for it, but the Romans had a word with better survival properties. Regardless of the word, what is now called intelligence has been talked about for at least 2000 years. And as long as 2000 years before the advent of attempts to measure intelligence, there seems to have been recognition of the fact that individuals differ in intellectual ability.

The earlier attempts at measuring were based on either of two quite distinct conceptions: the Galton–Cattell idea that intellectual ability manifests itself in simple, discrimination functioning, and the Binet notion that cognitive ability reflects itself in more complex functioning. The Binet concept proved to be more fruitful, and by 1925 there was on the market, in addition to various versions of the Binet scale, a flood of group tests of so-called general intelligence.

A few words about definition may be in order. First, it might be claimed that no definition is required because all intelligent people know what intelligence is – it is the thing that the other guy lacks. Second, the fact that tests of general intelligence based on differing definitions tend to intercorrelate about as highly as their respective reliabilities permit indicates that, despite the diversity of definitions, the same function or process is being measured – definitions can be more confusing than enlightening. Third, that confusion might have been anticipated is evident from recent re-examination of the problem of definition by Miles (1957). This British chappie found himself struggling with the awful fact that the word 'definition' itself has twelve definitions. Perhaps the resolution of this problem should be assigned to the newly formed Division of Philosophical Psychology, or maybe the problem should be forgotten since psychologists seem to have lost the concept of general intelligence.

Why has the concept been abandoned? Was it replaced by something else? By something better? Must we admit that the millions who have been tested on general intelligence tests were measured for a non-existent function? If it is possible that the notion of general intelligence is not lost but merely gone astray, in what corners of what psychological fields should we search for it?

REASONS FOR DISCARDING THE IDEA OF GENERAL
INTELLIGENCE

Apparently one reason why concepts are either discarded or modified beyond recognition is that too much is claimed for them. Among the supposed strikes against general intelligence are the following: the earlier false claims about IQ constancy; prediction failures in individual cases; unfounded claims that something innate was being measured by the tests; equally unfounded assertions that nothing but cultural effects were involved; the bugaboo that IQ tests reflect middle-class values; the notion that an IQ standing fosters undesirable expectations regarding school achievement; the idea that IQ differences are incompatible with democracy and lead to educational determinism; and, finally, the great stress on general intelligence caused us to ignore other possible abilities.

This last point leads us right into the problem of factor analysis. Spearman died in battle defending his theory of *g*. Under pressure he reluctantly conceded that factors other than *g* might exist, and he frequently said, in effect, I told you so as long ago as 1906. Actually, Spearman was on the run before the invention of modern factor analysis, but it was not until Thurstone's (1938) first major application of his centroid factor method that Spearman's *g* became, seemingly, non-existent. Thurstone said, 'We have not found the general factor of Spearman' and 'We cannot report any general common factor in the battery of fifty-six tests [p. vii].' As anticipated by some, Spearman was not prone to admit defeat. He reworked Thurstone's data and a *g* was found, plus some group factors. He charged that Thurstone's rotational process had submerged the general factor.

American factorists found Thurstone convincing. The description of abilities in terms of seven primaries was an attractive package. The so-called primaries were more amenable to specific definition than the old hodgepodge called general intelligence. Despite the fact that Thurstone was able to replicate his findings on samples from two other populations, thus giving credence to his method and results, there were a couple of events that led to some turbulence in his seven-dimension rarefied atmosphere. The first of these was a minor study, by one of his own students, based on the intercorrelations of 1916 Stanford–Binet items, in which the *g* refused to be rotated out. But rather than admit that this might be some kind of general intelligence, the author renamed it 'maturational level'. Incidentally, this illustrates the first cardinal Principle of Psychological Progress: *Give new names to old things*.

The second disturber of the neat little set of primaries, sans a *g*, resulted when Thurstone took the next logical step, that of constructing tests to measure the primaries. It was found that the primaries were themselves intercorrelated whereas it had, at the time, been expected and hoped that they would be independent. The Thurstones (1941, p. 26) readily admitted that a general factor was needed to explain the interrelatedness of the primaries. This eventually led to the idea of oblique axes, which axes were regarded as representing the primaries as first-order factors, whereas the general factor pervading the primaries was dubbed a second-order factor. It began to look as though Spearman was being revisited, except for the little matter of labelling: anything called second-order could not possibly be regarded as of much importance. Furthermore, it could always be said that, in the ability domain, it is less difficult to attribute psychological meaningfulness to first-order than to second-order factors, so why pay much attention to the latter? Thus it was easy for most American factorists to drop the concept of general intelligence and to advocate that tests thereof, despite their proven usefulness over the years, should be replaced by tests of the primaries. Hence the emergence of differential aptitude batteries, about which more later.

Meanwhile, our British cousins did not tag along with the factor methods preferred on this side of the Atlantic. After all, it is possible to use factor methods that permit a sizeable general factor, if such exists, to emerge as the very first factor. Being first, it is, presto, the most important, as indeed it is as a factor explaining, for the starting battery as a whole, more variance for more tests than attributable to any American-style primary factor. The methods preferred by the British also yield group factors, apt to bear the same name as the primaries, but of attenuated importance. Apparently the British are sceptical of the multitude of ability factors being 'discovered' in America. The structure of intellect that requires 120 factors may very well lead the British, and some of the rest of us, to regard our fractionization and fragmentation of ability, into more and more factors of less and less importance, as indicative of scatterbrainedness. This statement presumes that intellectual abilities are brain-centred.

In practically all areas of psychological research the demonstration of trivially small minutiae is doomed to failure because of random errors. Not so if your technique is factor analysis, despite its being based on the correlation coefficient – that slipperiest of all statistical measures. By some magic, hypotheses are tested without significance tests. This happy situation permits me to announce a Principle of Psychological Regress: *Use statistical techniques that lack inferential power.* This will not inhibit your power of subjective inference and consequently will progress you right back to the good old days when there was no strangling stat or sticky stix to make your insignificant data insignificant.

It may be a long time before we have an ivory tower, strictly scientific resolution of the issue as to whether a scheme involving primary abilities plus a de-emphasized *g* is preferable to one involving an emphasized *g* plus group factors. With bigger and better computers we will have bigger, though not necessarily better, factor analytic studies, but it seems unlikely that such further studies will, in and of themselves, settle the issue under discussion. Until such time as some genius resolves the broader question, so ably discussed by Lee Cronbach in 1957, of the place, if any, of correlational method in a science that aspires to be experimental, we may have to turn to the criterion of social usefulness as a basis for judging whether it is wise to discard general intelligence. Like it or not, much of our heritage in this area is that earlier workers, from Binet on, had as their motivation the solution of social problems, and currently many in the area have a similar motivation.

THE BEARING OF SOCIAL USEFULNESS

In practice, if you believe that the concept of general intelligence has outlived its usefulness, you may choose from among several differential, or multiple, aptitude batteries, which will provide measures of some of the so-called primary mental abilities. If you happen to believe that there is something to general ability, you can find tests to use. The novice looking for these latter tests may have to alert himself to the first Principle of Psychological Progress – the test labels may have changed from 'general intelligence' to 'general classification' or 'scholastic aptitude'. If you enjoy riding the fence, you might become a devotee of the practice of the College Board, and others, and measure just two abilities: Verbal and Quantitative.

This is certainly not the place to review the voluminous literature that amply demonstrates the practical utility of tests of general intelligence. Nor is it the place to catalogue the misuses of the Stanford-

Binet for purposes which Terman never claimed for it, or the misuses of the Wechsler scales for purposes which Wechsler *has* claimed for his scales. Neither the Binet nor the Wechsler provides a factorially pure, unidimensional measure of a *g*. The current Stanford–Binet was in reality constructed too early to benefit from the implication of factor analysis for test purity, whereas the Wechsler scales were based on the impossible premise that ten or eleven subtests can simultaneously provide diagnostic subscores and a meaningful total score. Of the many group tests that appeared between 1920 and 1945 it can be said that few, if any, provide unidimensional measures of general intelligence. The chief difficulty is that most of them lead to a total score based on a mixture of verbal and mathematical material. Thus, with two main sources of variance, marked qualitative differences can exist for quantitatively similar total scores. The College Board–Educational Testing Service people have justifiably refrained from giving a total score involving verbal plus math, but there are those who question the usefulness of the Board's math score and there are those who criticize the Educational Testing Service for failing to change over to a differential aptitude battery. [...]

Just how successful have the multitest batteries been? Since by far the most extensive social use of tests has been, and continues to be, in the schools, let us look at the evidence of validity studies therein. As indicated previously, little is known about the predictive usefulness of some of the seven batteries discussed above. The DAT of the Psychological Corporation is the only battery for which adequate predictive (and concurrent) validity data, derived from school sources, are available. It is also the battery that has fared best in the hands of the test reviewers; therefore if we allow the case for differential batteries to rest thereon, we will be looking at the best. So, what is the story?

Recall that the hoped-for advantage of a multitest battery over the old-fashioned general intelligence test was that it would have greater predictive power, a power which could manifest itself in higher validity coefficients for specific subject matter and, perhaps, for overall achievement. It was hoped that such a battery would be truly differential in that particular factors (or subtests) would correlate higher with achievement in some areas than in other areas. Presumably each factor (or subtest) should have unique usefulness. If a battery were truly differential, it would be a boon to school guidance personnel.

Now the manual of the DAT of the Psychological Corporation contains a staggering total of 4096 (yes I counted 'em) validity coefficients. With such a large pool to draw from, one could by gracious selection 'show' that the DAT is the answer to the prayer of every counsellor, male or female, or by malicious selection one could 'prove' that the DAT is far worse than any test ever published. The validity coefficients range all the way down to −0·37, which is presumably a chance deviation downward from 0, and all the way up to 0·90, which is likely as not a chance deviation downward from unity. But ranges tell us nothing. After a careful perusal of the 4096 correlations, it seems safe to summarize DAT validities as follows:

(1) Verbal Reasoning (analogies to most of you) is the best single predictor; Language Usage, as represented by a sentence test dealing with grammar and word usage, and admittedly more achievement than aptitude, is a close second.

(2) Numerical Ability, as measured by a test of simple arithmetic operations, designed to tap arithmetic reasoning without the usual verbal component, is the best predictor of achievement in school mathematics. It does not, however, correlate as well with grades in science as does Verbal Reasoning.

(3) Aside from the Numerical Ability test, the only other test that shows differential power as a predictor is the Spelling test – if you cannot spell you may have trouble learning shorthand.

(4) The remaining five tests in the battery simply fail to show compelling evidence that they are good in the differential predictive sense. For the Mechanical Reasoning and the Clerical Speed and Accuracy tests this may be understandable in that little of school curricula for Grades 8 through 12 requires such abilities, but one would expect that Abstract Reasoning and Space Relations would fare better than they seem to.

Such data as we have been able to locate for the other six multitest batteries tend to support these findings on the DAT. Aside from tests of numerical ability having differential value for predicting school grades in math, it seems safe to conclude that the worth of the multi-test batteries as differential predictors of achievement in school has not been demonstrated. Incidentally, the fact that the Verbal and Numerical tests stand out as the only two useful predictors tends to provide some support for the Educational Testing Service–College Board practice of providing scores for just these two abilities.

And now we come to a very disturbing aspect of the situation. Those who have constructed and marketed multiple aptitude batteries, and advocated that they be used instead of tests of general intelligence, seem never to have bothered to demonstrate whether or not multitest batteries provide better predictions than the old-fashioned scale of general intelligence. Be it noted that we are not discussing experimental editions of tests. Some may say that in so far as a test publisher provides validity data for a new battery it is not necessary to show that the validities are, for the given school condition, better than those of other tests. With this one can agree, but only in case no claims are made, explicitly or implicitly, regarding superior merits for the new battery.

It is far from clear that tests of general intelligence have been outmoded by the multitest batteries as the more useful predictors of school achievement. Indeed, one can use the vast accumulation of data on the validity of the Psychological Corporation's DAT to show that better predictions are possible via old-fashioned general intelligence tests. Consider the fact that a combination of the tests Verbal Reasoning (analogies) and Numerical Ability would be, in terms of content, very similar to many group tests of general intelligence. Consider also that an equally weighted combination of these two tests correlates in the mid-0·80s with the Otis S-A, Higher Form. Then, when you turn to a careful study of the empirical validities, as reported in the DAT manual, you will not be surprised at the outcome of the application of a little arithmetic, which leads to the definite conclusion that a simple unweighted combination of the Verbal Reasoning and Numerical Ability tests predicts as well as or, in most instances, better than any subtest taken singly, or in the differential sense.

The manual for the DAT contains the following statement (Bennett, Seashore and Wesman, 1952):

> Apparently the *Verbal Reasoning* and *Numerical Ability* tests can serve most purposes for which a general mental ability test is usually given in addition to providing differential clues useful to the counsellor. Hence, the use of the so-called intelligence test is apparently unnecessary where the *Differential Aptitude Tests* are already being used [p. 71].

Anyone who disagrees with this quotation could, with better justification, say that an intelligence test can serve nearly all, if not all, the purposes for which a multiple aptitude battery is given in the schools because the former, in general, is a better predictor and because, as we saw earlier, the differential clues are too fragmentary to be of use to the counsellor. And there is a bonus: one classroom period of testing, compared to six periods. A second bonus: much less costly. A third bonus: fewer scores to confuse the already confused minds of most school counsellors.

Thus, we come to the conclusion that general intelligence has not been lost in the trend to test more and more abilities; it was merely misplaced by a misplaced emphasis on a hope that a lot of us, including the speaker, once entertained, a hope that in turn was based on a misplaced faith in factor analysis: *the* hope that factors, when and if measured, would find great usefulness in the affairs of society. By the criterion of social usefulness, the multiple aptitude batteries have been found wanting. Now, I have no desire to furnish ammunition for those test critics who would have us stop all testing merely because they find a trivially faulty item in a standardized test. At a time when there is shouting about the tyranny of the testers and the brass of the brain watchers, at a time when school people are showing resentment at the disruption caused by too many national testing programs, at a time when federal and state legislators are all too willing to write legislation that places restrictions on the use of tests, and at a time when both majorities and minorities are being denied the benefits of test-based guidance because certain well-intentioned persons fail to realize that scores for the underprivileged minorities are useful indices of *immediate*, or present, functioning – at a time when all these and other forces are operating to throw out the tests, it is high time for the profession to establish a bureau of standards to test the tests instead of coasting down a road that is tinged with some of the trappings of Madison Avenue. Better to have informed internal control than ignorant, hostile, external control.

INTELLIGENCE ELSEWHERE?

Aside from the near loss of the idea that progress in school may depend on general intelligence, one wonders whether intelligence has come to be regarded as unimportant in other areas.

Any of you who have money invested in stocks and wish some reassurance regarding the intelligence level of business and industry managers should read Edwin Ghiselli's (1963) Bingham Lecture. His summary of his own work indicates that the average intelligence of those in the upper and middle management levels falls at the ninety-sixth percentile of the population. Thomas Harrell (1961) came to a similar conclusion. Furthermore, management level is correlated with intelligence – you can be too dumb to succeed as a manager. Also you can be too bright to be a managerial success! Now it must be admitted that little, if anything, is known about whether management success might be better predicted by measures of factor analytic defined abilities.

On this you are free to guess – most of you will have already guessed my guess.

A one-by-one cataloguing of what we know or do not know about what abilities contribute to success within various occupational and professional groups would merely add to the dullness of this presentation, so let us turn to some of the more esoteric fields of psychology to see whether the concept of general intelligence has or has had any relevance. One such field, and a very broad one, is creativity. Anyone who peeks over the fence into this field is apt to be astonished at the visible chaos. The definition of creativity is confounded by the diversity of subareas within the field, the criterion problems are far from licked, and so little is known about the creative process that measuring instruments are, seemingly, chosen on a trial-and-error basis. [...]

Let us turn to a criterion-based study (D. Taylor, 1961). The criterion measures for creativity and productivity were based on the checking by supervisors of statements that had been scaled by Thurstone's equal-appearing interval method. Creativity and productivity, so gauged, correlated 0·69 with each other on a sample of 103 researchers (electronic scientists and engineers). For this same group, intelligence, as measured by the Terman Concept Mastery Test (CMT), correlated only 0·20 or less with the criteria. Two Psychological Corporation tests and an American Institute for Research test did a little better. Creativity is slightly more predictable than productivity. In so far as these two criteria are themselves valid, the findings indicate that within a group of research workers, precious little of the variance in creativity, and still less in productivity, can be predicted by the tests.

A third study (MacKinnon, 1962) based on criterion (rated) measures of performance was concerned with the creativity of architects. Although the author reports that *within* a creative sample the correlation is essentially zero between intelligence (CMT) and rated creativity, it is not clear from the context what is meant by 'within' sample. If this means within the sample of forty creative architects selected as the 'most creative' in the country, then we indeed have such a drastic restriction in range on the *criterion* variable that little, if any, correlation can be expected for any and all predictors. Now the author says, without presenting any evidence, that 'Over the whole range of intelligence and creativity there is, of course, a positive relationship between the two variables [p. 488]'. One wonders just what is meant by creativity in architecture as rated either by fellow architects or by editors of architectural journals. If judged creativity reflects engineering-structural innovation, then intelligence would likely be a correlate; if judged creativity depends on new artistic designs, then the intelligence component would likely be of less importance. It would seem that when the author says we 'may have overestimated . . . the role of intelligence in creative achievement [p. 493]', he should have included some marked qualifications as to what type of creativity he had in mind.

That such qualification is indeed necessary is supplied by a finding of still another investigator (Barron, 1963). For a group of highly creative writers it was estimated, by way of the Terman CMT, that their average IQ is about 140, which we interpret as meaning that a high IQ is a necessary, though not sufficient, condition for outstanding success as a writer. On the basis of his own studies and those of other persons, this same investigator suggests that 'over the total range of intelligence and creativity a low positive correlation' of 0·40 probably obtains. This sweeping generalization is for all areas of creativity.

And speaking of sweeping generalizations, consider the suggestion in a 1961 study (Holland, 1961) that 'we need to use non-intellectual criteria in the selection of students for scholarships and fellowships [p. 146]'. The author did not say so, but presumably he meant in addition to intellectual ability; maybe he did not, since he had previously concluded that 'intelligence has little or no relationship to creative performance in arts and science . . . [p. 143]' at the high school level. His data back up this conclusion, as might have been expected when correlations are based on groups restricted in range to the top 1 per cent!

If the foregoing examples of criterion-based studies of creativity seem to indicate that general intelligence is relatively unimportant for creativity, it should be remembered that drastic but unknown or unspecified curtailment of range exists for both ability and criteria. Why do correlational studies under such adverse circumstances?

Next we turn to a few studies of creativity which cannot be criticized because of restriction of range on the criteria – these studies simply avoid this problem by never having actual criterion information. The approach is to claim that certain tests, which typically are scored for novel responses or novel solutions to problems, *are* measures of creativity, with no evidence whatsoever that the tests have predictive validity for non-test, real-life creative performance. This bit of ignorance does not prove to be a handicap to those who think that creativity can be studied without the nuisance of obtaining criterion measures. We reluctantly accept the test-based criteria solely for the sake of seeing what happens to general intelligence as a part of the picture. Time permits only three examples.

We first note that general intelligence has not manifested itself as a correlate of so-called creativity tests in the factor analytic studies of creativity. The explanation for this is easily found – no measures of general intelligence are used in these studies. When discussing his plans for studying creativity, a certain author (Guilford, 1950) said that 'we must look well beyond the boundaries of the IQ if we are to fathom the domain of creativity [p. 448]'. He went on to say, the conception 'that creative talent is to be accounted for in terms of high intelligence or IQ ... is not only inadequate but has been largely responsible for lack of progress in the understanding of creative people [p. 454]'. With a part of this one can agree, but does it follow that one should prejudge the role of general intelligence as a source of variance in creativity tests or factors derived therefrom? Does the failure to include an IQ test help one learn the extent to which one must go beyond the boundaries of the IQ to fathom creativity? Apparently the author, although willing to predict that the correlations between IQ and the many types of creativity tests 'are only moderate or low', was unwilling to include an IQ test for the sake of finding out. However, negation by omission is not very convincing.

That at least one test bearing the label 'creativity' is correlated more than moderately with IQ is evidenced by the value of 0.67 (average for boys and girls) for the carefully chosen sample of 15-year-olds in Project Talent (Shaycoft, Dailey, Orr, Neyman and Sherman, 1963). This sample-stable r (based on a total N of 7648) becomes 0.80 when corrected for attenuation.

In a recent extensive study (Getzels and Jackson, 1962), already extensively criticized, creativity is defined as the sum of scores on five tests (median intercorrelation of only 0.28). Although the investigators use the sum score for most of their analyses, they do not bother to report the correlation of creativity, so defined, with IQ. From the published report I have ascertained (via the correlation-of-sums formula) that creativity and IQ correlate to the extent of 0.40 for the total of 533 cases. Now this r of 0.40 has been greatly attenuated because of three things: first, the usual measurement errors; second, the cases were highly selected on IQ (mean of 132); third, the IQs are a mixture from the Stanford–Binet, Henmon–Nelson and Wechsler Intelligence Scale for Children (the use of regression-estimated Binet IQs from the other two scales aggravates rather than improves the mixture). We deduce that intelligence and the creativity tests used here have far more common variance than the authors believe.

Much is made of the finding that the creativity tests tended to correlate higher than did IQ with verbal-content school achievements. Again the IQ comes in for an unfair drubbing because of the same mixture of IQ scores and, what is more pertinent, because of explicit selective curtailment on the IQ variable and only incidental selection on the creativity variable.

Of more importance to the present paper is the analysis, by these same authors, based on a high IQ group and a high creative group, these groups being selected as the top 20 per cent for each variable but excluding those who were in the top 20 per cent on both variables. These two selected groups were then contrasted on total school achievement (and a host of other variables that are of no interest here). The mean IQ for the high IQ group was 150 whereas the mean IQ for the high creative group was 127, yet the achievement means of the two groups were 'unexpectedly' equally superior to the school population mean despite the 23-point difference in mean IQ. The authors say that it '*is* quite surprising' that the high creativity group achieved so well. From this it is concluded that the 'creative instruments account for a significant portion of the variance in school achievement [p. 24]', and the subsequent argument implies that creativity is more important for ordinary school achievement than is the IQ. Now anyone who is at all familiar with a three-variate problem will not be 'unexpectedly' surprised at the foregoing results – indeed, if the authors had bothered to give the three basic correlations among the three variables (IQ, creativity and total school achievement) for the entire group, any person versed in simple multivariate analysis could deduce the results. Furthermore, he could deduce a further result (and this one has been overlooked by the critics) which might be unpleasantly surprising to the thesis of these authors: namely, the high IQ and the high creative groups did equally well in school achievement despite an unreported difference in mean creativity that is of the same order as the much stressed difference in IQ. Utilizing the half-blind logic of the authors, one can say that creative ability is not as important as IQ for school achievement – just the opposite of their position.

Now the fact that seven of nine replications of this study confirm the original findings merely indicates that repetition of the same faulty design and false logic will lead to the same false conclusions. The design being used is such that, if two variables are equally correlated with a third, the conclusion will be reached that the two are actually unequally correlated with the third. This is the neatest trick of the decade for supplying educationists with an antidote for the IQ virus. I cannot refrain from saying at this point that, although discouraged, I am still hopeful that people who do statistical studies will first learn a modicum of elementary statistics!

Time does not permit a discussion of other studies in which creativity is defined in terms of test performance instead of being based on actual creativity of the sort prized by society. In summary of this brief on creativity studies, I would like to offer a few dogmatic-sounding observations. First, one need not be surprised at the fact that so-called creativity tests do not yield high correlations with IQ tests – but the correlations are generally far higher than those found in typical studies with range restrictions. I would anticipate that for normalized scores, the uncurtailed scatters for IQ versus creativity tests will be bivariate normal. Second, if we have honest to goodness criterion measures of literary or architectural or scientific creativity, the scatter diagram between IQ and such creativity (not normalized, since it makes sense to expect a skewed distribution for actual creativity) will be triangular in shape for unselected cases. That is, at the high IQ levels there will be a very wide range of creativity, whereas as we go down to average IQ, and on down to lower levels, the scatter for creativity will be less and less. Having a high IQ is not a guarantee of being creative; having a low IQ means creativity is impossible. Third, it remains to be seen whether or not the so-called creativity tests and/or factors derived therefrom have appreciable value as predictors of actual creative performance. Such tests may or may not yield better predictions than a test of general intelligence. Fourth, as far as I am concerned, to claim factorial validity for creativity tests, along with definitions of creativity in terms of tests, is an unwarranted avoidance of the fundamental problem of validity.

The recently renewed interest in 'gifted' children, along with the flurry of creativity studies, has led to a re-examination of methods for identifying the gifted. It has long been recognized that identification in terms of high IQ is too narrow – those gifted in such areas as art and music would be overlooked. The argument against the IQ is now (Torrance, 1962) being reinforced by the claim that the selection of the top 20 per cent on IQ would mean the exclusion of 70 per cent of the top 20 per cent on tested creativity. This startling statistic, which implies a correlation of only 0·24 between IQ and creativity, is being used to advocate the use of creativity tests for identifying the gifted. Be it noted that these creativity tests will also miss those gifted in art and music.

We are being told that it is important 'to identify creative talent early in life', hence you need not be surprised that the search goes down to the kindergarten level, with claims of successful identification. The creativity tests are presumed to be better for this purpose than the IQ tests because of the failure of the IQ to be constant, an argument that completely overlooks the fact that the IQ does have some constancy whereas absolutely nothing is known about the stability of standings on creativity tests. The IQ tests, known to be imperfectly valid as predictors of outstanding achievement in life, are to be replaced by the creativity tests, known to be of unknown validity as predictors. Anyway, progress, defined as change, is in the offing.

The IQ is being linked with *learning* as an outmoded educational objective; the new objective involves an emphasis on *thinking*. Somehow or other, creativity, not general intelligence, is being associated with thinking. The horrible idea of underachievers and overachievers, in terms of expectancies based on the IQ, will be abolished. But no thought is given to the fact that the use of creativity tests will simply define a new drop of under- and overachievers.

In an apparent zeal to rid us of general intelligence, it is argued that measured creativity is significantly related to ordinary school achievement. Maybe so, but never, never does one find complete data reported as to the relative sizes of validity coefficients. And, as we have seen, the technique being used will show that equal coefficients are unequal. Why not the full facts, free of fantasy?

An additional difficulty is not being faced by those who would replace IQ tests by creativity tests, or creative-thinking tests. The factor analytic studies indicate either no, or a trivially small, general creativity factor in these tests, yet these self-characterized 'bold, adventurous' reformers (see Torrance, 1963) do not hesitate to advocate a total score which is nearly devoid of meaning. Changing the curriculum to the teaching of creativity and creative thinking will not overcome this measurement difficulty. Again, I express the hope that the IQ is replaced by something better rather than by something worse.

There are other areas, such as reasoning, problem solving and concept formation, in which one might expect to find some consideration of intelligence as an aspect. One might also expect that investigators of thinking would have something to say about individual differences in thinking being dependent upon intelligence, but for some unintelligent reason these people seem never to mention intelligence. Surely, it cannot be inferred that thinking about thinking does not involve intelligence!

IN CONCLUSION

It has been the thesis of this paper that the concept of general intelligence, despite being maligned by a few, regarded as a second-order function by some, and discarded or ignored by others, still has a rightful place in the science of psychology and in the practical affairs of man. It has not been argued that the nature of general intelligence is well understood. Much, however, has been written about its nature. Over forty years ago, an editor secured and published the reasoned views of thirteen well-known test psychologists. Later, Spearman set forth his speculations about the nature of *g*. Prior to these, Binet had, of course, given much thought to the problem.

More recent discussions exist. Hebb (1949) has considered the problem from the viewpoint of neurology and brain functioning. Cyril Burt (1955), always a vociferous defender of the concept of general intelligence, has reviewed the evidence for a *g* and restated the idea, dreadful to some, that intelligence is innate. Perhaps it was inevitable that Raymond Cattell (1963), who has camped with the general intelligence contingent, should gaze into his crystal *n*-dimensional factor ball and find evidence for crystallized as opposed to fluid general intelligence. Joseph McVicker Hunt's (1961) book on *Intelligence and Experience* is in large part devoted to questions pertaining to the nature of intelligence.

By far the most provocative recent discussion that I have encountered is the closely reasoned 44-page paper by Keith Hayes (1962). He puts forth a motivational–experiential theory of intelligence. In essence, he presumes that there are hereditary differences in motivation. 'Experience-producing drives' and environmental differences produce differences in experience, which in turn, by way of learning, lead to differences in ability. Therefore, differences called intellectual are nothing more than acquired abilities. I think that Hayes has ignored the possibility of individual differences in learning ability, but if such a formulation leads to experimental manipulation of variables, we may eventually make progress in an area that has too long been dominated by ever increasing fractionization by factor analysis, with little thought as to how the fractured parts get put together into a functioning whole.

Abilities, or capacities, or aptitudes, or intellectual skills, or whatever you choose to call them, are measured in terms of response products to standardized situations. The *stimulus* is presented to an *organism* which by some *process* comes up with a *response*; thus any attempt to theorize and/or study intellect in terms of a simple stimulus-response (S-R) paradigm seems doomed to failure unless drastically modified and complicated by the insertion of O for organism and P for process.

There have been thousands of researches on the multitudinous variations from organism to organism, and the results fill books on individual differences. These studies can be roughly classified into two types. First, those that ascertain the intercorrelations among scaled response products to various stimulus situations, known as tests, have to do with the structure of intellect; and whether the resulting factors are anything more than dimensions for describing individual differences need not concern us here. The second type of study seeks the non-test correlates of test performance, and whether or not any of the found correlates can be regarded as explaining individual differences is not of interest here. Both types of studies certainly force one to stress the overwhelming diversity exhibited among the organisms.

But these studies of individual differences never come to grips with the *process*, or operation, by which a given organism achieves an intellectual response. Indeed, it is difficult to see how the available individual difference data can be used even as a starting point for generating a theory as to the process nature of general intelligence or of any other specified ability.

As a basis for a little speculation, let us conceive of a highly hypothetical situation in which the two members of a pair of identical twins, with identical experiences, find themsleves cast up on an uninhabited tropical island. Let us assume that they are at the supergenius level, far beyond that of your favourite man of genius. Let us also assume that, though highly educated in the sciences, they have been fortunate enough to have had zero exposure to psychology. In addition, we presume that, being highly involved and abstracted in the pursuit of science, they have never noticed what we call individual differences in abilities.

A quick exploration of the island assures them that food is plentiful, that shelter is available, and that clothing is not a necessity. To allay the boredom that they foresee as an eternity in this labourless heaven, they decide to spend their time in the further pursuit of science, but the lack of the wherewithal for constructing gadgets rules out any research in the physical sciences. Having had a college course in Bugs and Bites they proceed to study the life of the island's insects, then the habits of the birds, and the antics of a couple of monkeys. The manner in which the monkeys adjust to the environment leads them to set up some trial situations for more systematic observation. Needless to say, the monkeys show evidence of what we call learning and what we call problem solving.

Eventually they decide that attempting to outwit each other might be more fun than being outwitted by the monkeys, so they begin to cook up and use games and problems for this purpose. This activity leads each to speculate and introspect about how problems are invented and how solved. Then by cleverly designed experiments, preceded of course by theory, they set forth highly developed laws and principles about what we call reasoning and problem solving. Incidentally, they switch back and forth between the roles of experimenter and subject, there being no college sophomores available. They continue for years the study of their own mental operations, constantly on the alert for new phenomena to investigate.

And now with apologies to the ancient Greeks, who did have some ideas along these lines, we leave with you the 64-million drachma question: Will our two identical supergeniuses, being totally unaware of individual differences, ever hit upon and develop a concept of intelligence?

4

C. Burt (1940)

Why does the psychologist need factors?

The Factors of the Mind: An Introduction to Factor Analysis in Psychology (University of London Press), ch. 1, pp. 3–13

THE ORIGIN OF FACTOR ANALYSIS

It is impossible to understand the nature of a mental factor unless we first understand the nature of the technique by which it is derived. Historically what we now call factor analysis is a mathematical procedure developed by psychologists as an extension of the ordinary device of correlation: 'the commencement', says Spearman (to whom more than to anyone else the introduction of factorial methods is due), 'consisted in noting that, when any pair of abilities are correlated with each other, they can be regarded *as depending on a common factor*'. Correlation in its turn, or so it has generally been maintained, is merely a statistical application of what Mill called the 'method of concomitant variation'; and Mill's fifth 'canon' might well be taken to express the implicit assumption on which nearly all interpretations of factor analysis have been tacitly based: 'Whatever phenomenon varies in any manner, whenever another phenomenon varies in some particular manner, is either a cause or an effect of that phenomenon, or is else connected with it *through some fact of causation.*'

In psychology, as in the biological sciences generally, the processes are too involved for us to isolate, as a directly observable 'phenomenon', either a simple 'cause' or a simple 'effect': at most, we can only surmise that some underlying 'fact of causation' connects the visible changes we can actually observe. Hence statistical analysis has to be used to supplement or take the place of experimental analysis, in order that we may allow for the complex mass of irrelevant influences which, in the simpler sciences like physics or chemistry, we should usually be able to remove or control. And in general the psychologist is able to state the connections between the facts observed only in terms of

C

partial dependence, seldom if ever in terms of *perfect* dependence. The degree of such partial dependence is measured by a coefficient of correlation or its equivalent; and, as Spearman puts it, 'the system of correlation proposed by Galton and elaborated by Pearson . . . may be conceived as expressing the *hidden underlying cause* of the variations investigated'. To designate the supposed 'underlying cause' – Mill's 'common connecting fact of causation' – the name 'factor' is now regularly used in psychology.

An example from an early research will make the form of reasoning clear. On testing a group of children for the chief school subjects, it was found that, 'as a rule, those who are bad at reading are bad at spelling as well; their arithmetic is also below the average for their age, but by no means as bad as their reading or spelling'. Now, we cannot suppose that weakness in spelling is (to borrow Mill's language) 'either a cause or an effect' of weakness in arithmetic. Consequently, we infer that both are 'connected' through some more fundamental cause, which we term a 'common factor'. We suppose, for instance, that an underlying ability – 'general intelligence' – is mainly responsible both for progress and for weakness in all three subjects. If spelling and reading further vary together in a way that is not wholly accounted for by the factor common to all three subjects, we apply Mill's 'fourth canon' – the 'method of residues'; we eliminate what is due to the first factor, and decide by a fresh application of the method of concomitant variation whether or not there is yet another factor – verbal facility, for example – common to reading and spelling, but not shared by arithmetic.

THE MEASUREMENT OF FACTORS

To render the arguments more precise, we endeavour at every stage to *measure* the amount of 'concomitant variation'. This, of course, means that we must begin by measuring the mental abilities themselves. Standardized tests are employed; and, as a rule, implicitly if not explicitly, the examinees' performances in the tests are first translated into terms of the variability of the group that has been tested, i.e. into terms of their own standard deviation, which is treated as a universal unit of measurement: the resemblances between their performances can then be measured by the average product of all the pairs. This is Galton's 'index of co-relation' as calculated by the so-called product-moment method.

It is important, however, to realize that the preliminary standardization of the unit is not indispensable. All that is necessary for the calculation is that the measurements should be expressed as deviations from their own average. Then, even though the measurements have not been reduced to terms of their own standard deviations, we can still use the average product of the pairs to measure the amount of concomitant variation. The product-moment is then termed the covariance; and in theory all forms of factor analysis can be applied to tables of covariances just as well as to tables of correlations.

When the calculation is completed, the degree to which each test performance appears to depend on the fundamental ability or 'factor' supposed to influence it is finally stated in terms of a 'factor loading' or 'factor saturation', as it is variously called, that is, a similar coefficient or 'index' measuring the amount of resemblance (or 'co-relation') between the empirical test on the one hand, and the estimated measurements for the hypothetical factor on the other. Tests of significance are generally applied, not to the factor loadings or factor saturations, but to the coefficients of correlation or their residuals; and, as usual, they indicate, not the probability that the postulated hypothesis is true, but the probability that the figures tested may after all have arisen from the mere effects of random sampling, that is, from what is loosely called 'chance'.

THE FACTORS OF THE MIND

By applying calculations of this kind to the results of mental tests, psychologists have hoped to reach an inventory of what, in Spearman's phrase, have been described as 'the abilities of man'. Verbal ability, arithmetical ability, mechanical ability, retentivity, quickness, perseveration, oscillation of attention and above all a general factor of intelligence that enters into all we say or do or think – these, or qualities somewhat like them (for, to avoid misconception, the factorists prefer to designate their factors by letters rather than by concrete names), are supposed to be the 'primary abilities' that make up the human mind. Other psychologists have gone on to claim that, not only the intellectual or cognitive aspect, but also the emotional or conative aspect of the mind can be described in terms of definable factors. This branch of the work has attracted less attention. Nevertheless, it would clearly be a mistake to begin by identifying the 'factors of the mind', as Thurstone and Alexander appear to do, exclusively with cognitive 'abilities'.

The catalogue no doubt is still incomplete; but, we are assured, the number of 'fundamental traits' that have eluded discovery must now be very small. 'It seems to be a fact,' says a leading exponent of the

Spearman school, 'that there is only a limited number of such fundamental tendencies in the human being: Spearman has found five or so; Thurstone specifies seven; the Thorndike Unitary Traits Committee expects to find anything between one and twenty.' And the writer concludes: 'the implication is that these few fundamental factors account for, explain, or are the cause of, all human conduct'.

Still more recently, similar factors have been invoked to explain the resemblances, not only between test performances and temperamental traits, but also between human individuals – resemblances which tempt us to class them together in groups under the heading of 'mental types'. As before, the factors are deduced from sets of correlation coefficients or covariances: only now we start by correlating, not the measurements for two tests, but the measurements for two individuals, taking all possible pairs of persons, just as previously we took all possible pairs of tests. Unlike the 'trait factors', these 'type factors', it is declared, may be exceedingly numerous. 'There are,' so we are told, 'only a few fundamental tendencies in the human being, and therefore only a few unitary traits in the mind; but types exist in great numbers.'

It is frequently implied that these 'factors of the mind' are innate factors – fundamental elements in the individual's mental endowment handed on to him at birth. Thus, in one of the earliest investigations on intelligence tests, an attempt was made to show that the factor which they tested was not only general but also inborn. And some of the earlier investigations into type factors, particularly those that appeared to be associated with temperament, race or sex, suggested the possibility that the most fundamental of all would be those attributable to genetic elements, obeying Mendelian laws and producing traits either linked or segregating freely. It is, however, somewhat unfortunate that the term 'factor' is used for both conceptions – the statistical factors that we are discussing here and the genetic factors responsible for hereditary resemblances: the common name tempts the lay reader and the student to identify the two.

About the genetic factors that influence mental ability and temperament comparatively little is known as yet. Children undoubtedly resemble their parents in regard to general intelligence and many other mental factors, and that in a degree that cannot be wholly explained by post-natal influences. Yet the relation between the observable phenomena is exceedingly indirect, and typical of the remote and complex type of causal determination with which the correlationist has to deal in psychology. The most that we can say about mental inheritance with any assurance is that each individual apparently receives through his two parents a very large sample of a still larger number of unit-determiners; that this sample is mainly but by no means entirely random (certain groups of determiners, for example, being always carried on the same chromosome); that his subsequent development must involve a further sampling of this sample (or rather of its possible effects); and that his mental reaction in any given situation must depend on yet another process of selecting or sampling whatever tendencies have thus developed or survived. It follows that, with few exceptions, the overt mental types, which are all that the psychologist can detect with his tests and rating scales, are related only in a very remote and indirect fashion to inherited types or tendencies: they are, as the biologist would say, phenotypes rather than genotypes. Indeed, if there were any likelihood of establishing mental genotypes, factor analysis, I imagine, would hardly be the main line of approach which the genetic psychologist would adopt in his endeavours to discover them.

THE CRITICISM OF FACTORS

In seeking to demonstrate the existence of the mental factors I have described, different psychologists have employed different modes of calculation. As a consequence, they have reached somewhat discrepant conclusions. Each, therefore, has been tempted to criticize any method yielding results a little different from his own. So far, however, the validity of factor analysis as such has not been seriously questioned. The non-statistical psychologist, it is true, is always a little dubious of statistical demonstrations; but no systematic refutation of the procedure as a whole has ever been attempted. The detailed differences between the various devices hitherto proposed have been described and discussed with great impartiality and clearness by Professor Godfrey Thomson.[1] Hence their special features need not detain us here.

Thomson's book, however, has brought the chief issues to a head. Though he has never condemned the general method in itself, he has always been one of the most vigorous critics of the conclusions popularly drawn. The aims of factor analysis, as usually stated, he readily accepts: its objects, he says, are twofold – 'to arrive at an analysis of mind based on the mathematical treatment of experimental data obtained from tests of intelligence and of other qualities, and to improve vocational and scholastic advice and prediction by making use of this analysis in individual cases'. But whether the mental factors thus arrived at will be so few or so simple as is commonly maintained, he very much doubts.

[1] *The Factorial Analysis of Human Ability*, 1939.

From the first he has opposed the familiar theory that there is a single central factor pervading and dominating all the activities of the mind – 'Spearman's *g*' or 'general intelligence', as it is variously termed; and in his more recent discussions he goes farther still, and rejects the whole notion that the human mind may be constructed out of a small number of fundamental capacities or traits. 'Far from being divided up into unitary factors, the mind is a rich, comparatively undifferentiated complex of innumerable influences – on the physiological side an intricate network of possibilities of intercommunication.' The mathematical peculiarities exhibited by our correlation tables are attributable, so he believes, not to psychological laws, but to statistical laws: they are at bottom simply the result of sampling the innumerable factorial elements of which the mind is ultimately composed, elements which he apparently would identify with the 'neurone arcs' of which the central nervous system is built up.

It would seem, however, that what Thomson is treating as the ultimate factors are something quite different from what Spearman, Thurstone, Kelley, Alexander and most other psychologists have had in mind, namely, what they would call the primary intellectual abilities – *g*, *v*, *c*, *F* and the like. Spearman's 'basic components' are rather like the organs of the body; Thomson's are more like its cells; or (to adopt an analogy which both writers use) Spearman's are like the 'parts' of a motor car – the wheels, the lamps, the horn, the engine and the tank containing the petrol; Thomson's more like the ultimate molecules of which all the materials are composed. And there is this further difference between them: Spearman looks upon the mind as a heterogeneous structure built up out of a few essential mechanisms or components; Thomson insists that the mind is almost devoid of structure – a tissue of homogeneous cells rather than an organized whole of specialized parts.

THE REASONS FOR FACTOR ANALYSIS

What may be the ultimate structure of the mind, and whether its parts are numerous or few, and its elements similar or differentiated, are questions, so at least it seems to me, which must be eventually decided by other lines of research – physiological, biological, introspective and experimental. Our present crude distinctions between intellectual abilities may give way to distinctions between the functions of various cortical areas or cell layers (indeed, the chief group factors so far discovered rather suggest some such basis); and our distinctions between temperamental types may be resolved into biochemical differences produced by variations in the balance of endocrine secretions: so that in these directions factor analysis may turn out to be a mere makeshift – a temporary expedient that we may conveniently exploit while awaiting a more refined experimental technique. Since the field is highly complex, a direct advance by non-statistical methods is bound to be slow. Meanwhile, scientific curiosity demands at least a provisional solution; and the immediate needs of applied psychology call for working hypotheses and some practical device for determining the key characteristics of different individuals. It is these urgent demands that factor analysis endeavours to meet. How far can we trust it?

If I am correct, the main reason for the protracted controversies which have obscured the whole subject lies in the fact that the opposing parties, though nominally acknowledging the same general purposes, are interested each almost exclusively in one purpose alone – the theoretical analysis of the human mind in the one case, and the practical prediction of individual progress and development in the other. Spearman's original concern, as the title of his great work implies, lay in the abstract nature of intelligence and cognition; his aim was 'to discover the causal mechanisms of the mind and the general laws which they obey'. Thomson's starting point, as he himself has related, was an endeavour to improve the methods of selecting pupils for different types of school and career by scholastic examinations or by mental tests. I myself would rather place the initial emphasis on a third and somewhat lowlier purpose. It is one which, I am sure, both parties would accept as equally obvious, yet at the same time one which, just because it is so easily taken for granted and perhaps because it is less ambitious, has been continually passed by. In my view the *primary* object of factorial methods is neither causal interpretation, nor statistical prediction, but exact and systematic description. And I suspect that most of the confusion has arisen because factors, like the correlation coefficients on which they are based, have been invoked to fulfil these three very different purposes, and so have made their appearance at three very different levels of thought – like the famous legal firm of Arkles, Arkles & Arkles, which, 'more to its own satisfaction than that of its clients, canvassed three different lines of business in three small offices on three different floors'.

5

L. G. Humphreys (1962)

The organization of human abilities

American Psychologist, 17, pp. 475–83

I have been disturbed for several years at two related tendencies in the work on human abilities. One is the proliferation of factors as more and more experimental test batteries have been intercorrelated and factored. For example, Guilford (1956) now recognizes more factors than Thurstone (1938) had tests. The other is the continuing tendency to think of factors as basic or primary, no matter how specific, or narrow, or artificial the test behaviour may be that determines the factor. This criticism, by the way, is not directed solely at those who search for genetic mechanisms underlying factors. It is directed equally at those who look primarily for general laws of learning or at those middle-of-the-roaders who would look for laws of human development jointly dependent on nature and nurture. Just because a number of scores have been intercorrelated, the correlations factored, and some interpretable factors obtained, is no adequate basis for concluding that these are the primary factors, that these are the factors for which measuring devices should be constructed, that these are the factors which should henceforth be used in practice or in further research. In other words, to paraphrase Gertrude Stein, I object to the conclusion that a factor is a factor is a factor.

These twin difficulties have become even more pressing with the development and wide use of high speed digital computers, and particularly with the increasing use of programs with those computers that objectively rotate the initially computed factors to 'simple structure'. The result can be empiricism at its blindest. Except for the decision as to the number of factors to rotate, which is a very important subjective component in the procedure, factor analyses can now be ground out without having the basic data seen by human eye or touched by human hand.

Now I must admit that these criticisms of empiricism and objectivity come haltingly to my lips. My own orientation is highly empirical, but I can still detect misdirected empiricism. May I also remind you that I have been characterizing factor analysis for several years as a useful tool in hypothesis formation rather than as a method of hypothesis testing (Humphreys, 1952). Our ability to make probability statements concerning the outcomes of experiments, either for decision making or for estimation purposes, lies at the very heart of the scientific method. Factor analysis simply does not qualify on this score. Let us, therefore, use it for what it can do; and since it is an aid in hypothesis formation, let us not neglect other aspects of hypothesis formation. In particular, when we factor, we need a model of the nature of individual differences. The factor analytic techniques do not automatically provide such a model. It must be provided by the investigator.

I start with the assumption, which I think is by now well supported, that test behaviour can almost endlessly be made more specific, that factors can almost endlessly be fractionized or splintered. When two tests differ in only the slightest aspect so that by definition they are not parallel forms, but are almost as highly correlated as parallel forms, we have by present standards the definition of the ultimate primary factor. In order to construct systematically non-parallel tests that differ only in the slightest aspect, each must be made highly homogeneous. Following this pattern will lead to the collection of a very large number of tests, each of which might be scalable in the original Guttman (1944) meaning of that term. For each there would be a near parallel form. Such tests would define many factors, probably many more than Guilford (1956) is suggesting, but they would not be, in my book, candidates for the designation 'primary'.

HIERARCHICAL MODEL

One model that appealed to me several years ago as a way out of this morass, and one still applicable to a great deal of psychological data, is the hierarchical model in a single order that British writers, for example (see Vernon, 1950), have discussed for many years and for which Schmid and Leiman (1957) and Wherry (1959) have supplied computational solutions. Schmid and Leiman have also pointed out the algebraic identity between their hierarchical model and factoring in accordance with the simple structure model in several orders.

Vernon's structure has been supported by numerous British studies. Lack of support on this side of the Atlantic is due solely to the fact that American psychologists have been using a different model. At the top of Vernon's hierarchy is g, though Vernon interprets his factors in accordance with Thomson's theories rather than Spearman's. Below the major group factors are minor group factors. One is known as the verbal–numerical–educational factor and the other as the practical–mechanical–spatial–physical factor. The probable appearance of other factors at this level in the hierarchy is discussed, but such factors are not well known. Below the major group factors are minor group factors and below those the specific factors. The factor splintering that has taken place in recent test construction history, however, may introduce still further levels in the hierarchy between major and specific factors. Thus Vernon recognizes the need for factoring in at least three orders, since there are at least three levels of his hierarchy beyond specific factors, if the intercorrelations of ability measures are to be adequately described psychologically.

As compared to factoring in several orders, my preference for a hierarchy within a single order is based on rather simple grounds: it is easier to misinterpret factors in several orders. Most people assume that first-order factors are the primary ones just because they are first to appear. Second-order factors are rather mysterious because they are defined, not by tests, but by first-order factors. Third-order factors are completely incomprehensible. Thus Guilford (1954), in his revision of the *Psychometric Methods*, concluded: 'The writer reserves judgement with respect to the psychological validity of factors higher than the first-order ones.' In contrast, the hierarchy of factors in a single order places the primary emphasis on the broadest factors (those in the highest order) and all factors are defined by the original test variables. First-order factors are typically placed where they belong, far down in the hierarchy with small loadings on a small number of variables. Their lack of generality in the test battery is indicative of their general psychological unimportance.

A logical hierarchy of mechanical information

A hypothetical hierarchy from the field of mechanical information can be used to illustrate these points. I offer no apology for offering a 'cooked-up' example. Principles can be seen more readily in this way.

I shall assume that there are four discriminable levels of specificity of tests of mechanical information. These are as follows: (*a*) information about specific tools, e.g. the cross-cut saw or the socket wrench; (*b*) information about groups of tools having a common function, e.g. saws or wrenches; (*c*) information about areas of mechanical interest, e.g. carpentry or automotive; (*d*) general mechanical information, sampling from several areas such as carpentry, automotive, metal working and plumbing.

If certain reasonable assumptions are made concerning the inter-relationships of items and tests in this hierarchy, the logical hierarchy will become evident empirically. These assumptions follow: (*a*) Inter-correlations of items within a Level 1 test will be higher than correlations between items in different Level 1 tests, i.e. their homogeneity coefficients are higher than their intercorrelations. (*b*) Correlations between Level 1 tests involving the same group of tools will be higher than those involving different groups, which will be higher in turn than those involving different areas. (*c*) Correlations between groups of tools will be higher for those involving the same area than for those involving different areas. (*d*) Correlations between areas of mechanical interest will be higher than those involving any one area of such interest and other factor measures, such as verbal comprehension or spatial visualization.

This four-stage hierarchy of mechanical information tests will generate three different levels of factors. Intercorrelations of Level 1 tests will produce tool group factors. Similarly, intercorrelations of Level 2 tests will produce area factors, and intercorrelations of Level 3 tests will produce the general mechanical information factor. Note that if we were to extract factors from item intercorrelations a fourth and most specific level of factor would result, namely, tool factors.

Factoring hierarchical data

As an example of the consequence of the assumptions concerning this hierarchy of tests, a factor analysis model is presented. The first row of Table 5.1 contains arbitrary factor loadings, but so selected as to reflect the assumptions made, of a Level 1 test. The second and third row values were computed from the first row by assuming that all Level 1 tests have comparable loadings and that each test at the more general level is the sum of three tests at the preceding level. For the fourth row five separate area tests were assumed.

The illustration thus uses forty-five Level 1, fifteen Level 2 and five Level 3 tests. The orthogonal factor model includes fifteen tool-group factors, five area factors and one general factor. We will examine the consequences of factor analysing the forty-five Level 1 tests.

The correlational matrix in this example would define only fifteen factors, since there are no independent measures of anything but tool-group factors. Objective orthogonal rotations would neglect six important factors. The theoretical structure could be reproduced in orthogonal rotations only by extracting six additional factors (or adding six dimensions with zero loadings) and by rotating to meaningful positions. If twenty-one centroid factors were used in rotations, factors could not be treated as if they were all equally important; one could not simply try to approximate simple structure and achieve the desired result. The factor analyst instead would have to have a theoretical model in mind toward which his rotations would be directed.

TABLE 5.1. *Factor analysis model for the mechanical information area*

Type of test	General mechanical information	Area of mechanical interest	Tool group
Level 1	·4000	·4500	·5000
Level 2	·4645	·5225	·5806[a]
Level 3	·5721	·6435	·2439[a]
Level 4	·8418	·1894[b]	·0718[c]

[a] Indicates the loading which would be obtained on each of three factors of this type.
[b] Indicates the loading which would be obtained on each of five factors of this type.
[c] Indicates the loading which would be obtained on each of fifteen factors of this type.

If we use oblique axes, and obtain factors in all orders, we do not need to be as arbitrary. The fifteen first-order factors would define five second-order factors and the latter would in turn define a general factor in the third order. If we had decided to start our analysis from items rather than from homogeneous tests, all of these factors would have been pushed back one order with a set of forty-five tool factors being found in the first order. The original structure, in other words, is preserved in the full oblique solution.

It should be particularly noted, however, that fully meaningful psychological description is not obtained with oblique axes until factors at all orders have been exhausted. The factor analyst who uses oblique solutions and stops with the first order is not better off than the one who uses objective orthogonal rotations. The oblique solution in such a case can be distinctly less meaningful, on the other hand, than one obtained by subjective orthogonal rotations, i.e. by rotations directed toward a meaningful model.

Problem of sampling of tests

The solution, as in all cooked-up examples, is nice and neat. All of us recognize the difficulties that would be introduced by sampling errors alone. There is another sort of error, not generally recognized, that also makes the rotation and interpretation of factors difficult. Either by design or by accident, more tests are constructed in one area than another. Also, the more intensively an area is tilled, the more likely one will find a hierarchy of tests of varying degrees of specificity. Thus one fluency factor is divided into multiple fluency factors as a result of intensive test construction (Fruchter, 1948) and so on. Cattell (1952) seems to have been more aware of this problem than anyone else, but he does not have a solution to it. Cattell writes in terms of density of sampling of tests from a given population, but does not arrive at independent definitions of a population of tests and *density* of sampling from that population.

To follow along this line, let us suppose that our test constructor is more interested in and has more knowledge about carpentry and automotive mechanics than about other areas of mechanical information. Thus he constructs several, let us say nine, Level 1 tests in each of those areas with each set of nine tests covering three tool groups. He covers three other areas less intensively, not going beyond Level 2 in his test construction, and provides three such tests in each area to define possible factors.

TABLE 5.2. *Primary pattern – first order*

	Factors								
Variables[a]	I	II	III	IV	V	VI	VII	VIII	IX
1–3	6990	0000	0000	0000	0000	0000	0000	0000	0000
4–6	0000	6990	0000	0000	0000	0000	0000	0000	0000
7–9	0000	0000	6990	0000	0000	0000	0000	0000	0000
10–12	0000	0000	0000	7824	0000	0000	0000	0000	0000
13–15	0000	0000	0000	0000	7824	0000	0000	0000	0000
16–18	0000	0000	0000	0000	0000	7824	0000	0000	0000
19–21	0000	0000	0000	0000	0000	0000	7824	0000	0000
22–24	0000	0000	0000	0000	0000	0000	0000	7824	0000
25–27	0000	0000	0000	0000	0000	0000	0000	0000	7824

[a] Variables with identical factor patterns are grouped together for economy in presentation. Three variables of each type were assumed since three would ordinarily be necessary in order to determine communalities and define factors. The first nine variables represent tool groups in this example; the remainder are Level 1, or tool information, variables.

This matrix of twenty-seven variables generates nine factors in the first order, though the *a priori* orthogonal model which is an extension of Table 5.2 requires twelve factors. An objective rotation of orthogonal factors is obviously faulty so we shall proceed to the oblique solution. In this discussion, a first-order factor will refer to the computations made from the data of the example; reference to the *a priori* model will be in terms of tool-group factors, area factors, etc. The one-to-one correspondence between the model and factor orders observed in the first example does not hold in this case. Thus in Table 5.2 six first-order

TABLE 5.3. *Intercorrelations of first-order factors*

	I	II	III	IV	V	VI	VII	VIII	IX
I		4415	4415	3398	3398	3398	3398	3398	3398
II			4415	3398	3398	3398	3398	3398	3398
III				3398	3398	3398	3398	3398	3398
IV					5921	5921	2614	2614	2614
V						5921	2614	2614	2614
VI							2614	2614	2614
VII								5921	5921
VIII									5921
IX									

factors are tool-group factors and three are area factors; i.e. factors that were restricted to different orders in our first example now appear in the same order. Intercorrelations of these factors are shown in Table 5.3. When this matrix is factored, two of the three factors in the second order are seen to be area factors. The third is part of the general mechanical

TABLE 5.4. *Primary pattern – second and third orders*

First-order variables	Second-order factors			Intercorrelations of second-order factors			Second-order variables	Third-order factor XIII
	X	XI	XII	X	XI	XII		
I	6645	0000	0000	X	6646	6646	X	1·0000
II	6645	0000	0000	XI		4415	XI	0·6645
III	6645	0000	0000	XII			XII	0·6645
IV	0000	7695	0000					
V	0000	7695	0000					
VI	0000	7695	0000					
VII	0000	0000	7695					
VIII	0000	0000	7695					
IX	0000	0000	7695					

information factor. The one factor in the third order will pick up the rest of the general factor. The second-order factors, their intercorrelations and the third-order factor appear in Table 5.4.

In this example, which can be considered typical of many actual cases, even the oblique solution is messy. There are thirteen factors in all orders when the model requires only twelve. Two of the thirteen overlap in interpretation though they are in different orders. Different levels of factors appear in the same order. Without knowledge of the structure which produced these results, it would be difficult to make adequate interpretation of the findings as they stand.

Hierarchical transformation

In order to interpret factors in several orders, it is useful to transform, by the procedure described by Schmid and Leiman (1957), the oblique factors in all orders to a single orthogonal factor matrix with the number of factors equal to the sum of the factors in all orders. A matrix of this type is presented in Table 5.5. In the present example, if communalities for the third factor had not been accurately estimated, a further rotation would have been necessary after the transformation in order to collapse the two general factors into one. The choice of factors to rotate, however, would have been subjective; with accurate communalities the transformation automatically collapses the factors in question into a single factor. With this final orthogonal matrix there are no difficulties in trying to interpret factors in two or three orders – all factors are in the same order, all variables have a factor loading on each factor, and comparisons of loadings of different variables can readily be made.

The characteristics of the final transformed factor matrix can be likened to the growth of a tree. A main trunk, or trunks, branches into several limbs. These in turn branch into smaller limbs until, with a final branching, the twigs farthest from the trunk are reached. Each twig can be traced back to the main trunk along a single continuous path. This model is reproduced in Fig. 5.1.

One might ask at this point whether factor measures are desired for the factors at all levels of the hierarchy. One possibility, of course, is to use nothing but 'twig' tests since all the information contained in tests at other levels is available in the most specific. This course of action is not recommended for the obvious reason that there would simply be too many for the user to manage, or for the psychometrician to obtain adequate data on. The recommended procedure is to construct the broadest possible test, to move back toward the 'trunk' as far as possible,

TABLE 5.5. *Final orthogonal factor matrix in hierarchical order*

							Factors						
Variables	I	II[a]	III	IV	V	VI	VII	VIII	IX	X	XI	XII	XIII
1–3	4645	0000	0000	0000	5224	0000	0000	0000	0000	0000	0000	0000	0000
4–6	4645	0000	0000	0000	0000	5224	0000	0000	0000	0000	0000	0000	0000
7–9	4645	0000	0000	0000	0000	0000	5224	0000	0000	0000	0000	0000	0000
10–12	3997	0000	4495	0000	0000	0000	0000	4997	0000	0000	0000	0000	0000
13–15	3997	0000	4495	0000	0000	0000	0000	0000	4997	0000	0000	0000	0000
16–18	3997	0000	4495	0000	0000	0000	0000	0000	0000	4997	0000	0000	0000
19–21	3997	0000	0000	4495	0000	0000	0000	0000	0000	0000	4997	0000	0000
22–24	3997	0000	0000	4495	0000	0000	0000	0000	0000	0000	0000	4997	0000
25–27	3997	0000	0000	4495	0000	0000	0000	0000	0000	0000	0000	0000	4997

[a] This column represents the second-order general mechanical information factor which was merged with the third-order general factor by the transformation.

without sacrifice of differential validity for the prediction problem at hand. Thus we can form the following guidelines for the present example: When mechanical tests are used in an aptitude battery, it is probable that the general mechanical information test is sufficiently specific. For assessing current skills for placement purposes, the area test would be necessary. In a shop training course, an examination over a small unit might be at the group level.

One might also ask how the use of the orthogonal transformation is related to the principle of parsimony which is frequently considered a

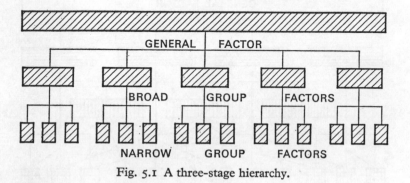

GENERAL FACTOR

BROAD GROUP FACTORS

NARROW GROUP FACTORS

Fig. 5.1 A three-stage hierarchy.

primary aim of factor analysis. The direct answer is that psychological meaning is considered primary; parsimony is secondary. The most parsimonious solution with respect to number of dimensions is the unrotated use of the principal components which account for some given percentage of the total variance. A second answer is that matrices of oblique factors and their intercorrelations are no more parsimonious than the orthogonal matrix presented here when additional factors simply reflect those intercorrelations. As a matter of fact, the oblique solution may duplicate information in successive orders which results in the loss of dimensions in the orthogonal solution. In this sense the orthogonal transformation may result in a more parsimonious solution than the complete oblique procedure.

Limitation of the model

Up until a year or so ago the preceding argument seemed very convincing, but unfortunately the hierarchical model is not sufficiently general. Consider, for example, the multitrait, multimethod matrix of Campbell and Fiske (1959). With traits along one dimension and with methods along another, as many tests are defined as the product of traits and methods. If one gets a single score, representing all methods, for each trait, a hierarchy of tests is obtained and the model seems adequate. But note that we get single scores for each trait only because we are usually interested in traits rather than in methods. It is also possible to add along the other dimension, obtaining a single score for each method, and obtain a second hierarchy. Twigs, to use the tree analogy, can no longer be traced back to a main trunk along a single path. Fig. 5.2 illus-

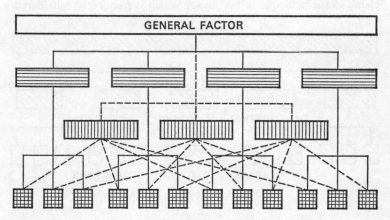

Fig. 5.2 A two-facet example.

trates this difficulty. Factoring of items would produce in the first order the tests of the trait-by-method matrix. Second-order factors would be both trait and method factors. The Schmid–Leiman transformation could still be used, but the resulting matrix of factor loadings would be quite complex. Even greater complexity is found if there are more than two dimensions whose product determines the test domain. With three dimensions, in place of two routes from twigs to trunk, there are six such routes. It becomes difficult if not impossible to define all of the factors in the second and higher orders that are logically present, and the hierarchical model breaks down.

FACET THEORY

I have moved on, therefore, to what I infer Guttman (1954b) means by facet theory. Whether he will recognize what I have to say about facets and elements is questionable, but he must be credited with the original stimulation. Perhaps, prior to Guttman, some credit must also be given to Thomson and Edward Thorndike because there is more than a superficial resemblance to their thinking. The contrast with the thinking of Spearman and Thurstone is also just as marked.

Definitions of facets and tests

Facets and the elements of facets are defined logically. Neither should be confused with factors. A facet is a logical dimension and its elements are the presence or absence of logically defined parts of that dimension. They must be manipulable by the test constructer. They are not even very psychological as defined. Thus item content might be considered a facet and words, numbers, figures and photographs would be its elements. A facet and its elements do not necessarily extend to all kinds of psychological tests. There is no necessity to strive for all-embracing categories. They may be restricted to a single domain such as achievement tests. A pragmatic test is applied to their definition, but this test does not refer to the behaviour of examinees. They should be useful to the test constructer; they do not need to make a behavioural difference in all populations, or even in a single existing population. In general, they should be selected so that they are potentially able to make a difference in behaviour, but whether they do may depend upon finding the right people who have the right genetic or environmental background. Thus they may or may not define factors.

Facet theory *is* used to define tests. The product of all elements of all facets defines a hypothetical universe of tests and makes possible the extension of content validity standards to the aptitude area. Many combinations result in completely feasible tests, other combinations may be difficult if not impossible to construct (I mentioned earlier that a given facet does not necessarily extend to all kinds of tests). This universe of tests is composed of highly homogeneous tests, though a homogeneous test is not a measure of a single element. Quite the contrary. The most homogeneous test contains a single element from each applicable facet. Tests of single elements are quite heterogeneous by either common sense or statistical standards since all other dimensions must be collapsed in order to obtain behavioural reactions to the single element. The best analogy here is to a complex factorially designed analysis of variance problem possibly with incomplete blocks. This is illustrated by Fig. 5.3, for a three-facet situation. In order to measure main effects one adds across all other dimensions. There are also interactions of various orders that are determined by the number of other dimensions over which one adds. Thus the facets and their elements not only determine a large number of quite homogeneous tests, but by collapsing one or more facets into a single score, by adding across dimensions, other broader tests are created.

For the example of Fig. 5.3 a test of a general factor results by obtaining a single score for items from all (or a random sample of) the ninety-six cells. A series of quite broad tests results by collapsing, in succession, pairs of dimensions. Thus one can construct four tests of the A facet, by collapsing B and C, then four of the B, by adding across A and C, and finally six of the C, by adding across A and B. These broad tests are followed by narrower ones obtained by collapsing only a single

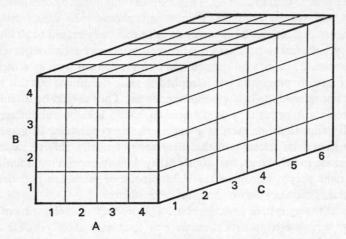

Fig. 5.3 Three facets creating ninety-six simple combinations
of elements.

dimension at a time. Thus there are sixteen AB tests, twenty-four AC tests, and twenty-four BC tests. The narrowest tests are those determined by the ninety-six independent combinations of $4 \times 4 \times 6$ elements of the three facets.

Relationships to simple structure and homogeneity

Consider the factoring of the set of tests, of all levels of homogeneity, systematically defined by facet theory. It is my prediction that simple structure would disappear. The beautiful examples of simple structure found with ability tests are by this reasoning the result of our test construction practices. Simple structure among human abilities reflects our ideas of what goes with what in a test. When I say that we get out only what we put in to the factor analysis, I realize that I am essentially repeating a favourite expression of Thurstone, but I also believe that my emphasis is different. I expect to find the tests constructed in accordance with these notions scattered throughout the factor space, with the exception that a positive manifold will still be found as long as negative item weights are not used, with a density depending largely on how systematically we vary the elements from test to test. The scatter will not be random, however; some elements, e.g. numbers, will produce more clustering than others will. It also follows that the simplex and circumplex patterns (Guttman, 1954a) among test intercorrelations will typically be more descriptive than factor patterns of the nature of human behaviour in response to test questions when we deal with tests constructed systematically in accordance with facet theory. This, however, is a long story which I do not have time to follow up in this paper.

From the facet point of view there are no 'pure' tests. One obtains better and better measures of an element by adding together as many elements on other facets as possible. Common variance associated with the element is increased while variance associated with other elements is decreased but cannot be reduced to zero by control of heterogeneity.

Facet theory thus gives one a new look at the concept of test homogeneity and the need for homogeneity. The implication for practice in test construction is deliberately to make the test as heterogeneous as possible within the limits of the definition of what you are trying to measure. This is what I meant in the preceding paragraph as 'control of heterogeneity'. An example of this point of view in practice might be the construction of a reasoning test. A good many tests are labelled reasoning, but one discovers in a particular example that the items are figures and only the analogies format is used. There are at least two facets of importance in reasoning: item content and item format. We can distinguish, as a minimum, the use of numbers, words, figures and photographs as elements in the item content facet and the use of analogies, series and classification as elements in the format facet. This 4×3 classification gives us twelve item types. All twelve should be used in the reasoning test, not just one. The only limitation on following this principle in this complete fashion is that of writing a feasible set of directions for the examinee. The deliberate introduction of maximum heterogeneity within the limits set by the definition of the test will result in a test with higher predictive validities than those with which we are familiar. Parenthetically, construct validity is not necessarily adversely affected by the lack of so-called purity. In my terms it would also be increased.

I have purposely neglected up to this point empirical studies of correlations among item types because I wished to stress the *a priori* analysis of facets and their elements. Correlational studies of what goes with what are, however, still useful and necessary. It may make little sense to construct all of the broad tests made possible by the facet approach, let alone many of the narrower ones, and part of the decision as to whether it makes sense is to determine whether the parts belong together empirically. Parts that don't belong together for one population at one point in time, however, may belong together in a different population or at a different point in time. Population differences may of course be either genetically or environmentally determined. Statistical analysis is important, but not controlling.

Nature–nurture problem

One cannot talk about abilities for any length of time without turning to the subject of their origin. In this case we ask about the causes for differential behaviour to the elements of facets. Facet theory basically has nothing to say about this question other than to recognize the opportunity for a lot of learning. Why should the switch from the analogies to the classification format make a difference in behaviour? Or from the analogies to the series? I find it difficult to believe that some people are 'born' to do series problems while others are born to do analogies. In general one would expect a specific learned component in every measure of each of the various element combinations. It is also possible, however, that good measures of functions likely to be genetically determined can be obtained by collapsing enough dimensions and adding together measures of enough specific element combinations. A general intelligence test constructed in accordance with this formulation would undoubtedly only partially resemble the Stanford–Binet or the Wechsler. I am certain that the 'standard' intelligence test contains much too much verbal material, but a particular combination of non-verbal materials is even farther from the answer. The largest genetic contribution will probably be found in the very broadest, most heterogeneous tests.

SUMMARY

I have called attention to two unfortunate tendencies in recent work on human abilities: the proliferation of factors and the tendency to think of only the first-order factors as the primary ones. An alternative model is to place factors in hierarchical order as advocated by the British psychometricians, especially Vernon. The application of the hierarchical model to a logical hierarchy of possible tests of mechanical information is presented, some hypothetical correlations are factored in several orders, and the Schmid–Leiman transformation is used to convert the factors back into a single orthogonal matrix manifesting the hierarchical principle. The test constructer and user is free to select, for measurement purposes, factors at any level in the hierarchy that suit his needs, though it will in general be found that broad tests high in the hierarchy are most useful. The narrow, relatively specific factors that appear in the first order are placed in the hierarchy in the relatively unimportant position that their size and generality warrant.

In certain kinds of psychological data the hierarchical model breaks down. This is illustrated with respect to the multitrait–multimethod matrix of Campbell and Fiske. As a more general way of thinking about psychological tests, facet theory of Guttman is suggested. Facet analysis would enable one to define a population of tests. It also clarifies and helps restate the need for homogeneity in a test. If a test is required for a selected element of a given facet, its homogeneity with respect to that definition is achieved only by striving for maximum heterogeneity along other facets. Controlled heterogeneity is the goal of test construction rather than maximum homogeneity in the statistical sense.

It would be nice to end this discussion with a listing of the facets and their elements that can be used in the construction of tests of human abilities. I have not spent the time on this problem that would be necessary to do an adequate job. It is also possible that my facets and elements would not be useful to another test constructer. Fortunately, Guilford has done a great deal of truly creative thinking about the structure of human intellect which can be adapted to the facet approach. Of course, he has been talking about factors rather than facets. As a consequence his definitions are frequently too psychological, and the elements are not as readily manipulable by the test constructer as they should be, but a good many ideas suitable for the task outlined can be found in his papers. One does have to read them from the facet point of view, always keeping in mind the main idea that we do not want separate test scores for the elements, but that knowledge of the elements is necessary in order to make wise decisions about the kinds of items that should be included in a given test score to be used for a given purpose.

6

J. L. Horn (1968)

Organization of abilities and the development of intelligence

Psychological Review, 75 (3), pp. 242–59

At the APA Convention of 1941 R. B. Cattell (1941) and D. O. Hebb (1941) presented papers based upon separate arguments but converging towards very similar conclusions; both concluded that two distinct concepts of intelligence should be recognized. In Hebb's theory the central ideas were expressed in the concept of an intelligence A, representing potential, and an intelligence B, representing realized intelligence. In Cattell's developments the somewhat similar ideas were represented in the concepts of fluid intelligence and crystallized intelligence. These papers aroused considerable discussion and debate. Yet surprisingly little has been done to bring the implications of the two statements into focus within general developmental and personality theory. The present paper is an attempt to rectify this (as the writer perceives it) unfortunate turn of events and thus to point the way towards more meaningful research on human intelligence.

The theory developed here will build primarily upon the Cattellian concepts of fluid and crystallized intelligence (abbreviated Gf and Gc respectively), rather than upon the Hebbian notions. There are several reasons for this. A major argument is that the Gf–Gc formulation is preferable to the Hebbian conceptualization because the principal concepts in this theory have specifiable and measurable behavioural referents, whereas in Hebb's theory intelligence A does not refer to measurable behaviour but to neurological potential. It is desirable for the behavioural scientist (in contrast, perhaps, to the physiologist, biochemist, etc.) to define intelligence in terms of observable, measurable behaviour, whence it may become possible to relate this variable to important variables of neurology, sociology, etc.

A major theme in this refinement of the theory of fluid and crystallized intelligence concerns the *development of abilities* and, more particularly, the development of a distinction between the broad patterns of abilities, Gf and Gc. It is hoped that this treatment of the topic will go some way toward achieving rapprochement between factor analytic research on human abilities and research and theory which has proceeded largely without benefit of factor analytic findings.

DEVELOPMENT OF FLUID AND CRYSTALLIZED INTELLIGENCE

In the earliest period of development no distinction can be drawn between fluid intelligence and crystallized intelligence. Indeed, one can seriously question the contention that intelligence (conceived of as a behavioural variable) is measured by tests developed for use in the first few years of life. The infant tests thus far developed seem to measure mainly a kind of sensory-motor alertness which bears little relationship to that which is identified as intelligence at later stages of development (Bayley, 1949, 1955, 1965; Hofstaetter, 1954; Hofstaetter and O'Connor, 1956). It can be argued that while such sensory-motor alertness sets limits on the rate at which intelligence can become manifest in behaviour, it is not an integral part of intelligence, *per se*.

However, granting that at least a small proportion of the variance on infant scales does represent measurement of intelligence as it is defined at later stages of development, the present theory argues that the relationship between early and later measurements of intelligence *cannot* be large for two principal reasons:

(*a*) Early in development intelligence is manifested in only one kind of behavioural function – what is called *anlage* function – whereas at later stages of development it is manifested not only in anlage function but also in functions which are referred to as *concept formation* and *attainment* (Bruner, Goodnow and Austin, 1956) and the use of *generalized solution instruments* or *aids* (Cattell, 1963; Ferguson, 1954, 1956). Although these kinds of function interact to some extent, one kind is not perfectly predictable from either or both of the other kinds and thus it is not possible for measurements which involve only one kind of function (namely, infant tests) to correlate highly with measurements which involve all three kinds of function (namely, childhood and adult tests).

(*b*) The influences of acculturation, maturation and damage to the physiological structures which support development of intelligence operate somewhat independently throughout development and with respect to the above-mentioned functions to produce distinct, measurably separate patterns of those abilities which, putatively, are said to indicate intelligence: the two principal patterns which emerge in this process are referred to as fluid intelligence and crystallized intelligence. But since the influences which produce these operate after the time that measurements on infants would have occurred and since many of these influences (excluding maturational influences more than the others) could not *in principle* be predicted from infant-scale measurements, the latter cannot be expected to correlate highly with childhood or adulthood measurements of either fluid or crystallized intelligence (much less a conglomerate of the two).

To clarify these points it will be necessary to more fully define the above-mentioned functions and to indicate the supposed process whereby fluid and crystallized intelligence become distinct.

Anlage function

This represents very elementary capacities in perception, retention and expression, as these govern intellectual performance. For example, span of apprehension – the number of distinct elements which a person can maintain in immediate awareness – is an elementary capacity and yet one which determines, in part, the complexity with which one can successfully cope in an intellectual task. It would seem that such capacities are not much affected by learning – anlage functioning is closely associated with neural–physiological structure and process – but that such functions operate to some extent in all intellectual performances and thus produce variance in all ability measurements.

The effects of anlage functioning can be felt in basically two ways in observed performances: (*a*) through a history of learning, which learning is then assessed in actual test performance, and (*b*) through demands imposed by the immediate task, *per se*, with little reference to previous learning. For example, a memory span test requires span of apprehension in the immediate testing situation more or less irrespective of prior learning, whereas a vocabulary test measures span less directly in outcomes which are results of this functioning over extended periods of learning.

In Hofstaetter's (1954) work a factor was defined primarily by test performances of the first two years of life. This could involve anlage function. However, anlage function is not to be equated with sensori-motor alertness. The latter refers to peripheral neural–effector–affector organizations which, although they may be important precursors of intellectual development, are not to be identified with it. Anlage function, on the other hand, involves central neural organizations which are integral to intellectual performances.

Generalized solution instruments: 'aids'

An aid is a technique which may be used to compensate for limitations in anlage capacities. For example, although most adults can retain no more than about seven distinct elements in the span of immediate awareness, they can nevertheless organize elements in such a way that they can effectively use considerably more than seven distinct elements in solving problems. Most of us remember a telephone number, for example, by coding the seven- or ten-digit number into sets of three and four digits, which sets are then called sequentially into immediate awareness. The formal rules of algebra are aids in this sense, as are many other problem solving techniques. Algebra represents a collection of aids which have been developed by many people, over a long course of human history, and deposited in what can be called the intelligence of a culture.

Concepts

The term concept, as used in the present theory, is in many respects similar to an aid. However, a concept is regarded as a category for classification of phenomena, whereas an aid is defined as a technique or method. In the formation of concepts one must perceive essential relations among phenomena and, on some basis of similarity, disimilarity, etc., categorize different things as the 'same'. For example, things which are perceived as similar with respect to 'leafiness', 'barkiness', etc., may be classified as 'trees' in distinction from other things which are classified as, say 'poles'.

A concept is not to be equated with a verbal representation of the concept. At any stage in development a concept may be known only idiosyncratically and not be represented in conventional language. A child may be aware of a distinction between trees and poles but have no conventional words with which to represent this awareness. However, idiosyncratic representations of concepts tend to become associated with conventional signs, such as the word 'tree'. When this occurs, it becomes possible to indirectly measure capacity for forming concepts by assessing ability to respond to conventional signs. This is the rationale upon which many items in intelligence tests are based. However, it must be recognized that one can be aware of more categories of phenomena than he is able to associate with conventional signs and that familiarity with such signs may not always indicate clarity of perception of the relations defining a concept. Indirect measures are bound to be somewhat invalid indications of capacity for forming concepts.

The accretion-transfer model

We need to conceive of how anlage functions, aids and concepts become welded together in the abilities which we measure and accept as indications of intelligence. J. E. Anderson (1939, 1940) has presented an accretion model which seems to account for some of the relevant facts. According to this, broad intellectual abilities are outcomes of an adding together (in development) of a series of specific abilities. In Anderson's mathematical representation of this idea each specific-ability accretion to the expanding store of skills is assumed to be independent of all others and no elements are lost as the process continues. If the development of an ability proceeds in this manner, one result will be a simplex matrix (Guttman, 1954a) of intercorrelations among test–retest measurements of the ability in question, as Humphreys (1960) has pointed out. Rather surprisingly, in view of the restrictiveness of the assumptions, this model has been found to work rather well to describe test–retest intercorrelations deriving from repeated measurements of intellectual abilities (Anderson, 1939; Humphreys, 1960; Roff, 1941). Hofstaetter and O'Connor (1956) have shown that by removing Anderson's second assumption, thereby allowing for the possibility that some additions in an early period could drop out in later measurements, the degree of congruence between predictions from the theory and test–retest intercorrelation data can be improved.

Ferguson (1954, 1956) has shown how principles of learning – in particular, transfer – can be utilized to help explain the way rather specific skills can be added together to form broad abilities. He points out that what is learned at one stage in development will tend to facilitate learning at later stages in development: the learning of one skill will tend to promote the learning of other similar skills and thus advanced learning in a particular area will be built upon less advanced learning. The end result will be a pattern of interdependent skills. But since this process would proceed in a somewhat different way for every individual, and it would proceed further for some than for others, the skills which enter into such a mutually facilitating pattern will correlate less than perfectly (even after eliminating error of measurement). Factors identified by means of factor analysis with ability-test performances represent such patterns of positively but imperfectly correlated skills. Thus the Ferguson theory provides an indication of the learning processes which operate to produce the well-replicated results of factor analytic studies of human abilities (as summarized by French, 1951; French, Ekstrom and Price, 1963; Guilford, 1967; Vernon, 1961). The Fleishman–Hempel (1954, 1955) studies (which Ferguson cites), and, more recently, the study of Duncanson (1964), illustrate how this kind of process operates over short periods of learning.

Several influences in addition to positive transfer in learning would operate in development to produce interdependence among skills and thus lead to the formation of the ability patterns identified by means of factor analysis. Skills learned under the aegis of a particular institution – a school, for example – would tend to be positively intercorrelated relative to skills learned in another setting – in a church, say – even in the absence of positive transfer. Similarly learned avoidance of particular educational situations and such influences as are represented by the promotion systems of schools and other institutions would tend to produce positive intercorrelation among skills which were not related by means of positive transfer. These processes are described in some detail by Horn (1965, 1967).

Separation of Gf and Gc through development

Any measured ability involves anlage function in the immediate situation and is a product of such functioning over the period of development which has preceded measurement. It would seem, in fact, that some primary-level ability factors, such as Memory Span (Ms), represent anlage function in fairly pure form. However, most primary-level factors (as established by the replicated research reviewed by French *et al.*, 1963, and Guilford, 1967) would appear to be compounds of anlage functions, concepts and aids welded together by the kind of development influences mentioned in the last section: surely the more general ability patterns, such as those indicated at the second order among primary-level factors or in the hierarchical bifactor (centroid) analyses described by Burt (1955) and Vernon (1961), are such compounds. This implies that a replicated ability factor, established at a primary or higher-order level, is an outcome of an orderly pattern of developmental influences operating in interaction with anlage functions. Such factors would thus be expected to appear only after a requisite period of development: Vernon (1961) and Guilford (1967) have pointed out that ability factors do not become distinct until relatively late in childhood. Also, some such factors would be expected to be relatively specific and cohesive, as, for example, many of those identified in the extensive research of Guilford and his co-workers, and others would be expected to be broad and diffuse, as in the case of the higher order factors said to represent fluid and crystallized intelligence. The question now before us is: What is the general nature of the orderly patterns of influence which produce Gf and Gc?

Acculturation constitutes a more or less orderly pattern of influences. These shape a crystallized intelligence factor. Of the myriad concepts and aids developed within a culture a relatively small number are seen to be sufficiently useful and/or interesting to pass from one generation to the next. These constitute what might be called the 'intelligence of the culture'. The major educational institutions of a society (including the home and its substitutes) are directed at instilling this intelligence in the persons (i.e. the young) who are expected to maintain the culture. The anlage capacities of individuals are thus harnessed, as it were, by the dominant culture for the purpose of maintaining and extending the 'intelligence of the culture'. This process is architectonic, building from a base of prerequisite concepts and aids to a superstructure of complex and esoteric concepts and aids by means of a promotion system which systematically increases the extent of acculturation of some and systemically reduces this for others. Thus, as development proceeds, individual differences in extent of acculturation will increase. Since many of the concepts and aids acquired under this pattern of influence are of a kind which, putatively, are said to indicate intelligence, the factor which results from this pattern of influence can be identified as a kind of intelligence. This is the factor representing crystallized intelligence.

However, it must be recognized that some of the learning which underlies expression of intellectual abilities and some of the basic processes involved in this expression, such as anlage function, are not very closely related to acculturation. For example, Piaget's (1950a, 1952a; Hunt, 1961) work indicates that the young child develops concepts and aids as a result of manipulations and experiments which are *not* arranged by those who would educate the child. Such incidental learning occurs throughout development. Although acculturation will depend upon this to some extent, the learning itself is not a product of acculturation and this latter is determined by many factors which are quite independent of the incidental learning. Similarly, to the extent that all persons in a society are exposed to comparable conditions for learning, individual differences in that which is learned need not be a product of acculturation. In these cases individual differences in learned abilities will be rather directly related to individual differences in the physiological structures which support intellectual functioning. It is apparent that influences which affect these structures occur largely independently of acculturation. Injuries to the brain are not determined by prior learning and although the effects produced by such injuries often will be felt in subsequent learning, they do not necessarily result in cessation of courses of learning already set in action, nor do they necessarily eliminate skills already learned (as Hebb demonstrated in 1941). The influences of heredity and maturation are likewise independent, to a considerable extent, of acculturation. Thus, to the extent that measured intellectual abilities involve primarily only anlage functions or aids and concepts which are products of incidental learning, the abilities will have been formed under a unitary set of influences affecting physiological functioning. If these abilities are of the kind which, putatively, are said to indicate intelligence, then the broad factor which involves them can be said to be a kind of intelligence – namely what, in this theory, is called fluid intelligence.

NEUROLOGICAL COUNTERPARTS OF FLUID AND CRYSTALLIZED
INTELLIGENCE

Both Gf and Gc reflect neural–physiological–heredity influences and both involve learned abilities. The essential difference is that a relatively large proportion of the reliable variance in fluid intelligence reflects a pattern of physiological influences and a relatively small proportion of this variance reflects acculturation, whereas the opposite emphasis occurs for crystallized intelligence.

Behaviourally, an intellectual ability is a compound of anlage functions, aids and concepts. Such a compound is represented in physiological function principally as a pattern of neurons which fire together (cf. Hebb, 1949). The firing of one neuron (or a small number of neurons) in such a pattern will tend to activate the entire pattern. Such patterns may be highly over-determined, as when a great number of neurons are linked together in mutually facilitating networks, or they may be relatively 'under-determined' – that is, involve only a few neurons, the firing of which is not over-determined by the firing of any one of many other neurons. The loss (as by brain damage) of a small number of neurons in a highly over-determined pattern may have virtually no influence on the overall functioning of the pattern, since the firing in the network is determined by the vast number of neurons still remaining. In an 'under-determined' pattern, on the other hand, the loss of a few neurons can result in loss of functioning of the entire pattern.

The behavioural counterpart of an over-determined neural pattern is a set of mutually supportive skills linked together through positive transfer. Crystallized intelligence is comprised of such sets of skills. The abilities of this factor should therefore not be greatly affected by brain damage and similar loss of efficiency of neurological function, provided, of course, that the damage or loss of efficiency is not extensive. The neurological counterpart of anlage function is a 'built in' network of neurons, probably not over-determined in the above-mentioned sense. Similarly, the patterns of skills acquired by incidental learning generally would be smaller and more isolated, neurologically speaking, than would the patterns of skills constructed through the architectonic process of acculturation. On this basis it is predicted that fluid intelligence will be more sensitive to changes in efficiency of neurological functioning than will crystallized intelligence.

SOME CONSEQUENCES AND EVIDENCE

A basic hypothesis deriving from this theory stipulates that if the inter-relationships among a wide variety of intellectual performances are analysed by means of covariational procedures such as factor analysis, there should be found two broad patterns, one involving performances which rather clearly indicate advanced knowledge of the culture and one in which this is not the case but which in other respects clearly indicates intelligence.

Extensive but rather tangential evidence relating to this hypothesis has been collected by Horn (1965). Studies designed specifically for the purpose of exploring implications of the hypothesis have been reported by Cattell (1963, 1967), Horn (1965, 1966), Horn and Bramble (1967), and Horn and Cattell (1966b). Humphreys (1967) has presented a critique of the Cattell (1963) study along with re-analysis of the data of this and the Horn–Cattell (1966b) studies. The general conclusion to be drawn from these investigations is to the effect that, indeed, two broad factors having the properties specified by the Gf–Gc theory are found among ability test performances. The specific nature of these factors is indicated in the summary of Table 6.1.

The factors of Table 6.1. are somewhat cooperative – that is, they involve some of the same tests. Each has about the same relationship to General Reasoning, for example. The factors are positively correlated.

TABLE 6.1. *Summary of some results from studies in which Gf and Gc factors have been identified*

Symbol	Behavioural indicant[a]	Approximate factor coefficient[b]		Symbol	Behavioural indicant[a]	Approximate factor coefficient[b]	
		Gf	Gc			Gf	Gc
CFR	Figural Relations. Eduction of a relation when this is shown among common figures, as in a matrices test.	·57	·01	Rs	Formal Reasoning. Arriving at a conclusion in accordance with a formal reasoning process, as in a Syllogistic Reasoning test.	·31	·41
Ms	Memory Span. Reproduction of several numbers or letters presented briefly either visually or orally.	·50	·00	N	Number Facility. Quick and accurate use of arithmetical operations, such as addition, subtraction, multiplication, etc.	·21	·29
I	Induction. Eduction of a correlate from relations shown in a series of letters numbers or figures, as in a Letter Series test.	·41	·06	EMS	Experiential Evaluation. Solving problems involving protocol and requiring diplomacy, as in a Social Relations test.	—·08	·43
R	General Reasoning. Solving problems of area, rate, finance, etc., as in an Arithmetic Reasoning test.	·31	·34	V	Verbal Comprehension. Advanced understanding of language, as measured in a Vocabulary or Reading test.	·08	·68
CMR	Semantic Relations. Eduction of a relation when this is shown among words, as in an Analogies test.	·37	·43				

Note: After Cattell, 1953, 1967; Horn, 1965, 1966; Horn and Bramble, 1967; Horn and Cattell, 1967.
[a] The referents here are primary factors, the names and symbols for which have been taken from French (1951), French, Ekstrom and Price (1963) and Guilford (1967).
[b] These are rough averages computed over the several studies in which the primary factor was used.

D

But it is clear that, in heterogeneous samples of older children and adults, the two patterns are distinct. Humphreys (1967) criticized Cattell's (1963) study on almost every count, and he found several points to question in the Horn–Cattell (1966b) study, but he concluded that the evidence indicated two broad patterns of the kind stipulated in the Gf–Gc theory.

Each factor in Table 6.1 contains tests which are accepted as measures of aspects of intelligence. The performances assessed by these tests can be seen to involve processes – of reasoning, perception of relations, eduction of correlates, abstraction, problem solving, etc. – which are widely recognized as integral to intelligence. Each factor thus indicates intelligence in an acceptable sense of this term.

But while both patterns indicate intelligence, they differ in noteworthy ways. The tests which are most characteristic of Gf are relatively culture fair in one of two senses: either the test materials are about equally common to all persons tested or else they are about equally novel. For example, the figural materials of the Matrices test are about as novel for college professors as for untutored labourers and the order of the English alphabet, as involved in the Letter Series test, is about as much over-learned by well educated as by poorly educated adults. In contrast, the vocabulary required in tests of verbal comprehension typically is that of a rather literate adult. Performance on such tests rather clearly indicates degree of acculturation. We cannot expect that any test will be perfectly culture fair or a perfect indicator of acculturation, but in so far as tests can be seen to involve one or the other of these emphases in measurement, they fall into the distinct patterns identified as Gf and Gc.

If anlage functioning is supported by relatively simple neural patterns and if abilities based upon incidental learning are supported by less complex cell assemblies than abilities based upon intensive acculturation, then fluid intelligence can be expected to show more impairment with loss of neurons than crystallized intelligence. If there are short-period, reversible fluctuations in the efficiency of neural functioning, producing an effect analogous to loss of neurons, fluid intelligence can be expected to show greater within-person variability over short periods of time than will crystallized intelligence. If ageing in adulthood is associated with loss of neurons, either because of accumulation of brain injuries or because of inherent degenerative processes, then the trend of change with age in adulthood for fluid intelligence will tend to be downward relative to the change with age for crystallized intelligence. It is on this basis that evidence on short-period fluctuations in abilities, changes accompanying brain injury, and changes associated with ageing can all be said to pertain to the construct validity of the general Gf–Gc theory.

The test performances which Hebb (1949) found to be most severely affected by brain injuries are of the kind which characterize the fluid intelligence, whereas the performances which he found to be least affected by neural damage are characteristic of crystallized intelligence. In the studies of Horn (1965) and Horn and Cattell (1966a, 1967), the age differences in the Gf and Gc factors, and in the separate tests which defined these, were found to be in accordance with the theory. That is, Gf was found to decline with age in adulthood, Gc was found to increase, and omnibus measures, involving about equal parts of the Gf and Gc functions, neither declined nor improved.

In the Horn (1966) study, the Gf and Gc patterns were identified in terms of variations *within* persons, as well as by the more usual R-technique correlational procedures. This is an important kind of evidence, for it indicates that not only do the various behaviours which define the Gf and Gc factors covary to distinguish one person from another, they also covary in a reliable manner within a person over short periods of time. Cattell (1957) has pointed out that this kind of evidence is necessary to establish that an observed phenomenon represents a *functional unity* – that is, a process within the person – but there have been relatively few studies designed to show this kind of evidence, and none in the area of human abilities. More pointedly, the evidence of this study suggested that of the reliable variance available in Gf and Gc a larger proportion of that for Gf pertained to short-period fluctuations within persons.

These studies thus suggest that several aspects of the Gf–Gc theory are in contact with reality. However, there are several points of controversy and several refinements of the theory which should be considered in the design of further research in this area.

COMPARISON WITH HIERARCHICAL THEORIES

Humphreys (1962, 1967) has pointed out that in many respects the Gf–Gc theory is congruent with hierarchical, group factor theories put forth (mainly in Britain) by investigators such as Vernon (1961), Burt (1949, 1955), and Moursey (1952). In Vernon's work, for example, a distinction is drawn between a broad 'abstract' verbal–numerical–educational factor (abbreviated V:ed), having properties similar to Gc, and an equally broad 'practical' mechanical–spatial–physical factor (referred to as k:m), which is somewhat similar to Gf. But while this theory is, in its broad aspects, similar to the Gf–Gc theory, it is different in the following rather important respects:

(1) In the V:ed–k:m theory mechanical abilities are regarded as 'practical' and thus integral to k:m, whereas in the Gc–Gf theory these abilities are regarded as very possibly an outcome of intensive acculturation and thus likely to fall into Gc, rather than Gf.

(2) In the most recent refinements of the Gc–Gf theory (as outlined below) a broad visualization function is regarded as distinct from Gf, whereas in the V:ed–k:m theory several tests involving visualization to a very considerable extent enter prominently in the definition of k:m.

(3) The operational definitions of Gf and Gc derive from factor analyses based upon the principle of simple structure (Thurstone, 1947) objectively determined (as specified by Horn, 1967), whereas the V:ed and k:m dimensions are defined by factoring procedures in some of which (bifactor procedures) the investigator makes subjective decisions concerning which variable goes into which factor and in all of which the principle of simple structure is not employed.

(4) Although it is mainly only a matter of semantics, not a crucial point in theory, it is perhaps worth noting that the 'abstract' versus 'practical' distinction which is drawn to characterize the difference between V:ed and k:m is not used and is not appropriate for distinguishing between Gc and Gf. Performance on the Advanced Matrices test demands a very high level of abstraction and this helps to define Gf, whereas performance on such tests as Associational Fluency requires a lower level of abstraction and such tests help to define Gc, but in both factors there are tasks involving rather high-level and rather low-level abstractions (cf. Hayakawa, 1949).

In his critique of the Horn–Cattell (1966b) work Humphreys (1967) pointed out that the answer to the question concerning the separation of visualization and fluid intelligence may depend rather crucially upon the answer to the (as yet) unsolved question of the number of factors which can be reliably determined in a factor analysis. In his reanalysis Humphreys found a distinction between the Gf dimension and a broad visualization factor, but only when he estimated five factors, not when he estimated a smaller number of factors. Perhaps this issue should be considered from a pragmatic point of view: 'Is it useful to maintain a distinction between visualization and fluid intelligence?'

As for the question about where the mechanical abilities fall in the higher-order relationships among all abilities, the existing evidence lends some support for both of the contending theories, as Humphreys (1967) pointed out. In the simple structure factor analytic solutions which Horn (1965) reviewed, the mechanical abilities had noteworthy relationships with both the Gf and the Gc abilities and this was also a finding in the Horn–Cattell (1966b) study. This indicates that Procrustean procedures are not required to get the mechanical abilities into a k:m-like dimension. However, it also indicates that these abilities involve components of crystallized intelligence. It would seem that the purely reasoning aspects of mechanical abilities may permit the use of fluid intelligence but that a substantial proportion of the observed variability in these skills must relate to the same kinds of intensive educational influences as determine other aspects of crystallized intelligence.

FURTHER REFINEMENTS

Sensory modality factors

Visual processes are instrumental in much of the learning upon which the development of intelligence is based. To a large extent, such processes govern the immediate expression of abilities, particularly in tests. If vision is lacking (as in the apes of Riesen's (1947, 1951) studies of early deprivation of sensory stimulation) some of the concepts and aids which otherwise might be developed simply cannot be developed. In so far as these are skills which enable persons to behave intelligently, the blind individual inevitably will lack this aspect of intelligence. Moreover, the figures, small printing, etc., which constitute the basic materials of tests are often such that if one is somewhat deficient in visualization, test performance can be expected to be impaired.

But visualization processes can be distinguished from central intellective functions. The ability to scan a visual display quickly is not to be equated with the ability to solve problems utilizing the information obtained from such scanning. Hence, while visualization will enter to some extent in the performances indicating both fluid and crystallized intelligence, it is possible that a visualization function can be distinguished from these intellective functions.

Although most current ability tests involve visualization to some extent, several involve this more than others. In particular, the tests of the primary factors known as Vz (Visualization), S (Spatial Orientation), Cs (Speed of Closure), Cf (Flexibility of Closure), explicitly require a subject to visualize movements of objects in space, find particular configurations imbedded within other configurations, bring about closure among disparate parts of a configuration, quickly scan configurations, etc. A central process seemingly involved in many of these tasks is one of visualizing in some sense of this term. Hence, if a broad visualization function pervades performance on many ability tasks but the above-mentioned primaries represent this to a greater degree than do other primaries, then a factor identified by these primaries can be expected to appear in a well-designed factor analytic study. The factor identified as Gv, visualization, in the analyses of Horn (1965, 1966), Horn and Bramble (1967), and Horn and Cattell (1966b) is interpreted on this basis (see also Smith, 1965).

The finding of a broad visualization influence pervading performances in ability tasks provokes the idea that analogous functions should exist to represent the influences of other sensory modalities, as, for example, audition and tactility. Such functions could not have been identified in the research thus far completed simply because the performances studied in this research were not of a kind that could be expected to involve systematic variance due to these factors. Holmes and Singer (1966) have found, however, that audition plays a rather important role in the learning of such crystallized skills as reading comprehension and that the influences represented by audition are somewhat independent of those represented by visualization. Similarly, Jones and Wepman (1961) have shown that sensory modality influences produce independent dimensions of variance in measurements of aphasia. If new tests were constructed which were otherwise like existing tests but involved auditory or tactile processes, rather than visual processes, then in factor analyses involving these and a broad sample of primary ability tests auditory and tactile factors might be identified and be shown to have variance in existing intellectual tests. If such functions were found to account for substantial portions of the variance in putative tests of intelligence, then it would be implied that truly balanced measures of intelligence (as Horn and Cattell, 1965, have discussed 'balanced') should contain items emphasizing use of audition and tactility, as well as visualization.

Speediness–carefulness factors

Questions about speed of performance, as it relates to intellectual functioning and speededness of test administration, have a long and complex history (cf. Morrison, 1960). It is not proposed that these questions be gone into in detail here. However, some of these questions have already come up in consideration of results obtained in previous research (Horn, 1965, 1966; Horn and Cattell, 1966b) and so must be recognized in the general theory.

Two broad factors identified in previous studies involved tasks wherein speed of performance was emphasized: these were labelled Gs (Speediness) and F (Fluency). One factor identified in previous work indicated a kind of opposite of speediness: this was labelled C (Carefulness). It will be worthwhile to consider these separately.

The Gs function was defined primarily by relatively simple tests in which virtually all subjects would get all problems correct if the test were not speeded. Tasks such as cancelling, copying (backward as well as forward) and simple numerical operations produced the principal variance in this factor. There is thus some suggestion that the speediness function is more closely related to temperament and/or effortfulness in the immediate testing situation than to a capacity to think quickly. However, the question implied here cannot be answered on the basis of existing evidence. More research is needed to clarify the possible distinction between involuntary and voluntary speediness and between speediness pertaining to central intellective functions and that associated with peripheral functions.

The broad fluency factor mentioned above was defined by the primaries Fa (Associative Fluency) and Fi (Ideational Fluency), but the factor also had variance in such tests as Vocabulary and Verbal Analogies. On logical and psychological grounds it might be expected that the fluency tests would correlate with speediness measures to represent a truly general speed-of-thinking function, but Gs and F were found to be largely independent. In the Horn (1965) study Furneaux's (1956) tests of intellectual speed had no appreciable correlation with F.

The F factor is not broad enough to represent intellectual speed, *per se*. Instead it seems to represent speediness only in tasks wherein it is necessary to bring concept labels (that is, words) from a long-term storage centre into immediate awareness. As Christensen and Guilford (1963) point out, such a function might relate to size of store of labelled concepts and/or to quickness in finding those concept labels which are stored, regardless of number.

That the latter accounts for some of the observed variance in the fluency function is indicated by the results from Horn's (1966) study of short-period fluctuations in abilities. One of the factors accounting for a substantial proportion of the reliable variability within persons over occasions was defined by associational and ideational fluency. This factor had a substantial *negative* correlation with fluent production of irrelevant associations, a variable which had substantial *positive* correlation with the F factor when this was identified among correlations based upon variation between people. Taken together, these results suggest that fluency may mainly represent an anlage function of ease of finding concept labels.

It should be noted, too, that the ideational and associational fluency primary factors which determine the second-order fluency factor are among those which currently are being discussed as indicative of creativity (cf. Getzels and Jackson, 1962; Guilford, 1962; Taylor, 1964). Moreover, some of this discussion seems to imply that creative ability – to be distinguished, theoretically, from motivation to create and creative temperament – may be functionally independent of intelligence. Thus it is possible that the factor identified as 'general fluency' is, in fact, a shadowy indication of a broad creativity function.

This hypothesis is made somewhat suspect, however, by results from recent research. The primary factor known as Figural Adaptive Flexibility (DFT), and sometimes discussed as indicative of creativity, was included in the Horn–Cattell (1966a) study, but it did not fall into the broad fluency factor and, in fact, had relatively little variance in common with associational and ideational fluency. In the Horn (1966) and Horn–Bramble (1967) studies, Mednick's (1962) Remote Association Test (RAT) was included. This is often referred to as a measure of creativity and is very similar to the tests which identify the factor O, Originality, also usually mentioned as indicating creativity (Guilford, 1962). Yet RAT did not come into the factor involving the fluency variables and, in fact, had relatively little variance in common with these. Instead the variance for this variable went into the Gc factor, suggesting that the 'originality' seen in remote associations may represent, primarily, crystallized intelligence. In any case, this evidence does *not* provide support for a hypothesis stipulating that the primary factors and variables said to be indicative of creativity do, in fact, indicate a unitary influence. It must be noted, however, that one of the areas most neglected in the sampling of factors in previous studies on the higher order structure of abilities has been in this area which contains the primaries that are said to be indicative of creativity.

Carefulness in an intellectual test is measured by subtracting the number of incorrect or irrelevant responses from a constant (the same constant being used for all subjects, of course), rather than by recording the number of correct responses, as is more usual (cf. Fruchter, 1950, 1953). If a test is speeded, so that not all people will attempt all items, the correlation between the carefulness score and the number-correct score can be less than 1·0. On first consideration, it might seem that carefulness in ability performances is merely the obverse of speediness. But the evidence does not support this notion. Speediness and carefulness in timed ability tests appear to be independent functions, although the correlation between them is slightly negative (-0.26 in the Horn–Cattell (1966b) results). The finding of a carefulness factor indicates that unwillingness to give incorrect answers is a fairly general characteristic, pervading a variety of intellectual tasks. This is one possible meaning of the concept of 'style' or 'strategy' in ability performances (cf. Bruner, Goodnow and Austin, 1956; Sigel, 1963).

When a test is scored by the constant-minus-wrongs procedure, the person who adopts a strategy of avoiding errors has the advantage; when the same test is scored by the usual number-correct procedure, the person who adopts a strategy of getting as many right as possible – even if this entails making a few errors – has the advantage. An interesting finding of the Horn–Bramble study was that if all of a set of primary factor variables are obtained in the first-mentioned way, the structure indicated by factoring the intercorrelations among these variables is very similar to that found by factoring among primaries measured by the usual number-correct procedure. This suggests that the same ability processes are mirrored in performances involving both careful and 'sloppy' strategies. Yet the Horn–Bramble results indicated that persons who score high on a factor when it is measured in a way which penalizes carefulness may score relatively low (as indicated by correlations of about 0.5) in a factor involving the same tests scored in a way which penalizes 'sloppiness'. Some interesting practical and theoretical questions are provoked by these results.

A hypothesis in the Horn–Cattell (1966b) study was to the effect that carefulness represents a kind of cautiousness such as might be determined by superego or self pride; but the evidence of this study provided little support for this hypothesis. It could be argued (after the fact) that really good measures of superego and self pride were not included in this study. In future studies it will be desirable to try out some new measurements of this kind, such as those identified (Cattell and Horn, 1963, 1964; Cattell, Horn and Butcher, 1962) among attitude variables as representing superego and self-sentiment functions.

It would seem that some of the observed variability in speediness and carefulness factors may stem from differences in motivation to achieve – that is, the kind of attribute which McClelland (1950, 1953) and his co-workers have described as need for achievement (n Ach). Similarly, it would seem that some of the variance in these factors might stem from an attribute similar to that which Atkinson (1958) has rather fully described as fear-of-failure (f-fail). It could be, too, that such n Ach and f-fail influences could represent states, not traits (cf. Horn, 1963, 1966; Horn and Little, 1965), engendered by situational factors. On *a priori* grounds it is reasonable to suppose that either the speediness, fluency or carefulness factor – or any two or all three – may represent variability which distinguishes individuals on a given occasion but is not a stable characteristic of any particular individual.

SOME GENERAL IMPLICATIONS

It is well known that even in rather homogeneous samples of subjects most tests which are accepted as measuring the intellectual abilities of humans have positive intercorrelations. Primary mental ability factors usually are found to be positively intercorrelated. The functions described in previous sections were positively intercorrelated in the studies cited. This well-documented finding of generally positive inter-correlations – a positive manifold – among intellectual abilities has been accepted widely as evidence in support of a hypothesis of a general intelligence factor underlying observed performances. While this evidence cannot be discounted and there is a sense in which it indicates a general intelligence, too much should not be inferred from it. Positive manifold is not equivalent to hierarchical order among intercorrelations (Spearman, 1927), although this seems to be assumed in some discussions of the concept of general intelligence. Hierarchical order may be interpreted parsimoniously as indicating one and *only* one influence, but positive manifold permits the possibility of many influences only loosely interrelated.

It is worth observing in this respect that not only do ability perform-ances intercorrelate positively, but also many non-intellectual person-ality factors fall into this same positive manifold. When anxiety tests are scored in the non-anxious direction, for example, they have generally positive correlations with ability measurements. Similarly, the self-sentiment and superego factors among attitude variables (Cattell and Horn, 1963, 1964; Cattell, Horn and Butcher, 1962) have generally positive correlations with ability tests. And, of course, social status and education are in the positive manifold. While it is reasonable to suppose that these several kinds of variables are mutually interdependent in rather complex ways, there is little to suggest that they all represent the operation of a single kind of influence. It is this kind of proviso which needs to be kept clearly in mind when interpreting the fact of positive intercorrelations among ability performances.

A practical implication of the theory and findings reviewed in this paper is that in educational and clinical settings we should move away from the idea of using a single ability test for the purposes of counselling, selection, diagnosis and prognosis. This does not mean that we should move to the other extreme of separately measuring every aspect of human intellectual ability, as seems to be implied by Guilford's theory. Nor does it mean that ability distinctions defined purely, or mainly, on the basis of logic alone – such as the verbal-quantitative distinction which McNemar (1964) seems to favour – should constitute a basis for applied use or theoretical formulation. Broad constructs of intellect should be based upon empirically established patterns of correlation in performance. Granted that the linear patterns established by linear factor analytic procedures are not ideal and are somewhat Procrustean, still they constitute reasonable first approximations of the more nearly ideal patterns and thus represent a useful first step toward accomplishing a truly adequate description of human abilities. In several ways, then, the position put here is a compromise of opposing positions currently extant in the field of human abilities.

A more argumentative implication of this review is that more future research should be directed towards bringing together results from studies pertaining to process and development, on the one hand, and results on structure (or correlational patterns) among performances in ability tests, on the other hand. For too long there have been too many invidious comparisons of work stemming from these sources, the implication sometimes being that one approach had the inside road to truth while the other was patent nonsense. When stated thus bluntly, of course, such extreme positions can be rejected rather easily. Nevertheless, there has been precious little cross-reference in the two major streams of research here indicated. Fortunately, many signs point toward removing communication barriers between these two. In this sense the Gf–Gc theory, with its emphasis on bringing factor analytic research on abilities into the context of developmental and process theories, is just one among several aspects of a Zeitgeist.

7

A. R. Jensen (1966)

Individual differences in concept learning

A. R. Jensen, *Analyses of Concept Learning* (Academic Press), pp. 139–54

To contemplate the problems of studying individual differences (IDs) even in relatively 'simple' forms of learning, such as conditioning, motor learning or rote learning, can be an unnerving enterprise. To have to think about IDs in *conceptual* learning is quite overwhelming!

If one of my graduate students were to tell me that he was thinking of doing his dissertation on IDs in concept learning and wondered if I could give him any help in getting started on this topic, my first impulse would be to give him two words of advice: 'First, if you want to study concept learning, try to steer as far clear of IDs as possible; second, if you want to study IDs in learning, then steer clear of *conceptual* learning.' This might appear to be cowardly counsel. But let me explain. I strongly advocate research on IDs in learning. I deplore the meagre state of our knowledge in this area, and I think it is high time that more differential and experimental psychologists launch large-scale, systematic research into this important realm of phenomena. The question I raise concerns the sequencing of our efforts. Practically all of the subject matter of experimental psychology is, of course, eventually going to have to be reworked from the standpoint of IDs. But it also seems reasonable to think that the state of the art in any particular substantive area must attain a suitable stage of ripeness before IDs in this realm can be successfully and fruitfully investigated. We must have some rather clear notions about the main parameters of our phenomena with regard to both the independent and dependent variables. Some degree of theoretical development that can afford a source of testable hypotheses is another sign of the kind of ripeness I have in mind. In so far as concept learning is viewed as being essentially continuous with other simpler forms of learning it shares in the same common body of theoretical development that has grown up around these other forms of learning. If we believe that many of the most basic and pervasive processes of learning are involved in conceptual learning and that some of these processes are the same as those involved in, say, conditioning, or discrimination learning, or verbal rote learning, or short-term memory, then it would seem reasonable to first try to investigate IDs in these more elemental processes in the purest and simplest forms in which they can be found. I believe that a great deal of what we are going to need to know in order to understand IDs in conceptual learning and in order to carry on worthwhile research on this topic will be most easily acquired through intensive investigation of IDs in simpler learning functions. Even here the difficulties are great. But it is my impression that, in general, the difficulties in studying IDs in learning increases disproportionately with the increase in the number of independent, intervening and dependent variables that are involved in the learning task. Conceptual learning is certainly at the 'high' end of this continuum.

Coming back to our hypothetical graduate student, what if he remains undiscouraged by what I have said and refuses to abandon the study of IDs in concept learning for either the usual kind of experimentation on the overall group effects of various independent variables on conceptual behaviour or for the study of IDs in comparatively simple learning processes? Is there anything I can give him by way of specific information or general orientation that could be of any value to him in his venture into this forbidding territory? Surely it is wide open virgin territory, and the student will find little evidence in the literature of previous investigators ever having explored very far into the interior. Nor will he have much company at the present time. He will find perhaps a few rather haphazard footprints around the edges, and perhaps a number of premature and abandoned efforts, but no clear-cut paths or signposts, at least, not into the region I would conceive of as the heartland of IDs in learning, conceptual or otherwise.

First of all, let us note some of the possible reasons for wanting to study IDs in learning. There are a number of justifiable aims in this area and these will in some degree determine our approach. It is hoped, of course, that these approaches will increasingly overlap as they are pursued and will converge in a common, systematic body of knowledge and theoretical formulation.

In the first place, we must do something about IDs in learning because, like Mount Everest, they are there. And they loom large in our research on learning; the more complex the type of learning, the more conspicuous and unavoidable are the IDs. If we are to develop a science of learning, we cannot ignore this vast continent of phenomena involving IDs. It is essential grist for our scientific enterprise, and it deserves higher priority in our investigative efforts than it is now receiving.

If we are primarily interested in prediction and diagnosis of conceptual abilities from a completely applied, practical standpoint, we can probably expect a fair degree of success without having to concern ourselves with many of the kinds of problems that will have to be faced by the investigator who hopes ultimately to achieve a scientific understanding of IDs in learning. Such understanding implies a great deal more than the achievement of a certain degree of actuarial prediction. The ability of psychologists to predict and control behaviour has, of course, always been far ahead of their understanding of behaviour. Knowing the correlation coefficient between two phenomena can always improve prediction of IDs from one phenomenon to the other, but the correlation may or may not add anything to our understanding of these phenomena. If someone tells me that a certain percentage of the 'between subjects' variance in a complex reaction time task can be 'explained' in terms of IDs in measured IQ, I'm afraid I am left with the dissatisfied feeling that nothing really has been explained, at least not about complex reaction time, though such a finding might afford some glimmer of insight into what might be the nature of 'intelligence' or whatever it is that the IQ test measures. I would hope that we can rapidly advance far beyond this level of thinking about IDs in learning.

Even the traditional experimental approach to the study of learning, based on statistical comparisons of experimental and control groups performing under different conditions of particular independent variables, cannot safely proceed very far without paying attention to IDs. The effect of an experimental variable on the performance of *individuals* can often be quite different from the *average* effect on a *group* of individuals. Where there are significant subjects × independent variable interactions, we should be wary of conclusions concerning the effects of a particular independent variable when these conclusions are based on group mean differences. When these differences are both large and statistically significant, there is less risk than if they are of negligible and insignificant magnitude. I wonder how many of the independent variables that have been relegated as unimportant on the basis of their producing negligible group mean differences in one of the standard experimental paradigms actually produce large and significant interactions with subjects. This 'between subjects' variance, of course, is usually just part of the error term in most experimental designs. Perusal of the analyses of variance in the experimental literature on concept learning indicates that some 50–90 per cent of the variance in the dependent variables in these experiments is due to IDs or to some combination of IDs and true experimental or measurement error. Because of IDs in learning-to-learn and because of changes in the factorial composition of IDs influencing learning at various stages of practice, the estimation of measurement error as distinct from variability due to IDs is itself highly problematic at the present time. This is one of the major methodological knots we must contend with in order to make progress in this field. It is troublesome enough in the study of IDs in rote learning. I wouldn't relish facing these problems on the level of concept learning. But they will surely and unavoidably be waiting there, larger than ever, for anyone who wishes to venture in this direction.

The fact of IDs is one of the strongest arguments I know of against the 'hollow organism' approach to research on learning. Research on IDs has the effect of making us think more about the inner structure of our 'black box' than we are inclined to do when we stick solely to investigating the effects of one independent variable after another. I think that this increased concern with the black box, which will result from paying more attention to IDs in learning, will have a beneficial effect on the development of our theories of learning. Knowledge of IDs in learning provides both a source of hypotheses about the nature of learning processes and a means of testing certain deductions from theoretical formulations. For example, a theory might postulate a single process as being involved in two phenotypically different concept learning tasks; and a computer simulation involving this single process could be made closely to approximate the performance of a human subject on both of these tasks. But what if we give these two tasks to a large number of persons and discover that the subjects show a reliably different rank order of ability on one task than on the other? Obviously our uniprocess model would have to be revised. In short, our models must be formulated and tested, not only with respect to group mean effects of independent variables or with respect to the performance of an individual subject (in which case IDs would never enter the picture), but with respect to the subjects × independent variable interaction. This class of data affords a rich and valuable source of constraints on our theories or models of any particular kind of learning. I dare say we will find out more about the nature of learning from the systematic study of the subjects × independent variable interactions than from the group mean differences resulting from the manipulation of independent variables. Both approaches are, of course, necessary for a comprehensive account of learning. And it is mainly through the manipulation of independent variables that we can discover and further investigate IDs in our dependent variables.

THE TAXONOMY OF CONCEPTUAL LEARNING

In order to make our subject matter amenable to research at all, it will have to be subdivided in some systematic fashion. Conceptual behaviour comprises a very broad class and no one can set out to study IDs in conceptual behaviour *per se*. Preliminary to any serious attempt to do research on IDs in concept learning, some kind of taxonomic analysis should be made of the whole field. For example, there are a number of fairly obvious broad classes of phenomena with which we are dealing here. Unless proper distinctions are made among these classes of phenomena, whatever results we may find in our study of IDs are apt to be quite blurred, possibly contradictory, and probably highly unsuitable for theoretical assimilation. We want to avoid, if possible, merely adding to the already overstocked store of uninterpretable psychological facts.

One basic distinction would seem to be that between concept *formation* and concept *attainment*. Underwood (1952) had some such distinction in mind when he distinguished between the initial *learning* of the elements that are involved in the concept and the *recognition* of elements comprising the concept. In the former case, the subject learns the concept almost from scratch, since at the beginning the relevant dimensions of the concept are not yet salient; the subject has not yet learned to discriminate the dimensions of the stimuli and has no readily available labels for whatever components of the stimuli he may be able to discern. Under these conditions we can speak of concept *formation*. In concept attainment, on the other hand, the subject comes to the task having already learned to distinguish and label all the stimulus elements; he simply has to discover in the concept attainment task which dimensions the experimenter has selected to be relevant for the attainment of the concept. It seems a safe guess that different processes and abilities are involved in these two forms of concept learning and they will, therefore, have to be kept clearly separated when it comes to studying them in relation to IDs.

Three other broad distinctions should also be kept in mind. First, there is concept learning on the basis of primary stimulus generalization. Whether or not stimulus generalization should be regarded as conceptual behaviour may in some cases be a rather arbitrary distinction. This does not matter so long as we are aware of the extent to which primary stimulus generalization as distinguished from other processes, such as semantic generalization, may play a part in our concept-learning tasks. The breadth and form of the gradient of primary stimulus generalization could, and probably does, involve IDs. This source of IDs would be important in concept learning only to the extent that the concept-learning task depended upon stimulus generalization.

A second kind of concept learning depends largely upon discrimination learning. Hull's experiment with Chinese pictograms is an example (Hull, 1920). Here different complex figures are presented, each of which does or does not contain some particular element. Throughout the learning trials only this single element of the complex stimulus is differentially reinforced until eventually it is discriminated by the subject, at least to the extent that it can serve as the cue for his identification of the complex figure as being a positive or negative instance of the concept to be acquired. This type of concept learning is closely akin to simple discrimination learning, so we might expect to find some of the same ID factors operating in both these forms of learning. Some of these factors would probably be much easier to discover in relatively simple discrimination learning tasks. Once found, their effects could then be sought in more complex concept-learning tasks of this variety.

The third main type of concept learning involves transfer of learning on the basis of symbolic mediating responses. The first two types of concept learning I mentioned – those based upon primary stimulus generalization and those based on discrimination – can also involve mediational processes. But they do not necessarily depend upon mediation. In this third category, however, I would include only those tasks in which the concept could not conceivably be attained except by means of symbolically mediated learning. This usually means verbal mediation. An example would be a sorting task in which such dissimilar objects as a watermelon, a potato chip and a glass of milk were exemplars of the concept. The concept could never be attained by the processes of primary generalization or by discrimination alone, but would depend upon the stimuli eliciting a common verbal mediating response, in this case the word 'food'. This type of concept learning introduces a host of sources of ID variance that are not apt to play a prominent role in simpler types of learning. Mediated concept learning will be affected to a large extent by transfer of learning from the subject's past experience. The subject's verbal repertoire, the structure of his verbal associative network, the strength of the subject's tendency to make verbal responses to non-verbal stimuli, and other such processes which are a mixture of nature and nurture will figure among the main determinants of IDs in concept learning of the mediated variety.

Finally we must distinguish between tasks that involve only concept identification, without any learning whatever being tapped by the task, and tasks that involve learning parameters. The Columbia Mental Maturity Scale (Burgmeister, Blum and Lorge, 1959) is a good example of a test of concept identification; it tests whether or not the subject has acquired a given concept at some time prior to the test. No learning is involved in the test itself. For example, the experimenter shows the subject a series of pictures – a locomotive, a ship, an automobile, a house and an airplane – and the subject is asked to pick out the one that is 'different'. Such a test taps past learning and recall rather than current learning. It is useful as a measure of status but not of process. It is, of course, generally easier to measure IDs in status than to measure IDs in processes, but it is the latter with which I am mainly concerned.

Beyond these broad categories concept-learning tasks can be analysed and classified in many other ways in terms of the degree of control over the various independent variables involved in the learning situation and the nature of the responses the subject is supposed to acquire. The innumerable independent variables that play a part in experimentation on concept learning should be classified in such a way that the investigator of IDs in any one type of concept learning or in any one experimental paradigm will be able to have some notion of the extent to which his findings can be generalized to other sets of conditions. For this purpose an index of similarity between concept-learning tasks would be useful; such an index could also help us in understanding relationships between specially contrived laboratory learning tasks and paradigms and their possible counterparts in 'real life' learning situations, such as in the classroom. One way of developing a taxonomy of concept tasks would be by the Q-sort method. Just as persons can be compared and classified by means of a Q sort, so could experiments on concept learning. In surveying the literature of this field one would note all the elemental characteristics of a large number of learning tasks and experimental arrangements. These would be put on cards to form the Q sort. Trained judges could then perform Q sorts on all kinds of concept-learning situations. We could, then, better answer such questions as 'Are tasks A and B more alike than tasks A and C?' Here are just a few of the kinds of variables that could be entered in our Q-sort deck: the form of the task, such as card sorting and successive or simultaneous presentation of stimuli; the number of dimensions in the stimuli and the number of values on each dimension; the number of relevant and irrelevant dimensions; the type of concept to be acquired – simple or unidimensional or involving two or more dimensions and whether these are conjunctive, disjunctive or relational; the sequencing of positive and negative instances and whether these are subject ordered or experimenter ordered; subject-paced versus experimenter-paced stimulus presentation; whether the subject gets feedback information after each stimulus or after scanning a succession of stimuli; the length of the feedback and postfeedback intervals; whether the stimuli are repeated in identical form throughout the learning trials or are never the same except for the relevant dimension; the length of exposure of each stimulus; the extent to which the experimenter makes available the information gained on past trials; the 'concept size' – that is, the ratio of the number of relevant dimensions to the total number of dimensions in the stimuli; and so on. This may seem wearisome, but unless some kind of taxonomy is worked out in this field and is worked out in a way that could permit quantitative comparisons among concept-learning tasks, research findings on IDs in relation to concept learning are apt to present a highly confusing picture. If ability X or trait Y correlates with speed of concept attainment in situation A but not in situation B, we can hardly draw any reasonable conclusion unless we know a good deal about how situations A and B differ. I decided in reviewing this literature that some kind of Q-sort method would help to cut through a good deal of the confusion that already exists. What are we to make of it when one investigator reports that, say, anxiety correlates $+0.40$ with speed of concept attainment and another investigator, using a different concept attainment task, reports a correlation of -0.40. Let us not settle for a box score or an average of the findings of a host of various experimental findings. This would be the ultimate in non-science.

CATEGORIES OF INDIVIDUAL DIFFERENCES

A useful distinction is that between intrinsic and extrinsic sources of IDs in learning. When we think of IDs in learning, we are usually thinking of extrinsic IDs. Age, sex, intelligence, motivation and personality are examples of extrinsic IDs that are sometimes correlated with performance in learning tasks. Extrinsic IDs are those which merely represent correlations with some measurable trait which does not bear any direct resemblance to learning or its inferred processes. Intrinsic IDs, on the other hand, are those which exist in the processes of learning. In other words, not all variance due to IDs is extrinsic in the sense that the totality of the 'between subject's' variance in a learning task can be accounted for in terms of variability in subject characteristics that lie outside the learning domain. Most of the variance in learning is not going to be accountable in terms of psychometric test scores, personality

inventories, age, sex and other extrinsic personal characteristics. Therefore we need to study IDs in the intrinsic processes of learning. This
means working out the dimensionality – the factorial structure – of the
IDs in learning which arise from all the various subjects × independent
variable interactions.

This is a big order, and the order gets bigger as the number of
possible independent variables that govern the learning process increases. In this sense conceptual learning is highly complex and is bound
to present considerable difficulty to the investigator who chooses to
study intrinsic IDs in this domain. There would be no problem, of
course, if subjects maintained the same rank order of ability in performance on every kind of concept-learning task. Then all we would
have to do would be to determine the extrinsic correlates of this unitary
concept-learning ability. We would 'explain' some of it in terms of
measured intelligence, some of it in terms of personality traits, and so
on. But unfortunately things are not that simple. We know that subjects do not maintain the same rank order of ability from one learning
task to another, or even within the same task under variations of the
independent variables. I am not speaking of unreliability of measurement, but of reliable changes in subjects' rank order of performance on
learning tasks under variations in the conditions of learning. This source
of variability seems not to be tapped to any appreciable extent by
psychometric tests. The process variables involved in a learning task are
very different from those involved in performing on a paper and pencil
test. When the learning depends on transfer from specific previously
acquired knowledge or skills, and when these forms of knowledge can
be assessed by psychometric tests, then we can expect to account for some
of the variability in our learning measures in terms of our psychometric
measures. Even under the best of conditions of this type considerably less than half the true ID variance in learning can be accounted
for by extrinsic factors. In fact, until we gain some understanding of
the dimensionality of IDs in intrinsic processes in learning, I doubt
if there is much to be gained from determining correlations between
single learning measures and extrinsic factors. The results are too uninterpretable, since some change in the conditions of learning can completely alter the pattern of correlations between learning measures
and extrinsic measures. My greatest hope is that some of the main
intrinsic factors that might be discovered in the realm of simpler forms
of learning might be able to account for much of the variability we find
in conceptual-learning tasks. These basic dimensions of learning ability,
I would imagine, can be more easily discovered in less complex forms

of behaviour than conceptual learning. At present, for example, I am studying IDs in learning at the level of short-term memory. Since short-term memory plays an important role in concept attainment (Dominowski, 1965), I would expect that the factors discovered in short-term memory tasks will also account for some of the ID variance in concept attainment tasks. This will, of course, depend upon the particular memory requirements of the concept attainment task.

THE NEED OF A THEORY OF INDIVIDUAL DIFFERENCES

Since there are such an enormous number of independent variables which in various combinations could interact with subject variables in concept learning, it would be practically hopeless to attempt to explore this realm without some theoretical conceptions about IDs in learning to guide our search. At present we have very little theory along these lines. We do not yet know the main dimensions of IDs in simple forms of learning. As these are delineated by our research we will have more basis for theorizing about the dimensions of IDs in concept learning.

It is my belief, which I have spelled out in greater detail elsewhere (Jensen, 1965), that the tremendous variety of IDs in phenotypically different types of learning has a limited number of genotypic sources. A subject's performance on any given task will be a product of his standing on these basic dimensions of learning and the degree to which the learning task involves these factors. Our job is to discover what these basic factors are and to devise means of reliably measuring them. Some of these basic factors might have labels such as rate of build-up of habit strength, susceptibility to various kinds of interference effects, such as proactive and retroactive inhibition, speed of formation and dissipation of reactive inhibition, breadth of generalization gradient, rate of consolidation of memory traces and so on. The most economical way to proceed at present seems to be to hypothesize some process that seems basic to a number of phenotypically different learning tasks, to measure IDs in performance on these tasks, and to determine by means of some appropriate form of multivariate analysis whether the various tasks are loaded on the hypothesized factor in the way one would predict. For example, I have factor analysed a number of simple learning tasks that were made up to differ in terms of the degree to which interference effects, such as proactive and retroactive inhibition, were thought to play a part in determining the subject's performance (Jensen, 1965). Tasks did, indeed, line up on certain factors in accord with the hypotheses. On the factor identified as susceptibility to interference, for example, the tasks hypothesized to involve a large degree of interference had larger factor loadings than did tasks hypothesized as being less influenced by interference. Actually three different kinds of interference factors were identified: one involving principally retroactive inhibition, one involving proactive inhibition, and one involving interference due to response competition. Dominowski (1965) has claimed that the memory effects in concept attainment can be regarded as involving both proactive and retroactive inhibition of short-term memory. So our proactive and retroactive inhibition factors might well be important basic sources of IDs in concept attainment. Subjects who score either high or low on our reference tests of these factors could be compared on concept-attainment tasks that differ in their memory requirements. Predictions would be made concerning the effects of IDs in proactive and retroactive inhibition on speed of concept attainment on these various tasks. A fundamental question would be whether or not the factors we have identified in short-term memory are referable to the same genotype as those we find in concept attainment.

There are a number of features of concept learning, however, such as strategies, which are not shared to any appreciable degree by simpler types of learning. These independent variables which seem more or less peculiar to concept learning also probably interact with subjects and will have to be investigated in their own right on the level of concept learning. I would make every effort, however, to analyse any type of concept learning down to its lowest possible denominator before studying it from the standpoint of IDs.

THE CURRENT STATE OF OUR KNOWLEDGE

I have saved a report on the current state of our knowledge till near the end, since it is a disappointing picture. As I have already indicated, we know next to nothing about IDs in simple forms of learning, much less concept learning. Only extrinsic IDs have been studied, principally age and intelligence and manifest anxiety. Findings are usually reported in the form of correlation coefficients, and I must say I derive little satisfaction from reading about these or from reporting them. The fact of the matter seems to be that you can obtain just about any kind of correlation you wish between concept-learning scores and scores on tests of intelligence or anxiety. The correlations in the literature spread over a range from about -0.60 to $+0.60$. Averaging the correlations would result in something close to zero for the correlation between 'concept learning' and intelligence or anxiety.

To find out how these ID variables interact with concept learning requires a highly analytical, experimental approach. Correlation coefficients alone cannot do the job.

The clinical literature provides most of what little we know about IDs in conceptual behaviour. Since it has been believed that various forms of psychopathology affect conceptual behaviour, we have a number of clinical tests of conceptual ability, such as the Goldstein–Scheerer tests, the Vigotsky or Hanfmann–Kasanin test, and the Wisconsin Card Sorting Test. Poor conceptual ability, as assessed by these tests, has been referred to by clinicians as 'concreteness' and is generally associated with mental deficiency and organic brain conditions. Payne (1961) has reported that five independent clinical measures of concreteness, when factor analysed along with tests of intelligence, had loadings ranging from 0·57 to 0·83 on g or the general intelligence factor. A seemingly opposite condition referred to as 'overinclusiveness', in which concept boundaries are extended far beyond their conventional limits, is characteristic of schizophrenic performance. Payne (1961) has thoroughly reviewed the literature on the clinical study of conceptual behaviour. Most of these findings and the clinical tests on which they are based are not sufficiently analytical to elucidate the workings of IDs in the realm of conceptual behaviour. Many dimensions of conceptual learning are involved simultaneously in these various clinical tests, and we have no way of knowing the precise locus of the effects of brain damage, of measured IQ, of anxiety, and so forth, on the processes involved in these complex tasks. Whatever their value in clinical diagnosis may be – and it is reportedly meagre – the scientific value of these tests as they are used in the clinic is practically nil.

INTELLIGENCE AND CONCEPT LEARNING

There can be little doubt that knowledge of everyday concepts and the spontaneous tendency to verbalize them, overtly or covertly, is highly correlated with measured intelligence. In fact, the Columbia Mental Maturity Scale, a test of general intelligence which was specifically made to correlate highly with the Stanford–Binet intelligence test, is based almost entirely on the subject's ability to recognize common concepts and classes of things in the natural environment.

When it comes to speed of concept learning the picture is much less clear. A study by Baggaley (1955) is rather typical of the psychometric approach to this problem. He correlated a composite measure of response time and number of errors in a concept-attainment task involving five bilevel dimensions with Thurstone's tests of Primary Mental Abilities. He found that level of concept learning had low but significant correlations with inductive and deductive reasoning ability (as measured by the figure analogies test) and with speed of perceptual closure (as measured by the embedded figures test). His conclusions were that level of concept attainment on a card-sorting task was positively correlated with inductive and deductive thinking, with strength and speed of perceptual closure, and with ability to concentrate on one aspect of a complex stimulus at a time. Here it seems to me we are attempting to explain one poorly understood complex process (concept attainment) in terms of a number of even more complex and less well understood processes. I believe that ultimately IDs in psychometric tests are going to have to be understood in terms of processes discovered in the learning laboratory rather than vice versa.

The type of analytical, experimental approach that is needed to make headway in this area is exemplified by two excellent studies by Sonia Osler (Osler and Fivel, 1961; Osler and Trautman, 1961). In these studies children at several age levels and of either average or superior IQ were compared on concept tasks that differed in the complexity of the stimuli and the number of potential hypotheses the stimuli were capable of eliciting. It was found that more intelligent subjects attained concepts by hypothesis testing based on verbal mediation of the concept. Their learning curves showed sudden rises as compared with the more gradual slope of the learning curves of less intelligent subjects. But here is the really interesting point. It was hypothesized that:

> If hypothesis testing is more frequent among superior than normal
> Ss, it should be possible to influence the performance of the superior
> group by varying the number of irrelevant dimensions, on which
> hypotheses can be based, in concept exemplars. For Ss of normal
> intelligence, who tend to achieve solution by the gradually building
> up of an S-R association, no systematic relation between the number
> of stimulus dimensions and speed of solution is anticipated (Osler
> and Trautman, 1961, p. 9).

It actually turned out that the high IQ subjects were slowed down, as compared with the average subjects, in attaining concepts when the stimuli were complex. The complexity of the stimuli made no difference in speed of concept attainment for the average IQ subjects. The superior subjects had to extinguish more erroneous hypotheses in order to attain the concept than did the average subjects. Thus it is possible experimentally to manipulate the correlation between IQ and concept-attainment ability. If the hypotheses or mediators needed to attain the concept were subtle or complex, the high IQ subjects would have shown up as markedly superior to the average subjects. The particular independent variables involved in any concept-learning task will strongly determine the nature of the interaction between performance on the task and the ID variables. For this reason it is impossible to draw any overall conclusion about the correlation between an ID variable and performance in concept-learning tasks in general.

MANIFEST ANXIETY AND CONCEPT LEARNING

The same thing seems to hold true for personality variables. The only personality measure that has been studied to any extent in relation to concept learning is anxiety, usually as measured by the Taylor Manifest Anxiety Scale. Some studies have shown a positive correlation between manifest anxiety and speed of concept attainment (e.g. Wesley, 1953), whereas others have shown an equally large negative correlation between anxiety and concept attainment (e.g. Beier, 1951). Again it appears that one can produce almost any correlation one desires between anxiety and speed of concept attainment by manipulating the conditions of the learning task. Concept attainment seems to be facilitated by high drive or anxiety when the relevant dimensions for the attainment of the concept are high in the subject's hierarchy of hypotheses or mediators. When the relevant dimensions are low in the subject's hierarchy of mediating responses, anxiety or high drive hinder concept attainment. This generalization is, of course, in accord with the Spence–Taylor hypothesis concerning the interaction of drive with performance on tasks that involve response competition. The evidence in the field of concept attainment is consistent with this formulation but is still too sketchy for it to be considered a settled issue.

IDS IN SPONTANEOUS VERBAL MEDIATION

In concluding, I wish to draw attention to one aspect of IDs in conceptual behaviour which has extremely important implications for education but which has not been subjected to thorough study. I refer to the tendency for non-social, non-verbal stimulus situations to elicit verbal mediational behaviour in subjects. Howard and Tracy Kendler (1962) have touched on this problem in their study of the mediational response in reversal and non-reversal shift learning. The tendency for concept learning to be verbally mediated increases with age. But at any age there seem to be IDs in subject's spontaneous tendencies to mediate verbally in learning and problem solving situations. Not only must concepts be learned, they must also be capable of being evoked by stimuli when the subject is not explicitly encouraged to look for or to verbalize the concept. Some pilot studies carried out in our Berkeley laboratory and in Martin Deutsch's Institute of Developmental Studies at New York Medical College indicate that there are large IDs in the tendency to use the concepts one has acquired. What are the determinants of this source of IDs in conceptual behaviour? Here is a simple example of IDs in the tendency to make use of a well-learned concept. A group of children is given practice to the point of over-learning in responding with the words 'same' or 'different' to a large number of pairs of stimulus figures in which the two parts of each pair are either identical or are different. The children thoroughly learn the concepts of *same* and *different* and eventually never falter in giving the correct verbal label to the pairs of stimuli. The children are then put into a different experimental situation in which equivalent pairs of stimuli are presented but no overt verbal responses are called for. The subject is rewarded for pushing button A when the stimuli in the pair are identical and is rewarded for pushing button B when the stimuli are different. Though all the children have learned to verbalize the concepts *same* and *different*, some of them do so in this non-verbal task and some of them do not. Those who verbalize learn the task immediately and are consistently rewarded. Those who do not verbalize learn very slowly, achieving consistently rewarded responses only after many trials. Apparently almost no use is made by these subjects of the previously acquired concepts of *same* and *different*. Age, intelligence and social class seem to be correlated with this phenomenon, which might be referred to as IDs in the threshold of verbal mediation in nominally non-verbal situations.

Finally, as I previously indicated, the subject of IDs in concept learning, indeed in any kind of learning, is virgin territory waiting to be explored by researchers with ingenuity and fortitude. At first the going will be rough and the initial hard-won advances may seem inelegant and meagre. But this is inevitable in pioneering. And since there are bound to be mishaps and casualties along the way, I think it important that many investigators commit their research efforts to this field if we are to see any substantial progress.

8

D. Zeaman and B. J. House (1967)

The relation of IQ and learning

R. M. Gagné (ed.), *Learning and Individual Differences*
(Charles E. Merrill Publishing Co.), pp. 192–207

The relation of learning and intelligence is a textbook problem of long tradition, but not one marked by clarity of theory or data. As we have noted earlier,

Theories of intelligence are often vague or inconsistent about whether MA, IQ, or both, should be related to learning. According to one view, it is MA score that is related to learning, because MA is a measure of the *developmental level* of the organism, and it is this level which limits learning ability. In these terms, IQ is *not* a measure of present learning ability, but rather a mathematical statement of the rate at which learning ability will change in time. An alternative view classifies the intelligence test as an achievement test of universally taught subject material. The MA score is then a measure of how much has been learned. If training is assumed to go on uniformly in time, the ratio MA/CA is the slope of a life-time learning curve, characteristic of the organism and recoverable in new, miniature learning situations. Consequently, IQ is the measure of present learning ability (House and Zeaman, 1960).

It would seem that the MA–IQ issue might in part be resolved experimentally: which of these two subject variables does in fact correlate with learning? Relevant data are available, of course, which we will review, but we plan to concentrate on just half the problem, the relation of learning and IQ, because our prime concern is with retardate learning.

The relation of retardation and learning can be translated in psychological terms to be the relation of a process (learning) and a trait (intelligence), or more specifically, learning and IQ, since it is IQ rather than MA that defines retardation. Despite the fact that intelligence is among the most frequently measured of all traits, and that learning is

116   *Readings in Human Intelligence*

surely the most popular target of research on basic behavioural processes, the conjunction of these two areas has been surprisingly under-
investigated. This may simply be the result of an arbitrary division of
labour: trait psychologists and process psychologists tend to live in
different skins. But the class of swinging psychologists (trait *and* process),
while relatively small, is neither null nor idle. Consequently, the research literature on the IQ–learning relation has grown sufficiently of
late to warrant a look at the current status of this traditional problem.

Two excellent reviews on IQ and learning appeared in 1963; Denny
(1963) and Lipman (1963) each have book chapters covering the retardation literature on intelligence and learning. It is unnecessary to
redo the job, so we shall restrict ourselves to an outline, a boxscore, and
an evaluation of positive and negative findings, including about twenty
new studies that have appeared in the last few years.

Delimiting the problem

MA, CA and IQ. If we wish to reason to the influence of IQ on learning,
it is necessary to control other relevant subject factors correlated with
IQ. MA and CA are the most likely relevant correlates. Theoretically,
IQ is independent of CA, but in a population of equal MAs, IQ is
negatively correlated with CA. And within a single age group IQ correlates positively with MA.

It is impossible, of course, to control both MA and CA simultaneously
and allow their ratio (IQ) to vary; but if CA were found to be irrelevant
for learning, the problem would be reduced to the influence of two separ-
able psychological variables, MA *v.* IQ. Since the logic of our later
arguments depends upon the assumption that CA is indeed an irrelevant
variable for learning, this might be the best juncture at which to
present some supporting evidence. Learning studies correlating performance with CA have reported unreliable, zero and negative correlations, unless accompanied by large MA differences. Instances include
Ellis and Sloan (1959), Stevenson (1965), Harter (1965) and House and
Zeaman (1960). Multiple correlations of learning with combined MA
and CA measures are not higher than those with MA alone (Harter,
1965); and the partial correlations of learning and MA with CA constant are not appreciably less than the first-order correlations of MA
and learning (House and Zeaman, 1960). The evidence on this matter
is not overwhelming, and may be variously interpreted, but we do
wish to suggest that our basic assumption of the irrelevance of CA is
not without empirical support.

To separate the effects of IQ and MA on learning (assuming CA irrelevant), three research strategies have been employed. (1) The simplest design compares the performance of two groups varying in IQ, but matched in MA. Comparisons of retardates with equal-MA normals are usually arranged for this. (2) Statistical control of MA has been employed using correlational techniques with populations having wide variability in IQ either in normal or retarded ranges. (3) Studies in which IQ and MA are confounded may fail to show relations with performance in learning tasks. These are relevant studies as negative instances, since it appears safe to assume that if IQ has no effect when correlated with MA, it would have no effect were it not. The usual source of this kind of negative evidence is from comparisons of normals and retardates of equal CA. All three sources of data will be considered.

LEARNING TASKS AND LEARNING MEASURES

A relation of intelligence to learning, unqualified with respect to task, implies some generality of learning ability across tasks. Woodrow (1946) reviewed the literature two decades ago and concluded that many observed low correlations between measures of learning in different tasks meant that no unitary learning ability existed. If the measures of learning were reliable and a wide range of individual differences observed, this would make a relation between general learning ability and intelligence impossible. The kinds of learning measures (gain scores) used by Woodrow have been criticized by other writers (Ruch, 1936, 1961; Tilton, 1949) for unreliability and attenuation of range, and for poor control of individual differences in starting level. Subsequent investigators have turned up moderate correlations between learning measures within certain task domains, such as discriminative learning (Stevenson, 1965; House and Zeaman, 1960).

With the task-to-task consistency of individual differences in learning in doubt, it may be instructive to collate the evidence on each of several broad classes of tasks separately, not only to describe more precisely the empirical boundaries of the IQ-learning relation, but also to provide tests of theories predicting task differences (we have proposed such a theory).

The broad classes of learning tasks to be considered are (a) classical conditioning, (b) discriminative learning, (c) verbal learning and (d) learning set. We chose these classes because they are broad and conventional classes with IQ-relevant experiments reportable on each.

To minimize the intrusion of processes other than learning, some further restrictions have been placed on the studies to be covered. Acquisition is the target variable here rather than extinction. Schedules of reinforcement give rise to motivational effects, so only 100 per cent schedules are considered. Transfer designs may introduce complex mediating processes, so only the original learning phases of such experiments are counted. Similarly, for studies whose prime focus is on retention, we include only original learning data.

While it would be naive to believe that such restrictions will guarantee unique theoretical interpretations of the process or processes underlying performance on learning tasks, we hope these will narrow things down a bit. It will turn out that there is complexity enough in the data even with these restrictions, and that despite them we end up inferring the intrusion of some other process than learning.

Classical conditioning

There is no relation between IQ and acquisition of simple, classically conditioned responses. The research literature (in English) is unequivocal on this point. The Russian literature, on the other hand, led one reviewer to quite the opposite conclusion. Razran (1961), after an extensive review of the large Russian literature on classical conditioning, concludes, 'Other things equal, the more intelligent the child, the more readily he forms the CR.' Not all Russian evidence is consistent with this view, however, since Razran (1933) earlier reviewed an experiment by Osipova in which retardates *exceeded* a group of equal CA normals in speed of conditioning finger-withdrawals with shock US. Whatever the balance of truth on this issue in the Russian literature, there have been half a dozen publications in English weighing heavily on the invariance side of the issue, i.e. conditioning is invariant with respect to IQ.

Let us look at the English literature. Six articles have appeared recently in which IQ was included as a parameter. Half of the studies conditioned in GSR with shock US: Birch and Demb (1959), Grings, Lockhart and Dameron (1962) and Baumeister, Beedle and Urquhart (1964). The remaining three studies conditioned the eyelid response: Cromwell, Palk and Foshee (1961), Behrens and Ellis (1960), and Franks and Franks (1962). All of the studies used retarded subjects to represent the lower ranges of intelligence, and most had normal control subjects. Reliable overall differences in CR acquisition between normals and retardates were not reported in any study, nor did IQ correlate with conditioning performance within the retardate range.

These studies cover a wide range of intelligence. Cromwell, Palk and Foshee report a correlation of 0·03 between IQ and CR frequency for a population of sixty-one retardates ranging from IQ 15 to 68. Grings, Lockhart and Dameron concluded, 'Apparently, autonomic conditioning is unaffected by intelligence over the IQ range employed (20–78).' Add to this the absence of normal retardate differences for both autonomic and non-autonomic (eyelid) conditioning and a more general invariance can be asserted.

A suggestion of contrary evidence is reported in a very early study by Mateer (1918) who measured anticipatory mouth-openings of children given candy on signal. But the *instrumental* features of this procedure are so obvious as to make it doubtfully classifiable (as it often is) as a classical conditioning study. The candy reinforcement was, after all, contingent upon opening the mouth, and this is the defining condition for instrumental conditioning.

None of the six studies mentioned above made equal MA comparisons at different IQ levels. The negative findings make such controls unnecessary. If subjects varying in both MA and IQ do not differ in conditioning, then it is a reasonable inference that IQ alone would be an ineffective variable.

Among the six published papers, of suggestive theoretical significance is the fact that only one measured *discriminative* classical conditioning (Grings, Lockhart and Dameron), as well as simple conditioning, and with the discriminative procedure there were some IQ differences favouring higher IQ subjects. This study confounds MA and IQ, so we cannot count it as positive evidence for IQ alone, but if the effect were replicable with equal MA controls, the finding would fit well with a theoretical interpretation (in terms of attention) that we will present later.

We have similar comparisons of lower and higher IQ retardates undergoing classical oculomotor conditioning in our laboratory at the Mansfield State Training School. In his dissertation research, R. Ramsey finds differences in performance corresponding to IQ for retardates classically conditioned to make eye movement anticipations of the occurrence of a peripheral light. The oculomotor response we regard as a peripheral correlate of attention.

Summary. Intelligence and simple conditionability are unrelated (at least for English-speaking subjects) over a wide range of intelligence. When discriminative features enter the classical conditioning procedures, however, a suggestion of a relation with intelligence appears.

Simple discriminative learning

In the area of discrimination learning, we have found eighteen studies relating IQ to performance with MA controlled. Twelve of these report positive results, with better performances from the higher IQ subjects (Baumeister, Beedle and Urquhart, 1964; Ellis, Hawkins, Pryer and Jones, 1963; Hoffman, House and Zeaman, 1963; House and Zeaman, 1958, 1960; Kass and Stevenson, 1961; Martin and Blum, 1961; Rieber, 1964; Ross, Hetherington and Wray, 1965; Rudel, 1959; Stevenson and Iscoe, 1955; Stevenson and Zigler, 1957), and nine report negative results with no reliable differences among the various IQ groups (Hetherington, Ross and Pick, 1964; Kass and Stevenson, 1961; Martin and Blum, 1961; Milgram and Furth, 1964; O'Connor and Hermelin, 1959; Sanders, Ross and Heal, 1965; Schusterman, 1964; Stevenson, 1960; Stevenson and Zigler, 1957). Three studies (Kass and Stevenson, 1961; Martin and Blum, 1961; Stevenson and Zigler, 1957) report both negative and positive results for different comparisons. With such discrepant results, the obvious question is how the two groups of studies differ. On the average, those with positive findings have higher IQ differences, and tend to include subjects of lower MA and IQ, but there is much overlap in these respects with the studies reporting negative findings. The big difference between the positives and negatives lies in the *difficulty of the task*. Six of the nine studies with negative findings had discrimination learning tasks which were far from optimally difficult, having been found too easy or too hard.

On the easy side were the following: An experiment by Hetherington, Ross and Pick (1964) reports almost no errors at all for their equal MA comparisons, using 'junk' stimuli in a 2-choice visual discrimination. Recognizing the possibility of a ceiling effect, these investigators increased the difficulty of their task in a later study (Ross, Hetherington and Wray, 1965) of size discrimination and obtained positive results. Studies by Milgram and Furth (1964) and Schusterman (1964) included 2-choice position discriminations which proved not only easy, but easier for retardates than normals. There are at least two other experiments in the literature (Weir and Stevenson, 1959; Osler and Trautman, 1961) which also show that for certain very easy discriminations, subjects of lower intelligence do better than brighter subjects.

On the hard side, the study by Martin and Blum (1961) used 3-choice oddity and the middle-sized problem, both of which turned out to be highly difficult for subjects of low developmental level. A 3-choice size discrimination by Stevenson and Zigler (1957) was even more difficult. Out of eighty-one subjects starting their second experiment, only eight learned the problem. Since a significantly greater proportion of retardates than normals were non-learners, we have classified this experiment as positive; it also appears in the negative list because reliable differences did not appear between the learners differing in intelligence. Floor effects may have been operating in the study by Stevenson (1960) with two complex discriminative tasks (a 3-choice size discrimination and a 7-item, non-verbal paired-associate discrimination). Here again, a majority of the subjects failed, both normal and retarded. Such studies are important in showing the complex interaction of task difficulty with the IQ–learning relationship (see Fig. 8.1).

High task difficulty cuts down on the size of the population contributing non-chance data and enhances the possibility of a Type II Error. In the study by Stevenson (1960), the normals in one of his experiments were superior to retardates of equal MA, but the p level was between 0·10 and 0·20. Such outcomes do not inspire confidence in the null hypothesis. A similar interpretation may also be likely for a study by O'Connor and Hermelin (1959), in which ten imbecile children required 25 per cent more training trials to reach criterion than did ten normal children of equal MA – a difference falling short of statistical reliability. To the degree that the correlation between IQ and performance in learning tasks deviates from unity, outcomes of this sort tend to be likely.

In summary, the bulk of the negative evidence may be the result of extreme levels of difficulty with consequent attenuation in the range of performance. The entire assemblage of data, both positive and negative, can be handled by the following assumption: *at least a low positive correlation exists between IQ (with MA controlled) and performance in visual discrimination tasks when a wide range of IQs is sampled and tasks of intermediate difficulty are used.*

The posited relations of performance and IQ for tests of varying difficulty are shown in Fig. 8.1. The ceiling and floor effects represented by the 'easy' and 'hard' tests are obvious enough in principle, but often hard to avoid in practice. The paradoxical inverse relation of IQ and performance for the 'very easy' condition has been observed by several investigators; a theoretical interpretation of this finding is considered later.

The magnitude of the correlation of IQ with visual discrimination learning has not been measured over the entire range of intelligence. A partial correlation of $-0·28$ ($p < 0·05$) has been reported by House and

E

Zeaman (1960) relating IQ (with MA constant) and log errors on a visual discrimination task. The population for which this relation held included seventy-one retarded children ranging in IQ from 17 to 67. A reasonable assumption would be that the −0·28 correlation suffers from attenuation due to range and that a higher – moderate – correlation exists between IQ and intelligence for an unrestricted range of IQs.

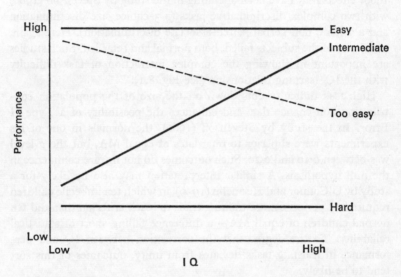

Fig. 8.1 Expected effects of IQ on performance in tasks at four levels of difficulty.

Verbal learning

The two major subdivisions of verbal learning, for which IQ-relevant data exist, are paired-associate (PA) and serial-position (SP) learning. In all, there are eleven studies either having equal-MA controls or showing no differences despite the lack of such control. More of the evidence in these studies is negative than positive. Nevertheless, we give less weight to the negative findings because these so frequently occur when either very hard or easy tasks are examined. As in the case of discriminative learning, a bias in favour of negative results may be caused by restrictions in the ranges of the independent variable (IQ) and the dependent variable (learning).

Let us list first the studies showing positive and negative results before evaluating them. The PA and SP articles are considered separately.

Paired-associate learning. Ten PA studies could be found with relevant findings; three of them contained positive evidence of a direct relation of IQ and performance in a PA learning task (Iscoe and Semler, 1964; Jensen, 1965; Johnson and Blake, 1960), seven of them contained negative evidence (Akutagawa and Benoit, 1959; Berkson and Cantor, 1960; Cantor and Ryan, 1962; Eisman, 1958; Girardeau and Ellis, 1964; Ring and Palermo, 1961; Vergason, 1964). Of the latter group, three were equal CA comparisons with no accompanying differences (Berkson and Cantor, Eisman, and Vergason). All of the studies used variations on standard PA verbal learning techniques, and all of them used visual stimuli (pictures, words or nonsense syllables) to be associated with verbal responses.

Serial-position learning. Only four SP studies supply pertinent data, three of them presenting positive evidence (Cassell, 1957; Girardeau and Ellis, 1964; Jensen, 1965), and two containing negative (Cassell, 1957; Johnson and Blake, 1960). As in the PA studies, the stimuli were all visual and the responses spoken.

Evaluation. Intelligence, or that aspect of it measured by IQ, can be varied over a wide range, and the greater the range of IQ in a particular study, the greater the likelihood of detecting a relation with verbal learning. The range of IQ differences in the set of eleven experiments above was from 12 points to 55. As might be expected, the study featuring only a 12-point IQ difference (Akutagawa and Benoit) reports negative findings; the study with 55 IQ points difference (Iscoe and Semler) yielded positive findings. This is not an arbitrary selection of cases. A biserial correlation of IQ differences versus positive–negative outcome for all the studies was computed at 0·86, showing a highly reliable tendency for the studies with higher IQ differences to yield positive results.

Restriction of range of the dependent variable may account for many of the negative results. Performance on verbal learning tasks will certainly be restricted if subjects who fail to learn at all are excluded in the analysis. Two of the studies (Cantor and Ryan, Berkson and Cantor) found normals and retardates not different in PA learning after having dropped failing subjects. In each case more retardates failed than normals – a finding hardly consistent with the conclusion that normals and retardates are not different in PA learning. These studies do establish the weakness, or absence, of an IQ–learning relation among normal and retardate *learners*, but do not permit generalization to the intact population, including non-learners.

A similar limitation can arise in studies which must set other entrance requirements closely related to verbal learning ability. Girardeau and Ellis (1964) and Cassell (1957) had to drop subjects not able to read, since they were using visual verbal stimuli. Cassell was forced to drop 100 subjects from a population of 152 retardates (but none from his normal group) as non-readers, and found marginal evidence (i.e. some positive, some negative) of a difference in SP learning between the normals and retardates remaining. Why should groups presumably equal in verbal learning be so different in ability to read?

In fairness to these experimenters, it should be recognized that if verbal stimuli are to be used in comparisons of this kind, it is difficult to think of alternative procedures. If the results of these experiments had been positive, there would have been no difficulty in interpretation.

A third way to restrict the range of the dependent variable is to have the learning task turn out to be too easy. In the studies of Eisman (1958) and of Vergason (1964), subjects learned in about six trials with group SDs in the neighbourhood of two or three trials. The effects of intelligence on learning may not be strong enough to show up with so little room.

Our reinterpretations of the negative results of the studies discussed are not intended as hindsight criticisms of experimental designs. It is much easier to know the boundary conditions of an empirical relation (such as IQ learning) *after* the research is done than before.

Of the ten PA studies listed above, four seem relatively free of the difficulties discussed. Ring and Palermo (1961) matched for MA a group of normal children (mean IQ 102) and retardates (mean IQ 76) and found no reliable differences in performance on a moderately difficult PA task. Johnson and Blake (1960) had similar matched groups (mean IQs 70 *v.* 102) and found normals better on two PA tasks, reliably so for one, but not the other. Varying IQ over a wider range, Jensen (1965) provided an equal-MA comparison for two groups of IQ 58 and 105 on two PA tasks and reported marked normal-retardate differences in both tasks in the expected direction. Finally, Iscoe and Semler (1964) arranged normal-retardate comparisons (mean IQs 109 *v.* 54, with MA controlled) using four PA tasks ranging in difficulty. A clear overall difference in favour of the normals was reported for this large IQ difference.

Of the four SP studies listed earlier, two provided clear tests of the underlying hypotheses. Johnson and Blake (1960) found no reliable difference in performance between groups of IQ 70 *v.* 100, while Jensen (1965) found normals (IQ 105) far better than equal-MA retardates (IQ 58).

Summary. IQ and verbal learning performance are positively related, in both paired-associate and serial-position tasks, for subjects of equal MA. The strength of this relation is dependent upon the magnitude of IQ difference. With differences of 40 or more points, a clear difference emerges between normals and retardates. With differences of 20–30 points, performance differences are marginal or absent. The effects of IQ can easily be obscured by restrictions on the range of variation of verbal learning performance, either by subject selection procedures or unhappy choice of task difficulty level.

Learning set

The relation of IQ to discrimination learning set has been investigated in five studies. While a larger number of experiments report on the relations of MA (and CA) to learning set, only five publications provide IQ comparisons with some control of MA. Three of these yield clearly positive findings (Girardeau, 1959; Harter, 1965, Wischner and O'Donnell, 1962), and two yield negative findings (Levinson and Reese, reported by Reese, 1963; Plenderleith, 1956).

It is not easy to explain the negative cases. Levinson and Reese had IQ differences restricted to the normal range, but Plenderleith did not. She used a wide range of IQs (53–112) and an MA level (6 years) approximating that of the positive studies. There is some question of the representativeness of her retardate sample, however. The levels of performance achieved by her retardates were astonishingly good compared with higher level subjects (cf. Harter, 1965).

A clear boundary condition on the IQ-learning set relation was established in a well-designed study by Harter (1965). She had subjects at three levels of IQ: 70, 100 and 130, at each of three MA levels: 5, 7 and 9 years, learning a series of 2-choice object discriminations. Learning-set performance was positively related to IQ at the MA 5 and 7 year levels, but the relation was weak at the MA 9 level due to a ceiling effect. Wischner, Braun and Patton (1962) observed similar limitations with object-quality learning-set tasks. Presumably, more difficult learning-set tasks could be found to provide adequate tests of the IQ-learning set relation at the higher MA levels. Despite the ceiling effects at the high MA levels, Harter reports the correlation of IQ and learning set (problems to criterion) as −0·57 with MA controlled. The multiple correlation of combined IQ and MA with learning set was a surprisingly high 0·73. The first-order correlation of performance with MA was −0·47.

In summary, this modest package of learning-set evidence is consistent with the view that between IQ and learning-set formation there exists a positive relation of a magnitude approximating that observed with simple discriminative and verbal learning.

SOME RELATIONS WITH THEORY

Learning theory

To show that intelligence is related to performance on some learning tasks is not sufficient to prove that intelligence is related to learning, if by learning we mean something like habit acquisition or growth of associative strength. Virtually all modern learning theorists distinguish learning and performance, and explicit theories provide rules for inferring learning from the data of learning experiments. A theorist such as Hull postulates that individual differences may occur in rate of growth of habit strength (his parameter, i), but no simple relation exists between i and the appearances of empirical learning curves. The reason is simple. Performance is theorized to be a function not only of habit strength but of other constructs such as drives and inhibitions as well. Individual differences can affect these. Which ones are responsible for individual differences observed in a particular set of empirical learning curves? A programme of research is necessary to find out. Hull's theory is sufficiently explicit to permit such a programme, and at least one serious attempt has been made to do this with some motor learning data (Zeaman and Kaufman, 1955).

Not enough data on the relation of motor learning and intelligence exist to make a Hullian analysis possible, but we have made a beginning on a similar programme in the area of visual discrimination learning.

Attention theory

We have published a theory of discrimination learning to account for the performances of retardates learning to solve 2-choice visual discriminations (House and Zeaman, 1963). The theory is formal and quantitative, and postulates a chain of two responses for problem solution: the first, an attention response to the relevant stimulus dimensions; and the second, a correct instrumental response to the positive cue of the relevant dimension. The theory is an extension and elaboration of Wyckoff's (1952) observing response model. Equations are written for the underlying processes of attention and habit acquisition, and parameters in these equations may in principle vary from subject to subject. The pertinent question here is: Can we tell from the data of our experiments whether observed individual differences in empirical learning curves are attributable to individual differences in rate of habit acquisition or some other underlying process such as attention? The answer is, we think we can.

Among our retardates wide individual differences are observed in their learning curves, with the higher IQ subjects doing better than the lower. The general form of the learning curves is S-shaped or ogival (if

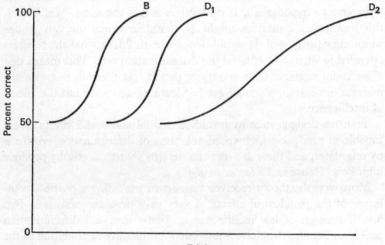

Fig. 8.2 Idealized forms of the empirical discrimination learning curves for brighter subjects (B) and two groups of duller subjects (D_1 and D_2). The data resemble the B and D_1 functions but not D_2.

plotted properly in the form of backward learning curves). Differences between brighter and duller subjects are observed to be not in the *slopes* of the rising portions of ogives, but in the length of the initial plateau.

Fig. 8.2 conveys the point. It is not the rate of improvement, once it starts, that distinguishes bright and dull, but how long it takes for improvement to begin. Improvement is uniformly fast once it begins.

Theoretically, this result could come about in a variety of ways, but the main contenders in this theoretical contest were two classes of parameters: (1) the θ parameters controlling individual differences in rate of acquisition and extinction, and (2) the $Po_{(i)}$ parameters controlling individual differences in initial probabilities of paying attention to the various (i) dimensions of stimuli. It was shown by computer simulation that θ differences would have tended to produce the kind of function depicted by D_2 in the figure – with low slopes in the transition zone. Differences in initial probability of attending to the relevant dimension ($Po_{(i)}$) would produce the differences exhibited by B and D_1 – the kind that were observed empirically.

The tentative conclusion was reached that intelligence level was associated with differences in attention (Po) rather than learning, in the sense of rate of habit acquisition (θ). The argument did not end there. Other consequences followed from this notion (which we called the 'θ-invariance hypothesis'). If dull subjects had the same θs as bright, this meant that conditions might be found in which the two groups would do equally well. It would depend upon Po, or what the subjects attended to when they entered the discrimination task. This means that if we could engineer their attention, that is, get them to focus on the relevant dimension, we could get fast learning and wash out the effects of intelligence.

Transfer designs such as intradimensional shifts and reversals are capable of producing high speed solutions of discrimination problems by retardates, and these are just the designs that theoretically produce high Po's (House and Zeaman, 1963).

Moreover, the theory receives support in providing a possible resolution of the paradoxical effects of very easy problems shown in Fig. 8.1. If subjects of low intelligence do badly in visual discrimination problems because they have a low initial probability of attending to the dimensions the experimenter has chosen as relevant, then the same retarded subjects ought to do better than normals if the experimenter should choose as relevant those dimensions the retardates *are* paying attention to. Analyses of error scores reveal that subjects of low developmental level tend strongly to respond to *position* in 2-choice tasks. If position is what retardates attend to, then our theory says that they should do better than normals on position discrimination learning, as Fig. 8.1 suggests, and some studies have shown. The limitations or boundary conditions of the intelligence-learning relation set by task difficulty are translated in our theory as an attention phenomenon. A difficult task is one the relevant dimensions of which have a low probability of being attended to at the start of training. For an easy task, all subjects, both bright and dull, have a high probability of relevant attention. Instrumental learning starts immediately, and under the θ-invariance hypothesis, all subjects will do equally well. The kinds of findings described by Fig. 8.1 are thus not unfriendly to attention theory.

To tidy up some of the other loose ends of data presented in our survey, let us ask whether the kinds of tasks which show and do not show IQ variation are at all consistent with theory.

Classical conditioning was the one area which most consistently failed to show IQ variations. All but one of these studies used non-discriminative classical conditioning. The experimenter presents a CS not in competition with other new stimuli, but in competition with a stable background. He turns on a light or sound. With only the adapted stimulation of a background as competition, such stimuli may reasonably be expected to have high attention value – for all subjects. If this analysis is true, the θ-invariance hypothesis says that no differences in conditioning should be observed between high and low IQ groups.

The one study which contained a suggestion of an IQ difference included a discriminative classical conditioning procedure (Grings, Lockhart and Dameron, 1962). These authors reason along lines similar to ours – they say:

> Certain results indicate a possible relation between intelligence and perception, if one includes orienting responses as perceptual behaviour. The following observations bear on the nature of this relation. If GSR response during the delay interval is used as an indication of orienting behaviour, the two IQ groups differ in the number of orienting responses to test and control stimuli (p. 27).

Extreme conditions are often regarded by methodologists as carrying special probative weight. Suppose we could show that subjects of low intelligence could regularly learn discriminations in a single trial. No one can do better. Hence, there is no room for an IQ-learning relation. We have arranged a set of experimental conditions in which retarded subjects have a fairly high probability of attending to the relevant dimensions (either colour or form) of the discriminative problems. We make the theoretical assumption that instrumental learning is complete in a single trial ($\theta = 1$) and try, then, to fit their learning functions with equations that make this assumption. Their empirical learning functions do not get to unity in a single trial because their $Po_{(i)}$, while high, is not $1 \cdot 0$. Theoretically, once they look at the relevant dimension, they learn immediately. The data of a coordinated series of six experiments were handled quantitatively by such assumptions (House and Zeaman, 1963). We were led to the amusing conclusion that retardates were slow learners who learned in one trial.

Our one-trial learning assumption has not been found inapplicable even for the verbal learning of retardates. House (1963) has shown that the retardate data of serial-position verbal learning tasks can be quantitatively described by a postulate set including a one-trial learning assumption. A doctoral dissertation by Kusmin (1964) has added further empirical support.

As in discrimination learning, the empirical verbal learning curves do not asymptote at unity in a single trial, but the items that are selected by the subject for learning on each trial are learned in one trial.

House (1963) has presented in detail evidence for a dual process of retardate verbal learning, following the Miller and McGill model, and has identified two parameters of the model with the process of learning and with the process of retention. Individual differences in intelligence were found to correspond with one but not both parameters. The interpretation was made that retardates vary in immediate memory ability as a function of intelligence but not learning ability.

The parallelism in our theoretical treatments of discriminative and verbal learning is close but not complete. Dual processes are inferred for both (attention and learning in discriminative tasks, learning and retention in verbal tasks), individual differences are found in only one of the component processes corresponding to intelligence, and in neither case is the process that of learning.

9

M. Wallach and N. Kogan (1965)

A new look at the creativity-intelligence distinction

M. Wallach and N. Kogan, *Modes of Thinking in Young Children: A Study of the Creativity-Intelligence Distinction* (Holt, Rinehart & Winston), ch. 8, pp. 287–303

For several years we have been concerned with two modes of thinking in young children, which, it turns out, bear directly upon what has assumed the proportions of a controversy in recent psychological history. The nature of the controversy might be put somewhat as follows: Is there an aspect of cognitive functioning which can be appropriately labelled 'creativity' that stands apart from the traditional concept of general intelligence? A close appraisal of the quantitative findings available on this subject led us to a pessimistic answer. We shall pass some of these findings quickly in review. Our examination of this literature opened up to us, however, the possibility of a valid distinction between creativity and intelligence that had not, in our view, been sufficiently pursued and developed. The next step, therefore, was empirical research in terms of this distinction. Finally, if creativity and intelligence could be validly distinguished, we were interested in studying the possible psychological correlates that might distinguish individual differences on these two dimensions considered jointly. Specifically, we were concerned with correlates in such areas as the child's observed behaviour in school and play settings, his aesthetic sensitivities, his categorizing and conceptualizing activities, his test anxiety and defensiveness levels. We can, of course, give but an overview of this work. For a complete presentation, see Wallach and Kogan (1965).

We began with a simple question: Does the relevant psychological literature support the assumption of a unified dimension of individual differences describing more and less creative cognitive behaviour? To put this question another way: Can one demonstrate the existence of greater and lesser degrees of a cognitive capability that is like intelligence in regard to being a pervasive, broad dimension, but yet is independent of intelligence, and which can appropriately be labelled 'creativity'? It is clear that to talk of 'creativity' is to imply a referent different from that of the general intelligence concept. If that is not intended, then the creativity label becomes quite superfluous. The typical evidence that we found on this issue led, however, to an opposite conclusion. Let us consider an example.

The volume by Getzels and Jackson (1962), *Creativity and Intelligence*, is perhaps the best known of recent efforts in the field. Five alleged tests of creativity were administered to large samples of students ranging in class from sixth grade through the end of high school. Four of the five creativity tests correlated significantly with IQ for the girls, and all five of these tests correlated significantly with IQ for the boys. Consider next the relationships among the instruments in the creativity battery – that is, the question of whether they define a unitary dimension of individual differences. The Getzels–Jackson results showed that the five creativity tasks are virtually no more strongly correlated among themselves than they are correlated with intelligence. To give some averages, for boys the mean correlation is 0·26 between the creativity battery and IQ, and is 0·28 among the tasks in the creativity battery; in the case of the girls, the corresponding mean correlations are 0·27 and 0·32. In sum, the creativity measures correlated with intelligence on the order of 0·3. There is no evidence, in short, for arguing that the creativity instruments are any more strongly related to one another than they are related to general intelligence. The inevitable conclusion is that little warrant exists here for talking about creativity *and* intelligence as if these terms refer to concepts at the same level of abstraction. The creativity indicators measure nothing in common that is distinct from general intelligence. Inspection of the creativity battery reveals a quite varied range of materials, including measures of the ability to devise mathematical problems, to compose endings for fables, to detect embedded geometric figures, to think up word definitions, and to imagine uses for an object.

Comparable examination of other research reports in the literature forced us to the same kind of conclusion. Our survey included the study of findings reported by Torrance and his co-workers (e.g. Torrance, 1960, 1962; Torrance and Gowan, 1963), Guilford and his collaborators (e.g. Guilford and Christensen, 1956; Wilson, Guilford, Christensen and Lewis, 1954), Cline, Richards and Needham (1963), Cline, Richards and Abe (1962), Barron (1963) and Flescher (1963). To give but one more example of the kind of outcome obtained, consider a recent study by Cline, Richards and Needham (1963). With high school students as Ss and seven creativity measures, the average correlation for boys between the creativity indexes and an IQ measure is 0·35, while it is 0·21 among the various creativity tests. For girls, the average correlation between the creativity tests and IQ is 0·33, while it is 0·24 among the seven creativity measures. Again and again in reviewing the research in this area, the evidence led to the conclusion that the various creativity measures utilized are almost as strongly, equally strongly, or even more strongly related to general intelligence than they are related to each other. The evidence in hand thus seemed not to permit the very type of conceptualization that Getzels and Jackson (1962) and other researchers were proposing: namely, that there exists a pervasive dimension of individual differences, appropriately labelled 'creativity', that is quite distinct from general intelligence. We should note that this same critical point has been made by Thorndike (1963) in a recent article.

Appropriate wielding of Occam's razor at this juncture thus dictated the tough-minded conclusion that little of any generality was being measured here beyond differences in the traditional notion of intelligence. Let us pose two issues, however, that made it seem premature to let the matter go at that. First, a potpourri of abilities was being assessed in the good name of 'creativity'; second, all of the work that we had seen failed to consider the implications of the social psychology of the assessment situation within which measurement of 'creativity' was attempted. Consider each of these points in turn.

If we return to the introspections of highly creative artists and scientists, one major focus emerges. The majority of the available introspective accounts have in common a concern with associative freedom and uniqueness. These accounts consistently stress the ability to give birth to associative content that is abundant and original, yet relevant to the task at hand rather than bizarre. The writer's classical fear of 'drying up' and never being able to produce another word, the composer's worry over not having another piece of music within him, the scientist's concern that he won't be able to think of another experiment to perform – these are but indications of how preoccupied creative individuals can become with the question of associative flow. Introspections about times of creative insight also seem to reflect a kind of task-centred, permissive, or playful set on the part of the person doing the associating. Einstein refers to 'associative play' or 'combinatory play'. The person stands aside a bit as associative material is given freedom to reach the surface.

We would propose that the essentials of the creative process may be contained in the two elements just considered: first, the production of associative content that is abundant and that is unique; second, the presence in the associator of a playful, permissive task attitude. Given a task clear enough that bizarre associative products do not readily occur, and given a permissive context within which the person works, two variables should permit us to index individual differences in creativity: the number of associations that the person can generate in response to given tasks, and the relative uniqueness of the associations that he produces.

One implication of this view is that productivity and uniqueness of associates should be related variables. Defining uniqueness as a relative infrequency of a given associative response to the task at hand for a sample of Ss, we would then expect stereotyped associates to come earlier and unique associates to come later in a sequence of responses. Such an expectation would also be consistent with recent work by Mednick (e.g. 1962). If unique associates tend to come later in time, then it becomes clear also that an appropriate assessment context will require freedom from the pressure of short time limits, and perhaps freedom from any temporal pressure at all. The postulated need for a permissive, playful attitude also implies the desirability of freedom from time pressure. Such temporal freedom is one aspect of what a permissive situation would involve. Permissiveness further connotes a relative lessening of evaluational pressures – that is, a focus upon the task rather than upon the self, a relaxed entertaining of the possible rather than tense insistence upon an answer that must be correct if one is not to lose face. The Taoists, as discussed by Rugg (1963), have called such a relaxed attitude a state of 'letting things happen'. Clearly, we are describing a type of situation in which the individual does not feel that he is being tested, and hence does not feel that what he does will have a bearing upon his self-worth in the eyes of others.

The foregoing analysis of creativity hence suggests a concentration of assessment attempts in the area of associational processes, in contrast to the quite heterogeneous types of tasks that have received the 'creativity' label in studies of the kind touched upon earlier. This theoretical analysis also suggests that the assessment context must be quite different from the kind utilized in the studies that we have reviewed; there should be freedom from time pressure and there should be a playful, game-like context rather than one implying that the person is under test. Interestingly enough, the kind of context present in the case of *all* of the studies on creativity that we reviewed earlier has borne strong connotations that a test or examination is at issue; the creativity procedures invariably have been referred to as 'tests', they have been administered to large groups of students in a classroom, and temporal constraint has been present – either explicitly, through the use of relatively brief time limits, or implicitly, through the use of group administration procedures. In all of this work, there has been the evident assumption that a testing context, with its implication that the respondent is being evaluated in terms of some success–failure criterion, is quite appropriate for studying creativity. The associative approach to creativity that we have taken, however, with its emphasis upon an attitude of playful entertaining of possibilities in a task-centred rather than ego-centred environment, suggests otherwise.

At this point we were ready to begin some experimentation of our own. Following the prescriptions just stated, could one empirically define a dimension of individual differences that concerned the ability to produce many cognitive associates, and many that are unique? Would this dimension possess a substantial degree of generality across differences in types of tasks – for example, verbal $v.$ visual kinds of procedural formats? Such a contrast was of special interest since the general intelligence concept is defined with respect to a kind of ability that manifests itself in visual (performance) as well as verbal types of tasks, and we were presuming to assess a characteristic possessing approximately the same level of generality as conventional intelligence. Finally, and most important, would the foregoing dimension of associational ability be independent of individual differences in the traditional area of general intelligence? If research findings could provide affirmative answers to these questions, then, and only then, would one be in a position to talk about a kind of thinking ability appropriately labelled *creativity*, with the evident implication of a characteristic different from general intelligence, but yet a characteristic which also possesses a substantial degree of generality across task variations.

Our work, conducted with 151 children comprising the entire fifth grade population of a suburban public school system in a middle class region, took great pains to establish a game-like, non-evaluational context for the administration of procedures. The Es, two young women, were introduced as visitors interested in children's games, and spent two initial weeks with each class gaining rapport with the children. This initial period of familiarization also provided the basis for observations leading to ratings of the children's behaviour on various dimensions, to be discussed later. Great effort was expended in communicating to the children that the presence of the Es did not concern examinations or tests. The teachers and principals, furthermore, did their utmost to dissociate the *E*s from any concern with intellectual evaluation. Finally, it was our view that the establishment of a game-like context required the *E*s to work individually with each of the 151 children. We sedulously avoided group administration with its academic testing implications.

Five procedures formed the basis for our exploration of creativity in these children. They concerned the generation of five kinds of associates. Two variables were measured in the case of each: uniqueness of associates, and total number of associates. Some of the procedures were verbal, others were visual in nature. One verbal procedure, for example, requested the child to generate possible instances of a verbally specified class concept, such as 'round things', or 'things that move on wheels'. Here and for every other creativity procedure, the child is given as much time on each item as he desires. Number of unique responses to an item is defined as the number of responses given by only one child in the sample of 151 to the item in question. Total number of responses offered to an item is, of course, self-defining. For 'round things', for example, 'life savers' is a unique response, while 'buttons' is not. Another verbal procedure requests the child to think of possible uses for various objects presented orally, such as 'shoe' or 'cork'. 'To trap a mouse in', is a unique use suggested for 'shoe', while 'to throw at a noisy cat' is not. A third verbal procedure asks the child to propose possible similarities between two objects specified in verbal terms. For instance, one pair is 'train and tractor', another is 'milk and meat'. A unique response to 'milk and meat' was 'they are government-inspected', while 'they come from animals' was not unique. The visual procedures, in turn, request the child to think of possible interpretations or meanings for each of various abstract visual patterns and line forms.

These procedures obviously owe a debt to the Guilford group. They are administered, however, in a carefully constructed game-like context, with each child taken individually and encouraged to spend as much time as he wishes, in a relaxed atmosphere, on every item. These administration arrangements were very different from those employed by the Guilford group. It should be emphasized, furthermore, that the use of a game-like context did not lead to a violation of the task constraints present in the various items of the procedure. Bizarre or inappropriate responses were exceedingly rare.

To assess the traditionally demarcated area of general intelligence, ten indicators were utilized. These included verbal and performance subtests from the Wechsler Intelligence Scale for Children (Wechsler,

1949); the School and College Ability Tests, which provide measures of verbal and quantitative aptitude (Cooperative Test Division, 1957a, 1957b); and the Sequential Tests of Educational Progress, which provide yardsticks of achievement in various academic content areas (Cooperative Test Division, 1957c, 1957d, 1959).

The ten creativity indicators – a uniqueness and a productivity measure for each of five procedures – proved to be highly reliable, in terms of both split-half and item-sum correlations. The reliabilities of the ten intelligence instruments, in turn, are known to be quite high. We now were in a position, therefore, to study the dimensionality of the creativity and intelligence indexes. The findings were as follows. Whether examining results for the sample as a whole, or separately for the seventy boys and the eighty-one girls, the ten creativity measures proved to be highly intercorrelated, the ten intelligence measures proved to be highly intercorrelated, and the correlation *between* the creativity and the intelligence measures proved to be extremely low. To provide an idea of the correlational magnitudes involved, the average correlation among the ten creativity measures is on the order of 0·4; the average correlation among the ten intelligence indicators is on the order of 0·5; and the average correlation between these two sets of measures is about 0·1.

We may conclude, therefore, that a dimension of individual differences has been defined here which, on the one hand, possesses generality and pervasiveness, but which, on the other hand, nevertheless is quite independent of the traditional notion of general intelligence. This new dimension concerns a child's ability to generate unique and plentiful associates, in a generally task-appropriate manner, and in a relatively playful context. It is a considerable surprise that such a dimension should prove to be quite independent of general intelligence, and it seems indeed appropriate to label this dimension 'creativity'. The independence of this dimension from general intelligence seems all the more intriguing for two reasons: first, the creativity procedures almost inevitably call upon verbal facility in some degree, and verbal facility is a very basic element of the general intelligence concept; second, the independence in question is found for elementary school children, and one would expect young children to show less differentiation in modes of cognitive functioning than adults.

In a sense, all that has been described thus far constitutes a prelude. Having isolated a mode of thinking in children that is pervasive, independent of intelligence, and appropriately described as a dimension of individual differences in 'creativity', we now wish to understand its psychological significance. The appropriate research strategy at this point seemed to require consideration of individual differences on the creativity and the intelligence dimensions taken *jointly*. That is, a child's location had to be defined with respect both to general intelligence and to creativity as we have conceived of it. It was necessary, in other words, to compose four groups of children within each sex: those high in both creativity and intelligence, those high in one and low in the other, and those low in both. In order to define these groups, a single creativity index score and a single intelligence index score were obtained for each child. These index scores were the summed standard scores of the ten measures in each respective domain. The distributions of creativity index scores and of intelligence index scores then were dichotomized at their respective medians, within sex, to yield the groups that exemplified the four possible combinations of creativity and intelligence levels. The two sexes, incidentally, were quite similar with regard to the distributions of these index scores. Since all cases were retained, rather than just the extremes, it is evident that the procedure used for composing creativity and intelligence combinations was a conservative one.

Consider now some of the psychological differences that we found to distinguish children who are both creative and intelligent, creative but not intelligent, intelligent but not creative, and neither creative nor intelligent.

To begin with, we turn to the behaviour of these several groups of children in the school environment. The two *E*s made independent ratings of the children along specifically defined behavioural dimensions during an initial two weeks of observation in each class. This work was carried out prior to any further contact with the children, so that the ratings could not be influenced by the performances of the children on the various experimental procedures used in our research. Furthermore, no other possible sources of information about the children were made available to the raters during the observation period. In short, every effort was made to insure that the ratings would be unbiased.

It should also be mentioned that these rating dimensions possess high inter-rater reliability, a very important point that the use of two independent observers permitted us to establish. Without this kind of reliability, investigation of individual differences on these behavioural dimensions would have been fruitless.

The judges rated each child's status on a given dimension in terms of a nine-point scale. For example, one characteristic was defined in terms of the following question: 'To what degree does this child seek attention in unsocialized ways, as evidenced by such behaviour as speaking out of turn, continually raising his hand, or making unnecessary noises?' The first, third, fifth, seventh and ninth points on the rating scale for this question were given the verbal labels 'never', 'seldom', 'sometimes', 'usually' and 'always', respectively. Other questions rated in the same manner included: 'To what degree does this child hesitate to express opinions, as evidenced by extreme caution, failure to contribute, or a subdued manner in a speaking situation?' 'To what degree does this child show confidence and assurance in his actions toward his teachers and classmates, as indicated by such behaviour as not being upset by criticism, or not being disturbed by rebuffs from classmates?' 'To what degree is this child's companionship sought by his peers?' 'To what degree does this child seek the companionship of his peers?'

The preceding questions were focused upon issues of social behaviour. Several questions of an achievement-centred nature also were included. These inquired about such matters as the following: 'How would you rate this child's attention span and degree of concentration for academic school work?' 'How would you rate this child's interest in academic school work, as indicated by such behaviour as looking forward to new kinds of academic work, or trying to delve more deeply into such work?' For these questions, the first, third, fifth, seventh and ninth points of the rating scales were labelled 'poor', 'below average', 'average', 'good' and 'superior', respectively.

Let us look in some detail at the results for the girls. Those high in both creativity and intelligence show the least doubt and hesitation of all the groups, show the highest level of self-confidence, and display the least tendency towards deprecation of oneself and one's work. Concerning companionship, these girls are sought out by their peers more eagerly than is any other group, and this high intelligence–high creativity group also seeks the companionship of others more actively than does any other group. There is reciprocity in social relationships for the members of this group. With regard to achievement, this group shows the highest levels of attention span, concentration and interest in academic work. In all of these respects, the high–high group obviously is reflecting highly desirable modes of conduct in both the social and the achievement spheres. Interestingly enough, however, this group also is high in regard to disruptive, attention-seeking behaviour. The high–high children may well be brimming over with eagerness to propose novel, divergent possibilities in the classroom, in the face of boredom with the customary classroom routines. Against the context of classroom programmes that emphasize equal participation by class members and academic values that are likely to centre around the traditional intelligence dimension, the cognitive behaviour reflected in high creativity levels in the case of these girls may well possess a nuisance value and exert a rather disruptive effect in the classroom situation.

Consider next the group high in creativity but low in intelligence. In many respects it turns out that this group is at the greatest disadvantage of all in the classroom – and, indeed, under more of a disadvantage than the group which is low in both creativity and intelligence. Those of high creativity but low intelligence are the most cautious and hesitant of all the groups, the least confident and least self-assured, the least sought after by their peers as companions, and in addition are quite avoidant themselves of the companionship of others. There is a mutuality of social avoidance in the case of these girls. In the academic sphere, they are the most deprecatory of their own work and the least able to concentrate and maintain attention. In terms of the ratings for disruptive attention-seeking, however, these girls are high, and in this one respect similar to the high-creativity-high intelligence group. Most likely, however, the attention-seeking of these two groups is quite different in quality, given the highly different contexts of other behaviours in the two cases. While the disruptive behaviours of the high–high group suggest enthusiasm and over-eagerness, those of the high creative–low intelligent group suggest an incoherent protest against their plight.

It affords an interesting comparison to turn next to the group low in both intelligence and creativity. These girls actually seem to be better off than their high creativity–low intelligence peers. The low–low group possesses greater confidence and assurance, is less hesitant and subdued, and is considerably more outgoing towards peers in social relationships than is the high creative–low intelligent group. The low-low group members appear to compensate for their poor academic performances by activity in the social sphere, while the high creative-low intelligent individuals, possessing seemingly more delicate sensitivities, are more likely to cope with academic failure by social withdrawal and a retreat within themselves.

Finally, we turn to the group high in intelligence but low in creativity. As in the case of the high–high group, these girls show confidence and assurance. In terms of companionship patterns, however, an intriguing difference emerges. While sought quite strongly as a companion by others, the girl in this group tends not to seek companionship herself. She also is least likely to seek attention in disruptive ways and is reasonably hesitant about expressing opinions. Attention span and concentration for academic matters, in turn, are quite high. The impression that emerges, then, is of a girl who is strongly orientated towards academic achievement, is somewhat cool and aloof in her social behaviour but liked by others anyway, and is unwilling to take the chance of over-extending or over-committing herself; there is a holding back, a basic reserve.

These results make it clear that one needs to know whether creativity in a child is present in the context of high or low intelligence, and one needs to know whether intelligence in a child is present in conjunction with high or low creativity. It is necessary to consider a child's joint standing on both dimensions. One must seriously question, therefore, the Getzels and Jackson (1962) procedure of defining a 'high creative' group as children who are high in creativity *but* low in intelligence, and defining a 'high intelligent' group as children who are high in intelligence *but* low in creativity. If one wishes to establish generalizations about the nature of creativity and of intelligence as distinct characteristics, one cannot afford to ignore those children who are high in both and who are low in both.

Let us consider now some evidence in a different area – that of conceptualizing activities. This evidence will cast light on differences among the groups of boys. In one of our procedures, the child was asked to group pictures of everyday physical objects, and was requested to give the reason for his grouping in each case. Among the fifty objects pictured were, for example, a rake, a screwdriver, a telephone, a lamppost, a candle. The groupings were to be carried out in terms of putting together things that seem to belong together. When this phase was completed, reasons for grouping were obtained. These reasons later were content analysed – blindly, of course, with respect to the identities of the children – and the reliability of the content analysis system was evaluated by having all materials scored by two independent judges. Reliability was found to be quite high. Consider briefly now one of the content analysis distinctions employed.

We were interested in contrasting relational or thematic reasons for grouping with reasons based upon abstracted similarities among the objects. In the latter type of reason, every object in the group is an independent instance of the label applied, whether the labels refer to shared physical properties or to shared conceptual properties. An example of the physical-descriptive type of category would be the label 'hard objects' for a group consisting of a lamppost, a door and a hammer. An example of the conceptual-inferential type of category would be the label 'for eating' in the case of a group containing a fork, a spoon, a cup and a glass. By a relational or thematic type of reason, on the other hand, we refer to a label deriving from the relationship among the objects in the group; no single object is an independent instance of the concept, but rather all of the objects in the grouping are required in order to define it. An example of a thematic category is the label 'getting ready to go out' for a group consisting of a comb, a lipstick, a watch, a pocketbook and a door.

The distinctions just made derive from work carried out by Kagan, Moss and Sigel (1960, 1963), with certain modifications necessitated by the nature of the stimuli. It has typically been assumed by these investigators as well as by others that responding on a relational or thematic basis represents an intellectually inferior manifestation. This may well be true when the stimuli to be grouped are few in number and their thematic characteristics highly salient, as has been the case in the studies just cited. Thematizing under such circumstances may represent a passive, global approach to the materials provided. In the procedure that we employed, however, a large number of stimuli – fifty in all – were present, and their nature as well as the instructional context were such as to reduce markedly the *Eindringlichkeit* or prominence of thematic relationships. The child was encouraged to group in terms of abstractions, since the instructions implied to him that similarity be used as the basis for sorting. In addition, the objects were commonplace physical things, and there were many of them. Under these circumstances, it might well be the case that relational or thematic grouping would constitute a free-wheeling, unconventional type of response to the given task, in contrast to the more customary practice of sorting the objects in terms of common elements, whether such elements be physical or conceptual. Constraints arising from the nature of the stimuli would be considerably stronger in the case of groupings based upon shared physical or conceptual properties. Groupings based on relationships or themas, on the other hand, would permit greater free play for the evolving of unique combinations of stimuli. With these considerations in mind, let us turn to some results.

The findings for males point to a particularly clear phenomenon. The group of high intelligence but low creativity stands out as avoiding the use of thematic or relational bases for grouping. Rather, they concentrate on conceptual common elements. For whatever reasons – and the reasons may differ in the case of different groups – the other three groups are more willing to indulge in thematic forms of conceptualizing. It is the high intelligence–low creativity group that shows a disproportionate avoidance of thematizing. Such a finding reinforces the hypothesis that thematic responding may, under the conditions of the present procedure, represent a more playful, imaginative approach to the grouping task than does strict common-element sorting.

To suggest that the low incidence of thematizing by the high intelligence–low creativity group is evidence for an avoidance reaction, however, is to imply a further distinction. In principle, a low incidence could reflect either an inability to thematize or an avoidance of it. In another experimental procedure, however, we assessed the ability of the children to integrate a set of words into a unified theme in story telling: that is, in this new task, thematizing was required of the child. Under such conditions, the high intelligence–low creativity group thematizes as well as the group high in both creativity and intelligence. It is when the option not to thematize is available that thematizing drops out of the behaviour of the high intelligent–low creative group. Such evidence, then, suggests that we are dealing with a disinclination to thematize on the part of this group, not an inability to thematize.

It has typically been proposed in work on cognitive development (e.g. Bruner and Olver, 1963) that the most mature cognitive functioning involves inferential abstraction – the kind of organizing that would be reflected in terms of sorting objects on the basis of shared conceptual properties. Thematizing has been considered a developmentally primitive response. Our findings suggest, however, that a more critical consideration may be the relative balance between conceptual-inferential and thematizing tendencies. Consider the results for the various groups of boys on the sorting task in somewhat more detail. For both of the high creativity groups, the relative incidence of thematizing *and* inferential-conceptual grouping is fairly high. For the high intelligence–low creativity group, the relative incidence of thematizing is quite low, while the relative incidence of inferential-conceptual sorting is quite high. Finally, for the low intelligence–low creativity group, the relationship is reversed; the incidence of thematizing is high, while the incidence of inferential-conceptual sorting is relatively low.

In sum, the creative boys seem able to switch rather flexibly between thematizing and inferential-conceptual bases for grouping; the high intelligence–low creativity boys seem rather inflexibly locked in inferential-conceptual categorizing and strongly avoidant of thematic-relational categorizing; finally, the low intelligence–low creativity boys tend to be locked within thematic modes of responding and relatively incapable of inferential-conceptual behaviour. Parenthetically, it might be well to offer the reminder that the incidences of thematic and inferential-conceptual groupings both can be high since there also exists the third scoring category of grouping in terms of common physical elements.

When we consider some of our data concerning sensitivity to the expressive potential of visual materials, a result similar to the thematizing findings is obtained for the high intelligence–low creativity group of girls. With line drawings of stick figures in various postures as stimuli, various emotional states were proposed to the child as possibilities for one or another figure, and the child indicated a willingness or disinclination to entertain each possibility. Let us focus our attention upon two kinds of affective labels for each stick figure: a label constituting a highly likely, conventional suggestion, and a label representing a quite unlikely, unconventional possibility. Unconventional and likely emotional attributions for the various stick figures were defined with reference to the consensus of adult judges. Each of some twenty-four stick figures was offered to the child with one affective label upon each presentation. A different type of label would be proposed each time a given figure was presented, and a given figure was repeated only after all the others had been shown. More inappropriate and more appropriate kinds of labels for the various figures would be offered on a random schedule. Note that a choice is never forced between these two classes of emotional attributions. Each presentation involves one stick figure and one label, with the child requested to accept or reject the label as a descriptive possibility. The child thus is free to accept appropriate and unconventional emotional attributions, to reject both kinds, or to accept one kind and reject the other.

The main results with this procedure for the girls were as follows. Although the four groups did not differ in regard to their acceptance of appropriate or likely affective attributions for the stick figures, they differed in a particular way regarding acceptance of the unconventional attributions – the group high in intelligence but low in creativity exhibited a conspicuously low level of such acceptance. Although the rate of acceptance of such attributions by the other three groups was generally quite low (about 5 per cent), the high intelligence–low creativity group accepted virtually none at all. The comparability among the groups regarding acceptance of appropriate attributions acts as a control, indicating that the differential acceptance behaviour just described relates to the entertainment of unconventional attributions in particular, rather than simply to the acceptance of any kind of affective labels. Furthermore, there is no relationship between degree of acceptance of unconventional and of appropriate attributions. It is safe to conclude, therefore, that an acquiescence or 'yea-saying' response set cannot account for the differential acceptance of unconventional attributions.

The implications of the present findings appear to be quite similar to the thematizing results considered before in the case of the boys. In both cases, the high intelligence–low creativity group is intolerant of unlikely, unconventional, types of hypothesizing about the world. This particular group appears conspicuously loath to 'stick its neck out', as it were, and try something that is far out, unconventional, and hence possibly 'wrong'. It is of particular interest that the high intelligence–low creativity group of girls avoids entertaining the possibility of unconventional emotional attributions under the present experiment's conditions. Recall that the entertainment of such possibilities has no effect upon the availability for acceptance of the likely and highly appropriate possibilities; it is not an 'either–or' situation. The high intelligence–low creativity girls seem to be so attuned to error that even where appropriate responses are not sacrificed they refuse to deviate from a critical standard of 'correctness'.

Consider next some of the other findings in the domain of expressive sensitivity. Included in this domain were tasks requiring free descriptions of stimuli with implicit emotive significance. We content analysed these free descriptions in order to determine the extent to which a child would confine his descriptions to comments upon the physical and geometric characteristics of the various stimuli, as contrasted with the extent to which he would 'go beyond' such physical categories and discuss the affective or expressive connotations of such materials. In the case of both sexes, the ability to range beyond the physical and into the realm of affective content tended to be maximal in the group high in both creativity and intelligence. That creativity and intelligence both could contribute to such physiognomic sensitivity – responsiveness to 'inner' feeling states on the basis of perceivable externals – suggested that two processes could be jointly involved in the display of this sensitivity. On the one hand, the capacity to make inferential translations from one mode of experience to another seems to be reflective of the general intelligence concept; on the other hand, the associational freedom implied by the creativity concept evidently enhances the range of experience available for making inferential linkages.

Let us turn now to some evidence on how the children describe themselves with respect to general anxiety symptoms and to those symptoms experienced under the stress of tests or examinations. Consider the findings for the boys. Standard materials for assessing manifest anxiety and test anxiety were employed, deriving from the work of

Sarason, Davidson, Lighthall, Waite and Ruebush (1960). The results are suggestive of a Yerkes–Dodson function. They are of the same nature for both general manifest anxiety and test anxiety. The level of anxiety is lowest for the group that is high in intelligence but low in creativity. Anxiety level is middling for the two groups that are high in creativity, regardless of intelligence level. Finally, anxiety level is highest for the group that is low in intelligence and low in creativity. The allusion to the Yerkes–Dodson law is made since creativity is found to be maximal in the presence of an intermediate level of anxiety. If anxiety is either too low or too high, then creativity is reduced. Just as interesting, however, are the particular conditions under which anxiety level is lowest. It is the group high in intelligence but low in creativity who, by self-report, are least anxious. At the other end of the dimension, with the highest anxiety scores, stands the group low in both intelligence and creativity.

What are the implications of these findings? First of all, they force us to question whether creativity should be conceptually associated with a state of maximal freedom from anxiety symptoms. It is not those children who are lowest in anxiety level, but those who report a moderate degree of anxiety, whom we find to be most creative in their thinking processes. Traditional conceptions of mental health place considerable emphasis upon anxiety as a debilitator of cognitive performance and as a signal of inappropriate or ineffective adjustment. This no doubt is true when anxiety reaches quite high levels. We need only remember that the strongest degree of anxiety is found in the most cognitively deprived group of children – those who are low both in general intelligence and creativity. However, it may also be the case that a modicum of anxiety is reflecting more the presence of sensitivity to internal states than the presence of disturbance. This should not be construed, of course, as acceptance of the old saw that neuroticism breeds creativity. However, the data in hand do suggest that it is equally unrealistic to assume that the most creative children are the happiest children. There may well be elements of obsessiveness present in the kind of associative freedom that leads to high creativity status. A playful contemplation of the possible, but also an obsessive, task-centred reluctance to put a problem aside may be involved in the production of many associates and of a large number of unique associates. Creativity need not be all sweetness and light, therefore, but may well involve a tolerance for and understanding of sadness and pain. To think otherwise is to fall prey to the rather widespread American stereotype that suffering is always a bad thing and is to be avoided at all costs.

One possible cost of the avoidance of suffering is evident in the group whose levels of general anxiety and of test anxiety are lowest – the group high in intelligence but low in creativity. This result may well stem from the fact that the group in question is the most closely attuned to the demands of the classroom environment. In that environment, traditionally defined intelligence and its manifestations in the form of high academic achievement most likely are heavily rewarded, while creativity may well be viewed as more of a disruption than a boon. The mode of operation of the high intelligence–low creativity child, therefore, may be such as to minimize the sources of possible conflict between himself and the school environment and to maximize the sources of reward from that environment. It is not surprising that such a close fit between individual and social context would be reflected in a minimal level of anxiety.

From the kinds of results that have been passed in review, pictures begin to emerge concerning the psychological nature of the children in the four cognitive groupings: high creativity–high intelligence, high creativity–low intelligence, low creativity–high intelligence and low creativity–low intelligence. In addition to our quantitative studies, clinical accounts describing various children in the sample also have been prepared, and these clinical materials have tended to reinforce the conclusions derived from the experimental work. The case studies can be summarized in terms of the generalizations presented below. These will also serve to underline the major points of congruence between the clinical and the experimental sources of information concerning the four creativity and intelligence groupings.

High creativity–high intelligence: These children can exercise within themselves both control and freedom, both adult-like and child-like kinds of behaviour.

High creativity–low intelligence: These children are in angry conflict with themselves and with their school environment, and are beset by feelings of unworthiness and inadequacy. In a stress-free context, however, they can blossom forth cognitively.

Low creativity–high intelligence: These children can be described as 'addicted' to school achievement. Academic failure would be perceived by them as catastrophic, so that they must continually strive for academic excellence in order to avoid the possibility of pain.

Low creativity–low intelligence: Basically bewildered, these children engage in various defensive manoeuvres ranging from useful adaptations such as intensive social activity to regressions such as passivity or psychosomatic symptoms.

In conclusion, this presentation has traced in outline form the history of our research on two modes of thinking in young children; modes which constitute quite different, but yet quite pervasive, dimensions of individual differences. Our work progressed from the definition and operationalization of the cognitive types in question to an investigation of their correlates in such areas as observable social and achievement-relevant behaviours, ways of forming concepts, physiognomic sensitivities and self-described levels of general anxiety and test anxiety. From the findings obtained, it seems fair to conclude that the present definition of creativity denotes a mode of cognitive functioning that matters a great deal in the life of the child. Most critical of all for advancing our understanding is a consideration of the child's *joint* status with regard to the conventional concept of general intelligence and creativity as here defined.

10

J. P. Guilford (1967)

The nature of problem solving and creative production

J. P. Guilford, *The Nature of Human Intelligence* (McGraw-Hill Book Co.), pp. 316–31

MOTIVATION FOR CREATIVE THINKING

Intellectual drives

There has been a growing realization that the utilitarian drives of hunger, thirst, sex and pain or fear are not by any means sufficient to account for much instigation of intellectual activity. Some animal psychologists who have observed exploratory behaviour of rats and other animals have accepted a drive of curiosity; some have not been willing to go even that far. Others see even more than curiosity behind some animal behaviour. E. L. Thorndike (1931) once suggested that the normal functioning of an organism in any respect is satisfying. The organism has certain equipment that is able and ready to accomplish certain purposes, and there is a natural urge to exercise that equipment. Having an unusual endowment of equipment in the form of brain cells, man has a natural urge to use that facility, as shown by an interest in having new experiences, in being the cause of movements, and in having ideas and playing with them to his satisfaction. Havelka (1956) noted that even rats sometimes show consistent preferences for solving problems on their way to reaching food. It may be recalled that some of Köhler's apes (1925), having solved a problem of making a long stick out of two short ones, seemed to take delight in using the new-found tool to rake in all sorts of things, letting the eating of food go until a bit later.

A number of psychologists have noted a similar source of motivation. White (1959) asserts that organisms have a natural desire to grow and develop, to master their environments by developing knowledge and skills. In other words, he posits a general drive to achieve competence. Berlyne refers to an 'epistemic' curiosity, that '. . . activates a quest for knowledge and is relieved by acquisition of knowledge' (1962, p. 27). Epistemic curiosity is instigated by conceptual conflict, by discrepancies in beliefs, attitudes and thoughts. In speaking of motivation for creative performance, Golann (1962) says that it is in the form of a desire to make the most of one's own perceptual, cognitive and expressive potentials. J. McV. Hunt (1965b) makes a good case for the thesis that cognition has its own intrinsic motivation and that drive is increased by discrepancies between input and stored information.

The study of recognized creative people demonstrates well the conclusion of Rossman (1931) that inventing carries its own intrinsic rewards. Inventors whom he studied often spoke of an exhilaration and a feeling of mastery and superiority on the successful conquering of problems connected with a new invention. So much is this true that the inventor looks for new problems so that he may again experience a similar reward. There is apparently little thought about the desire to benefit humanity, as much as some observers would like to think so. Roe (1952) found this to be true in general of her outstanding scientists, an exception being that some social scientists indicated the humanitarian kind of motivation. The creative producer probably derives secondary satisfactions from the fact that others do approve, and he experiences satisfaction from knowing that what he does is beneficial. On the other hand, there are those of other dispositions who derive sadistic satisfaction from the torture and destruction their inventions make possible.

Secondary sources of satisfaction

There are other secondary rewards derivable from creative productions. Hadamard (1945), in discussing creative people in different fields, remarked that artists often have the desire to do something different just because it is different. A similar hypothesis was tested experimentally by Houston and Mednick (1963). They hypothesized that highly original individuals have a strong preference for novel responses, as such. To express the hypothesis in a negative way, original persons have an urge to avoid the trite and the banal. The experimenters' results tended to support the hypothesis, but it was difficult to say whether the positive or the negative statement of the hypothesis is the more realistic.

Barron (1953, 1958) has found that artists as a group and other creative people in different professions exhibit preferences for complex visual designs over simple, regular or symmetrical designs. One hypothesis is that the complex designs offer challenges to the comprehension abilities of the creative person and to his facility for establishing order out of disorder. This interpretation is close to the idea of a general drive for competence or intellectual mastery. From results obtained by Kincaid (1961) and Burkhart (1962), who do not find this kind of preference on the part of children, it appears that the preference for complexity is something that develops with age and experience. It may be that the individual at any age prefers a level of complexity that is neither so easy as to be beneath his coping powers nor so difficult as to be frustrating. The right level of complexity offers opportunities for the person to grow.

It has often been noted that creative people are likely to be independent thinkers. They have their own scales of values and are on the nonconforming side. Such a feature has been demonstrated experimentally by Crutchfield (1959), by use of the Asch–Crutchfield test of conformity. In this test, the examinee hears four of his associates render a judgement, e.g. of lengths of lines, before he gives his own judgement. By design, the four give a judgement that is in error. The score for the examinee is the number of times he goes along with group opinion. Crutchfield found a significant negative correlation between this score and an assessment of originality.

Factors of interest in thinking

Interests are motivational traits. They represent tendencies to be attracted to certain kinds of activities. A number of dimensions of interest in different kinds of thinking, including interest in reflective thinking, logical thinking, autistic versus realistic thinking, convergent thinking, divergent thinking, and a factor of tolerance of ambiguity, have been demonstrated (Guilford, 1961).

Scores for these interest variables and for other motivational traits have been found to correlate significantly but low with scores on some of the divergent-production tests (Merrifield, Guilford, Christensen and Frick, 1961). Associational-fluency tests correlated with need for adventure and with tolerance for ambiguity. It may be recalled that a leading test for factor DMR asks for a variety of synonyms. A long list can be obtained only if the examinee allows himself considerable leeway in accepting doubtful responses that occur to him. Expressional-fluency tests correlate with liking for reflective thinking. Originality tests correlate positively with liking for divergent thinking, tolerance of ambiguity and reflective thinking; they correlate negatively with need for meticulousness and with need for discipline. These associations are all reasonable. Taken together with other sources of drive considered in previous paragraphs, these facts demonstrate the great complexity of motivation for creative thinking and problem solving.

THE ROLE OF INFORMATION

On the need for a good supply of information for successful creative production, there is practically unanimous agreement. Information is not sufficient, but it is necessary. Brain (1948) asserts that a genius excels ordinary men in his having a wealth of *schemata*, a term that we may translate as stored products of information. Agnew (1922) concluded after studying composers that auditory memory is very important. After years of study of behaviour in the visual arts, Meier (1939) concluded that visual memory is one of the most important assets for the artist.

As to the role of stored information, there are differences of opinion. Some seem to agree with Welch (1945) that there is nothing new in creative products except the arrangement: a kind of kaleidoscopic hypothesis. Such a view is favoured by those who are partial to an associational theory. There is reluctance to admit that there is much change in the associative structure that is impressed upon the organism by his environment. There is preference for believing that most recall is replicative. The informational view is that there is considerable transfer recall and there is considerable transformation activity in the emerging of new products of information.

The role of systems

Among the products of information, one of the most important in creative production is that of the system. In the field of mathematics, Hadamard (1945) advises that it is well for the mathematician to start with some kind of schema. It may be vague in form and outline, but it is needed to give unity to the thinker's efforts. In the field of music, Cowell (1926) asserts that the flow of music that the composer hears in auditory imagery centres in a theme. In her study of the writing of poetry, Patrick (1941) reported that about two-thirds of the poets had general ideas from the beginning of their periods of incubation and that all of them were involved with a general idea by the time of illumination. Those who began with some specific item, perhaps a single word, found a general conception growing out of such a beginning.

Arnheim, Auden, Shapiro and Stauffer (1948) also noted that poems typically begin in skeleton form; the poem is sketched out as a whole, with the structure becoming clearer with illumination later. In the paintings of artists and non-artists, Eindhoven and Vinacke (1952) found that a motif is established early. The subject matter and the composition may be changed a number of times, but the first steps involve an outlining of the working space, with rough arrangements, the details coming later.

THE ROLE OF INCUBATION

Observationally, incubation is a period during which there is no apparent activity on the part of the individual towards the solution of his problem but during which and at the end of which there is often evidence of material progress towards a solution. The period of incubation may be a matter of minutes, days, months, and even years. The evidence of some progress in the interim calls for explanation. Such progress is associated with a persistent desire to solve the problem, perhaps with an intention to come back to it. Even without such an intention, problems seem to haunt some individuals, in a kind of perseveration.

The only known experiments designed specifically for investigation of the phenomena of incubation were those of Patrick (1935, 1938). She had subjects working on poems or on scientific problems in the laboratory. Periods of incubation occurred when an individual dropped one idea or strategy for a time and returned to it later. There was not complete cessation of problem solving effort in these instances, but such pauses might be in somewhat the same category. Better examples were obtained when Patrick had half of the subjects planning experiments in the laboratory and the other half at home, with lapsed time for incubation. Although such an experiment runs great risk of losing control over conditions of work, the result was suggestive when she found that the group with the incubation period produced somewhat better ideas.

Hypotheses concerning incubation

Numerous creative people will testify to the benefits of incubation, if not to its necessity. In efforts to explain those benefits, many writers follow the lead of Poincaré (1913) when he stated that during incubation unconscious problem solving is going on. This hypothesis tells us practically nothing, of course. We still do not know what the unconscious psychological operations are, if nothing more is said.

F

A fatigue hypothesis has been suggested: the problem solver becomes tired, suffering a decrement in performance, and the period of incubation gives him a rest, after which his performance level is higher. The fatigue must be a very specific one, however, for the individual often turns to other work that should be just about as tiring. This hypothesis also fails to account for apparent benefits derived from delays of time intervals much longer than are needed to recover from fatigue.

Woodworth (1938) favoured the hypothesis that taking up the problem again after a period of incubation provides an opportunity for a new start on the problem. Before the problem solving effort has been dropped, certain wrong directions have gained such recency value that they inhibit the trying of other directions. During the lapsed time of incubation, such information loses its recency value and more fruitful recalls can be effected. This hypothesis is the same as that often favoured in accounting for the benefits of spaced practice in learning. The two psychological problems, incubation and spaced learning, seem to have much in common. But it remains to be seen whether the same principles will account for both.

A transformation hypothesis

It can be proposed as a new kind of hypothesis that during incubation some transformations of information, transformations that take time to bring about, are taking place. On the basis of studies by D. R. Davis and D. Sinha (1950a, 1950b), it may be concluded that products of information in memory storage are not immune from interactions with new input. They may become modified or transformed. There is the possibility that interactions among stored products also occur, under the influence of somatic input from motivational sources. Bernard Weiner (1966) has assembled a great deal of evidence from various sources that indicates the effects of motivation upon memory traces.

That modifications take place unconsciously is incidental and gives no special superiority to an assumed 'unconscious mind'. The fact that so many so-called inspirations come into conscious view full-blown suggests that the transformations had occurred before the moment of inspiration or had been developing towards that moment. Such unconscious mental activity should not be surprising. Organized speech that rolls off the tongue so glibly is perpetually being formulated unconsciously.

Our best prospect of learning more about the role of incubation seems to be in the direction of discovering the principles governing the occurrence of transformations, conscious or unconscious. There must also be notable individual differences with respect to persistence of motivation to solve problems. There are 'incubators' who do and others who do not carry around with them much unfinished business, making considerable difference between those who create and those who do not.

THE ROLE OF INSIGHT OR INTUITION

To most observers, the most dramatic aspect of creative production is the moment of 'illumination', when the individual takes a notably large step in his thinking and it comes suddenly. Westcott (1961) refers to this step as the 'intuitive leap'. Although a number of experimental studies on the problem of intuition or insight can now be cited, we are still much dependent upon anecdotal information regarding the phenomenon in connection with what is called inspiration.

Emotional aspects

Many of the anecdotal reports regarding the moment of inspiration mention emotional accompaniments, sometimes with the implication that emotional aspects have something to do with the birth of the idea. C. R. Rogers (1962) speaks of the 'Eureka feeling', also of a feeling of anxiety and an urge to communicate to others. Patrick (1937) reported that painters, professional and non-professional, during painting in the laboratory sometimes experienced emotional excitement along with insights, sometimes not.

It can be hypothesized that the amount of emotion occurring with illumination depends upon several conditions: the strength of motivation of the individual, the amount of frustration he may have endured for lack of progress, the size of the intuitive leap and the importance of the outcome. How much the emotional component contributes to the success of the creator is problematical. Motivation, of course, should be a contributor.

The nature of insight or intuition

There can be no doubt about the fact of sudden arrival of increments of progress towards solutions, even when they are not complete. Intuitive ideas come with various degrees of clarity and completeness and with no apparent effort. Sometimes the intuited idea is only the nucleus of the eventual structure, but it is a key idea, and by working out the suggested implications the whole can be developed. Sometimes the intuited conception is rather evanescent, like a memory after-image. It is apparently quite common for the idea to be over-valued rather than properly evaluated, but later corrections will possibly take care of that error.

Maier (1931) demonstrated some of the characteristics of insight in experiments with his famous string problem. In this problem, the subject is shown two strings hanging from the ceiling of a room, so far apart that when he attempts to tie the ends together, as instructed, he cannot reach both strings at the same time. Four solutions are possible: using a heavy object to anchor one string while the other is brought to it; lengthening one string temporarily with an extension; pulling one string over with a pole while holding the other; and, with the use of a weight, making a pendulum of one string, swinging it within reach. Various objects needed for these solutions are lying about, but some have to be put to unusual uses, e.g. using pliers as a weight to make the pendulum.

Maier reported that the solutions came as wholes in 75 per cent of the cases. The self-observer rarely is able to catch any steps in his thinking immediately preceding the insight. The solution emerges like the hidden figure in a puzzle picture.

Mental state during intuition

From anecdotal information, there is unanimous agreement that there is an abandonment of controlled thinking, a resort to free association in a kind of daydreaming state (Beveridge, 1950). Composers, especially, speak of this type of experience (Griswold, 1939). Both Mozart and Brahms spoke of doing their best creations in dream-like states or of ideas coming as in vivid dreams. Tchaikovsky is quoted as saying: 'There is something somnambulistic about this condition.' César Franck is said to have been wandering in a trance-like state while generating his ideas. But there is also frequent mention of a very strong urge to create something and of much preparation and hard work preceding incubation.

It has long been known that relaxation is a favourable condition for recall of information. The dream-like, dispersed type of attention may mean that there is a relaxation from a restrictive use of a search model, which results in a broadening of the scanning among stored items of information, providing a condition of improved probability of arriving at the needed information. The wide search may favour more remote transfers. This hypothesis needs investigation. Also to be answered is the question of why the relaxed and dispersed search does not bring about total recall. The creative product is, after all, a result of selective recall.

Environmental conditions

A number of creative people have attested to the need for complete quiet during the period of illumination, while others do not find this essential. There is a greater agreement that lack of distractions and freedom from interruptions, even from threats of interruptions, are important conditions. Some idiosyncratic conditions are also reported. For example, it is said that Ben Jonson needed a purring cat, orange peel and plenty of tea to drink; Balzac required much black coffee at night; Zola drew shades in the daytime and worked in artificial light; Kipling demanded black ink only; and Freud was a chain smoker (McKellar, 1957). Such conditions are often in the category of fetishes, something that many creators apparently get along without. Incidental stimulations may add their contributions, as in the case of Keats, writing 'Ode to a Nightingale' after hearing one sing, and of Mendelssohn, who was inspired by the sight of a trumpet vine. Then there was Newton and the falling apple.

Some personality differences and intuition

Westcott (1961, 1964) has approached the problem of intuition from the standpoint of individual differences in personality traits other than intellectual aptitudes. He has been particularly interested in tendencies to take risks in reaching inferences on the basis of limited information. Westcott used problems of the following type:

$$4:2 \qquad 9:3 \qquad 25:5 \qquad 100:10 \qquad 64:8 \qquad 16:\text{------}$$

S is given these clues one at a time and is told to give an answer whenever he feels that he has had sufficient information. The number of clues that S requests is his *demand score*. The number of correct conclusions is his *success score*. The ratio of success score to demand score is an index of his efficiency of intuition. The demand and success scores correlated near zero; so there can be four types of individuals, those combining low demand with low success, low demand with high success, high demand with low success, and high demand with high success. The four categories of individuals are characterized as 'guessers', 'intuitive leapers', 'poor problem solvers' and 'steady, logical thinkers', in the order as just stated.

From independent assessments of personality traits of his subjects, Westcott (1964) found that those with high demand for information, regardless of success, were inclined to be cautious, conservative and compliant. The high-demanding and successful *S*s were not rigidly conservative or compliant and were willing to question things. The high-demanding and unsuccessful *S*s were defensive and rigidly moralistic. The low-demanding and successful were composed and unafraid. The low-demanding and unsuccessful were inclined to be depressed, despondent and even without hope. These associations seem reasonable, but there remains the question of which is cause and which is effect, if causal relationships are involved.

Role of previous experience

It is important to investigate the relation of insight to past experience because of its theoretical significance, among other reasons. Some psychologists with associational bias have been too ready to dismiss insight as being completely accounted for on the basis of previous learning, by which they probably mean a direct dependence upon learned associations that are revived in replicated recall in the insight situation (McGeoch and Irion, 1952). In holding such a view, there seems to be a self-blinding to the new elements involved in an insight.

Birch (1945a) did a transfer experiment in which six young chimpanzees were first tested to determine whether they could use a hoe to bring in food from a distance. Two of the apes succeeded. All were given training in the act of hauling in things by using plain sticks and were then retested on the hoe problem. All of them succeeded very quickly on the second hoe test. The conclusion that practice with plain sticks transferred to the use of the hoe seems to be justified. But even more significant is the fact that two apes could develop insight into the use of the hoe without the training with sticks. The associationist's answer would be that the two apes had had other prior incidental experiences to account for their early insights in the hoe problem, but it is highly unlikely that they had had raking experiences with a hoe. They may have had other experiences that transferred to success in the hoe problem on its first presentation, but that would be transfer recall, not replicative recall.

Several studies have been concerned with the way in which additional given information pertaining to a problem may help in solving it. With graduate students, Maier (1931) first taught separately three principles that would be needed in solving a complex problem that involved all three. In five different groups of *S*s he presented the complex problem, giving different numbers of hints in different groups. Only nine of the eighty-four *S*s got the correct solution, and eight of these were in the group receiving the most hints. Thus, experience of the kind that Maier gave may not be sufficient to bring about solutions. Something more was necessary, as in the form of hints that helped *S*s to use the previously given information. Maier (1940) thought that the 'something else' is what he called 'direction'. A little further thinking would have brought him to the conclusion that what was needed was the formation of a new product of information, an integration of the given principles into a system.

Weaver and Madden (1949), who took up the study of Maier's hypothesis of direction, found difficulty with the concept, because all *S*s, regardless of what information is given them, seem to have some direction. They concluded that 'directions' involve strategies, which point towards the formation of structures (systems) to which the goal idea is a contributor. In the process, we can say that perceptual and conceptual changes (transformations) occur.

That scattered items of information can have their bearings upon successful insights is suggested by some results of Judson, Cofer and Gelfand (1956). Students who had previously memorized lists of words some of which pertained to the Maier string problem, e.g. ROPE, SWING, PENDULUM, were more likely to reach the pendulum solution to the problem than *S*s who had not memorized such a list.

Saugstad and Raaheim (1957) used a more complex concrete problem, which offered possibilities of more varied amounts of helpful information. The additional information was in the form of some short lists of unusual uses for the objects that were needed in solving the problem. Briefly, the problem was to move some steel balls from a glass to a cylinder, both at some distance from *S*. Objects available for use included a nail, pliers, newspapers, rubber bands and string. The expected correct solution involved (1) making a hook out of the nail, using the pliers; (2) making a 'fishing line' from the hook and string; (3) hooking the frame on which the glass of balls rested; (4) pulling the frame within reach; (5) rolling newspaper into a tube, holding it in place with rubber bands; and (6) rolling the balls through the tube into the cylinder.

The subjects were 149 high school students who had had a course in physics. The kind of information given about the objects to be used was a list of five alternative uses for each object (three for the rubber bands), one of the uses being adaptable to solving the problem. Five experimental groups were given different amounts of information, some for one object and some for two. A control group had none of this kind of information. The results were that for the groups receiving information about two objects, 90 per cent solved the problem; for the groups receiving information about one object, from 25 to 57 per cent solved the problem (least for the tube uses, most for the hook uses); and of the control group, only 19 per cent succeeded. There had been no matching of groups on problem solving ability of any kind.

In a similar experiment with sixth grade children (Saugstad and Raaheim, 1959), it was found that the younger subjects were less able to make use of the given information and that memory for it seemed less stable in that they showed more solutions when the delay of the test was fifteen minutes than when it was thirty minutes.

Role of motivation in insight

There is little information regarding degree of motivation as a condition of probability of insight. Birch (1945b) reported one such study with six young chimpanzees as subjects. These young apes solved a number of string problems differing in the degree of insight needed, six different degrees of food deprivation being involved, including deprivation for two, six, twelve, twenty-four, thirty-six and forty-eight hours. Results, although based upon a small sample, were rather consistent. With two, thirty-six and forty-eight hours without food, the success in problem solving was no better than chance. The best scores were obtained with six and twenty-four hours of deprivation. The condition of twelve hours of deprivation should not be considered because it was largely occupied with a period of sleep, no meal actually having been missed. At the shorter intervals of deprivation, there was such lack of interest in food that S was easily distracted from his task. At thirty-six and forty-eight hours S had such a strong hunger drive that he paid too much attention to the goal and not enough to methods of arriving at the goal. Being frustrated to the point of screaming and tantrums, he was in poor mental condition for problem solving.

A moderate degree of hunger drive was therefore optimal for these apes. This tells us very little about the relationship between motivation and insight in human individuals where the motivation is more intrinsic to the task, but it is likely that there, also, motivation can be too strong as well as too weak for best results. Creative producers attest to the need for strong effort followed by relaxation as being favourable for inspirations.

In addition to the problem of the relation of degree of motivation to insights, there is the problem, as yet unmentioned and unexplored, of how the specific nature of the motivation may affect the shaping of solutions, producing possible transformations during the state of incubation and at other times.

THE ROLE OF FLEXIBILITY

There are three different kinds of flexibility in thinking, each with its distinct place in the structure-of-intellect model. One is flexibility with respect to classes, the readiness to shift from class to class; a second has to do with transformations in divergent-production activities; and the third type pertains to redefinitions or transformations in connection with convergent production.

Flexibility of classes

A factor first interpreted as spontaneous flexibility later became known as divergent production of semantic classes. The essence of the factor is the ready shifting from class to class in searching for information. It was demonstrated by Frick *et al.* (1959) that tests of tendency to perseverate within a class have strong negative loadings on this factor, where tests like Brick Uses (shift score) and Alternate Uses, which forces the examinee to go from class to class, have strong positive loadings. More recently, tests requiring *E* to classify the same set of items of information in different ways have also measured the factor, justifying its place in the SI model. The factor is not the same as Spearman's factor of perseveration (in reverse), for he regarded his *P* factor as being completely general, like *g*. It is now recognized that the same kind of spontaneous-flexibility factors pertain to figural and symbolic information, with parallel kinds of tests serving to demonstrate those factors.

It is likely that other writers have been coming close to the same conception as the idea of flexibility with classes. For example, in his book on teaching how to think creatively, W. J. J. Gordon (1961) stressed the importance of tackling a problem at a high level of abstraction. This could very well mean that the thinker's search model (a class idea) is very broad. Such a mental set should widen the scope of the search among stored information, thus increasing the probability of finding something useful. Narrowing the scanning operation within a limited class at the beginning might exclude the very information that is wanted.

Arnold (1962) gave an example of this approach to a problem. He considered the problem of thinking of an entirely new type of printing device. In order to ensure a broad consideration of the problem, he recommended that printing equipment be defined to include all devices for producing multiple copies of permanent visual records in readable form. This is an abstract definition of a common, concrete object. Four main attributes or dimensions are recognized: (1) carrier of information, (2) method of information transfer, (3) visual rendering and (4) production of multiple copies. This delineation provides a broad search model.

Arnold goes on to recommend that differentiations be made along each of the four dimensions to form what is essentially a morphological model, like the SI model. Then, by combining each distinguished step in a dimension with all other possible steps on other dimensions, a whole systematic set of hypothetical devices is generated. The ordinary printing press is one such combination. Anne Roe (1952) may have been considering the same breadth-of-scanning habit when she concluded that the top scientists whom she had studied seemed to be generalizers. Generalizing works towards larger, more inclusive classes, within which one can go from one subsidiary class to another.

It is interesting that too much familiarity with an object can work against a broader, more abstract view. Arnold (1962) cited an example of this. Employees of the AC Spark Plug Co. were found to have difficulty in listing the attributes of a spark plug, but they had little difficulty in listing the attributes of a bicycle. Listing attributes of an object means becoming abstract about it. On the other hand, employees who were making heavy machinery had little difficulty in listing attributes of a spark plug.

Thus, it is difficult to become abstract about familiar things. It is reported that Albert Einstein made a practice of denying his understanding of the obvious, in order that he might obtain a new look at things. It has also been reported that when a group is engaged in generation of ideas to solve a problem, it is sometimes the tyro or amateur who comes up with the key to the adopted solution. Experts in the field sometimes develop what has been called a 'disease' of hardening of the categories. Flexibility with respect to classifications is an important asset for the creative thinker.

Flexibility and divergent production of transformations

The conception of divergent production of transformations arose first in the form of a factor recognized as adaptive flexibility, the characteristic test for which is Match Problems. It was later recognized that the factor first identified as originality is an adaptive flexibility in dealing with semantic information and that both factors pertain to transformations. Because the Match Problems items involve considerable trial-and-error behaviour, the first interpretation was that adaptive flexibility is a matter of changing strategy, a habit-breaking disposition. Tests involving a tendency to persist along the same line of attack were found to have negative loadings on factor DFT (adaptive flexibility), supporting that interpretation (Frick *et al.*, 1959). But an alternative interpretation was later given, in line with the identification of this factor with transformations. The change of strategy entails changes in the meanings and roles of lines in the Match Problems figures and changes in meanings or interpretations in tests of originality. The tests of persistence can be regarded as measures of resistance to transformations.

The mention of persistence brings to mind the kind of rigidity that Luchins (1942) has investigated so extensively. The task involved in his famous Water Jar test is to measure out a specified quantity of water, given two jars with specified capacities. The first five problems are solvable by the same formula, which it is presumed most examinees will discover and adopt as a stock kind of solution for the items after item 5. But the later items can also be solved by shorter formulas. Will *E* (if we assume he has gained insight into the stock solution) continue to use the same formula, or will he shift to simpler ones?

A group form of the Water Jar test was analysed along with tests of flexibility factors (Frick *et al.*, 1959). The test had a loading of only 0·18 on factor DFT and a loading of $-0·09$ on factor DMT (originality). It is therefore not a measure of either figural or semantic divergent production of transformations. Whether it will be found to be loaded on factor DST, when that factor has been demonstrated, remains to be seen. A large part of the test's true variance was accounted for by two factors not in any flexibility category, however, both of them dealing with semantic content. Although the problems in the Luchins test require operations with numbers, they are like arithmetic-reasoning tests in general, in which the conceptions of the problems and of the strategies for solving them may well be in terms of semantic content. The failure to find any kind of flexibility variance in the Water Jar test indicates that the wide use of this test as a measure of rigidity is highly questionable.

Redefinition and functional fixedness

The redefinition factors are in the operation category of convergent production, the kind of product being transformation. Three such abilities have been demonstrated. Logically, a low degree of these abilities is identifiable with the phenomenon of functional fixedness, a rigidity in the use of objects or in the definition of information. Functional fixedness has been noted most particularly with solutions in the Maier string problem and similar problems, in which the subject has to desert the common use of an object, e.g. pliers, in order to employ the object in some unusual way: in the string problem, as a weight for a pendulum. Such rigidity is not the same as that proclaimed in connection with the Luchins Water Jar test; in other words, it is not the same as the Einstellung effect, for Adamson and Taylor (1954) found only a small, insignificant correlation between scores for the Maier and Luchins tests.

A number of experimental studies have been done to determine under what conditions functional fixedness (FF) is increased or decreased. Such experiments give *S*s some prior tasks in which they employ in various ways the object that is to be redefined. For example, in the string problem, Birch and Rabinowitz (1951) used an electric switch and an electric relay, both of which were suitable for becoming the weight of the contrived pendulum and were available during the solution of the problem. Prior to giving the problem, the experimenters asked one group of *S*s to use the switch in constructing an electric circuit and another group to use the relay for a similar purpose. The hypothesis was that recent uses of objects in conventional ways would make redefinition more difficult in solving the string problem. It turned out that way. All ten of the *S*s having experience with the relay chose the switch to make the pendulum; seven of the nine with the switch experience chose the relay to make the pendulum; a control group was evenly divided in uses of the two objects.

Flavel, Cooper and Loiselle (1958) gave their *S*s prior experience in terms of *unusual* uses of objects, with the expectation that this would facilitate redefinition in solving the string problem. One group was given prior experience with the *usual* use of a switch, and four other groups were given experiences with *unusual* uses. In the string problem test later, only three of twenty-four *S*s having had the usual use of the switch employed it. Of those having had differing amounts of unusual uses, in increasing order, eight, nine, thirteen and twelve employed the switch in making the pendulum. It appears unnecessary for an individual to have had much experience with unusual uses to prepare him for other unusual uses.

Other experiments add confirmatory and varied information bearing on the same hypothesis. Maltzman, Brooks, Bogartz and Summers (1958) found that experiences with unusual uses of a string, a screwdriver and balsa wood were followed by less FF behaviour in solving the string problem. Bond (1955) found that it is necessary only for S to *observe* unusual uses of an object to help prevent the FF type of behaviour in solving the problem.

Adamson and Taylor (1954) tested the hypothesis that effects of training affecting the FF behaviour would decrease with a lapse of time, as in normal forgetting. The time interval between training and the FF test was varied from one minute to one week. The training was in *usual* uses of switch and relay. After different time lapses, the percentages *not* employing the previously used object were: after one minute, 70; thirty minutes, 70; one hour, 65; one day, 53; and one week, 50. Thus, the FF effect due to training in habitual uses of objects can wear off almost completely in a day's time, since the 53 per cent was close to the chance level.

D. M. Johnson (1962) has demonstrated another condition that affects FF behaviour: the degree of embeddedness of the needed information. This should be a very fruitful hypothesis, because tests of the redefinition abilities characteristically present embedded objects: hidden figures or faces and hidden words. Johnson worked with hidden words; hence his Ss were dealing with symbolic information. Three degrees of embeddedness were represented: (1) single words presented for S to judge them for pleasantness versus unpleasantness (no embedding); (2) words in phrases, also to be judged; and (3) words in sentences. The task following required S to build anagrams in which the previously exposed words could be useful. From condition 1 to condition 3, the Ss did more poorly in using the pre-exposed words. In another experiment, words used in the exposed instructions could be useful in solving anagrams. Ss apparently did not make any use of this potential information that was continuously exposed to them.

Youtz (1948) has demonstrated the operation of rigidity in problem solving with a somewhat different kind of experiment. Women students first solved a series of arithmetic-reasoning problems, all of which could be solved by using a certain principle. Three groups had 10, 20 and 40 such problems as exercises. Then all were given a new set of problems that were solvable by a different principle. In the exercises, improvement was continuous and regular; those with the most practice problems were solving the problems most rapidly by the termination of practice. In the later test problems, the more practice on the first kind of problem, the slower were the solutions, indicating some kind of inhibition or interference. This interference could have been in failure to give a new interpretation (redefinition) to the test problems or in failure to transform the problem solving strategy. In either case, failure to discriminate between systems or failure to effect transformations was involved.

THE ROLE OF IMPLICATIONS

Thus far, we have seen that various SI operations and products enter into problem solving in various ways. The role of units is ubiquitous. Classes play their roles in recall of information, and they have a unique function in connection with one of the kinds of flexibility versus rigidity. Systems seem to be the culminating goals for much of creative production, and strategies in problem solving are also in the category of systems. Transformations were given a special role in connection with incubation, and they are basic to two kinds of flexibility, adaptive flexibility and redefinition.

Wallas's stage of verification in creative production evidently involves both elaboration and evaluation. Although elaboration, which is basically a matter of implications, is more characteristic of later phases of problem solving after a skeleton-like system has been generated, it can occur at any place along the way. For whenever there is an inference, there is an implication. An illustrative problem, borrowed from Helson and Helson (1946), is very pertinent. It was offered by them as an example of productive thinking in the area of symbolic information to supplement Wertheimer's many illustrations (1945) in the figural or concrete area of information.

The problem statement was: 100 people attend a cinema, men for 30 cents each, women for 20 cents each and children for 1 cent. The money received for tickets one afternoon was $10. How many men, women and children attended the cinema on that afternoon?

In approaching the problem algebraically, two simultaneous equations each involving three unknowns were set up, for x women, y men and z children:

$$x + y + z = 100 \qquad (1)$$
$$20x + 30y + z = 1000 \qquad (2)$$

Setting up the equations may be regarded as the convergent production of symbolic systems, each a set of relations. The difficulty in solving these equations is that there are three unknowns and only two equations. The first tactic is to follow the usual treatment of simultaneous equations. With foresight (cognition of symbolic implications) it can be seen that one unknown can thus be eliminated, but it is still unknown. Since the zs have the same coefficient, a subtraction yields the equation

$$19x + 29y = 900 \tag{3}$$

There is now the task of solving for two unknowns, but with only one equation.

The next tactic is to look for properties of the elements in this equation that might be utilized. It was noted that 900 is a multiple of both 9 and 10 (cognition of symbolic classes) and that 19 and 29 can be subdivided into the same two values (more class cognition), leading to the breakdown (a symbolic transformation) in the next equation:

$$10x + 9x + 20y + 9y = 900$$

With regrouping (further transformation),

$$10(x + 2y) + 9(x + y) = 900 \tag{4}$$

The Helsons then made some further useful inferences (implications). It was noted that two of the terms in equation (4) are multiples of 10; therefore the third term must also be a multiple of 10. This is the term $9(x + y)$. Since 9 is not a multiple of 10, $x + y$ must be a multiple of 10 (another implication). In other words the number of men plus the number of women must be a multiple of 10. Another implication is that $x + 2y$ must be a multiple of 9, making the first term of (4) a multiple of 90, which is true of the other two terms.

This information, convergently produced and therefore logically sound, makes possible the next tactic, which is to introduce two new variables, p and q, in writing the equations

$$x + 2y = 9q$$
$$x + y = 10p \tag{5}$$

By solving for x and y,

$$x = 20p - 9q$$
$$y = 9q - 10p \tag{6}$$

Substituting equations (5) in equation (4), we have

$$90p + 90q = 900$$

and from this, the information that

$$p + q = 10$$

One could now test various combinations of integers, each summing to 10, to see which combinations give non-negative values for x and y. The Helsons short-circuited this procedure by using inequalities, finding that $p = 4$ and $q = 6$. From these values x is found to be 26 (women), y to be 14 (men) and z to be 60 (children), which satisfy the original equations.

The point illustrated here is that, besides the cognitive insights involving classes and relations and in addition to the transformations produced, there are other insights involving implications. These implications are in the form of deductions leading to additional information implied by the statement of the problem and also in the form of implied tactics to use next. Sometimes the tactics are recalled from the memory storage, based upon learned mathematical operations, but sometimes they have to be invented to fit the particular situation.

THE ROLE OF EVALUATION

Evaluation is another aspect of Wallas's stage of verification, with the implication that it occurs near the end of the total creative process.

Suspended judgement

One of the main features of Alex F. Osborn's brainstorming method (1963) is its intentional suspension of evaluation during the idea-generating sessions of group thinking on a problem. One experiment designed to test for the benefits of this condition in creative production was reported by Meadow, Parnes and Reese (1959). One group of subjects generated ideas with suspended judgement and another without. Additional steps were taken to use reinforcement, in the form of penalties for low-quality ideas. The problems called for thinking of unusual uses for a wire coat hanger and for a broom. In scoring the performances of the two groups, all responses were weighted for quality, applying the criteria of uniqueness and usefulness. The group with suspended judgement (with negative reinforcement for failure) produced an average of 7·9 high-quality ideas and the other group only 3·9. The two conditions were alternated in the two problems. The group having the suspended-judgement condition first did better under the other condition when it came second.

Suspension of judgement is not always an advantage where numbers of high-quality responses are concerned. Christensen *et al.* (1957) gave the Plot Titles test to some groups of adults without any mention of cleverness and in comparable groups with the explicit instruction to list clever responses. It was hypothesized that under the second type of instruction the examinee would impose some degree of censorship or evaluation, reducing his output. The result was rather decisive. Under the instruction to be clever, the total quantity of responses decreased but the total number of clever-rated responses increased, as did the average degree of rated cleverness.

There can be no doubt about the last two conclusions. But of the first conclusion, regarding total quantity, there can be some doubt. Under the instruction to be clever, we do not know how many titles *E* generated but discarded, not taking the trouble to write them down. There may have been some of this behaviour under the other instructions, but it was probably not so common. We cannot say that there was a condition of complete suspension of judgement in the case of the instructions without mention of cleverness, but the difference would be in that direction. A group especially instructed to let itself go and record all possible responses would be needed to round out the experiment.

The results of the last-mentioned experiment were supported by similar results from the work of Weisskopf-Joelson and Eliseo (1961). They had groups brainstorming new names for a cigar, a deodorant and an automobile, half of them with instructions to be critical and half of them not. The non-critical groups gave responses of higher quantity, but the critical groups gave a higher proportion of high-quality responses. This tendency may develop with age of the individual, for Torrance (1962) found that instructions to give 'clever, unusual, and original' responses tended to increase quantity of production at the fourth-grade level but to decrease it slightly above that grade.

Reactions to criticism

A number of studies have dealt with two kinds of criticism, constructive versus destructive, applied by self versus applied by others, with adults and with children. In one of them, Torrance (1965) instructed one group of graduate students to read previous research reports with a constructive attitude and another group to read the same reports with a critical, fault-finding attitude. After these readings, the students were asked to list new ideas for research suggested by their readings. The number of high-quality ideas produced by the constructive-reading group exceeded that produced by the critical-reading group.

In another study, three groups of students were given three different instructions to apply in their reading: (1) to retain ideas they read about, (2) to evaluate them, and (3) to improve upon them (Torrance, 1960). They were later given four types of examinations: cognitive (multiple-choice items), memory (completion items), evaluative and creative (new applications). The creative-set group had the highest mean on the creative items, the evaluative-set group had the highest mean on the evaluative items, and the memory-set group had the highest mean on the cognitive and memory items. These results highlight the fact that the kind of preparation has a bearing upon the score made in examinations with different kinds of items. In general, many students have learned to prepare for the kinds of examination they expect, and such slants in preparation determine what kind of mental exercise they derive from that effort.

Hyman (1964) has made a preliminary report of a systematic experiment on two kinds of criticism combined with self-criticism and with criticism of others. The subjects (students) were to offer solutions to the problem of how to improve education in spite of a shortage of teachers. There was an early attempt at solving the problem in which S listed his proposed solutions. The obtained solutions were criticized, some by the subject himself and some by other Ss. In either case, some Ss were to evaluate the solutions constructively, and some were to criticize them destructively. Then there was a second attempt with the problem to see what effect prior evaluative activity had had on later generation of solutions.

Several conclusions could be drawn. Ss who evaluated others' solutions constructively and their own destructively made the most changes in quantity and quality of solutions. Ss who evaluated others' solutions destructively and their own constructively were next best in the second attempt. Ss who made the same kind of evaluation of self and others, whether constructive or destructive, changed significantly but less than the others. Both were better than the control group. In terms of quality, the destructive–destructive group was the poorest of the four. The major finding, which was somewhat surprising, was that those who made both kinds of evaluation gained more from the evaluation experiences than those who made evaluations of the same kind when that kind was constructive. The hypothesis coming out of this conclusion is that there is more to learn by making both kinds of evaluation and that what is learned is probably in terms of ways of applying standards and criteria of judgement. In this way Ss gain more skill in discriminating good and poor solutions. A general comment was that one should be cautious in drawing blanket conclusions in the area of evaluation; there are likely to be interaction effects.

From extensive studies with evaluation exercises with schoolchildren, Torrance (1965) has a number of generalizations to offer. He has concluded that too frequent application of evaluation during practice sessions, regardless of type, tends to interfere with subsequent performance on similar tasks. Unevaluated or off-the-record practice tends to produce greater originality, more elaboration, and more sensitivity than does evaluated practice. One exception was at grade 6. When peer evaluation is constructive, it promotes more creative development than when it is critical, especially at grades 4 to 6. But even constructive suggestions can be worse than no evaluation at all, for they seem to call the children's attention to evaluation, as such, which works against suspended judgement. Thus, with children, also, there are interaction effects.

II

R. B. Cattell and H. J. Butcher (1968)

The prediction, selection and cultivation of creativity

R. B. Cattell and H. J. Butcher, *The Prediction of Achievement and Creativity* (The Bobbs-Merrill Company), pp. 281–306

SECTION I: THE GENERAL PROBLEMS IN FOSTERING CREATIVITY

We may conclude that four main tasks await those who would foster creativity:

(1) Selecting persons who can safely be predicted to be highly creative
(2) Educating thought processes to maximize creativity
(3) Setting up special institutions to support creative work
(4) Providing suitable working conditions and incentives in such institutions and elsewhere.

Because no facet can be well understood in isolation, and because selection cannot be accurately undertaken unless we know the conditions for which we are selecting, we shall begin with a discussion of institutions and conditions and later work back to the first two points.

From the Middle Ages until this generation, the university has been looked upon as the institution for cherishing and stimulating creative work in scientific and philosophical, and to some extent in literary and artistic, fields. For much of this time, the churches also played their part, with varying felicity, according to whether a Michelangelo or a Galileo was involved. Because of the conservatism or inadequate organization of such institutions, however, creative genius has always had to make its own way, alone and largely unsupported. Increasingly, however, since the foundation of the Royal Society in Britain and of the Academy in France in the seventeenth century, scientific, literary and artistic societies have been offering some moral and even material support to highly creative individuals. But it is certain that these institutions have succeeded in giving opportunities for successful expression to only a fraction of the talented people available.

So much has been written about wasted talent, and so rapid has been the growth of universities in recent times, that it would be easy to assume complacently that the needs of creative ability will henceforth be well met. The chief reasons for doubting this are:

(1) Human reactions to disturbing new ideas have changed very little.

(2) The universities, though often explicitly founded for both 'the advancement and the propagation of knowledge', have always been dominated by the second, i.e. the teaching function. The students are always there, and the ideas are not. Furthermore, the rapid increase in this generation in the endowment of universities and the consequent astonishing increase in the percentage of the population taught in them have brought a corresponding increase in attention to the teaching function.

The prosperity of our times is not primarily the result of better education, and still less of any great improvement in conducting business intelligently, but is largely the result of scientific discoveries by a few creative men. It is, therefore, a matter of simple self-interest to any community – quite apart from more lofty considerations – to plough back an appreciable proportion of this increased wealth into the support and encouragement of creative scientists.

To a gratifying degree in the United States, Germany, Russia and Sweden, and to a recognizable degree in Australia, Britain, France, Italy and other countries, a fraction of the community gain has been fed back to the goose that lays the golden eggs. Not all this fraction has been fed in the right way to the right geese. A great deal of money for research, both in Britain and America, goes to professors too harassed by heavy loads of teaching and administration to make the best use of it. Admittedly, some enterprising universities (neither Harvard and Yale nor Oxford and Cambridge excel in this respect) have set up research professors in their science departments and leading painters and composers in their art and music departments. But even these relatively few and apparently fortunate individuals are only too often isolated in the wrong sense in universities as they are currently organized. Relative freedom from administrative duties frequently means that the administrative machine pays little regard to their interests. Almost universally, too, they find it impossible to climb the university promotion ladder without veering abruptly between alternate spells of research and teaching. This situation has arisen from adherence to the rarely challenged shibboleth that the best teacher is also the best researcher and creative scholar. The time has come for an objective and unprejudiced examination of this bland formula. For whom and for what is this sedulously fostered type of intellectual amphibian 'best'? Is it true that the best teacher from the standpoint of the under-graduate's needs (in large classes that every high school graduate may attend) is also the most original scholar? If it is good for the teacher to be a researcher, is it also necessarily good for the researcher to be a teacher? These are questions that urgently require dispassionate re-consideration – reconsideration unhampered by traditional precon-ceptions. There is no reason why they should not be answered by psychological and educational research.

SECTION 2: FOR WHAT WORKING CONDITIONS ARE WE SELECTING CREATIVE INDIVIDUALS?

What then is the best environment for creative work? Certainly, the current academic environment has serious drawbacks. Teaching traffic may disturb and distract from research concentration, and, in particular, the simplified, dramatized presentations of undergraduate teaching may conflict with the subtlety and tolerance of ambiguity necessary in research. It may well be, therefore, that as far as research is concerned, the role of the university should be that of a proving ground, in which the good researcher and the good teacher can give demonstration of their respective talents. Between the ages of 30 and 40, the individual of proven flair in research should perhaps be directed to an institution shaped purely for research work. Such institutions, exemplified in the Rockefeller Institute, the Max Planck Institutes in Germany, and the various pure research centres formed by private enterprise, e.g. the Salk Institute and the Stanford Research Center, have sprung up rapidly, as experiments in a new form of organization, in the last fifty years.

Some appreciable light on the conditions required for creative work has been thrown by experimental investigation in the last few years. This has supported, as far as the main outlines are concerned, reports in the autobiographies of a series of creative men – Poincaré in mathe-matics; Kekulé in chemistry; Cannon, Carrel and Pasteur in physiology; Rutherford in physics; and many a literary and artistic genius.

These men describe a period of immersion in the problem, in which they familiarize themselves with all the relevant facts (or, in the case of the artist, the moods and half-unconscious indications). At this stage, they deliberately avoid any premature solution and try to hold in balance a rich variety of alternative directions of solution. Of this stage, Kuhn (1963) well says 'ability to support a tension that can occasionally become almost unbearable is one of the prize requisites for the very best sort of scientific research'.

After this, a period of withdrawal from the problem ideally follows. This incubation period, however, must not be filled with any strenuous mental activity of a different kind. It is an intellectual gestation period, in which even vigorous discussion of the problem itself with others would be as inappropriate as acrobatics for a woman in late pregnancy. During this period energy is needed in the unconscious, to develop, to rearrange, to wipe out the errors of conscious logic and those 'errors of the market place' and common semantics described by Francis Bacon. From this period of consolidation and unconscious invention there will finally spring into consciousness, if the creative process goes well, the inspirational solution. And as these creative persons have recorded, it may come at the most untimely places – as the behaviour of his bath water brought the cry 'Eureka!' from Archimedes. [...]

In science, and in existing research institutions, surveys have been made of the conditions that people consider desirable. The needs of genius are not unique; they are largely echoed by anyone doing research work of any importance. As Taylor (1964), Knapp (1963), Thistlethwaite (1963), Chorness and Nottelmann (1957) and others indicate, individual freedom to follow the problem wherever it may lead is highly prized. So also is that freedom from interruption that we have seen to be essential to the incubation process. But in the existing institutional situations we see also some problems of organization and incentive not stated by the freelance scientist.

SECTION 3: DEFINING THE CREATIVITY CRITERION

The reader will realize that although various modes of estimating the criterion from tests exist, such as, for example, the adjustment model and the effectiveness calculation, the psychologist can get nowhere without a firm criterion to predict. Seldom has psychology been asked to undertake so ambitious a task as that of defining the creativity criterion. If getting a reliable criterion for 'success as a bus driver' has its difficulties, it will be evident that obtaining a criterion score on 'creativity' to check the predictive power of our tests is going to present formidable conceptual and practical problems.

For safety, one should perhaps first work with creativity separately and operationally defined in each specific field. However, the fact evidenced below that substantially the same personality factors predict creativity as defined in science and art strongly suggests that because the criteria themselves are so positively correlated we shall find them to contain a strong common factor, i.e. creativity may prove a very similar thing across many fields.

When we seek to apply the criterion of adaptiveness across all fields of cultural creativity, we at once encounter the unfortunate fact that it is far easier to apply in science, in mechanical invention and in politics, than it is in literature, art or music. A moon rocket works or it does not. Whether a painting on the wall of the Guggenheim Museum deserves to be there or not may be determined by which school of art is politically in the ascendant. At best, one can take a poll of the percentage of people who claim a spiritual experience from it. One may be convinced that there really is a sense in which a work of art reaches certain adaptive standards and thereby achieves a potent emotional message, but, as psychologists, we must admit that today we do not know how to evaluate this criterion and that our attempts to be objective are premature.

Present treatment of the criterion must therefore be confined to scientific creativity, and even here the difficulties are great.

Taylor's (1957) correlation and factor analysis shows at least eight sources of criterion evaluation with practically zero intercorrelation, as follows.

(1) Originality and significance of reports as rated by experts (this also has loading in patent rate and effective suggestions within the laboratory).

(2) Creativity as seen by head people in the same organization.

(3) Ratings of personal qualities of flexibility, independence, co-operativeness, as made by immediate supervisors.

(4) Productivity rated in the laboratory by peers.

(5) Creativity counted by publications. This also loads consultantship activities and *un*cooperativeness as rated by supervisor.

(6) Awards, participation in conference papers, number of people supervised (with some negative relation to originality in the first source mentioned).

(7) Quality of finish in organizational reports.

(8) Popularity and likeableness.

The above analysis is based on 166 scientists at government basic research centres. As Taylor observes, the feature that strikes one most is the poor agreement even between such sources of evaluation as supervisors and laboratory chiefs. Other less extensive data, e.g. our own and Harmon's (1963), suggest that Taylor's orthogonal analysis has removed a slight general positive relation among these sources, but that with this proviso his conclusions are probably typical. The theory of instrument factors (Cattell, 1961) should reconcile us to the expectation that different groups and situations of raters will throw in prejudiced observations from each special angle. Similarly, the theory of ipsative scoring should make us realize that whenever there is a limiting total shared by all scores – in this case that there are only twenty-four hours in a day – the correlations of diverse performance will approach a negative value. In simple words, although a general potential excellence may exist in men, if more time spent on X involves less time spent on Y, the result will be that excellence in actual performance over a diversity of fields will not be general.

SECTION 4: CREATIVITY PREDICTION BY PSYCHOLOGICAL TESTS AIMED AT A 'CREATIVE TYPE'

It is necessary to bear in mind the distinction between *adjustment* and *effectiveness* calculations of fitness for a task. In the former, we ask what characteristics distinguish the person in the job from those in other jobs. In the latter, we obtain regression coefficients of personality, ability and motivation factors upon a criterion of effectiveness or efficiency among those actually in the job. Both these criteria have been used in research on creativity. With a few exceptions, however, both have very often been studied with *ad hoc* scales and supposed measures of creative ability of unknown factor composition and meaning, so that psychological insight and generalization have been impaired. Among the exceptions are the studies of Drevdahl ('adjustment' criterion), Jones, Chambers and Tollefson ('effectiveness' criterion).

The first study using primary personality factors was carried out by Drevdahl (1956) with graduate students. His criterion was the creativity shown by these students in essays, research and class discussion, as evaluated by professors familiar with them. He found statistically significant differences between students of high and low creativity on the 16 PF test in that the former were more schizothyme (A—), self-sufficient (Q_2), desurgent (F—) and radical (Q_1).

The more extensive study that was next made was concerned specifically with creativity in the scientific field. A careful search was made for forty-six leading research physicists, forty-six distinguished re-search biologists and fifty-two productive researchers in psychology (all selected by committees in their particular fields, and all of whom completed both A and B forms of the 16 PF Questionnaire). A full account of this investigation is given elsewhere (Cattell and Drevdahl, 1955), but chief among the questions that can be asked are:

(1) In what way does the personality profile of the creative scientists differ from that of the average man?

(2) How does it differ from persons of equal intelligence and similar education whose eminence is in teaching or administration rather than research?

(3) How is the profile of those talented in science different from that of innovators in radically different areas, as in art and literature?

The answer to the first question is shown in Fig. 11.1, from which it will be seen at once that the personality profile is very different from that of the average man (indicated by the central dark band), no fewer than five factors deviating at a $P = 0.01$ significance or beyond. Moreover, the differences in every case support, through measures on contemporary research leaders, the kind and direction of deviation we had inferred from the biographical accounts of historically important researchers. Notably, the researcher is decidedly more sizothyme, more intelligent, more dominant and more inhibited or desurgent. As we pass towards the bottom of the diagram, into dimensions we have not previously discussed, we notice other divided peaks and troughs indicating that researchers are also significantly more emotionally sensitive ($I+$), more radical (Q_1+) and somewhat more given to controlling their behaviour by an exacting self-concept. It is noteworthy that in so far as the conclusions from our different instruments can overlap, Anne Roe's results and our own are in essential agreement.

As far as comparison with the general population is concerned, physicists, biologists and psychologists are close together and form one family. However, if space permitted, we could study some interesting minor differences, e.g. the finding that the physicists are even more sizothyme than other researchers, and the psychologists (perhaps we should say with embarrassment!) more dominant and less desurgent.

In answer to our second question, it is clear that, when compared with the general population, eminent researchers have a good deal in common with those who have achieved an outstanding reputation for teaching and administration. For example, both are decidedly above the population

Personality dimension label at lower pole.	Mean stens	PLOTTED MEAN STEN SCORES 1 2 3 4 5 6 7 8 9 10	Personality dimension label at upper pole	
A – Sizothymia	3.36		Affectothymia	A+
B – Low intelligence	7.64		High intelligence	B+
C – Low ego strength	5.44		High ego strength	C+
E – Low dominance	6.62		High dominance	E+
F – Desurgency	3.15		Surgency	F+
G – Low group superego	4.10		High group superego	G+
H – Threctia	6.01		Parmia	H+
I – Harria	7.05		Premsia	I+
L – Low protension	5.36		High protension	L+
M – Praxernia	5.36		Autia	M+
N – Simplicity	5.50		Shrewdness	N+
O – Low guilt-proneness	4.38		High guilt-proneness	O+
Q_1 – Conservatism	7.00		Radicalism	Q_1+
Q_2 – Low self-sufficiency	7.52		High self-sufficiency	Q_2+
Q_3 – Low self-sentiment	6.44		High self-sentiment	Q_3+
Q_4 – Low ergic tension	4.91		High ergic tension	Q_4+

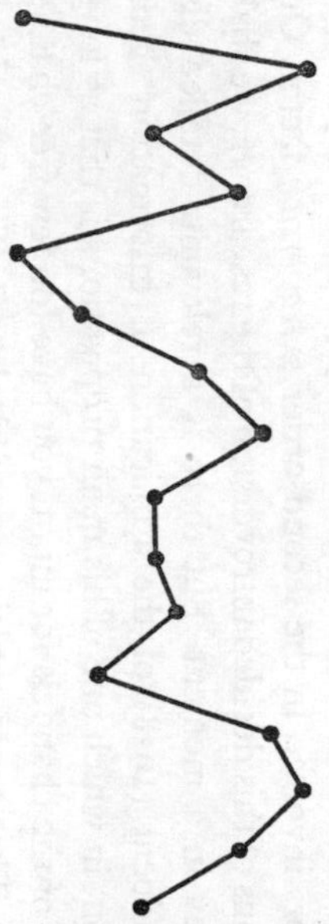

Fig. 11.1 Mean 16 PF profile of eminent researchers ($N = 144$) in physics, biology and psychology.

average in ego strength, intelligence, dominance and social obligation as shown in the self-sentiment. Nevertheless, it would be foolish to leave out of our calculations, or our selection formulas, whatever makes for high achievement *as such*, regardless of field. In separating the potential creative researcher from the equally able administrator and scholar, we must discern where to drive in the wedge. At the one per cent significance level, researchers are more sizothyme, less emotionally stable, more self-sufficient, more bohemian and more radical than are successful administrators and teachers. Compared next with the general college population from which they come (using the general undergraduate population norms), researchers are again more sizothyme and more intelligent, more self-sufficient, more withdrawn, more paranoid and anxious, and more inhibited (F−).

When we consider second-order personality factors, the most striking fact is that the researcher is uniformly lower on all primary personality factors involved in the second-order *extraversion* factor. On the implications of this decided introversion of the researcher, we shall have more to say in a moment. But there is a relevant, detailed discussion by Broadbent (1958) of the application of information theory to brain action, in which one of his main propositions is that as long as you use a lot of the channels for input, you have too few free channels for scanning. That could explain a good deal here. The typical extravert conceivably has too many channels taking in information – or at least, alert to the external trivia of everyday life – and not enough for scanning accepted material.

Let us turn to the third question, namely, 'To what extent are creative persons in one field like those in another, e.g. those in science like those in the arts?' (or, in other words, 'Is the creative personality a recognizable type despite differences in the area of operation?').

As more research on creativity is done, increasing the accuracy of determination of personality by using two or more forms of the 16 PF, and by extending measurement to include motivation factors in the MAT, it will become appropriate to concentrate on what test factor weights determine creativity in different fields. At present, we have to deal only with 'indications' of differences, but the common pattern is strongly evident. The latter is not necessarily that of an accommodating and popular personality, and its qualities of independence and forthrightness would commonly evoke the criticism 'tactless'. As Lowell Kelly's results with medical men show, this pattern of personality tends to be subjected to group antipathy and derogation. Central in it is a dominant independence, E, some high inhibition (in F, not unlike

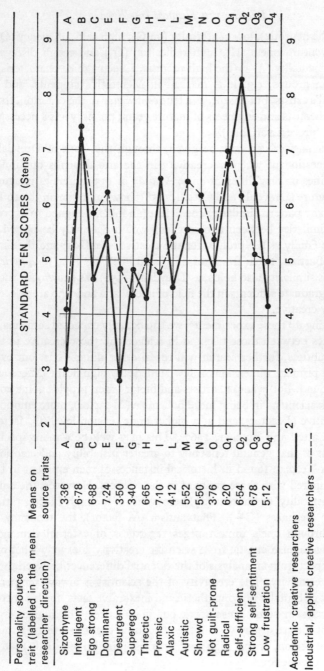

Personality source trait (labelled in the mean researcher direction)	Means on source traits								
Sizothyme	3·36	A							
Intelligent	6·78	B							
Ego strong	6·88	C							
Dominant	7·24	E							
Desurgent	3·50	F							
Superego	3·40	G							
Threctic	6·65	H							
Premsic	7·10	I							
Alaxic	4·12	L							
Autistic	5·52	M							
Shrewd	5·50	N							
Not guilt-prone	3·76	O							
Radical	6·20	Q₁							
Self-sufficient	6·54	Q₂							
Strong self-sentiment	6·78	Q₃							
Low frustration	5·12	Q₄							

Academic creative researchers ———

Industrial, applied creative researchers -----

Fig. 11.2 Profile of basic and applied (industrial) researchers.

that in the neurotic), low conformity (on G), high self-sufficiency (Q_2), high adventurousness (H), high radicalism (Q_1) and tough disregard for sentimentality (A—) (the high premsia, I, seems to be characteristic of certain groups, e.g. it is marked in Meredith's students, and in Drevdahl's artists, but absent, as a true *contributor* to the criterion, from Jones's chemists and engineers of mature years; possibly it is a necessary youthful 'process variable').

A clear answer can now be given, through the work of Drevdahl, to the question of whether creativity in the arts depends on similar personalities or very different ones. A study of 153 writers of imaginative literature (Drevdahl and Cattell, 1958) shows a profile on the 16 PF that, by any pattern similarity coefficient (an index designed to express overall similarity between two profiles), would definitely be placed in the same family as the profiles for the creative scientists; and the same is true of artists, taken from persons listed in *Who's Who in American Art*. This similarity also holds, as Drevdahl (1956) has shown, for those who are graduate students in the field of liberal arts and who are selected as highly creative.

In setting up these experiments, we had actually expected some major differences between those talented in science and those creative in the arts. Doubtless, further search will reveal other dimensions, but even on these primary dimensions a few statistically significant differences can be found. For example, artists and literary men provide some contrast with scientists in being more bohemian (M factor), more emotionally sensitive (I factor), and at a higher ergic tension level (Q_4 factor) (Cross, Cattell and Butcher, 1967). This may well be a more specific statement of that general tendency to greater instability and emotionality that Terman found in historical instances of men eminent in the arts, compared with those eminent in the sciences. However, the emotional 'instability' or 'immaturity' here is that of the high I factor rather than ego weakness (C—). That autism (M factor), the tendency to follow through one's inmost urges regardless of external demands, should distinguish artistic from scientific creativity is exactly what one would expect from an analysis of the essential differences between these types of creativity. The creativity of the scientist is always tempered by a host of brutally unsympathetic and inexorable facts, for his theory must always in some sense work out in practice. The higher ergic tension of the artist may sustain the conclusion that the artist is a more frustrated person, or that high anxiety is less inimical to artistic than to scientific production.

Although such differences of personality and motivation between artistic, scientific and other areas of creativity can be found and will doubtless continue to be found in more refined studies, the really remarkable feature of these research findings, especially for our present concentrated survey, is the high degree of similarity and consistency of the personality picture across *all* areas. It would almost seem as if the differences between science, art and literature are differences of particular skills and interests only, and that the fundamental characteristic of the creative, original person is a type of personality.

It is on this basis that we have argued above that the diversity of criterion factors found by Taylor is likely to converge on one general second-order creativity factor, loading particularly his primaries 1 and 7, for in all these diverse fields of performance there is evidently something substantially in common.

SECTION 5: CREATIVITY PREDICTION BY REGRESSION ON A CRITERION OF EFFECTIVENESS WITHIN A RESEARCH GROUP

So far we have asked what distinguishes the *type* of the creative student, in terms of abilities and personality traits, from the average one, or from the equally intelligent but uncreative adult. But let us now turn to the alternative examination by a *weighting of attributes* calculation. The weakness of the adjustment criterion is that it merely defines who stays in the job, and that it indicates not only those who are good at that job but also inevitably to some extent those who have failed alternative jobs. For example, it used to be not uncommon to find among psychology students some who had wanted to follow a science but had failed the mathematics necessary for chemistry or physics. And we have all heard of academic men who became administrators because they failed to find a successful research trail.

It is conceivable, of course, that a person in research is a failed teacher, but there are reasons for believing that the selection that has produced the personality profile typical of research workers is not, in the main, a backfiring selection. It is a selection tending to concentrate in the field the people who are better at it. However, the defects in the 'job adjustment' profile assumptions make it vital also to have data showing the relation of personality factors and actual research effectiveness. We need, in fact, data in terms of regression of personality measures upon a criterion of research productivity. Usually, we seek at first a linear regression equation, but it can progress to non-linear prediction. What data we have so far are as precious as they are fragmentary. But at least these exploratory studies, e.g. by Jones and Cattell (1965), Tollefson (1961) and Chambers (1964) on predictors and by Taylor (1955, 1957) and his colleagues on the criteria, are highly encouraging.

Among the first studies of research efficiency or productivity measured on the job, one should note that of Van Zelst and Kerr (1954), who found, among other characteristics of productive researchers, a disbelief in egalitarian 'committee-like' practices in research groups and a need for withdrawal and cogitation. This finding again appears reasonably in line with the personality characteristics we have already shown to be typical.

A first study to deal with well-known, replicable personality factors is that of Tollefson (1961), measuring fifty-three Ph.D. chemists in the research department of a nationally known oil company. Here the indicated correlations between primary factors on the 16 PF and rated magnitude of contribution to research were as in the following specification equation:

$$\text{Research performance} = 0.25B + 0.46C + 0.32E - 0.46I + 0.33N \\ + 45Q_1 + 0.29Q_2 - 0.35$$

Here B is General Intelligence, C is Ego Strength, E is dominance, I is Emotional Sensitivity, N is Shrewdness, Q_1 is Radicalism, Q_2 is Self-Sufficiency. The criterion in this study was based partly on the number of papers produced and partly on their rated importance. This is reasonably in line with what would be expected from the differences between researchers and other academics listed in the preceding section, except for Source Trait I, Premsia-versus-Harria, which needs comment. Evidence is accumulating that the I source-trait dimension is related to early home background. It appears that 95 per cent of the variance arises from environmental determination and only 5 per cent from hereditary determination. So far as preliminary evidence can show, the increase of Premsia, i.e. of protected emotional sensitivity, has to do with over-protection and indulgence in childhood. Because this factor was found by Cattell and his associates to be negatively related to various kinds of achievement, and by Cattell and Stice (1960) to be related to 'hindering' and 'self-centredness' in small group behaviour, it is hard to interpret the rather high I found in academic researchers (not, be it noted, with industrial researchers) as advantageous. More likely, we are dealing here with an incidental and non-useful characteristic of academic selection!

However, before any dependable conclusions can be drawn about the causes of differences of pattern between job adjustment profile and the criterion performance profile, it is necessary to study further groups;

one can readily conceive that the specification equation quoted will apply to all kinds of research performance. The work of F. E. Jones has provided us with fairly substantial checks on the personality and ability regressions for industrial research creativity, and the planned continuation of his work to larger, cross-checking samples and the inclusion of motivation measures such as the MAT may yield still more complete predictive powers.

Working with an exploratory sample of forty-five research chemists of mature years, in industry, he found that Ego Strength (C), Dominance (E), Parmia (H), Radicalism (Q_1), stronger Self-Sentiment (Q_3) and Low Ergic Tension (Q_4-) were significantly related to the rating criterion of creativity and, in fact, gave a multiple correlation of 0·8, even with intelligence omitted (actually, 63 per cent of the variance of the criterion was accounted for by these source traits in chemists, and 52 per cent in engineers). Later (Jones and Cattell, in preparation), with a mixed group of eighty-eight researchers in the U.S. Rubber Co., and using a creativity criterion composed of twelve ratings (originality, self-reliance, etc.) by twenty-five observers (pooled) he obtained the relations shown in Table 11.1.

TABLE 11.1. *Specification of creativity in industrial research chemists by personality and ability measures*

Personality factors	Correlation with creativity
Ego strength (C factor)	+·25
Dominance (E factor)	+·36
Parmia (H factor)	+·24
Guilt-proneness (O factor)	−·31
Radicalism (Q_1 factor)	+·35
Ability factors	(not available for whole group but approximate)
Fluid general intelligence (Culture Fair test)	+·30
Logical reasoning	+·31
Mathematical reasoning	+·29
Ideational fluency	+·33

The reliabilities on both sides of the correlations in Table 11.1 are sound, that of the criterion being +0·88 and that of the personality factors being about the same, due to the experimental thoroughness of using all three equivalent forms (A, B and C) of the 16 PF at once. It is worthy of note that the above measures are the survivors – the
G

highest correlating tests – but of no fewer than fifty-three tests tried by Jones, on the suggestion of one experiment or another that they would be predictors of creativity. Most – notably the personality scales – correspond to factors having only the usual slight correlations of oblique factors. But behind the personality factors there stand the general ability factors, though the correlations show that their predictive power arises appreciably from specific reasoning and ideational fluency.

It is not surprising that with this degree of independence of predictors, multiple correlations have been obtained by Jones with this battery as high as 0·95 for chemists and 0·83 for engineers, though in the group here cited and with correction for such bias as might enter a second sample, the R is 0·67. Trying the weighting formula on ten new research chemists, Jones found that the 'rank order of the [estimated] creativity scores divided the cases at the median exactly in accordance with the [performance] rating division'.

Further work along the same lines has been done by Chambers (1964), who took 400 chemists and 340 psychologists and compared personality and biographical data for the top and bottom 50 per cent of each. This division may have confounded eminence with creativity, which should be taken into account when considering Table 11.2. The personality factors distinguishing the more from the less creative were: A—, E, F, I, Q_1 and Q_2, the strongest emphases being on E and Q_2.

SECTION 6: THE BROADER CONTEXT OF THE PREDICTIVE PROBLEM

If we may, for a first approximation, make a certain discount of differences, such as that in the I factor, found by the 'adjustment' approach, we can use the Drevdahl and the Jones evidence (Fig. 11.2) as the basis for a biserial correlation. Thus we can derive from Table 11.2 rough estimates of weights for various personality factors, combining the above with the Tollefson, Jones and Chambers regressions.

The consensus of these studies on the importance of B (General Intelligence), C (Ego Strength), E (Dominance), Q_1 (Radicalism) and Q_2 (Self-Sufficiency) is considerable. A number of *ad hoc* scales, such as Ghiselli's initiative scale, have also shown significant relations in single studies, but because the 16 PF is founded on the total personality sphere it is highly probable that these are substantially correlated with 16 PF scales and therefore included in its predictions. And because

TABLE 11.2. *Overview of evidence on approximate relative weights of personality factors in predicting creativity*

Research	A	B	C	E	F	G	H	I	L	M	N	O	Q_1	Q_2	Q_3	Q_4
4 groups by Drevdahl and Cattell	−4	+5	+2	+2	−2		+1	+1		+1			+3	+4	+1	−1
1 group by Jones	−3	+5	+1	+2	−1									+1		
1 group by Tollefson		+3	+5	+3				−5			+3		+5	+3		
1 group by Jones			+3	+4			+3					−3	+4			
1 group by Chambers			+4	+4										+4		
Suggested present best compromise of weights:	−·3	+·5	+·3	+·3	−·2		+·1				+·2	+·1		−·1	+·4	+·3

they do not correspond to frequently investigated personality structures, it is not easy to see what such specific scales are doing.

If the main emerging personality associations in the measurement approach are compared with qualitative personality observations, e.g. those of Roe, or with those of the systematic studies of Knapp, the agreement is obvious. Knapp (1963), for example, finds his creative researchers stating that they were solitary, felt more distant from parents and others, and recorded fewer group activities. They were more cautious and realistic (desurgent), aimed at more distant goals, and were more assertive (dominant) and authoritative, whereas the uncreative controls were more acquiescent and submissive. They are also more consistent in the rewards they sought (Q_3, Self-Sentiment) and had more well-differentiated value hierarchies.

Before asking about the dynamics of our formula, however, we should recognize that another source of prediction resides in the situational, biographical data, as found in the work of Knapp, Chambers and Taylor. Some differences exist among these studies and, for example, those of Parnes and Meadow (1963), regarding the predictive value of grades. The latter, for example, found a triserial r of $+0.06$ between undergraduate grades and research merit; but Chambers found that in high school the creative scientists far more frequently had a straight A average (the selection differences may well account for the predictive differences). Chambers found creative scientists graduating from high school at a younger age, given to wider reading, and less interested in religion and community affairs. Knapp's extensive work shows very clearly that *scientific* creativity is apt to arise more often relative to creativity in art and music, in lower middle-class than in upper middle-class homes. It may be that art and music are easier, more immediately emotionally appealing expressions of intelligence for those in more protected or indulgent environments, such as tend to produce high I-factor scores. Knapp also shows that scientific creativity is higher in Protestant and Jewish than in Catholic backgrounds, and that in the Protestant family background it frequently occurs in the transition from a disciplined, restrictive religious ethos towards agnosticism. [...]

SECTION 7: 'TRAINING FOR CREATIVITY'

A great array of evidence, not assignable to sources in a brief survey, suggests that training for creativity is far more a personality than a cognitive matter, and that we are not going to offset by some 'intensive training courses in creativity' what may be fundamentally wrong in our values and way of life. 'Training for creativity' is about as hopeful as training to be intelligent, when intelligence is defined as 'handling well a situation that you have had no previous training to meet'. However, when we have selected by wise psychological testing the most creative individuals, they could probably be helped by educational direction towards:

(1) Learning how to manage their necessary nonconformity without being delinquent. For example, for a child who grasps a principle at once it would be reasonable to do only ten out of forty examples set for homework and to show that he has independently read further afield by doing examples in more advanced or specialized principles.

(2) Avoiding being dragged into race-track competitiveness – it has been justly said that 'competition, like alcohol, though it begins by stimulating, ends by bringing all to the same dull level', i.e. it brings all into the same track or race channel, instead of favouring exploration. This requires a high degree of inner security, such as we recognize in the Q_2 (Self-Sufficiency) factor.

(3) Learning to spend time alone, reading and thinking, despite the temptation to constant social life. Nowadays, this would include breaking the habit of sitting for hours passively before the television 'idiot-box'.

(4) Developing certain almost purely cognitive techniques, notably: (a) a habit of intensive study and discussion of the elements in a problem, followed by arranging an undisturbed incubation period in which one's energies but not one's conscious thought are devoted to the problem; (b) declining to take too seriously the conventional verbal terms in which the problem is commonly debated. Compared with visual imagery and mathematical symbolism, words involve a mode of reasoning that ties one to public views. They are relatively more tied to the symbolism of popular thought, and make it difficult to move from a common coin of alleged 'logic' to an uncommon mould; (c) keeping close to reality. Although much creative thought must be of the nature of dreaming, rather than (initially) explicit logic, and although it avoids social checking, it should not become subjective in the sense of avoiding reality. Many theorists merely substitute for the existing public theory a highly individual and subjective statement that is equally insensitive to reality and equally unoriginal in being precast in conventional verbal terms, e.g. it may be merely the exact opposite – a mirror image – of the current public theory. Creativity requires an objectivity, in the sense that the mind is withdrawn from conventional, social formulations

but is by no means withdrawn as is the psychotic. On the contrary, it must be devoted to realism.

When all is done that education (in the schools) can do, it will still probably remain true that more can be contributed to increasing creativity in our society by selection than by education. For one thing, certain of the ability and personality factors now known to be important for creativity appear from nature–nurture research (Burks, 1928; Burt and Howard, 1956; Cattell, Blewett and Beloff, 1955; Eysenck and Prell, 1951; Freeman, Holzinger and Mitchell, 1928; Gottesman, 1963; Vandenberg, 1956) to have substantial hereditary components. This is true of Intelligence (B factor: 80 per cent), Dominance (E factor: possibly 60 per cent), Parmia (H factor: probably 70 per cent), Autism (M) and Self-Sufficiency (Q_2 factor: probably 50 per cent), though not, of course, of Desurgency (F), Ego Strength (C), Radicalism (Q_1), etc.

Although, as far as the social need for scientific creativity is concerned, it is true that vastly increased numbers are now supported in research, it is probable that a proper return on this support will be gained only if research is organized so that much of it is directed by the most outstanding research workers. The need to recognize and choose the best is here greater than in almost any other field. With the weaknesses in the criterion that we have discussed in already published research, it would not be appropriate to offer a specification equation taken to two decimal places. Besides, the equation must be finally modified for the age, range of ability, etc., in the group concerned. But from the above contributions of Drevdahl, Jones, Tollefson and others, we can propose centrally, in the school range:

$$\text{Creativity} = -0.3A + 0.6B + 0.3C + 0.3E - 0.2F + 0.1G$$
$$+ 0.1H - 0.1I + 0.2M - 0.1O + 0.4Q_1 + 0.3Q_2 - 3.85$$

The weights are so adjusted that with stens (standard scores) for A, B, etc., the creativity score will also come out in stens (the constant, -3.85, being added to bring the mean creativity score at the sten mean of 5.5).

Undoubtedly, as research proceeds, the ability contribution will need to be increased, as the work of Jones and Sprecher shows, by adding special ability measures (Thurstone's Reasoning Factor, the 'ideational fluency' factor of Guilford and Cattell, and several of Guilford's other factors). Also, the proceeding work will add motivation factors. As to personality factors, although the above shows significant weights on only twelve of the sixteen in the 16 PF (or the fourteen in the High School Personality Questionnaire), it is probably that more exact work will show slight weights on the others. In any case, if the maximum prediction is required, it is best – and more convenient in testing and scoring – to use the whole 16 PF or HSPQ.

SUMMARY

(1) Before selecting for creativity, we ought, as part of the criterion definition, to ask about the conditions under which the creativity is to be exercised. The assumption that the combined teacher-researcher – long the ideal of the academic world – is the most desirable product of education, for this purpose, is questioned. Teaching and research may require, in part, different skills and ways of life. Society is likely to see an increase of institutes devoted purely to research. Selection for creative work must take into account these conditions and also the conditions of 'freelance' creativity in art and literature.

(2) In predicting creativity, the assessment of creative performance itself offers unusual difficulties. Originality cannot be equated with oddity. Psychopathology also results in oddity, and this is one reason for the folklore assertion of a kinship between genius and insanity. Actually, men of genius have a lower-than-average incidence of mental disorder, and the creative product has involved a process of objective adjustment. It is 'odd' only because it has not been reached before.

(3) Literary and artistic genius is known to have lesser emotional stability and freedom from pathology than has scientific genius. In other respects, however, the personality profiles found for leaders in art and science have a marked similarity, which suggests that selection for creativity can proceed along much the same lines in both.

(4) The criterion is more easily examined in the scientific field, whereupon it is discovered that it contains several distinct instrument (source of evaluation) factors, such as the number of good research articles produced, evaluation by supervisors, popularity and esteem among laboratory associates, role in national science association politics, originality as rated by senior research leaders and shown in patent inventions. Two of these seem essentially to exemplify creativity and may be positively correlated.

(5) The relation of personality and ability measures to the creativity criterion shows that the psychologist possesses substantial predictive resources. Moreover, the meaning of the factors found agrees well with that emerging from the qualitative, biographical approach of the

preceding chapter. Creative individuals are more 'introverted' (actually, sizothyme, desurgent, self-sufficient), more dominant, radical and autistic than persons of the same intelligence and education who have made a name in teaching or administration.

(6) The relationships have been examined by both the 'adjustment' and the 'effectiveness' types of criteria. The former can proceed in practice with the pattern similarity coefficient, r_p, and the latter by the factor specification equation. A general specification equation is set out for use in schools, universities and industry, but ultimately it will need to be tailored to particular groups.

(7) Although a high level of creativity must depend on a high level of intelligence, because the final capacity to educe relations depends on fluid ability, and although special reasoning and ideational fluency measures contribute significantly to prediction, the selection in any professional group of the more creative persons depends decidedly more upon personality characteristics. Creativity in a one-hour examination-like situation may depend more on abilities, but creativity over years, in the life situation, is clearly more determined by personality as a way of life, and by motivation factors yet to be measured.

(8) The cultivation of creativity may turn out to be the development of personality – nothing less. However, cognitive habits play some role, and minor increments may result from suitable 'training'. Four major ways are suggested for the cultivation of creativity. They may be so disruptive of ordinary classroom procedures as to be best reserved for selected individuals only, and at the upper mental-age levels.

(9) Creativity in any individual varies with age and circumstance. By age, productivity is higher at an early period in relatively abstract studies such as mathematics and modern physics, and at a later age in biology, history, politics, etc., where large realms of fact and experience have to be absorbed (Lehman, 1953). However, any peak at any early age is partly an artefact (Dennis, 1958) and partly a failure to free outstandingly creative persons in later life from excessive organizational responsibilities. Creativity differences are far more the result of individual than of age differences. Even with the rapid increase of research support, it is as important as ever (some personality factors in creativity being relatively innate) to select for creativity, regardless of age, and to organize increased research resources around the selected individuals.

12

D. E. Broadbent (1966)

The well ordered mind

American Educational Research Journal, 3, pp. 281–95

At the beginning of George Eliot's great novel *Middlemarch*, the heroine's uncle inquires how one of his friends arranges his documents, and is told 'in pigeonholes'. 'Ah,' says the uncle, 'pigeonholes will not do. I have tried pigeonholes, but everything gets mixed in pigeonholes: I never know whether a paper is in A or Z.' 'I wish you would let me sort your papers for you, Uncle,' said Dorothea, 'I would letter them all and then make a list of subjects under each letter.' Many of us who have to deal with a fair number of written documents are only too thankful if we have somebody like Dorothea to bring some system and method into the task, not merely of keeping and preserving the documents, but of finding the one we want on the occasion when we want it. It is a matter of harsh everyday experience that one need not worry very much about losing things in the sense of destroying them accidentally or sending them off to some other person; what you really have to worry about is being able to find them without going to every document on your desk and every file in the cabinet.

This difficulty is inherent in the whole idea of storing information for later use. But we ourselves are equally systems which store information for later use, just as the files in our offices or the libraries of our academic institutions are. It seems likely, therefore, that our own nervous systems must encounter problems closely similar to those which appear in files or libraries. Indeed, I was interested to note that, in a hearing before a subcommittee of the United States Senate, a distinguished senator from North Carolina remarked that he did not confess to his constituents who see his desk that his mind is in the same disordered condition as his desk. The record showed laughter at this point, but those of us who, like myself, do not altogether adhere to the principle of the clean desk, may experience some unease at the analogy, and may regard it as far too threatening and serious a matter for laughter. Consequently, it occurred to me that there might be some others with consciences as guilty as my own, who might conceivably welcome the opportunity to think about the organization and operation of memory. One slight snag in this intention is that I rapidly realized that I could provide little information as to the best way of achieving the well-ordered mind; but then it is such a blessing to the man who fails to recall names or references, or to remember how to differentiate the product of two quantities, if the sufferer can only realize that other people are in just the same mess as he is himself. Furthermore, there are nowadays a number of lines of attack on the problems of retrieval which might conceivably shed some light on human memory, so that even if there are no answers, there may at least be a profitable language in which to ask the questions. In what follows, therefore, I am going to raise queries about memory, and toss them about a bit, but hardly, I fear, answer them.

Perhaps the most obvious naïve view of memory with which many of us started our lives, before we became interested in education or psychology, is that it is simply a record within the brain of the series of events which have occurred to a man during his life, laid down in the order in which they happen. When at some future date I wish to know what happened at some time in the past, I consult the appropriate portion of this record. Of course, even the most naïve view of memory will rapidly recognize that the record is highly selective, so that some things are never even noticed at the time they happen, and consequently do not get stored away in memory. It is also true that some things which are noticed and which produce a reaction, may not be recorded in memory; the record of a particular episode may consist only of a few key items together with a knowledge of the probable structure of all such episodes, so that one remembers to a large extent what is probable. Sound as these principles are, they do not by themselves alter the naïve picture of the cinematograph film or the magnetic tape storing a sequence of experiences: they merely tell one more about the form of the storage.

If, however, we consider a relatively orthodox academic library, we can see that the chronological storage of the incoming information is by no means the whole story. Usually the books do tend to be added to shelves in the order in which they are published. This may be particularly true of one's own domestic library: it saves a lot of work rearranging all one's books just because a new one has come into the house. However, the usual technique in any substantial library is rather to keep a number of separate storage places, each of which accumulates books in the order of publishing, but each of which is devoted to a certain class of books. A widely used criterion of division is the subject matter of the book, so that one may find that part of the library is devoted to the sciences, and another to the arts; that within the sciences there is a distinction between physical and biological, and so on. The well-known Dewey Decimal System of Classification is a method of this kind. It depends upon a series of successive subdivisions, and once one has entered one particular subdivision, one cannot get across to other books outside it. For example, in the Cambridge University Library, within the shelves devoted to psychology, large psychological books accumulate for convenience on different shelves from small psychological books. The same distinction is made within other subjects. It is not, however, possible to find any single shelf on which all large books, regardless of subject matter, are being placed. That perhaps is of little moment, but it is more serious that the inquirer for a book does not usually arrive at the library armed with the date at which the book entered the library and with its subject matter, but rather knows other information about it which has not been used in placing it on a particular shelf. For example, he knows the name of the author and the title of the book. There is therefore in the library another record, which does not contain the books themselves, but rather consists merely of authors and titles, arranged in an order which is quite different from that of the books. If you look up the author and find the right book in this index, you get the address which refers you to the right place on the right shelf where you can find the book itself. If I may labour just one last obvious point about libraries, the existence of this index shows that each book, when it arrived, has been examined by a librarian. Not only has he put it in a geographically quite separate storage which depends on the subject of the book and therefore its content, but also he has extracted some of the information about the book and put it in the index.

All these points are very familiar and obvious, although I'm afraid we all take them rather for granted if we are not professional librarians. I emphasize them, however, because each of us is in many ways meeting a problem like that of a library: he receives a long stream of incoming information from his senses, from birth to death. He encounters problems at one time which can be solved by reference to earlier information, and he therefore has to extract this earlier information. In the case of libraries, however, it does not appear to be very useful simply to arrange the incoming information in order of arrival, and it is not sufficient even to divide it up into a number of separate stores each of which then is separately arranged in order of arrival. With such a system, if one receives a query for some information without knowing the exact date of time at which it was received, one must scan the whole of the relevant store. You might feel that this process could be made tolerable by a sufficiently fine subdivision of subject matter, so that there were only a few items in each of the ultimate stores. In that case, however, there is a very high probability that the item was put on its arrival in a store other than the one one now thinks appropriate. Consequently it does seem essential, for efficient retrieval, to maintain a quite separate storage system organized in a different way, which allows one to select the right item from memory from among all the other irrelevant items. This is indeed a truism of contemporary retrieval system theory; yet in the analysis of human memory relatively little attention is paid to the intermediate file or index which might be supposed necessary if selection of the right item from memory is to be easily possible. If our memories are like the gradually increasing rows of books on the shelves of a library, then what corresponds to the index?

At this stage, let me heave a sigh of relief, and turn from these rather general considerations towards experiments. One of the most influential papers recently advocating the analogy between human recall and the search of some non-human store of information is one by Yntema and Trask (1963). They were concerned with an experiment in which the person being studied wore earphones, with each ear receiving quite separate information. He was given a whole list of items, say half a dozen, with half the items arriving at one ear and the other half simultaneously at the other ear. He was then asked to reproduce all the items. I should perhaps explain that this general type of experiment had been launched about twelve years ago by myself: in the version I used originally, all the items the man had to remember were digits (Broadbent, 1954). He might receive, say, 723 on one ear and 645 simultaneously on the other ear and he had to remember them all. He tends to find this very difficult, unless he hits on the idea of reproducing everything from one ear first, and then going over to the other ear and giving you what reached that ear. If you make him try to produce the digits in some other order, he does badly.

Now I had interpreted this result as being due to something which had nothing whatever to do with the problem of retrieval which we are discussing today. I had rather argued that the phenomenon was due to the similar but distinct problem of dealing with all the information that is striking one's senses at any one moment. There is so much information that the nervous system is almost obliged to hit on various techniques for economizing its efforts, and one of these I suggested was to analyse only those patterns of stimulation striking some of the senses at one time. Thus two spoken digits, one on each ear, were too much to be dealt with simultaneously, and the brain had to select only the information coming in through one ear if it was not to be overloaded in its task. This selection, I felt, would take time to change and it was therefore easier simply to select all the information from one ear, and then afterwards to collect the other information from some kind of buffer or temporary storage attached to the other ear.

Now, there are a large number of other ways in which one can do this experiment. The particular modification with which Yntema and Trask were concerned was one in which you do not use six items belonging to the same general class, such as digits, but rather have some items belonging to one class and other items to another class. For example, you can have three digits and three letters of the alphabet, or three digits and three colour names. If you mix up the two classes of items on the two ears, so that each ear receives two items of one type and one item of the other type, then it is no harder to reproduce the three letters first and then the three digits, or the three digits first and then the three letters, than it is to produce the signal on one ear first and then the signal on the other ear. This fact is one of the best and most widely repeated in the literature: while Yntema and Trask were doing their experiments, others were being conducted by Gray and Wedderburn (1960) at Oxford, by Broadbent and Gregory (1964) at Cambridge, by Bryden (1964) in Montreal and most recently of all by a group of workers in Indiana (Emmerich *et al.*, 1965). Everybody agrees on the answer, and there is no question that a mixture of classes of item changes the character of this experiment considerably.

Yntema and Trask argued that this difference suggested a different view of the original effect. Perhaps its explanation lay in the recall process and not in the original intake of information. They suggested that each item, as it was received, was given a 'tag' which could identify it if selective recall was desired. If all the items were essentially of the same type, the only different tags that could be given to different items would be those corresponding to the sense organ by which they arrived. Consequently, when recall was carried out, the organization of recall was likely to separate the items into those arriving at one ear and those arriving at the other. One might suppose that the recall operation takes the form of retrieving all items with a certain tag, and then going on to retrieve items with another tag. If, however, the items fall into two classes, if there are some letters and some digits, or some digits and some colour names, then there may be tags attached to the items on this basis also, as well as on that of the sense organ originally stimulated. Under these circumstances, the recall may be the colour names first and then the digits. Such at least is the type of theory which Yntema and Trask have put forward.

This kind of theory is undoubtedly much nearer the problems of a library or filing system than are most traditional theories of memory. It will explain other experimental results as well, such for instance as the phenomena of clustering which has been noticed by Bousfield in free recall of words (Bousfield and Cohen, 1953). That is, if you give somebody a list of words and ask him to produce them in any order he pleases, he tends in fact to remember certain words together, because they are associated in his mind. This may happen regardless of the fact that you may not have presented them together, and that they are not required to be recalled in any particular order. This phenomenon would fit in very well with the idea that memory is divided into a number of separate storage areas, and that we can recall the items from any one of these areas fairly easily without disturbing other areas.

As we shall see in a moment, I do not think there is any doubt that selection does take place in retrieval, and that consequently its properties are of very considerable interest. Nevertheless, before I go on to that point, I ought perhaps to digress to say that I do not believe the original phenomenon which Yntema and Trask were considering to be one which disproves the existence of selection during perception as well as during retrieval. This is quite important, because the problem of the brain in perception is really very similar to that in retrieval: in both cases it is faced with far more information than it needs, and has to pick out some of it. The two selective processes may be closely similar, and although we are primarily interested in retrieval from memory on this occasion, I would not like to leave you with the impression that there is no selection at the time when information actually strikes the sense organs and goes further on into the brain.

The reasons for continuing to believe in the importance of selection during perception depends on facts which were not available to Yntema and Trask at the time when they put their theory forward. The key point is that the efficiency of recall in one order rather than another may depend upon experimental conditions at the time the material was presented, and these conditions must have had their effect during presentation rather than during recall. For example, suppose that some of the material presented is not going to be required in recall. Perhaps a man's voice and a woman's voice may be heard, and the experimenter asks only for the information spoken by the man. It makes a big difference to the efficiency of recall whether the person memorizing knows this at the time of presentation, or only just before recall is required.

(Broadbent, 1952; Broadbent and Gregory, unpublished.) Therefore there must be a difference in the way the information is received and not just in the way it is recalled. Again, the speed at which material is presented affects these processes. To take one example, suppose I say to you 7 J 3 Q 9 R 5 A; this is harder to remember than J Q R A 7395 provided that the speed of presentation is high. (Broadbent and Gregory, 1964.) It is hard to receive incoming items of different kinds in alternation at high speeds, but not at low. In terms of the library analogy, the librarian has to look at each book as it comes in, and if they arrive fast it is easier for him to put a whole group into one store before turning to a group of books for another store. There is selection in perception as well as in memory.

Let me now get back on to the main track of my argument, and recapitulate a bit about where we have got to. I started by drawing attention to the discrepancy between the organization of an actual library and the naïve view of memory as a continuous cinematograph film or tape recording of the series of events through which a man has lived. More sophisticated accounts of memory would alter our view about the detailed nature of the record, suggesting that it is composed of associations of input and output, and that it may economically consist of general rules together with particular crucial information-bearing items, but in many of us these sophistications leave the original analogy of the cine film untouched. In a library, however, the storage of materials may be physically in many different places, each of which is accumulating over time rather than in a single series. Furthermore, a second store is usually kept, arranged on a different basis from the ultimate store, and giving the place where one should look, the address, for each item under some reference tag such as the author's name. Yntema and Trask have suggested a similar organization of human memory, because if you present people with material of two different kinds all mixed up, they can recall it separated out into the two kinds. At that point I digressed to argue that in fact the particular experiment which they were considering can now be interpreted rather as showing that the nervous system actually selects one type of material during presentation rather than during recall. It is, in terms of our library, as if the librarian on receiving a batch of books separates them by subject matter and then goes off to place on the shelves the books belonging to one topic before he comes back to deal with the remaining books. The grouping of items is produced to some extent during presentation rather than during retrieval.

Let me now take up the main theme again, and say that nevertheless Yntema and Trask's suggestion does seem to me to be correct for certain

other situations. It is an addition to the selection of material in perception, but it is nevertheless a real effect. If we remain faithful to our
previous arguments, we can show this by finding cases in which conditions at the time of presentation do not affect the efficiency of retrieval. One particularly interesting example of this is the case in which
one presents six items, three to one ear and three to the other ear, but
staggers the presentation so that each item on the left ear arrives at a
time when there is in fact silence on the right ear, between two items.
It was demonstrated some years ago by Moray (1960) that under these
conditions people can very readily reproduce the six items in the actual
order in which they arrived, rather than giving everything from one
ear first. The explanation is presumably that in this case the listener
does not adopt the rather artificial strategy of neglecting one ear and
concentrating on the other, but rather behaves in a more normal fashion
and listens to both ears simultaneously. In this situation he will not
overload his perceptual mechanisms if he accepts the input from both
ears at the same time. The interest of this situation from our point of
view, however, is that selective recall can take place even though the
listener was not aware at the time the material was delivered of the
order in which it would be required. That is, we can either tell the
listener to reproduce one ear first, or to reproduce in the actual order of
arrival, and it makes no difference whether we tell him which we want
before he hears the items or only at the time when we want him to recall them (Broadbent and Gregory, 1961). This kind of selection must be
operating in recall, and it certainly suggests that the items have been
stored with a tag indicating the ear by which they were delivered. The
process of retrieval can select the items that reached a certain ear, or
the items that arrived first in point of time, with equal ease.

Here then we have a clear case of storage of information under particular tags or headings, by which it can later be retrieved. It is as if
there were two shelves in our library, one marked 'Right ear' and one
marked 'Left ear', so that each item can be stored in a separate place,
and the contents of one store or shelf retrieved at one time. The more
alert of you may have noticed a fault in the argument at this point, to
which I shall return, but broadly speaking the picture of memory as
organized in separate files under separate labels may be accepted for the
moment.

At this point, perhaps I should digress to point to an analogy with the
languages that are now used to programme computers. One can draw
an analogy not only between the human nervous system and the library,
but also between a computer and a library. Incoming information to a

computer is placed in different regions of storage, just as different books are placed on different shelves, and subsequent operations may be carried out by extracting information from one area of storage, performing some operation upon it, and perhaps putting the result into some other area. In early machines the different areas of storage, the different shelves in the library, were known only by an arbitrary machine code, just as the shelves may be known as No. 3 North Wing or something of that sort. Nowadays, however, it is more usual to provide a system of communication with the computer whereby the programmer can attach labels of his own to certain areas of storage, and can then make statements using the labels in various combinations. He may for example make a statement such as 'Area = Length × Breadth'. This will be interpreted by the machine as an instruction to extract the information stored in that part of store which is labelled as 'Length', to do the same for the part of the store labelled 'Breadth', multiply them together, and put the result in the part of store which is labelled 'Area'. In some cases, what is stored under a given label may include a reference to another label, and the contents of this second area of storage may include a reference to a third area, and so on. Very large amounts of information can be stored in this way, and the system of data may expand indefinitely, which possesses considerable advantages for many purposes. The information contained under a particular label may take the form of instructions to perform some operation, as well as consisting of data such as numbers, so that by using a label such as 'S Q R T' the programmer may call up a sequence of operations involved in finding a square root.

It seems to me a plausible analogy that human languages behave to some extent in similar ways, so that the making up of a simple affirmative statement to a man causes him to store in a labelled region of his memory information that has previously been available only under some other label. Thus, when I say to you 'Mary is blonde' I am instructing you to transfer to the store labelled 'Mary' the information which at present you keep under the label 'blonde'. Parenthetically, this may include not simply neutral data, but also behavioural tendencies to react in certain ways to Mary. On this view, the importance of names and/or words in general is not so much the traditional point that they are stimuli which will replace the original real object, or 'signs' of some real object in that sense, but rather that they indicate the location in memory of the information relevant to a certain topic or concept. Of course, not all labels for regions of memory need be of linguistic type; as I have just said, in computers the address of a particular area of storage may be either in a machine code, or in a name assigned by a public language usable by many machines. In a library, the address of a particular part of storage may be 'No. 3 North Wing' (machine code) or 'The Linguistics Section' (public or user code). Equally in human beings one would suppose that there are some variables which are in a code private to a particular individual, and consist perhaps of particular sensory qualities difficult to put into any public language and communicate to one's fellow men. There are many people for whom certain numbers are associated with certain colours or shapes, and, for example, a smell may call up in one man memories of extreme significance while his neighbour is unaffected.

The point is an important one, because retrieval is not always perfect, either in human beings or in the man-made systems which we have been considering. It is extremely plausible that, in picking out a particular address in storage, one will occasionally go to the wrong address. But the errors which are made will presumably not be random, but rather will be linked to the way in which the different possible addresses are organized together. If one looks up a telephone number hastily in the book, it is the number above or below the one one wants which one is likely to get by mistake, rather than a number on the opposite page. If now labels for different parts of storage are to be used as means for picking out some memories rather than others, they too must be organized like the alphabetical order of names in a telephone book, so that a particular label will rapidly lead one to the correct memory. It is therefore not terribly surprising that, when a Conservative politician in Britain was being interviewed recently on television by a Socialist journalist, called Paul Johnson, the politician persisted in referring to his interrogator as Howard Johnson. Nor is it surprising that most of us get the right message when we are told by Lewis Carroll that 'The slithy toves did gyre and gimble in the wabe'. When labels are closely similar, information under one will often be called up by the use of the other. Indeed, this kind of dependence of retrieval upon the structure which links together different labels for different types of storage can be illustrated from much of the classic psychological literature on human learning.

The view that I have been putting forward is not of course completely contradictory to, but rather a development of, the classic analysis of learning in terms of stimuli and responses. Although for reasons of time I have been talking mostly about experiments in a different tradition, this is not to deny the importance of the other stream of experimentation. Classic paired-associate experiments in human learning show

that the extent to which two items of previously learned materials interact varies with the similarity of the stimuli which elicit the items. Thus,
for example, it is difficult for an English-speaking person to remember
that the letter 'C' on a bathroom tap in France does not mean 'Cold';
and we probably have more difficulty with this than would a German
to whom 'C' on a tap means nothing previously. It is easy to remember
that 'trottoir' is a word for 'sidewalk', but hard to remember that 'couloir'
is not a word for 'refrigerator'. Similar effects appear of course even
within one's own language: there are people who think that the adjec-
tive 'vicarious' means 'belonging to a minister of the Church of England'.
These positive and negative transfer effects can be readily interpreted in
terms of retrieval from memory of items stored in regions adjacent to
the one desired.

By looking therefore at sources of difficulty in memory, we may hope
to find some signs of the way in which the storage is in fact classified
and organized. One especially striking example of this has been giving
rise to a good deal of work on both sides of the Atlantic during the past
two or three years. One can present visually to a person certain information, and then compare the errors that he makes in remembering
it with the errors that are made by other experimental subjects listening
to the same information acoustically against a background of noise. The
pattern of errors turns out to be closely similar in the two cases; that is
to say, if a man is trying to remember a sequence of letters of the alphabet containing letters such as B, C and D, he is likely to produce as mistaken items in his recall the letters V, G and P. I may add that in the
United States they also produce ZEE whereas we never do, because we
call it ZED. All this is despite the fact that the letters have been presented visually and their shapes do not appear particularly similar; it is
I think universally agreed that the person who is trying to remember
them has converted the visual information to a memory that is structured
acoustically, or, if you will, that he has said them to himself. A number
of these studies have been carried out by Conrad in Cambridge, England
(Conrad and Hull, 1964), and it has been established by Wickelgren
(1965) in Cambridge, Massachusetts, that the effects of transfer and
interference, which I mentioned earlier, are in short-term memory
especially serious if the new material is acoustically similar to the old.
Thus we have here an example of the way in which the memory for
visual events is laid out according to acoustic qualities, just as the names
in a telephone book are laid out alphabetically.

I am leading up finally to an unpublished experiment, and would like
to recapitulate my argument thus far. First, the problems of memory

are not only those of storage, but also those of finding the right material again when you want it. Second, in man-made information retrieval systems it is essential to divide storage into many different categories, and also to construct an index. Third, experimental work on perception shows selection of particular classes of incoming information not only by sensory channel or arrival, but also by the category to which a word belongs. Fourth, a similar form of selection appears to operate not only during perception but also during recall. We can, therefore, to some extent think of memory as divided into separate stores from each of which we can retrieve separately by finding the right label. Fifth, the errors of retrieval shed some light on the classification into which memories are fitted, and in short-term memory the acoustic qualities, which an item would possess if it had been heard instead of seen, are relevant to such errors.

Let me now take up again the point which I said earlier had been loose in my argument. We can think of memories relevant to different topics as being stored in completely different places – say, on different shelves in a library. We may then think of retrieval as producing for recall the contents of one particular store, with a certain probability of extracting adjacent stores by mistake. But this carries with it the difficulty I mentioned earlier in connection with actual libraries, namely that one cannot operate on some other classification. If one store contains items A, B, C and D, and another items R, S, T and U, then it is difficult to retrieve a combination which consists of items B and S. But I mentioned an experiment in which words were presented in rapid alternation to two ears. I said that in that case it was possible to retrieve either in chronological order, or selectively by ears, as you pleased. This suggests rather that the items are stored, not in quite separate cells, but rather in a multidimensional lattice so that one can extract by different classifications.

In human terms, let us take the analogy of a set of personnel records which involves some male members of staff and some female ones. One might keep two separate sets of cards, one in one drawer of a cabinet and the other in another drawer. Inside each drawer, the cards might be arranged alphabetically or by length of service, but the two sexes would never meet. In an alternative arrangement, one might mix the cards within one drawer, but have a tag sticking up on the right hand side for male cards, and on the left hand side for female cards. The actual order of cards could be alphabetical or chronological as before. The advantage of this latter system is that it might well simplify extracting an alphabetical or chronological classification if one wanted such a grouping, while still making it possible to select by sex if one wished to do that. But the penalty which would be paid is that one might well, in selecting male cards beginning with the letter A, extract also the occasional female card because it happened to be adjacent to the male cards one wanted.

Let us now return to a psychological experiment by Broadbent and Gregory (unpublished). The technique was to flash on a screen eight items, all letters of the alphabet, but four in red and four in black. The subject was to be asked after presentation to recall either the four red items or the four black items but not both. Two conditions were compared, in each of which the same items were actually recalled. The difference between the two conditions lay in the irrelevant items, the ones that were not in fact recalled. In one condition these irrelevant items consisted of letters which had names acoustically very similiar to the ones that were to be recalled. In the other condition, the irrelevant items had names which sounded quite different from the names of the items which were to be recalled. Now, if the memory of the red items and the memory of the black items had been stored completely separately, as if it were in different drawers of a filing cabinet, there should have been no effect upon the efficiency of recall from the properties of those items which were in the other store. In fact, however, it is found that similarity between the red and black items in acoustic quality did increase the number of intrusions from the unwanted set of items into the ones that should have been recalled. In other words, short-term memory appears to be organized like the kind of personnel file in which the cards for men and women are kept in the same sequence, but with some mark on each card which allows one to pick out men only if one should wish.

Notice that we know this, not just because there are intrusions from the wrong set of items; that might simply mean that the labels from the two stores were hard to discriminate, or in concrete terms that the difference between red and black was hard to remember. But the number of intrusions increases when the items are close together on a quality which has nothing to do with the label by which the set of items is indicated. Going back to our analogy of the personnel file, if the male and female cards were kept in separate drawers and in order of length of service, we might get some female cards when we wanted male cards just by going to the wrong drawer. But we would not expect to find that this happened more often if men tended to have the same length of service as women, as compared with the condition when they had different length of service. An effect like that must mean that both male and female cards were ordered together by length of service. Similarly in our experiment, memory for red and black letters must be arranged in store according to the acoustic qualities as well as to the colour of the letters.

It is not at all surprising in fact to find that memory is not organized in a large number of quite separate stores divided up by successive classification like the Dewey Decimal System Classification in a library. Even in libraries, such a system of classification is found unsatisfactory when pushed to the limit (Vickery, 1965). For example, a particular book may seem to be appropriate to Psychology, and yet also to have relevance to Education, to Computer Science and to Library Retrieval. If it is put in only one of these subjects, it will not be retrieved by a system using only the single hierarchical classification. It is more general to say that each book has a number of characteristics, drawn from a large vocabulary of possible features which a book might have. The various terms which say what characteristics a book may have are known as the descriptors of the book, and the hierarchical classification is a particular case in which the presence of one descriptor implies the presence of certain others and the absence of others. Thus in the hierarchical system if a book is described as Physics, it must also be Science, and is not allowed to be Biology.

In fact one can make a very large number of different hierarchies from any given set of descriptions by allowing some combinations and disallowing others. For example, one might have a hierarchy in which one decided first of all if a book was psychological or not, and then divided those books which were psychological into those which were fact and those which were fiction, rather than doing it the other way around. Some people might think that this was a much more reasonable hierarchy. Indeed, instead of thinking of a library as divided into a vast number of small separate and completely independent sections by subjects, one might almost equally think of each book as potentially describable by a vast array of different adjectives, which indicate its characteristics. Sophisticated retrieval systems of the present day recognize this fact; they may well take account of restrictions between particular descriptors, such as the fact that in a given library there may be no books which are both Science and Fiction. But such restrictions are largely a function of the population of items that have to be classified for retrieval, and are not absolute properties like those in a traditional hierarchical classification. This allows one to cope with the modern situation in which a book on, say, the structure of the RNA molecule may be regarded as Physics *and* Biology.

Our simple little experiment, therefore, on the effects of acoustic confusions between material that is primarily classified by its colour, goes to show that human memory is similar to these more sophisticated forms of information retrieval from libraries, and not to the simple hierarchical classification. In short-term memory, over a period of a few seconds or minutes, direct sensory qualities such as acoustic confusion, colour, time of arrival, and so on, are of great importance for the classification of memory. Relationships of meaning, which are not reflected directly in sensory quality, are relatively less important: the words 'tranquil' and 'serene' are similar in meaning, while the word 'rugged' is similar to neither. Experiments by Baddeley and Dale (1966) in Cambridge show that similarities of this sort have relatively little effect on short-term memory, and thus cannot be supposed to form part of the system or structure in which the memories are located. In long-term memory, however, lasting over several days, this is not the case at all. Similarity of meaning then becomes exceedingly important in deciding whether there should be transfer or interference between old and new learning.

Thus the organization and labelling of memories which have been firmly established seems to be rather different from that of memories of recent acquisition and short duration. All the same, it seems likely that in long-term memory also it is possible to extract information by many different routes, rather than having it located purely in a single separate store. Let me take up in this connection a point I made earlier about the likely role of words as labels for particular forms of storage, and remind you of the remarkable properties of word association. If you say to most people the word 'black' and ask them to say the first word which comes into their head, they will tend to say the word 'white'. At first sight you might think that this represents a frequent conjunction in experience, but if you think about it, it is rather odd that word associations of this sort very rarely represent, for example, prepositions or other functional words. In ordinary English sentences, one may talk frequently of 'The house in the valley' or 'The house by the sea', but if you say to a man 'House' he is most unlikely to reply 'In' or 'By'. It is quite a good bet that he will reply 'Garden', which is a word that could hardly ever have occurred as the next word in a sentence. Such associations are unlikely therefore to be explained simply by frequency of occurrence in succession in past experience. What they do resemble, as has been pointed out by Vickery, is the restriction of relationship which may exist in retrieval systems between commonly used descriptors. If information is wanted about houses, it may well be filed under the heading of Garden. More specifically, if a man inquires at a library for information under a certain heading, relevant material may be searched for not only under that heading, but also under terms which are opposite, superordinate or subordinate to the heading and so on – just as the common word associations to a stimulus word are often opposite, superordinate or subordinate to the original stimulus. The network of associations between words which human beings possess looks not so much like the contents of a book when it is opened, as the cross-referencing of a subject index which is being used to find a book. If this is indeed the case, it would confirm the picture of words as labels for stored information which I presented earlier.

I said in the beginning that I would not be able to give many answers to the problems of the organization of memory. My argument has pointed, however, to the process of learning as similar to that of a librarian coping with his library. As the information comes in, it has to be stored in an active fashion which requires some analysis and transformation of what has occurred. Thus visual information may be stored in acoustic fashion, and no doubt vice versa. The storage may be under different headings depending upon the subject matter which is being presented, and above all when retrieval takes place, it is not necessary for the person recalling to have available the one correct label under which a particular item has been stored. Rather one can reach the same item through different characteristics, and one may be reminded of an event in one's childhood sometimes by a smell, sometimes by the song of a bird, and sometimes by a spoken phrase. But in the long term, it is the links between words which make available one type of memory when another has first been recalled.

In some sense, the whole of this discussion represents a meditation on the awkward question which was asked me recently by a distinguished classicist. The question was 'What are we doing when we educate somebody?' The answer is not at all obvious, because almost certainly we are not really establishing any great store of information. I do not now recall very much about the Punic Wars, and my daughter's homework reminds me only too well how much I have forgotten of the theorems of Euclid. In education, therefore, we are not loading books into the library. Could it be that we are writing the Index?

13

M. Minsky (1966)

Artificial intelligence

Scientific American, 215 (3), pp. 246–60

At first the idea of an intelligent machine seems implausible. Can a computer really be intelligent? In this article I shall describe some programmes that enable a computer to behave in ways that probably everyone would agree seem to show intelligence.

The machine achievements discussed here are remarkable in themselves, but even more interesting and significant than what the programmes do accomplish are the methods they involve. They set up goals, make plans, consider hypotheses, recognize analogies and carry out various other intellectual activities. As I shall show by example, a profound change has taken place with the discovery that descriptions of thought processes can be turned into prescriptions for the design of machines or, what is the same thing, the design of programmes.

The turning point came sharply in 1943 with the publication of three theoretical papers on what is now called cybernetics. Norbert Wiener, Arturo Rosenblueth and Julian H. Bigelow of the Massachusetts Institute of Technology suggested ways to build goals and purposes into machines; Warren S. McCulloch of the University of Illinois College of Medicine and Walter H. Pitts of M.I.T. showed how machines might use concepts of logic and abstraction, and K. J. W. Craik of the University of Cambridge proposed that machines could use models and analogies to solve problems. With these new foundations the use of psychological language for describing machines became a constructive and powerful tool. Such ideas remained in the realm of theoretical speculation, however, until the mid-1950s. By that time computers had reached a level of capacity and flexibility to permit the programming of processes with the required complexity.

In the summer of 1956 a group of investigators met at Dartmouth College to discuss the possibility of constructing genuinely intelligent machines. Among others, the group included Arthur L. Samuel of the International Business Machines Corporation, who had already written a programme that played a good game of checkers and incorporated several techniques to improve its own play. Allen Newell, Clifford Shaw and Herbert A. Simon of the Rand Corporation had constructed a theorem-proving programme and were well along in work on a 'General Problem Solver,' a programme that administers a hierarchy of goalseeking subprogrammes.

John McCarthy was working on a system to do 'commonsense reasoning' and I was working on plans for a programme to prove theorems in plane geometry (I was hoping eventually to have the computer use analogical reasoning on diagrams). After the conference the workers continued in a number of independent investigations. Newell and Simon built up a research group at the Carnegie Institute of Technology with the goal of developing models of human behaviour. McCarthy and I built up a group at M.I.T. to make machines intelligent without particular concern with human behaviour (McCarthy is now at Stanford University). Although the approaches of the various groups were different, it is significant that their studies have resulted in closely parallel results.

Work in this field of intelligent machines and the number of investigators increased rapidly; by 1963 the bibliography of relevant publications had grown to some 900 papers and books. I shall try to give the reader an impression of the state of the field by presenting some examples of what has been happening recently.

The general approach to creating a programme that can solve difficult problems will first be illustrated by considering the game of checkers. This game exemplifies the fact that many problems can in principle be solved by trying all possibilities – in this case exploring all possible moves, all the opponent's possible replies, all the player's possible replies to the opponent's replies and so on. If this could be done, the player could see which move has the best chance of winning. In practice, however, this approach is out of the question, even for a computer; the tracking down of every possible line of play would involve some 10^{40} different board positions (similar analysis for the game of chess would call for some 10^{120} positions). Most interesting problems present far too many possibilities for complete trial-and-error analysis. Hence one must discover rules that will try the most likely routes to a solution as early as possible.

Samuel's checker-playing programme explores thousands of board positions but not millions. Instead of tracking down every possible line of play the programme uses a partial analysis (a 'static evaluation') of a

relatively small number of carefully selected features of a board position
– how many men there are on each side, how advanced they are and
certain other simple relations. This incomplete analysis is not in itself
adequate for choosing the best move for a player in a current position.
By combining the partial analysis with a limited search for some of the
consequences of the possible moves from the current position, however,
the programme selects its move as if on the basis of a much deeper
analysis. The programme contains a collection of rules for deciding
when to continue the search and when to stop. When it stops, it assesses
the merits of the 'terminal' position in terms of the static evaluation. If
the computer finds by this search that a given move leads to an advantage
for the player in all the likely positions that may occur a few moves
later, whatever the opponent does, it can select this move with confidence.

What is interesting and significant about such a programme is not
simply that it can use trial and error to solve problems. What makes for
intelligent behaviour is the collection of methods and techniques that
select what is to be tried next, that size up the situation and choose a
plausible (if not always good) move and use information gained in
previous attempts to steer subsequent analysis in better directions. To
be sure, the programmes described below do use search, but in the
examples we present the solutions were found among the first few
attempts rather than after millions of attempts.

A programme that makes such judgements about what is best to try
next is termed heuristic. Our examples of heuristic programmes demonstrate some capabilities similar in principle to those of the checkers
programme, and others that may be even more clearly recognized as
ways of 'thinking'.

In developing a heuristic programme one usually begins by programming some methods and techniques that can solve comparatively
uncomplicated problems. To solve harder problems one might work
directly to improve these basic methods, but it is much more profitable to try to extend the problem solver's general ability to bring a
harder problem within reach by breaking it down into subproblems.
The machine is provided with a programme for a three-step process: (1)
break down the problems into subproblems, keeping a record of the
relations between these parts as part of the total problem, (2) solve the
subproblems and (3) combine the results to form a solution to the
problem as a whole. If a subproblem is still too hard, apply the procedure
again. It has been found that the key to success in such a procedure
often lies in finding a form of description for the problem situation (a

descriptive 'language') that makes it easy to break the problem down in a useful way.

Our next example of a heuristic programme illustrates how descriptive languages can be used to enable a computer to employ analogical reasoning. The programme was developed by Thomas Evans, a graduate student at M.I.T., as the basis for his doctoral thesis, and is the best example so far both of the use of descriptions and of how to handle analogies in a computer programme.

The problem selected was the recognition of analogies between geometric figures. It was taken from a well-known test widely used for college admission examinations because its level of difficulty is considered to require considerable intelligence. The general format is familiar: Given two figures bearing a certain relation to each other, find a similar relation between a third figure and one of five choices offered. The problem is usually written: 'A is to B as C is to (D_1, D_2, D_3, D_4 or D_5?).' The particularly attractive feature of this kind of problem as a test of machine intelligence is that it has no uniquely 'correct' answer. Indeed, performance on such tests is not graded by any known rule but is judged on the basis of the selections of highly intelligent people on whom the test is tried.

Now, there is a common superstition that 'a computer can solve a problem only when every step in the solution is clearly specified by the programmer'. In a superficial sense the statement is true, but it is dangerously misleading if it is taken literally. Here we understood the basic concepts Evans wrote into the programme, but until the programme was completed and tested we had no idea of how the machine's level of performance would compare to the test scores of human subjects.

Evans began his work on the problem of comparing geometric figures by proposing a theory of the steps or processes the human brain might use in dealing with such a situation. His theory suggested a programme of four steps that can be described in psychological terms. First, in comparing the features of the figures A and B one must select from various possibilities some way in which a description of A can be transformed into a description of B. This transformation defines certain relations between A and B. There may be several such explanations 'plausible' enough to be considered. Second, one looks for items or parts in C that correspond to parts in A. There may be several such 'matches' worthy of consideration. Third, in each of the five figures offering answer choices, one searches for features that may relate the figure to C in a way similar to the way in which the corresponding features in B are related to those in A. Wherever the correspondence, if any, is not perfect, one can make it more so by 'weakening' the relation, which means accepting a modified, less detailed version of the relation. Fourth and last, one can select as the best answer the figure that required the least modification of relations in order to relate it to C as B is related to A.

This set of hypotheses became the framework of Evans's programme (I feel sure that rules or procedures of the same general character are involved in any kind of analogical reasoning). His next problem was to translate this rather complex sketch of mental processes into a detailed programme for the computer. To do so he had to develop what is certainly one of the most complex programmes ever written. The technical device that made the translation possible was the LISP ('list-processor') programming language McCarthy had developed on the basis of earlier work by Newell, Simon and Shaw. This system provides many automatic services for manipulating expressions and complicated data structures. In particular it is a most convenient method of handling descriptions consisting of lists of items. And it makes it easy to write interlocked programmes that can, for example, use one another as subprogrammes.

The input for a specific problem in Evans's programme is in the form of lists of vertices, lines and curves describing the geometric figures. A subprogramme analyses this information, identifies the separate parts of the figure and reconstructs them in terms of points on a graph and the connecting lines. Briefly, the programme takes the following course: After receiving the descriptions of the figures (A, B, C and the five answer choices) it searches out topological and geometric relations between the parts in each picture (such as that one object is inside or to the left of or above another). It then identifies and lists similarities between pairs of pictures (A and B, A and C, C and D_1 and so on). The programme proceeds to discover all the ways in which the parts of A and B can be matched up, and on the basis of this examination it develops a hypothesis about the relation of A to B (what was removed, added, moved or otherwise changed to transform one picture into the other). Next it considers correspondences between the parts of A and the parts of C. It goes on to look for matchings of the A-to-B kind between the parts in C and each of the D figures (the answer choices). When it finds something approaching a match that is consistent with its hypothesis of the relation between A and B, it proceeds to measure the degree of divergence of the C-to-D relation from the A-to-B relation by stripping away the details of the A-to-B transformation one by one until both relations (*A*-to-*B* and *C*-to-*D*) are essentially alike. In this way it eventually identifies the *D* figure that seems to come closest to a relation to *C* analogous to the *A* and *B* relation.

Evans's programme is capable of solving problems considerably more complex or subtle than the one we have considered step by step. Among other things, in making decisions about the details of a picture it can take into account deductions from the situation as a whole. No one has taken the trouble to make a detailed comparison of the machine's performance with that of human subjects on the same problems, but Evans's evidence suggests that the present programme can score at about the tenth grade level, and with certain improvements of the programme that have already been proposed it should do even better. Evans's work on his programme had to stop when he reached the limitations of the computer machinery available to him. His programme could no longer fit in one piece into the core memory of the computer, and mainly for this reason it took several minutes to run each problem in the machine. With the very large memory just installed at M.I.T.'s Project MAC the programme could be run in a few seconds. The new capacity will make possible further research on more sophisticated versions of such programmes.

The Evans programme is of course a single-minded affair: it can deal only with problems in geometrical analogy. Although its ability in this respect compares favourably with the ability of humans, in no other respect can it pretend to approach the scope or versatility of human intelligence. Yet in its limited way it does display qualities we usually think of as requiring 'intuition', 'taste' or other subjective operations of the mind. With his analysis of such operations and his clarification of their components in terms precise enough to express them symbolically and make them available for use by a machine, Evans laid a foundation for the further development (with less effort) of programmes employing analogical reasoning.

Moreover, it is becoming clear that analogical reasoning itself can be an important tool for expanding artificial intelligence. I believe it will eventually be possible for programmes, by resorting to analogical reasoning, to apply the experience they have gained from solving one kind of problem to the solution of quite different problems. Consider a situation in which a machine is presented with a problem that is too complicated for solution by any method it knows. Ordinarily to cope with such contingencies the computer would be programmed to split the problem into subproblems or subgoals, so that by solving these it can arrive at a solution to the main problem. In a difficult case, however, the machine may be unable to break the problem down or may become lost in a growing maze of irrelevant subgoals. If a machine is to be able to deal, then, with very hard problems, it must have some kind of planning ability – an ability to find a suitable strategy.

What does the rather imprecise word 'planning' mean in this context? We can think of a definition in terms of machine operations that might be useful: (1) Replace the given problem by a similar but simpler one; (2) solve this analogous problem and remember the steps in its solution; (3) try to adapt the steps of the solution to solve the original problem. Newell and Simon have actually completed an experiment embodying a simple version of such a programme. It seems to me that this area is one of the most important for research on making machine intelligence more versatile.

I should now like to give a third example of a programme exhibiting intelligence. This programme has to do with the handling of information written in the English language.

Since the beginnings of the evolution of modern computers it has been obvious that a computer could be a superb file clerk that would provide instant access to any of its information – provided that the files were totally and neatly organized and that the kinds of questions the computer was called on to answer could be completely programmed. But what if, as in real life, the information is scattered through the files and is expressed in various forms of human discourse? It is widely supposed that the handling of information of this informal character is beyond the capability of any machine.

Daniel Bobrow, for his doctoral research at M.I.T., attacked this problem directly: How could a computer be programmed to understand a limited range of ordinary English? For subject matter he chose statements of problems in high school algebra. The purely mathematical solution of these problems would be child's play for the computer, but Bobrow's main concern was to provide the computer with the ability to read the informal verbal statement of a problem and derive from that language the equations required to solve the problem (this, and not solution of the equations, is what is hard for students too).

The basic strategy of the programme (which is named 'Student') is this: The machine 'reads in' the statement of the problem and tries to rewrite it as a number of simple sentences. Then it tries to convert each simple sentence into an equation. Finally it tries to solve the set of equations and present the required answer (converted back to a simple English sentence). Each of these steps in interpreting the meaning is done with the help of a library (stored in the core memory) that includes a dictionary, a variety of factual statements and several special-purpose programmes for solving particular kinds of problems. To write the programme for the machine Bobrow used the LISP programming language with some new extensions of his own and incorporated techniques that had been developed by Victor H. Yngve in earlier work on language at M.I.T.

The problems the machine has to face in interpreting the English statements are sometimes quite difficult. It may have to figure out the antecedent of a pronoun, recognize that two different phrases have the same meaning or discover that a necessary piece of information is missing. Bobrow's programme is a model of informality. Its filing system is so loosely organized (although it is readily accessible) that new information can be added to the dictionary by dumping it in anywhere. Perhaps the programme's most interesting technical aspect is the way it cuts across the linguist's formal distinction between syntax and semantics, thus avoiding problems that, it seems to me, have more hindered than helped most studies of language.

The remarkable thing about Student is not so much that it understands English as that it shows a basic capacity for understanding anything at all. When it runs into difficulty, it asks usually pertinent questions. Sometimes it has to ask the person operating the computer, but often it resolves the difficulty by referring to the knowledge in its files. When, for instance, it meets a statement such as 'Mary is twice as old as Ann was when Mary was as old as Ann is now', the programme knows how to make the meaning of 'was when' more precise by rewriting the statement as two simple sentences: 'Mary is twice as old as Ann was X years ago. X years ago Mary was as old as Ann is now.'

Bobrow's programme can handle only a small part of the grammar of the English language, and its semantic dictionaries are quite limited. Yet even though it can make many kinds of mistakes within its linguistic limitations, it probably surpasses the average person in its ability to handle algebra problems stated verbally. Bobrow believes that, given a larger computer memory, he could make Student understand most of the problems that are presented in high school first-algebra textbooks.

As an example of another kind of intelligence programmed into a machine, a programme developed by Lawrence G. Roberts as a doctoral thesis at M.I.T. endows a computer with some ability to analyse three-dimensional objects. In a single two-dimensional photograph of a solid object the programme detects a number of the object's geometrical features. It uses these to form a description in terms of lines and then tries to analyse the figure as a composite of simpler building blocks (rectangular forms and prisms). Once the programme has performed this analysis it can reconstruct the figure from any requested point of view, drawing in lines that were originally hidden and suppressing lines that should not appear in the new picture. The programme employs some rather abstract symbolic reasoning.

The exploration of machine intelligence has hardly begun. There have been about thirty experiments at the general level of those described here. Each investigator has had time to try out a few ideas; each programme works only in a narrow problem area. How can we make the programmes more versatile? It cannot be done simply by putting together a collection of old programmes; they differ so much in their representation of objects and concepts that there could be no effective communication among them.

If we ask 'Why are the programmes not more intelligent than they are?' a simple answer is that until recently resources – in people, time and computer capacity – have been quite limited. A number of the more careful and serious attempts have come close to their goal (usually after two or three years of work); others have been limited by core-memory capacity; still others encountered programming difficulties. A few projects have not progressed nearly as much as was hoped, notably projects in language translation and mathematical theorem proving. Both cases, I think, represent premature attempts to handle complex formalisms without also somehow representing their meaning.

The problem of combining programmes is more serious. Partly because of the very brief history of the field there is a shortage of well-developed ideas about systems for the communication of partial results between different programmes, and for modifying programmes already written to meet new conditions. Until this situation is improved it will remain hard to combine the results of separate research projects. Warren Teitelman of our laboratory has recently developed a programming system that may help in this regard; he has demonstrated it by re-creating in a matter of hours the results of some earlier programmes that took weeks to write.

The questions people most often ask are: Can the programmes learn through experience and thus improve themselves? Is this not the obvious path to making them intelligent? The answer to each is both yes and no. Even at this early stage the programmes use many kinds of processes that might be called learning; they remember and use the methods that solved other problems; they adjust some of their internal characteristics

H

for the best performance; they 'associate' symbols that have been correlated in the past. No programme today, however, can work any genuinely important change in its own basic structure. (A number of early experiments on 'self-organizing' programmes failed because of excessive reliance on random trial and error. A somewhat later attempt by the Carnegie Institute group to get their General Problem Solver to improve its descriptive ability was based on much sounder ideas; this project was left unfinished when it encountered difficulties in communication between programmes, but it probably could be completed with the programming tools now available.)

For a programme to improve itself substantially, it would have to have at least a rudimentary understanding of its own problem solving process and some ability to recognize an improvement when it found one. There is no inherent reason why this should be impossible for a machine. Given a model of its own workings, it could use its problem solving power to work on the problem of self-improvement. The present programmes are not quite smart enough for this purpose; they can only deal with the improvement of programmes much simpler than themselves.

Once we have devised programmes with a genuine capacity for self-improvement a rapid evolutionary process will begin. As the machine improves both itself and its model of itself, we shall begin to see all the phenomena associated with the terms 'consciousness', 'intuition' and 'intelligence' itself. It is hard to say how close we are to this threshold, but once it is crossed the world will not be the same.

It is reasonable, I suppose, to be unconvinced by our examples and to be sceptical about whether machines will ever be intelligent. It is unreasonable, however, to think machines could become *nearly* as intelligent as we are and then stop, or to suppose we will always be able to compete with them in wit or wisdom. Whether or not we could retain some sort of control of the machines, assuming that we would want to, the nature of our activities and aspirations would be changed utterly by the presence on earth of intellectually superior beings.

14

C. Burt (1966)

The genetic determination of differences in intelligence: a study of monozygotic twins reared together and apart

British Journal of Psychology, 57, pp. 137–53

I THE COMPLEXITY OF THE PROBLEM

Individual psychology and psychogenetics might themselves be fairly described as fraternal twins: they were begotten by the same father, Sir Francis Galton, and they emerged almost simultaneously as vigorous offspring of the mother science. Unfortunately they became parted soon after birth. Consequently, as Professor Darlington has remarked, 'despite their common origin, psychology and genetics, whose business it is to explain behaviour, have failed to face their task together'. One reason suggested is that general psychology has so far been unable to supply the genetic psychologist with any clear conception of what is commonly called the mind, or of its structure and development, such as might serve as a working basis for his researches. He has therefore to shoulder the preliminary task of determining for himself what particular traits or tendencies he shall select for observation and assessment.

In the case of the human species the variations with which the student of individual psychology is commonly concerned have proved to be extremely complex. In the first place, as Galton pointed out, a person's success in almost every walk of life depends on at least three distinguishable types of mental quality – cognitive, affective and conative: 'he must possess the requisite abilities; he must respond with eagerness and zeal; and he must sustain the necessary effort'. Secondly, statistical studies based on factorial techniques have demonstrated pretty clearly that we can no longer be content with the traditional notion of a motley assortment of cognitive 'faculties' or 'primary abilities', such as Thorndike at one time postulated and many educational and psychological writers still tacitly assume, nor yet with the over-simplified hypothesis of a single 'general factor' which Spearman proposed to substitute. The evidence – biological and neurological as well as purely statistical – suggests that the brain, or rather the central nervous system, is an organized hierarchy comprising both a 'general cognitive factor' and a number of more specialized 'group factors' of varying extent or breadth; but of these the 'general factor' is by far the most important, especially during early years. Thirdly, 'a vast mass of evidence, which I have summarized in previous papers, suggests that differences in this factor are largely the effect of the individual's genetic constitution – the product of the particular set of genes which each pair of parents transmits to their offspring – and that the mode of transmission conforms to the general principles worked out by Mendel and his followers for unifactorial and multifactorial inheritance (Burt, 1912, 1958).

This threefold distinction – between cognitive characteristics and motivational, between general characteristics and the more specialized, and between genetic characteristics and those that are acquired – leads to the concept of an 'innate, general, cognitive factor', each of the adjectives being defined in a somewhat technical sense. The problem for the psychologist therefore has been to decide, by means of appropriately planned research, whether such a factor really exists, and if so, what is its practical significance. To designate this concept it is more convenient to use one word instead of four, and Spencer's term 'intelligence' has been adopted (perhaps a little unwisely) as a popular label. Differences in this hypothetical ability cannot be directly measured. We can, however, systematically observe relevant aspects of the child's behaviour and record his performances in standardized tests; and in this way we can usually arrive at a reasonably reliable and valid estimate of his 'intelligence' in the sense defined. But it is clear that what we thus observe or calculate is a somewhat artificial abstraction, and, developmentally at any rate, decidedly remote from the aggregate of biochemical tendencies transmitted at the time of sexual reproduction.

Of late, however, an increasing number of British psychologists and educationists have vigorously challenged, not so much the bare fact of mental inheritance, but the idea that it has any appreciable importance as compared with environmental influences. Most of their criticisms rest, not on any fresh evidence or new researches of their own, but chiefly on armchair arguments from general principles. There are two obvious ways in which the questions thus raised can be met and dealt with.

(1) First, we can compare the performances of children who *differ in their presumable inheritance*, but have been brought up in much the same environment – children, for example, who have been removed

soon after birth to an orphanage or other institution. With the present problem largely in view, I and my colleagues under the London County Council carried out a series of investigations on such cases (Burt, 1943). Two main results emerged. (i) In spite of the uniformity of the environment, the individual variation in intelligence was at least as great as that of a random sample of children living in their homes. (ii) These variations showed a fairly close correlation (about 0·5), with the variations in the intelligence of their parents. Some of the most striking instances were illegitimate children of high ability; often the father (as the records showed) had been just a casual acquaintance of the mother, well above her own social and intellectual status, who had taken no further interest in the child, and whom the child himself had never even seen. In such a case it would be out of the question to attribute the child's exceptional intelligence to the cultural opportunities of his home, since his only home had been the institution to which he had been sent.

(2) Secondly, however, we may compare the performance of children who have the *same genetic constitution*, but have been brought up in widely different environments. Galton (1883) was apparently the first to recognize that the occurrence in man of so-called 'identical' twins 'makes it possible to show, more clearly than in other animals, the relative influence of differences in genotype and in environment respectively' (Darlington and Mather, 1949, p. 349). 'Monozygotic' or 'uniovular' twins are derived from the splitting of a single fertilized egg or zygote. Since they are developed from the same cell-nucleus, it follows that (barring accidents to the chromosomes, which are by no means unknown) they must have the same outfit of genes. However, the cytoplasm of the cell, as well as its nucleus, can occasionally influence heredity; and, unlike the splitting of the nucleus, the splitting of the cytoplasm could introduce a slight genetic difference (Spiegelman, 1946): hence the description 'identical' may be somewhat misleading. In the paper just quoted Darlington noted 'what an extraordinary success this [line of research] has had as a means of comparing the effects of a difference in heredity and in environment'; but he went on to warn the psychologist against the hasty inferences and simplifications often made in interpreting such data, not so much by Galton himself as by some of his over-enthusiastic successors.

In most of the investigations in which 'identical' twins have been distinguished from 'fraternal' the two members of each pair have nearly always been brought up together, usually in their own homes. Now it is well known that identical twins tend to keep together far more than fraternal twins, particularly since about half the fraternal twins are of different sex. The environmentalist therefore naturally argues that the higher correlation for intelligence found in the case of identical twins can be fully explained by the greater similarity in their life histories. To meet this criticism my co-workers and I decided to make a special study of cases in which the members of such pairs had been brought up in entirely different environmental conditions.

In our earliest survey of children in L.C.C. schools and institutions we reported a number of case studies in which 'identical' twins had been separated during the first few months of life (Burt, 1921); and over the years the number has steadily increased. Other writers, chiefly geneticists, have described isolated instances in which the members of a single pair were reared apart: of these the earliest is perhaps the most instructive (Popenoe, 1922; cf. Muller, 1925). Three group studies, in addition to our own, have since been published (Newman, Freeman and Holzinger, 1937; Juel-Nielsen and Mogensen, 1957; Shields, 1962); and the total number thus investigated now amounts to well over a hundred. Strange to say, however, apart from our own, nearly all the inquiries have been concerned, not so much with children, but with adults; and for adults of course it is far more difficult to secure complete or accurate data.

During the last ten years or so the inferences drawn from these and similar studies have been repeatedly questioned by several writers, notably by Halsey (1959), Stott (1956), Lewis (1957), Maddox (1957) and Woolf (1952). The most recent and the most outspoken is McLeish (1963). He cites and criticizes the work both of Newman and myself. The correlations obtained, so he tells his readers, show that 'identical twins reared apart resemble each other on intelligence tests about as much as do fraternal twins reared together'; (this is by no means accurate as a glance at the figures will show; see Table 14.2). At all events, he says, 'the best studies (which these are he does not specify) render the initial assumptions of the tester obsolete or highly questionable'; and the idea that 'identical twins are endowed with the same genes' is itself 'an assumption open to question' (on what grounds we are not told).

On the other hand, Shields (1962) has recently reached conclusions which are much the same as my own. In his review of 'previous reports' he refers to a wartime paper of mine on 'Ability and income', in which I quoted data from our first London survey (Burt, 1921), and included correlations between children related in various degrees (including a small group of monozygotic twins reared apart) whose after histories had been followed up for fifteen to twenty years (Burt, 1943). He regrets that I have 'given no other information about the twins brought up apart'. The paper which he cites, however, was concerned primarily with the 'influence of innate ability and parental income on entrance to universities', and the mention of twins was merely incidental. For further information I expressly referred to previous L.C.C. Reports, and explained that my own research students were still 'working on data obtained for twins up to the outbreak of the war'. After the war a fuller account was printed (Burt, 1955), and the statistical evidence set out in some detail by my co-workers and myself in one of the more technical periodicals (Burt and Howard, 1957; Conway, 1958). Both the earlier and the later publications, however, seem to have escaped Dr Shields's attention.

Meanwhile, largely as a result of these various discussions, further cases of separated twins have been brought to our notice, and more information has now been obtained for the earlier cases from the follow-up inquiries. The main purpose of the present paper therefore will be to bring together the evidence now available both from our studies and those of more recent investigators, and at the same time to answer the questions and criticisms raised by Dr Shields, Dr McLeish and other writers.

2 DATA ON TWINS REARED APART

The tests employed have been fully described elsewhere (Burt, 1921, 1933). Except for three children living in rural areas who had to be visited during the holidays, all the tests were applied in school. They consisted of (i) a group test of intelligence containing both non-verbal and verbal items, (ii) an individual test (the London Revision of the Terman–Binet Scale) used primarily for standardization, and for doubtful cases (iii) a set of performance tests, based on the Pintner–Paterson tests and standardized by Miss Gaw (1925). The test results, which generally covered other children in the school as well, were submitted to the teachers for comment or criticism; and, wherever any question arose, the child was re-examined. It was not practicable for the same person to test every child. I was helped by three principal assistants, and in a few cases by research students, all of whom had been trained by me personally. The methods and standards therefore remained much the same throughout the inquiry. If any divergence occurred, it would tend to lower rather than to raise the correlations. The reliability of the group test of intelligence was 0·97; of the Stanford–Binet 0·95; of the performance tests 0·87. For school attainments we used the group tests constructed and standardized for London children (Burt, 1921). Assessments of eye colour, head length and head breadth were obtained for all twins, but only random samples (fifty of each sex) in the case of the ordinary siblings: measurements for height and weight were corrected for sex and age. The number of children in each of the categories to be compared is shown at the top of each column in Table 14.2.

Most writers (e.g. Shields, 1962, pp. vi, 9) apparently suppose that 'monozygotic twins who have been separated from early childhood are of great rarity'. This we believe to be founded on a misconception. At the time of our main survey the number of twins among children born in London (excluding those who were not British) amounted to 1·4 per cent; and of these nearly a quarter must have been monozygotic. This follows because among twins generally about 38 per cent are of unlike sex; and among dizygotic twins the number of pairs of like sex must be approximately equal to the number of unlike sex. Monozygotic pairs are always of the same sex. Hence about $100-2 \times 38 = 24$ per cent of all twins must be monozygotic. Twins brought up together usually attend the same or neighbouring schools; and, even after full allowance has been made for the higher mortality of twins during preschool years, the proportion discoverable by school visiting alone is far less than would be expected from the number of those born. What happens is fairly clear. Many mothers are unable or unwilling to rear two children at the same time; but they are generally reluctant for it to be known that they have arranged for one of the children to be removed at or soon after birth. Since the actual placements are often carried out by the local authority or by some public body, a psychologist or social worker who is also a member of staff can usually obtain full particulars for a large number of such cases. Hitherto most of the published researches have been undertaken by outside investigators who have no access to these confidential records. May we therefore urge that other educational psychologists, who have the advantage of being on the staff of a local authority, should conduct similar inquiries along much the same lines?

From Table 14.2 it will be seen that the number of monozygotic pairs we have studied now amounts to 148, of whom fifty-three have been reared apart. Of the ninety-five pairs who were reared together, the majority attended London schools; thirty-seven came from areas outside London: nearly half of these were encountered during an investigation I was asked to carry out for the Birmingham Education Authority; several were discovered in the Warwickshire area, where my family lived; and the rest were cases to which our attention was drawn by colleagues or correspondents. In each of the fifty-three pairs reared apart one child at least was a Londoner in all but eight cases. All had been separated either at birth or during their first six months of life (in our initial report we included three who were separated considerably later; but they were subsequently omitted).

To determine 'zygosity', i.e. to distinguish 'identical' from so-called 'fraternal' twins, no one criterion is sufficient. A difference of sex is of course decisive; such a pair cannot be monozygotic. With the younger children, particularly those born in the area in which the investigator was working, we were frequently able to secure detailed records of the mother's pregnancy and birth; and it is generally agreed that twins reported as born in a single chorion are monozygotic. When twins brought up together can be seen side by side, the impressionistic judgement of an expert observer is likely to be correct in nineteen cases out of twenty; but a few dizygotic twins are remarkably alike. Height, weight and right- or left-handedness are unreliable; hair colour, eye colour, fingerprints and palm prints are more helpful. In doubtful cases the most valuable check is provided by an investigation of blood groups and serum groups. This had not been introduced when we started our inquiries; and, though in half-a-dozen of our later cases where slight doubts existed, it was adopted as an extra precaution, we were unable to carry it out as a routine procedure. We think it highly unlikely that any misclassifications have been made; but, if they have, their effect would be to reduce the differences between the correlations for monozygotic and dizygotic pairs (see Essen-Möller (1941) and Penrose and Smith (1955) for a discussion of the peculiar methodology of the problem).

One argument often advanced by our critics is that, although our separated pairs may have had a different environment from the day of birth or shortly afterwards, they must have had 'the same pre-natal environment, equally favourable in some cases, equally unfavourable in others'. But this, if correct, would apply to dizygotic twins almost as strongly as to monozygotic twins: the mere fact that the latter are enclosed in the same membrane, as well as in the same uterus, could not of itself account for the far higher correlations they provide. However, the assumption on which the argument rests are not borne out by the actual facts. To begin with, the position of the foetuses within the uterus, and the time (and often the mode) of delivery will be different. Moreover, the immediate cause of the twinning process appears in most instances to be some temporary setback at the outset of gestation; and this may affect the different foetuses in different degrees. Before splitting the two portions of the developing embryo generally develop at different rates. When the splitting occurs at a fairly late stage, the twin derived from the less developed half tends to be both smaller and weaker. If the splitting occurs after the embryo has begun to assume bilateral symmetry, then, in certain anatomical details, one twin may even be the mirror image of the other. In conjoined or 'Siamese' twins, where the splitting occurs so late as to remain incomplete, reversals seem the rule rather than the exception. Among our own cases we noted that mirror reversals (opposite handedness, reversed patterns in fingerprints and palm-prints, contrary directions in the crown whorl of the hair, etc.) were nearly four times as frequent with monozygotic pairs as with dizygotic. It was among pairs in which, on these and other grounds, we inferred late splitting that we discovered the largest discrepancies in the estimates for intelligence; as a rule, the child delivered second turned out to be the feebler of the two both in mind and in physique: and, as gynaecological records show, it is the one most frequently still-born.

The biggest differences of all were found among low-grade mentally defective twins in L.C.C. institutions. Here, out of twenty-six cases in which deficiency occurred in a monozygotic twin, there were twenty-one in which the other twin was *not* mentally deficient. These were likewise the cases in which physical differences were most conspicuous. When the deficiency was of a high-grade type, unaccompanied by physical defect, both twins were commonly affected to much the same degree; and among those pairs in which the physical defect occurred in one twin only, the correlation between intelligence and the extent of the physical damage was decidedly low. We therefore concluded that intra-uterine conditions are, if anything, more likely to diminish the resemblance between twins than to increase it, and that, apart from the rare cases of marked pathological deficiency (not included in our present series), their effect on mental capacity is comparatively slight (for fuller details see Burt and Howard, 1956, pp. 123 f.).

In the records for our cases various reasons were given for the separation of the twins. In nine cases the mother had died either in childbirth or shortly afterwards; in the others the parents generally explained that they had felt unable to bring up both the children 'in a proper way'. In twelve the ground alleged was the mother's poor health; in six she was unmarried; in the remainder the chief or only ground was economic: e.g. the father was dead, out of work, or weak in health, and the mother was the main wage-earner; often, it was said, the family was already too large for the resources of the home; in the better classes the parents frequently declared that they could not afford the cost of educating both children in the way they deserved.

Since our object was to compare twins brought up in different environments with those brought up in similar circumstances, we included in our group of separated twins no cases in which both had been brought up by a relative, except for five in which one relative lived in a town and the other in the country. For our fifty-three separated cases the occupational categories of the parents and foster parents are shown in Table 14.1. The classification of occupations is the same as that adopted in my previous reports (for details see Carr-Saunders and Jones, 1937, pp. 55 f.). The descriptions on the left indicate the occupational category of the children's own parents in cases where one child was brought up by them (the vast majority); in the few remaining cases that of the relative who adopted one of them, or the better type of foster parent. These figures should dispose of one of the commonest explanations advanced by thoroughgoing environmentalists – namely, that the high correlations for the separated twins is due to the way the foster parents were chosen.

TABLE 14.1. *Occupational categories of parents and foster parents*

		Foster parents						Residential institution	Total
	Parents	I	II	III	IV	V	VI		
I	Higher professional, etc.	0	0	0	I	2	0	0	3
II	Lower professional, etc.	0	0	I	0	4	2	2	9
III	Clerical, etc.	0	I	I	I	3	I	0	7
IV	Skilled	I	I	0	0	2	I	0	5
V	Semi-skilled	2	0	2	I	5	2	3	15
VI	Unskilled	I	I	0	0	7	3	2	14
	Total	4	3	4	3	23	9	7	53

Halsey (1959), for example, criticizes the inferences which my co-workers and I originally drew on two main grounds. First of all, he believes, the practice of 'selective placement' would suffice to account for the similarities found between twins who have been reared apart – an explanation also put forward by Hudson (1965). Secondly, it is said, our cases 'do not represent the full range of the social and cultural scale'; hence the effect of environmental differences have not been allowed a fair opportunity to reveal themselves. Both criticisms are apparently derived from the notion that (as another critic has put it) 'official surveys confined to pupils in the ordinary elementary schools of the Council would not at that date have included children from the professional or well-to-do classes, nor those who are mentally deficient': with a wider range in the cultural background of the homes, so Dr Halsey maintains, we should have found a wider range in the children's intelligence; and in that case, particularly had defectives also been included, much larger discrepancies would have been discovered.

However, it can, I think, be safely stated that none of these objections is warranted. Had our critics referred to the original reports they would have seen that many of the children included among the twins reared apart were not in fact pupils at elementary schools. Three pairs were children of parents in the highest professional category; and the two brightest twins were sons of an Oxford don who had died just before they were born (their story is told in full by Conway, 1958, p. 186). Moreover, there was a disproportionately large number from the 'lower professional' category: parents of this class, when the family increased in size, often found it hard to preserve the standard of appearance they thought proper to their station and to give their children the type of education they deserved, since in those days education at a grammar school entailed payment of fees.

In arranging placements it is undoubtedly true that an endeavour is usually made to find foster parents of the same social class as that of the original parents, but such efforts frequently fail. Parents in the skilled classes are not only reluctant to have their own twins separated, but also disinclined to accept foster children from other families. Parents in the unskilled classes can seldom provide suitable foster homes. On the other hand, childless couples who are well-to-do are often eager to adopt a child; and many of the children thus chosen are healthy and attractive-looking infants from the lower occupational categories. The consequence is that, contrary to Halsey's assumption, the average environmental difference between separated twins is actually greater than it would have been, had the homes been selected purely at random: only nine of the fifty-three separated twins were placed with foster parents of the same social class as their own parents.

As regards range of intelligence, our group included a couple of mental defectives from special schools (IQ 66), and, at the other end of the scale, two scholarship winners (IQ 136 and 137) – a difference of 71 points, which is wider than the range one might normally expect in a sample of only fifty-three (namely, 4·5 SD). However, for correlations to be comparable, what are really important are not so much the *ranges* as the *standard deviations*. The standard deviation of the group of separated monozygotic twins was 15·3; and that of the ordinary siblings was 15·0. The American groups, it is true, showed a bigger range with standard deviations rising to 17·3; but the correlations now generally printed are nearly always corrected for this disparity (see Woodworth, 1941).

3 RESULTS

Means and correlations

The average intelligence of the twins measured on a conventional IQ scale (SD = 15) was 97·8 for the separated monozygotes, 98·1 for monozygotes brought up together, 99·3 for the dizygotes as compared with 100·2 for the siblings and 100·0 for the population as a whole. The fact that twins – particularly uniovular – tend to have a lower average ability than ordinary children of the same social background has since been confirmed in several large-scale investigations carried out by Husén (1959), Sandon (1959) and others. The intra-class correlations obtained with the various groups for the different measurements and estimates are set out in Table 14.2. Since several writers (e.g. Heim, 1954; Hudson, 1965) have stated that the figures reported by Newman *et al.* (1937) for American children imply different conclusions from those drawn in my previous reports, I have appended the corresponding correlations obtained from their inquiry: their raw figures were corrected for age and range by McNemar, and the slight changes this involves have been accepted by Holzinger.

(a) Intelligence

(1) *Twins reared together.* It will be seen that, both in our own inquiries and in those of Newman, there are large and significant differences between the correlations for 'identical' and for 'non-identical' twins, when both members of the pairs have been brought up in their own homes. Between 'non-identical' twins (at any rate with our own data) the correlations are much the same as those between ordinary brothers and sisters; Newman reports slightly higher figures, as might be expected from the types of test employed. Shields obtained a coefficient of only 0·51 for his dizygotic twins, which is even lower than ours. There is a small positive correlation between the assessments for unrelated children brought up in the same home (0·27). This would seem attributable to the efforts (not very successful) to place these children in foster homes corresponding to those of their parents. Still more recent results, chiefly American, fully confirm our main finding. Using composite scores from tests for 'primary mental abilities' Blewett (1954)

obtained correlations of 0·75 and 0·39 for monozygotic and dizygotic twins: but the size of his samples (twenty-six pairs in each group) prevents the difference from being fully significant. Nichols (1965) used composite scores obtained from the National Merit Scholarship Qualifying tests: pairs differing in school, sex or health records were excluded, and the correlations obtained were 0·87 for monozygotic twins (687 pairs) and 0·63 for dizygotic twins (482 pairs).

(2) *Twins reared apart.* Comparisons of the foregoing type are commonly dismissed on the ground that 'identical' twins naturally keep together much more closely than other siblings. I find it hard to believe that this of itself could account for the large differences observed. However, the study of cases in which twins of identical constitution have been separated almost from birth is likely to carry far more conviction. Unfortunately the number of investigations is extremely small.

In our own set of results the outstanding feature is undoubtedly the high correlation for 'intelligence' between monozygotic twins even when reared apart – 0·87 as compared with 0·54 for dizygotic pairs reared together – a difference which is over four times its standard error. With children picked at random the average difference between their IQs is approximately 17 points, with 'fraternal' twins 12 points, and with 'identical' twins, when reared apart, just under 6 points. The correlations reported by Newman (last 2 columns of Table 14.2) show similar but somewhat smaller differences. Shields (1962) reports a correlation of 0·77 for separated monozygotes age 8–59 years (the figure is actually higher than that for monozygotes brought up together 0·76), and a correlation of 0·51 for dizygotes brought up together; but, owing to the small samples, the difference, taken by itself, is too small to be statistically significant. The reader will find it instructive to note how closely the various correlations for intelligence resemble those for most of the physical characteristics. Those for weight, however, are evidently affected by environmental conditions.

In most other researches on twins the investigators have not been in a position to secure the information needed to discriminate between monozygotic and dizygotic pairs. They have therefore merely recorded separate correlations for pairs of like and of unlike sex. Maxwell (1953, p. 144) has collected data from earlier studies; to these we can now add the figures recently reported by Vandenberg (1956), Sandon (1959) and Husén (1959). This yields seven independent researches, based on well over 1000 pairs of like sex and nearly 1000 of unlike. For intelligence the average correlations are 0·76 and 0·57 respectively. Applying the formula given above (p. 224) and using Fisher's z-transformation, the probable

TABLE 14.2 Correlations for mental, educational and physical characteristics

	(A) Burt et al.						(B) Newman et al.		
	Mono-zygotic twins reared together	Mono-zygotic twins reared apart	Dizygotic twins reared together	Siblings reared together	Siblings reared apart	Unrelated children reared together	Mono-zygotic twins reared together	Mono-zygotic twins reared apart	Dizygotic twins reared together
Number of pairs ★...	95	53	127	264	151	136	50	19	51
Intelligence									
Group test	0·944	0·771	0·552	0·545	0·412	0·281	0·922	0·727	0·621
Individual test	0·918	0·863	0·527	0·498	0·423	0·252	0·881	0·767	0·631
Final assessment	0·925	0·874	0·534	0·531	0·438	0·267	—	—	—
Educational									
Reading and spelling	0·951	0·597	0·919	0·842	0·490	0·545	—	—	—
Arithmetic	0·862	0·705	0·748	0·754	0·563	0·478	—	—	—
General attainments	0·983	0·623	0·831	0·803	0·526	0·537	0·892	0·583	0·696
Physical									
Height	0·962	0·943	0·472	0·501	0·536	−0·069	0·932	0·969	0·645
Weight	0·929	0·884	0·586	0·568	0·427	0·243	0·917	0·886	0·631
Head length	0·961	0·958	0·495	0·481	0·506	0·110	0·910	0·917	0·691
Head breadth	0·977	0·960	0·541	0·510	0·492	0·082	0·908	0·880	0·654
Eye colour	1·000	1·000	0·516	0·554	0·524	0·104	—	—	—

★ Figures for boys and girls have been calculated separately and then averaged. In columns 3, 4, 5 and 6 the correlations for head length, head breadth and eye colour were based on samples of 100 only.

averages for the monozygotic and dizygotic pairs respectively work out
at 0·89 and 0·56. In a survey just published, Wiseman (1964, p. 99) has
computed estimates from data obtained in Manchester schools, using a
rather different method; his figures are 0·92 for 'identical' twins and
0·51 for 'fraternal'. All four estimates, it will be observed, are in close
agreement with our own, where the zygosity was determined by direct
empirical evidence.

(b) Attainments

The differences obtained with the scholastic tests present a striking
contrast with those for intelligence. In our own investigation the correlations for non-identical twins and for siblings reared together (0·83 and
0·80) are far higher than those for identical twins reared apart (0·62)
and nearly as high as those for identical twins reared together (the
difference is even larger with Newman's groups). For siblings reared apart
the correlation sinks to 0·53. Here, therefore, the influence of environment is unmistakable. The coefficients which are most conspicuously
increased are, as one might expect, those for verbal attainments.

Criticisms

The inferences which my colleagues and I drew from our earlier studies
of twins (as well as from other lines of evidence) have been sharply
criticized by those who favour an environmentalist theory. But the
objections advanced rest almost entirely on armchair arguments: hardly
any of the critics cite first-hand evidence of their own. Heim (1954),
for example, observes that, even when so-called 'identical' twins have
been brought up together, the correlations for intelligence 'still fall short
of unity', and she contends that this tells against the genetic hypothesis.
But no tests or assessments can claim perfect reliability; and the correlations she cites are almost, if not quite, as high as those obtained from the
same individuals on two different occasions. Quoting Newman, she tells
us that 'when monozygotic twins are separated . . . the differences
between their scores are as great as those between unseparated dizygotic
twins'. But here there is clearly a mistake. Newman's average difference
for dizygotic twins is 9·2 points, but for the separated monozygotic
twins only 8·2 points – a reduction which certainly cannot prove the
superior importance of environment.

Maddox (1957), Halsey (1959) and Hudson (1965) are still more
emphatic in their rejection of genetic influences. Like so many writers,

however, they speak of 'differences in *intelligence*' and 'differences in *scores from intelligence tests*' as though the two were synonymous, and tacitly assume that what is true of one type of test – a verbal group test, for instance – holds good of all other assessments. In Newman's investigation the average difference between the separated twins is considerably increased by the big differences obtained in a very small number of pairs. There were four in which the difference amounted to at least 17 points; and in each there was marked difference in the amount of schooling received – ranging from 4 to 15 years. Gladys, for instance, brought up in an 'isolated part of the Rockies where there were no schools', obtained an IQ of only 92, whereas her twin sister Helen, who had been to college, obtained an IQ of 116 – a difference of 24 points. Hudson quotes the case of Mary and Mabel where the difference was 17 points; here there was four years difference in schooling. But what does all this prove? Not that the innate intelligence of the twins was widely different, but merely that predominantly verbal tests, like the Otis and the Stanford–Binet, do not furnish very accurate assessments, when the schooling and cultural background are so dissimilar. Newman's own conclusion is very different from that drawn by our various critics. He observes that, even where there was a large discrepancy in the actual scores, it nevertheless seems probable that 'the twin with the lower IQ had an *inherited capacity* to reach the rating of the other, had he or she enjoyed the same opportunities'; on the other hand, 'even with a good education the poorly endowed person does not reach the level of a potentially able but poorly educated person' (Newman *et al.*, 1937). And in a later summary of his main results he remarks that, 'throughout the whole study of identical twins reared apart', he was, as a geneticist, 'much more impressed with the very great intra-pair *similarities* of the twins, after they had been exposed to all sorts of environmental differences, than with the *differences*' (Gardner and Newman, 1940).

Environmental influences

I have never maintained, as McLeish (1963) implies, that environment has no effect whatever. I have always insisted that genetic and environmental factors are continually interacting from the very start. In our own data the environmental influences are most obvious in the case of group tests. And with every type of test or assessment a *small* portion of the correlation still seems to be attributable to environmental conditions. However, to demonstrate the importance of environmental opportunities it is quite misleading to pick out, as Dr Hudson and other critics

234   *Readings in Human Intelligence*

have done, just one or two striking instances where a large discrepancy in the test results is accompanied by a marked difference in home circumstances: one can always counter such an argument with cases, like that of 'George' and 'Llewellyn' (see Conway, 1958, p. 186), where, in spite of an exceptionally wide difference in upbringing, both twins happen to score almost exactly the same IQ. The only satisfactory method is to correlate the *differences* between the various mental or scholastic assessments for each member of a pair with the *differences* in the material and cultural conditions (see Conway, 1959, pp. 8 f.).

For this purpose we have assessed the economic and cultural conditions of the homes in terms of a conventional scale similar to that employed for assessing intelligence and educational attainments, namely, one in which the mean is 100 and the standard deviation is 15. The correlations thus obtained are shown in Table 14.3.

TABLE 14.3. *Correlations of differences for monozygotic twins reared apart*

Test results Differences in intelligence	Home conditions	
	Differences in cultural conditions	Differences in material conditions
Group test	0·43	0·21
Individual test	0·26	0·16
Final assessment	0·15	0·18
School attainments	0·74	0·37

Coefficients over 0·29 are significantly different from zero ($P < 0.05$)

It will be seen that differences in educational attainments are highly correlated with differences in the cultural background: there is also a significant correlation between cultural differences and differences in the scores for the group test taken as they stand. But the correlations for the individual test and for the final assessment are so low as to be non-significant with a sample of this size. The differences in educational attainments show a small but significant correlation with differences in material conditions, chiefly no doubt because the latter are responsible for differences in the children's physical health and school attendance.

The multifactorial hypothesis

Most of the critics who seek to belittle the importance of mental inheritance seem content to examine just one particular investigation and base their arguments on the weaknesses they discern in that. They ignore the fact that the hereditarian's conclusions rest, not on a single research however elaborate, but on inferences drawn from a wide variety of different approaches – all leading to a systematic theory of mental inheritance, very similar to that arrived at by contemporary geneticists working in entirely different non-mental fields.

Accordingly, it seems desirable by way of conclusion to compare the correlations obtained from twins and siblings with those obtained from other pairs related by various degrees of affinity. The figures compiled from our London surveys are set out in Table 14.4. We have endeavoured to select the individuals composing the groups so that they should, as far as possible, be genuinely representative of the population as a whole. With the smaller groups this has not been easy; but for all of them the standard deviations, which range from just under 14 to a little over 16 IQ points, are much the same. To compare or correlate figures for adults with those obtained from children may seem a questionable procedure. But many of the pupils tested between 1914 and 1924 have since grown up; and it has often been possible to trace and retest them as well as to test their own children. In that way correlations between assessments for these children and similar assessments secured from their parents when they were children can be computed. On the whole, they fully confirm the values obtained in the usual way.

For purposes of comparison I also give medians for results reported by other investigators and the hypothetical values to be expected in accordance with what may be called the neo-Mendelian theory of mental inheritance. To calculate the latter the method used is a modification of that originally developed by Fisher (1918) in his study of body measurements. The formulae (Burt and Howard, 1956, pp. 115–16), unlike those used by most other writers, allow for two facts commonly ignored: in the case of intelligence there is (i) ample evidence for assortative mating between parents, and (ii) some evidence for a slight but incomplete amount of dominance. To some extent these two opposing influences tend to neutralize each other; but the net result is usually to raise the theoretical figures somewhat above those generally published, which tacitly assume that dominance is absent and that mating is perfectly random. In that case with simple multifactorial inheritance the theoretical correlations would be – with parents 0·5, with grandparents

TABLE 14.4. *Correlations between relatives*

	Burt		Other investigators		
	Number of pairs	Corre-lation	Number of investi-gations	Median corre-lation	Theore-tical value
Direct line					
With parents (as adults)	374	0·49	13	0·50	0·49
With parents (as children)	106	0·56	—	—	0·49
With grandparents	132	0·33	2	0·24	0·31
Collaterals					
Between monozygotic twins					
Reared together	95	0·92	13	0·87	1·00
Reared apart	53	0·87	3	0·75	1·00
Between dizygotic twins					
Same sex	71	0·55	8	0·56	0·54
Different sex	56	0·52	6	0·49	0·50
Between siblings					
Reared together	264	0·53	36	0·55	0·52
Reared apart	151	0·44	33	0·47	0·52
Between uncle (or aunt) and nephew (or niece)	161	0·34	—	—	0·31
Between first cousins	215	0·28	2	0·26	0·18
Between second cousins	127	0·16	—	—	0·14
Unrelated persons					
Foster parent and child	88	0·19	3	0·20	0·00
Children reared together	136	0·27	4	0·23	0·00
Children reared apart	200	−0·04	2	−0·01	0·00

0·25, with cousins 0·125, i.e. $(\frac{1}{2})^n$ for correlations between relatives of the nth degree. With intelligence we believe that unifactorial as well as multifactorial modes of transmission operate. And slight indications of sex-linkage, chiefly associated with the former, also seem discernible, particularly in the correlations for dizygotic twins. However, both these further influences, if they operate at all, are relatively small, and were consequently neglected in deducing the formulae used.

Erlenmeyer-Kimling and Jarvik (1964) have reported the results of a somewhat similar review of the literature. As they point out, 'while behaviour theory as yet makes few provisions for modern genetic concepts, the literature of the past half-century contains far more information than is generally realized about the relation between genotypic similarity and performance on mental tests'. They have located fifty-two such studies yielding 'over 30,000 correlational pairings from eight countries in four continents', and present the main results in the form of an instructive diagram, which exhibits according to the degree of relation every correlation in their collection, together with the median for the various groups. Within some of the groups, particularly those where members of the same family have been brought up together, the coefficients exhibit a fairly wide range, e.g. for siblings they range from just over 0·30 to a little over 0·70. The reasons are fairly obvious. The low values have usually been obtained with somewhat unreliable tests, occasionally from but a single unvalidated test; often, too, the groups are fairly homogeneous. The high values are generally derived from heterogeneous samples, varying considerably in home background and education, and the tests are frequently verbal group tests, such as would be appreciably affected by differences in education. For most of the comparisons, however, there is a clear concentration of values near the mean or median. My own list includes a number of studies, chiefly British, which do not appear in the American collection; and with the writers' permission I have now added to my own earlier compilation data from several inquiries which they quote and which had escaped my notice.

In Table 14.4 I have given median values only; and I have indicated the number of investigations on which the medians are based. It will be seen that the values reported by other investigators tend to be somewhat higher than my own, presumably because many based their correlations on scores obtained from tests of a predominantly verbal type. If allowance is made for this, then, it will be seen that (except perhaps in the case of first cousins in my own research) both the figures obtained in the London inquiry and the medians of the figures published by other observers are in close agreement with the theoretical values we have calculated according to the neo-Mendelian hypothesis.

4 SUMMARY AND CONCLUSIONS

(1) Various mental and physical characteristics have been measured for persons related in different degrees, and the correlations compared both with each other and with those obtained by other investigators, as well as with the values to be expected in accordance with the modified theory of multifactorial inheritance outlined in an earlier paper (Burt and Howard, 1956). In particular, an intensive correlational study has been made of monozygotic twins reared together and apart.

(2) For assessments of 'intelligence' the correlations from unrelated pairs of children brought up together are positive but comparatively

small; those from related pairs increase progressively according to the closeness of family relation. The correlation for monozygotic twins reared in separate environments amounts to as much as 0·87, and is but slightly increased where such twins have been reared together. On the other hand, the correlations for school attainments vary closely with similarity in environmental circumstances. From this it may be inferred that individual differences in 'intelligence', particularly when the assessments have been carefully checked, are influenced far more by genetic constitution, or what is popularly termed 'heredity', than by post-natal or environmental conditions.

(3) The detailed values for the different groups obtained both in my own investigations and in those of other writers, agree satisfactorily with the view that the genetic tendencies which are responsible for individual differences in intelligence are in the main (though probably not exclusively) transmitted in accordance with a multifactorial or polygenic hypothesis, due allowance being made for assortative mating and partial dominance.

15

D. H. Stott (1960)

Interaction of heredity and environment in regard to 'measured intelligence'

British Journal of Educational Psychology, 40, pp. 95–102

I INTRODUCTION

Discussion of the relative contributions of heredity and environment to 'measured intelligence' seems to have reached a point where the value of the dichotomy has been called in question owing to the demonstration of a certain degree of correlation. This correlation, it was pointed out (Maddox, 1957), is due to the sociological fact that high test intelligence of the parents is associated with high cultural stimulation of the child. Maddox also suggested, from the analogy of chicks, that the manifestation of a hereditary characteristic might be dependent upon post-natal environment.

The object of the present contribution is to draw attention to a body of comparatively recent work in experimental biology which has demonstrated yet another and, indeed, far closer type of interaction, further complicating the heredity–environment dichotomy.

2 CONGENITAL MALFORMATIONS IN ANIMALS AND MAN

It has been known for a generation that the subjection of the pregnant female to certain exogenous stresses was liable to produce malformations in the young. But these were held to be 'phenocopies', resulting from an arrest of embryonic development similar to that produced by a genetic anomaly (Goldschmidt, 1937). The exogenous factors were thought of as alternative to the genetic, and hence the unconvincing attempts to classify individual malformations as either environmentally or as genetically induced. Among the supposed latter sort there was a notable failure to establish a Mendelian pattern of inheritance. Some were attributed to dominant, some to recessive genes, and some to both (Warkany, 1947; Penrose, 1951); but whichever pattern was held to operate did not do so consistently. However, this variable 'expressivity' of gene influence was a common phenomenon in genetics, and was accounted for by two special explanations – that of the 'phenocopy' mentioned above, and 'penetrance', the latter being essentially no more than the statement that an apparently gene-determined tendency achieved morphological manifestation only in a proportion of cases. These terms bear more than a trace of 'explanation by label'. Moreover, the 'copying' implied in the phenocopy not only implies an agent, but perpetuates the concept of an agent *distinct from* the gene; while the concept of penetrating some unspecified barrier goes beyond methodological parsimony. Both terms have been rendered superfluous by evidence that genetic and environmental factors may interact to produce the malformations formerly attributed to the one or the other.

A wide range of unfavourable environmental factors during pregnancy can produce malformation in the offspring. The type of stress applied – chemical, vitamin deficiency, mechanical, irradiation – is immaterial so far as the type of malformation is concerned; the latter seems to depend upon the stage of gestation and, as mentioned below, upon dormant hereditary propensity. Whereas species of animals vary somewhat in their susceptibility to different stresses, the same general tendency is found in all. For example, vitamin deficiencies have been made to produce congenital malformation in the chicken, turkey, duck, pig, cow, rat, mouse and guinea pig (Giroud, 1954). No verification by controlled experiment is, of course, possible in man, and except for German measles there is as yet no agreement as to what are the noxious agents. Mumps is under suspicion and so is influenza, but apart from a recent epidemic there has been no good opportunity to enable the guilt of the latter to be tested. In fact, attempts to relate malformation to physical illnesses during pregnancy have been surprisingly unrewarding. Recently, psychological factors have been adduced (Ingalls, 1947, 1956; Stott, 1957, 1958). The sharp rise in the incidence of congenital malformations from the beginning of the war and in the early post-war years in Germany are attributed by German workers in part to emotional shocks and stresses (Gesenius, 1952; Klotz, 1952; Grebe, 1953; Grebe and Windorfer, 1953).

Despite disagreement as to which types of maternal stress are responsible, all authorities are agreed that the pre-natal environment plays a large part in the production of human congenital anomalies. It is hard to account otherwise, for example, for the enhanced risk of mongoloid defect and of other malformations with both advancing maternal age, and also in first births (Murphy, 1947; Record, 1956; MacMahon and McKeown, 1953; Alwyn Smith and Record, 1955), for the higher incidence of anencephaly (lack of cerebral cortex) among first births conceived during the summer months (McKeown and Record, 1951), or for the association between mental defect and conception during hot summers (Knobloch). The terms 'congenital' and 'innate' have consequently to embrace pre-natal environmental influence as well as heredity.

It was during the experimental work with animals that the more specific evidence of genetic–environmental interaction was forthcoming. Observing the incidence of diaphragmatic hernia in rats, Anderson (1949) observed that, in a strain which does not spontaneously show hernia, a diet deficient in vitamin A could produce only 9·9 per cent, but in another strain, which showed 2·7 per cent hernias even with a diet rich in vitamin A, the deficiency produced 19 per cent. Similarly, Fraser and his colleagues (1951, 1954), inducing cleft palate in mice, found that the incidence varied from 4 per cent to 100 per cent, according to the genotype of the mother and the foetus. Thus, the impairment would seem to result from a hereditary predisposition which was *facilitated*, that is, brought into morphological manifestation, by environmental stress during gestation. Facilitation constituted a unitary theory which explained both the undoubted tendency of certain malformations to run in families and their erratic and also sporadic appearance, without recourse to special explanations such as those of phenocopy or penetrance.

3 'INTELLIGENCE' AND PRE-NATAL ENVIRONMENT

This new biological concept promises to be relevant to current thought about 'intelligence'. There is a certain amount of evidence (Pasamanick and Lilienfeld, 1955; Knobloch and Pasamanick, 1956; Stott, 1957, 1958) that human mental impairment is related to adverse prenatal environment. This might well explain why the prediction of a decline in national intelligence was controverted by the Scottish survey. The fall of IQ with increase in family size observed therein has its counterpart in the higher incidence of several malformations in later-born children of large families. Anderson, Baird and Thomson (1958) found a correlation between fatal malformation of the central nervous system and adverse social conditions, notably in large cities. If the neural structures upon which mental ability depends are similarly subject to lesser impairment, we should expect a rise in the mean 'measured intelligence' of a population with improvement in social conditions. In effect, mental impairment due to adverse conditions of pregnancy would

seem to explain certain trends in the statistics of the Scottish Mental
Survey that its authors were at a loss to account for. When the fall in
test score with family size is examined closely, it is seen that this was
most striking among the 'white collar' groups, and within them at that
family size – four or five – at which the latest addition may have been
unwanted. The intellectual inferiority of children of mothers of 21 or
less is also largely confined to the first four social groups. This can
hardly be due to the greater risks of first births, since the trend virtually
disappears in the manual worker groups. It has been estimated (Wimperis, 1960) from the Registrar General's Statistical Survey that two-
thirds of legitimate children born to mothers of under 20, and 24 per
cent of those of 20–24, are premaritally conceived; and a significant
proportion of the children of the mothers of 21 or under covered by the
Scottish Survey would, presumably, be illegitimate. It is reasonable to
infer that extramarital conception would be more frequent among those
young mothers belonging to the higher social classes, and the mental
stresses associated therewith would be greater among them for cultural
reasons. That children of one child families living in grossly overcrowded conditions should be mentally inferior even to those of larger
families in similarly overcrowded conditions again suggests the effects of
illegitimacy. There is consequently some reason for inferring that the
mental impairment following adverse conditions of pregnancy is not
limited merely to that of the occasional production of mental defect (the
'ineducables' were excluded from the survey), but may apply to the
merely sub-average.

The hypothesis of the facilitation of genetic tendencies by environmental influences would also explain the failure of mental defect in
general, and above all of feeblemindedness, to conform to genetic expectations (Penrose, 1949). A further important study has been published by Brandon (1957), who followed up the children of female
mental defectives who had at one time been inmates of the Foundation
Hospital, London. Ninety-nine of the 109 children still alive were
apparently mentally normal. Only six of the ten subnormals consistently
scored below IQ 70, and only four below 65. This is higher than would
be expected in a general population, but probably about the same as
would be found in a slum or other culturally disorganized community.
Some three-quarters of the children in question were born out of wed-
lock and in circumstances unlikely to afford the mother a trouble-free
pregnancy or the child an optimal post-natal environment, so that it is
open to conjecture what proportion of the 9 per cent subnormality was
due to heredity.

In a sample of 450 mentally normal children the present writer (Stott, 1957) found that, after stressful pregnancy, one child in three suffered serious non-epidemic illness before the age of 3 years (compared with one in nine after a reported clear pregnancy). The stresses in question were similar in type, although probably on the whole somewhat less acute, than those followed by mental subnormality and/or malformation. The risk of either of the latter types of impairment following a stressful pregnancy can be roughly estimated on the basis of the incidences quoted at between 1:30 and 1:40. This study must rank only as an exploratory one, but the findings are consistent with the theories of facilitation, and help to explain why mental subnormality is more prevalent in poor neighbourhoods. These findings add infantile ill-health to the 'continuum of reproductive casualty' hypothesized by Pasamanick and Lilienfeld (1955), Warkany (1947) and others.

4 TWINS

Facilitation has a quite particular bearing upon the twin studies which are currently regarded as a means of isolating the genetic component of 'measured intelligence'. Maddox (1957) has already suggested that identical twins, even though separated from near birth, will probably have more similar environments – by way of placement with relatives or in selected foster or adoptive homes, etc. – than a random sample of children, so that the whole of the correlation cannot be attributed to heredity. To this we must now add a sharing of the foetal environment, for whatever stresses the mother was subjected to would apply to both. Furthermore, twinning in itself presupposes heightened maternal stress and a greatly heightened foetal risk, as instance the high perinatal mortality of twins. If, therefore, pre-natal environment can exercise a general influence upon mental development apart from the production of definite defect, this will also tend to contribute to the correlation of measured intelligence in separated twins.

The Scottish Survey (1953) found that the mean IQ of twins was 4·83 points lower than for all non-twins (5·55 points lower for boy twins). The inferiority of boys to girls among twins (3·06 points compared with 1·77 for non-twins), which the authors of the report comment upon with surprise, is in conformity with the greater general vulnerability of male infants to pre-natal impairment (Stott, 1957). The intellectual inferiority of twins is borne out by Sandon's (1957) study of the relative proportions of twins and of non-twins who get through the selection examination for Birmingham grammar schools. Of the twenty-four twins per 1000 live births, he estimates that sixteen reach examination age. But only eight twins could be discovered in every 1000 of the successful. This might have been due in part to the failure to trace some of them, but he also found the examination marks of twins to be significantly lower than those of non-twins, and it was probable that the deficiency was more pronounced in the case of the monozygous.

It is possible in short, that the observed higher correlation of 'measured intelligence' between monozygous twins compared with heterozygous twins and non-twins may be accounted for, at least in part, by the theory of facilitation. Given a pregnancy-stress, impairment depends in the first place upon the genetic vulnerability of the foetus to the impairment in question. It would also seem to depend upon the genetic proneness of the mother to withstand stress, and presumably upon her acquired vulnerability thereto. Thus, in monozygous twins, not only the genetic constitution but also – subject to the qualification below – the foetal environment is similar; for heterozygous twins, the genetic constitution differs but the foetal environment is by-and-large similar; and of course, for non-twin sibs the genetic constitution again differs, while the pre-natal environment (same mother, different pregnancy) will vary more than that for fraternal twins (same mother, same pregnancy). The above is in conformity with the hierarchy of correlations found for children of the above groups reared apart. In addition, monozygous foetuses share the same membrane, whereas the heterozygous do not. Hence, one would suppose that for monozygous twins the pre-natal environment would be somewhat more similar than for fraternals. It is again interesting that the Scottish survey found that like-sex twins, both boys and girls, were inferior to unlike-sex twins. The difference is slight, but if it represents an inferiority of the monozygous, as Sandon suggests from a similar result in his own study, it must be multiplied by two, since these would only constitute about half of the like-sex twins. In summary, there would seem to be environmental factors making twins as a whole more similar in mentality than non-twin sibs, and monozygous twins more similar than heterozygous, however soon after birth the twin pairs are separated. It seems thus unfortunately not to be true, as Warburton (1958) avers, that in 'identical' twins Nature has provided us with the means to measure the genetic component.

5 THE INDIVIDUAL'S ALTERNATIVES OF MENTAL DEVELOPMENT

The value of the hypothesis of facilitation is that it suggests a process by which the interaction of heredity and environment can affect mental development. If it may be assumed that a significant part of the genetic influence is of the facilitatable sort, it is possible to envisage broadly the range of alternatives of mental development open to an individual embryo. At each critical stage of embryonic life, there will be different, genetically determined, pronenesses to impairment. Whether any of these are triggered off, to produce the impairment characteristic of the genotype, depends upon the intra-uterine environment at that particular stage. It is also realistic to think of impairment, not as a lowering of a general 'level of intelligence', but as damage to the neural structures which make mental operations of certain sorts impossible. This does not necessarily mean that certain *tasks* are made impossible, since we know that similar tasks are often performed by different individuals by very different mental processes. Hence, the alternative process upon which an impaired individual falls back may be just as good, or nearly so, as the primary one. On the other hand, impairment in the form of an inability to form general concepts, or – as suggested below – of intrinsic motivation, may have no substitute and so result in poor general mental functioning. Whether the individual can, in fact, fall back upon alternative processes depends upon whether the environment in which he grows up allows him to exploit the next most suitable alternative, or the next after that, as the case may be. The developmental potential of any individual can thus be likened to the path of a traveller who runs the risk of having to take diversions, each of which offer a variety of obstacles; his ability to surmount any one becomes important only if he is forced to take the path upon which it lies. If he suffers from congenital night-blindness, and gets drowned by falling into a deep pool, his demise might be attributed mainly to a hereditary factor; but if he had been killed by treading upon an unexploded bomb in taking a short cut despite warning notices his death could have been said to be due mainly to environmental factors in the form of defects in his education or upbringing. If one likes to conceive of the roles of heredity and environment in terms of quantitative contributions, it is consequently seen that the (pseudo-)ratio heredity/environment not only varies from individual to individual, but according to the turn which his development has taken. The value of a general estimate of the ratio, when the variance must be so large, surely becomes meaningless.

6 MOTIVATION AS A DETERMINANT OF 'INTELLIGENCE'

Nor, unfortunately, have we exhausted all the complications. 'Measured intelligence' is a sample of an individual's behaviour. Being such, it depends not only upon the possession of an aggregate of neural structures such as make certain mental operations possible, but upon the extent to which the individual is actually motivated to perform them. This is not simply a question of how the subject feels at the time towards the test and the tester. For the whole of his life he will have been variously motivated to think thoughts of a certain type; he will have acquired particular readinesses or mental sets, and the general type and level of his concept-formation – the systems by which he has coded information – will depend cumulatively upon his congenital plus environmentally conditioned motivation.

Now, when we study the behaviour of mentally subnormal individuals without preconceptions about a self-operating quantity of 'intelligence', we observe that impairment of motivation, alias 'emotional factors' (Clarke and Clarke, 1958), is a large element in their poor performance. In some, one suspects, failure or distortion of motivation (in very unresponsive or hyperactive defectives) could be the only factor. In such children nutritional motivation may evoke good perceptual discrimination and appropriate response, but mental activity vanishes when it is no longer a question of eating or drinking; it is as if they had suffered congenital prefrontal lobotomy (Brazier, 1950; Lashley, 1935). Other defective children, although active, have no interest in human relationships, and never learn speech or social adaptation. A good proportion of any group of educationally subnormal children suffer from 'unforthcoming' temperament, *alias* under-motivation. Other things being equal, this would make for poor concept-formation, since the child would not have performed the mental operations upon which conceptualization is based. In Piaget's (1951) terminology, there would be a shortage of the anticipatory schemata which are built upon previously existing classifications and other learned relations. Our general failure to appreciate the importance of motivation in this building up of the mental equipment is due to the conventional separation of the cognitive and conative fields.

Impairment of motivation – whether it be 'unforthcomingness', disorganization (inability to concentrate), lack of response to personal stimuli or other abnormality – must therefore be reckoned a component of 'measured intelligence'. In so far as it is congenital, there is some evidence that it can be facilitated by pregnancy-stress in the same way as can cognitive disability (Stott, 1959). This adds a third dimension of alternatives to the possibilities of an individual's mental development.

7 IS 'INTELLIGENCE' SUBJECT TO ALLOCATION?

At this point it may be well, in summarizing the argument, to see what remains of the concept of relative contribution when it is translated into the language of interaction. The contemporary view of genetic determinants is that they are built-in 'instructions' for the development of the organism within the range of environment for which it is fitted. To ask whether given individual variations are more due to the variability of the instructions or to that of the environment is not to ask one question, but a thousand or a hundred-thousand – according to where we stop following the alternatives. It would, no doubt, be feasible, in dealing with an individual at a given stage of mental development, to study retrospectively which of the alternatives of interaction were in fact followed, and so be able to say *of that individual* that heredity or environment played the major part. For example, it might be said of a child of an academic family that his mental development was greatly stimulated by his environment, and that if he had been born in an unacademic family he would have remained intellectually undistinguished; or of a child suffering from a congenital mental impairment that no matter how good the environment his mental development would always have remained low. But to try to assess either of the two types of influence as percentages, even in individual cases, would be merely rhetorical quantification.

Moreover, we are driven to the point of recognizing that we are not asking an answerable question. If an organism failing to solve a problem by one sort of mental behaviour is free within certain limits to utilize other skills; if the relevance of each of the alternative skills depends upon the type of problem; if the primary mode of solution, or the calling into play of the alternative approaches, depends upon the strength and quality of the individual's motivation; if the skills themselves owe their existence in large part to the motivation which has instigated the skill-forming practice – then we are forced to question the value of subsuming the resultant individual differences in mental behaviour within a concept of 'intelligence'. Our ability to measure specified individual differences does not justify us in assuming that there is any unitary factor underlying them, which can be conceived of as a quantity. In our term 'intelligence' we have in fact taken over the popular and traditional reification of these individual differences, which exists not in the mind of the subject, but in that of the observer. Theoretically speaking, the term 'measured intelligence' does not save us, for the attempted measurement of an animistic concept no more conjures it into reality than two wrongs logically ever make a right. By extension, it is also impermissible to pose queries as to the relative quantitative contributions of heredity and environment to mental efficiency unless we specify efficiency in what and in which person, and even then the question only makes sense in broad clinical assessment of etiology.

16

C. J. Bajema (1963)

Estimation of the direction and intensity of natural selection in relation to human intelligence by means of the intrinsic rate of natural increase

Eugenics Quarterly, 10, pp. 175–87

INTRODUCTION

The great changes now taking place in the social structure of human societies undoubtedly have an effect on the direction and intensity of natural selection. Whether a given human characteristic, such as intelligence, is favoured or discriminated against in terms of reproductive performance may very well be a function of the social practices prevailing at the time. It is desirable, therefore, to investigate reproductive differentials in a variety of human societies at frequent intervals in order to assess the biological consequences of various social practices.

Cole (1954), in his discussion of the theoretical consequences of life history phenomena, has clearly demonstrated the necessity of taking into account the total life history pattern of the population being studied if an accurate estimation of the direction and intensity of natural selection in relation to a particular trait is to be made. The probability of making an erroneous conclusion concerning the direction and intensity of natural selection in relation to a behavioural trait such as intelligence is greatly increased if subtle differences in such factors as generation length, mortality rates and the proportion of non-reproductive individuals are ignored. Anastasi (1956), in her review of the literature concerning the relationship between intelligence and fertility, has pointed to the fact that, since the observed correlations between intelligence and fertility are generally quite low, the operation of a very small selective factor could produce a completely spurious result.

In the past, investigators have sometimes erred in their estimates of the direction and intensity of natural selection in relation to intelligence because they failed to consider one or more of the variables which affect

I

population growth. Differentials in the following variables must be taken into account when measuring natural selection:

(1) Number of offspring per fertile individual.
(2) Proportion of non-reproductive individuals.
(3) Mortality rates up to the end of the childbearing period.
(4) Generation length.

The life table method, which involves computing the intrinsic rate of natural increase, provides the only means currently available whereby all of the biological variables affecting population growth can be taken into account simultaneously. During the early part of this century Lotka (1907a, 1907b, 1922, 1925; Lotka and Sharpe, 1911) devised a statistic, r_m, called the intrinsic rate of natural increase – or the Malthusian parameter – by which differentials in fertility, mortality and generation length can be taken into account simultaneously when determining the growth rates of various segments of a human population. Although several biologists (Cole, 1954; Crow, 1962; Fisher, 1958) have urged the use of this statistic to estimate the direction and intensity of natural selection in relation to different genotypes, it has yet to be applied to human data for this purpose.

This investigation proposes to estimate by means of the intrinsic rate of natural increase the direction and intensity of natural selection in relation to human intelligence among a group of native white individuals born in 1916 or 1917.

METHODS AND MATERIALS

Type of population under study

Terman Group Intelligence test scores were obtained on 1144 native white individuals born in 1916 or 1917 and tested in the sixth grade by the Kalamazoo Public School system. The average age at time of testing was 11·6 years. The study was restricted to individuals born in 1916 or 1917 because this was the youngest age group for which completed fertility data were available. It was necessary to choose all individuals born in two successive years in order to obtain a sample of sufficient size.

Data collecting procedures

The following life history data were collected for 979 of the 1144 individuals in the population under study: (1) date of birth; (2) number of siblings (excluding stepsiblings) who lived past the age of one; (3) marital status; (4) number of offspring produced who lived past the age of one; (5) date of death if the tested individual was deceased; and (6) place of residence.

The following sources of information were utilized in locating and obtaining information about the individuals included in the study:

(1) Relatives and close friends.
(2) Telephone directories.
(3) City directories.
(4) School records – transcripts and census records.
(5) Marriage records.
(6) Birth records.
(7) Death records.
(8) Records of funeral directors.
(9) College alumni offices.
(10) Present and former employers.

The individuals included in the study were interviewed personally whenever possible. An attempt was made to interview in person all individuals living within a 200 mile radius of Kalamazoo. Questionnaires were sent to seventy-seven individuals whose life histories could not be ascertained personally by the investigator.

Definitions and formulas

In the present study, the symbol r_m always represents the intrinsic rate of natural increase for the total sample of 979 individuals, including both males and females.

The age-specific rates of survival, l_x, and fertility, m_x (where $x =$ age in years), are defined as follows:

$$l_x = \frac{\text{number of individuals surviving from age of testing to age } x}{\text{number of individuals tested}} \quad (1)$$

$$m_x = \frac{\frac{1}{2} \text{ times the number of offspring surviving to age one who were born to individuals of age } x}{\text{number of individuals tested who survived to age } x} \quad (2)$$

The intrinsic rate of natural increase, r_m, is the value of r which satisfies the equation:

$$\sum_{x=0}^{x=\infty} l_x m_x e^{-rmx} = 1 \quad (3)$$

The average generation length, T, is obtained from the relation:

$$T = \frac{Ln(\sum l_x m_x)}{r_m} \qquad (4)$$

The relative fitness, W_i of subgroup$_i$, is defined as

$$W_i = \frac{e^{r_{mi}T}}{e^{r_{mh}T}} \qquad (5)$$

where e is the base of the Napierian logarithms, T is the average generation length for the total sample, Ln is the Napierian logarithm, r_{mi} is the intrinsic rate of natural increase for the ith subgroup of the sample, and r_{mh} is the intrinsic rate of natural increase for the subgroup of the sample having the fastest growth rate (i.e. the largest value of r_m).

The estimate of the population growth rate per individual, e^{r_mT}, is derived from the relationship:

$$N_T = N_O e^{r_mT}$$

where N_t is the number of individuals alive at time T, N_O is the number of individuals alive at time O, r_m is the intrinsic rate of natural increase calculated by equation (3), and T is the average generation length of the total sample calculated by equation (4). If N_O is taken as unity, then e^{r_mT} is the population growth rate per individual for a period of time equal to the average generation length of the total sample.

The intensity of phenotypic selection in relation to a trait is defined as

$$I = 1 - \frac{\overline{W}}{W_O} \qquad (6)$$

where $\overline{W}$ is the fitness of the total population under study and W_O is the fitness of the optimum phenotype.

RESULTS

Characteristics of the sample

Life histories were compiled on 979 (85·6 per cent) of the 1144 native-born white individuals in the population under study. This included seventy-two individuals who died before reaching the age of 45 as well as sixty-one individuals out of seventy-seven individuals who were contacted by mail.

The average test score of the sample was 101·46 IQ points, and the standard deviation of a random observation was 12·66 IQ points. The

979 individuals had 2189 offspring who lived past the age of one – or an average of 2·24 offspring per individual.

Possible biases

The sample was taken at random from the population under study only in so far as the methods used to locate individuals were unbiased. The sample was compared with the population from which it was taken to determine the presence and/or the importance of three types of biases: (1) differences in the sex ratio; (2) differences in the distribution of IQ scores; and (3) differences in place of residence (living in Kalamazoo County versus living outside of Kalamazoo County).

It was thought that females might be underrepresented in this sample because they change their last names at time of marriage. Table 16.1, which gives the sex ratios of the population under study and the sample, clearly indicates that the sample is not biased in relation to the sex ratio.

TABLE 16.1 *Sex ratio of the population under study and of the sample*

	Male	Female
Population under study	575	569
Sample	493	486

Table 16.2, giving the per cent of the original population contained in the sample with respect to the five IQ groups into which the sample was broken down, shows that the inclusion of an individual in the sample was not a function of his intelligence test score.

TABLE 16.2. *Proportion of individuals in population under study included in sample in relation to IQ*

IQ range	No. included in sample/ No. in population	Per cent included
⩾120	82/91	90·1
105–119	282/327	86·2
95–104	318/377	84·4
80–94	267/312	85·6
69–79	30/37	81·1
Total sample	979/1144	85·6

The sample is definitely biased with respect to place of residence. Since it can be safely assumed that almost all of the 165 individuals not contacted do not reside in Kalamazoo County, the bias in the average number of offspring per individual due to place of residence might adversely affect any conclusions concerning the relationship between intelligence and fertility. A 2 × 5 analysis of variance with disproportionate subclass numbers, as discussed by Snedecor (1956), was used to test the effect on fertility of the two residence categories within the five IQ groups (Table 16.3). This analysis indicated that the effects on fertility due to place of residence and interaction between place of residence and IQ were negligible.

TABLE 16.3. *Average number of offspring per individual suriviving to age 45 by place of residence in relation to IQ*

	Living in Kalamazoo Co.		Not living in Kalamazoo Co.	
IQ range	No.	Av. no. of offspring	No.	Av. no. of offspring
≥ 120	32	2·56	47	2·66
105–119	164	2·52	99	2·09
95–104	200	2·14	92	2·05
80–94	176	2·49	71	2·73
69–79	21	1·57	5	2·00
Total sample	593	2·35	314	2·31

Thus it can be concluded that the sample of 979 individuals does not deviate significantly from the population in terms of sex ratio or test score distribution and that the average number of offspring per surviving individual is not significantly different for place of residence within the five IQ groups.

Average number of offspring in relation to intelligence

The data were subdivided into five groups in relation to test scores: IQ ≥ 120; 105–119; 95–104; 80–94; and 69–79. These subgroupings were chosen so that (1) one of the groups (IQ 95–104) encompassed the average IQ of the sample; (2) the bimodal nature of the data would be apparent (IQ ≥ 120 and IQ 80–94); and (3) to maintain sufficient numbers within each group without including too wide an IQ range.

The average number of offspring per individual in relation to IQ is given in Table 16.4. A one-way analysis of variance showed that the average number of offspring per individual for the five IQ groups is significantly heterogeneous at the 1 per cent level of significance (F = 4·136 > 3·32).

Further statistical analyses were performed using the Duncan Multiple Range test (Duncan, 1955) with corrected tables (Harter, 1960). This test maintains the protection level against making a type II error (asserting that a mean comes from the same population as another mean

TABLE 16.4. *Average number of offspring per individual in relation to IQ*

IQ range	No. reporting	No. of offspring per individual
≥ 120	82	2·598
105–119	282	2·238
95–104	318	2·019
80–94	267	2·464
69–79	30	1·500
Total sample	979	2·236

when in reality both means come from different populations) at the same level that it is in the Student's *t* test which protects against the type I error (asserting that the two means come from two different populations when in reality they come from the same population) at the 95 per cent level. The results of the Duncan Multiple Range test indicate that the average number of offspring per individual for the IQ ≥ 120 group is not significantly greater than that of the IQ 80–94 group, and that the average number of offspring per individual for the highest two reproductive groups (IQ ≥ 120 and IQ 80–94) in the bimodal relationship between IQ and fertility are both significantly greater than the IQ 69–79 group and the average IQ group (95–104) but are not significantly greater than the IQ 105–119 group.

Table 16.5 compares the results of this study with those of Higgins *et al.* (1962) using the IQ subgroupings employed by them in their investigation. While the results of the study by Higgins *et al.* also indicate a bimodal relationship between IQ and fertility, it is not so pronounced as the bimodal relationship found in this study. Both studies provide strong evidence for the existence of a high reproductive rate for the IQ > 130 group which is probably a quite recent development. No other previous studies have reported a bimodal relationship between IQ and fertility, and it is doubtful that the biased techniques employed in the past could have completely obscured a high reproductive rate of the high IQ group.

TABLE 16.5. *Comparison of the results of this study with those of Higgins et al. (1962)*

IQ range	Higgins et al. (1962)		This study	
	No.	Av. no. of offspring	No.	Av. no. of offspring
>130	25	2·96	23	3·00
116–130	269	2·45	107	2·51
101–115	778	2·26	344	2·08
86–100	583	2·16	427	2·30
71–85	208	2·39	75	2·05
56–70	74	2·46	3	0·00
0–55	29	1·38	—	—

Since both studies indicate that a bimodal relationship exists between IQ and fertility, Penrose's equilibrium model (Penrose, 1948, 1950a, 1950b), which assumes a very high reproductive rate among the low-normal IQ groups and a very low reproductive rate among the high IQ groups, cannot be used to explain the current relationship between IQ and fertility nor any changes that could occur in the mean IQ of the population due to this relationship. Penrose assumed that differential fertility in relation to intelligence was a permanent phenomenon. The results of Higgins *et al.* (1962) and this study contradict Penrose's assumptions and support the position that the relationship between IQ and fertility is a dynamic one.

Intrinsic rate of natural increase in relation to intelligence

Life tables were compiled for each of the five IQ groups as well as for the total sample. The data were programmed, and the computer facilities at Michigan State University were utilized to find the value of the intrinsic rate of natural increase for each group that satisfied equation (3). The values of the intrinsic rate of natural increase for each of the five IQ groups and for the total sample are given in Table 16.6. The bimodal nature of the relationship between IQ and total reproductive performance (including the effect of generation length as well as fertility) is indicated by the r_m values for the IQ $\geqslant$ 120 and IQ 80–94 groups.

The value of r_m for the total Kalamazoo sample was only $+0.004$. The fact that r_m was extremely small for this study can be explained by the characteristics of the population under study which are known to affect fertility in a negative way and thus would reduce r_m. The population under study consisted of: (1) white individuals only; (2) native-born Americans only; (3) individuals with above-average educational attainments; (4) predominantly Protestant individuals; (5) individuals who spent almost all of their potentially most productive childbearing years during the Great Depression and World War II; (6) individuals who spend most or all of their lives in an urban environment. The urban nature of the population under study is probably the major reason for finding such a small intrinsic rate of natural increase. It is a well-known fact that the complete fertility of the total urban population (age 45 and older) of the United States has been below replacement level in the past (Grabill, 1959).

TABLE 16.6. *The intrinsic rate of natural increase and the average generation length in relation to IQ*

IQ range	Intrinsic rate of natural increase r_m	Average generation length T
$\geqslant$ 120	$+0.008885$	29.42 years
105–119	$+0.003890$	28.86 years
95–104	$+0.000332$	28.41 years
80–94	$+0.007454$	28.01 years
69–79	-0.010001	28.76 years
Total sample	$+0.003915$	28.49 years

Generation length in relation to intelligence

The almost universally held hypothesis that the generation length of the lower IQ groups is shorter than the generation length of the higher IQ groups has been supported by casual observations and by data compiled by Conrad and Jones (1932), who correlated the intelligence of the parent with the age of the parent at the birth of the first, second, third and fourth child and found that the age of the parent at the time of birth of his children is positively correlated with IQ (the higher the IQ, the older the parent at the time of birth of his children). However, no exact estimates concerning generation length (given in years) in relation to IQ have been made.

Table 16.6 gives the average generation length, T, calculated from equation (4) for the five IQ groups as well as for the total sample. The results indicate a very slight positive relationship between IQ and generation length. The IQ 69–79 group is the only IQ group deviating from this positive relationship. The average generation length for the total sample approximately agrees with the estimated average generation length for the population of the United States (29–30 years).

Relative fitness in relation to intelligence

Relative fitness is defined in this paper as the ratio of population growth rate per individual of a particular phenotype (IQ group) to the population growth rate per individual of the optimum phenotype (IQ group) for the same trait. The optimum phenotype is that phenotype which has the highest population growth rate per individual (IQ $\geqslant$ 120 in this study).

The relative fitness of each of the five groups using the average number of offspring per individual as the measure of population growth is given in Table 16.7, while Table 16.8 gives the relative fitness of the five IQ groups using e^{rmT} which takes all the variables affecting population growth into account. Note that because the IQ $\geqslant$ 120 group has the longest generation length, the relative fitness of each of the other four IQ groups is increased when e^{rmT} is used to measure relative fitness instead of the average number of offspring per individual. This indicates the importance of generation length as a variable which can affect the population growth rates of several phenotypic classes of a particular behavioural trait unequally.

As pointed out by Dobzhansky and Allen (1956), 'fitness' is meaningful only in relation to a particular environment. The relative fitness values given in this paper pertain only to the population under study and cannot be assumed to be the same for IQ groups in different environments.

Intensity of natural selection in relation to intelligence

When measuring the effect of natural selection on a trait, it is interesting to determine the population's phenotypic load or the proportion by which the population fitness is decreased in comparison with the optimum phenotype. This reduction in the fitness of the population relative to the optimum phenotype is called the intensity of natural selection (Haldane, 1954; Spiess, 1962). The intensity of natural selection in this study is measured by subtracting the relative fitness of the total sample (where fitness is measured by e^{rmT}) from one (equation 6).

TABLE 16.7. *Relative fitness in relation to IQ using the average number of offspring per individual as the measure of population growth*

IQ range	Relative fitness
⩾ 120	1·0000
105–119	0·8614
95–104	0·7771
80–94	0·9484
69–79	0·5774

The intensity of natural selection in relation to intelligence in man was found to be 0·13 in this study where the optimum phenotype is the IQ ⩾ 120 group. The fitness (reproductive performance) of the population under study, therefore, is 0·13 less than what it would be if all the IQs were in the optimum range (IQ ⩾ 120). That is to say, the phenotypic load due to variability in intelligence is 13 per cent.

Correlation analyses

The negative relationship between the IQ of an individual and the size of the family from which the individual comes has been observed many times and is one major evidence used to support the hypothesis that the IQ of the population is declining. The correlation coefficient between the IQ of an individual and the size of the completed family from which he comes is −0·2599 for this study and is significantly different from 0 at the 1 per cent level. This agrees with the results of other studies on samples of a similar nature which have found the negative correlation

TABLE 16.8. *Relative fitness in relation to IQ using e^{rmT} as the measure of population growth*

IQ range	Relative fitness
⩾ 120	1·0000
105–119	0·8674
95–104	0·7838
80–94	0·9600
69–79	0·5839

to be between $r = -0.20$ and $r = -0.30$. However, when the IQ of an individual was correlated with his subsequent completed fertility in this study, the correlation coefficient is $+0.0503$, significantly greater than 0 at the 6 per cent level by a one-tailed test. Thus the mean IQ of the population under study has probably increased slightly due to the small positive relationship between IQ and fertility.

The fact that in this study the IQ of an individual is positively correlated with the number of offspring he produces but is negatively correlated with the size of the family from which he comes appears to be paradoxical at first. However, these observed correlations are due to the operation of two factors.

First, the correlation between the IQ of an individual and the size of the family from which he comes has an inherent defect which makes any estimation concerning the relationship between intelligence and fertility based on it subject to considerable error. That part of the population which leaves no offspring (20·2 per cent in this study) is completely ignored. The results (Table 16.9) indicate that the relationship between

TABLE 16.9. *Proportion of individuals who left no offspring in relation to IQ*

IQ range	Number	Per cent leaving no offspring
⩾ 120	11/82	13·41
105–119	48/282	17·02
95–104	70/318	22·01
80–94	60/267	22·47
69–79	9/30	30·00
Total sample	198/979	20·22

the intelligence of an individual and the size family from which he comes is biased in a negative direction due to the fact that as intelligence decreases the probability of leaving no offspring increases. The results of this study show that the probability of leaving no offspring is more than two times as great for the IQ 69–79 group compared with the IQ ⩾ 120 group. A comparison of Table 16·9 with Table 16.10 indicates that this is primarily due to differentials in childbearing as opposed to the differentials in marriage rates, which were found by Higgins *et al.* (1962) to be the important factor in their study. The correlation coefficient between the IQ of individuals who were not childless and the number of offspring they produced was found to be $+0.0077$

– not significantly different from 0 at the 10 per cent level, and a shift in the negative direction from $r = +0.0503$. Thus it can be concluded that the relationship between the intelligence of an individual and the size of the family from which he comes has an inherent bias in the negative direction at the present time.

Secondly, the relationship between intelligence and fertility is definitely a dynamic one and appears to be changing rapidly. Higgins *et al.* (1962) and this study have shown that a bimodal relationship exists between IQ and fertility at the present time. It is doubtful that the

TABLE 16.10. *Proportion of individuals who never married in relation to IQ*

IQ range	Number	Per cent never married
⩾ 120	5/82	6·10
105–119	14/282	4·96
95–104	21/318	6·60
80–94	15/267	5·62
69–79	3/30	10·00
Total sample	58/979	5·92

biased techniques employed by previous studies could have completely obscured a high reproductive rate of the high IQ group. Therefore, it is highly probable that fertility is more positively correlated with intelligence than at any time during the past seventy-five years. It is a well-known fact that a tremendous change has taken place with respect to family size in the United States. There has been a decrease in the proportion of unmarried individuals, childless families and one-child families in addition to a decrease in the proportion of families having five or more children (Grabill, 1959). In this study the correlation between the size of the family from which an individual comes and the number of offspring produced is quite low ($r = +0.07$). Thus a positive change in the relationship between intelligence and fertility occurring simultaneously with the great changes taking place with respect to family size could help explain the observed positive correlation of intelligence with the number of offspring produced and the negative correlation of intelligence with the size of the family that the tested individual comes from.

Estimation of the change in the frequency of the genetic factors favouring high intelligence in the population under study

It is generally held that a major part of the variation in intelligence is due to genetic factors usually considered to be primarily quantitative in nature. It is highly probable that at least 50 to 60 per cent of the total variation in intelligence is due to hereditary factors. Vandenberg (1962a), for instance, has found that approximately 60 per cent of the variation in numerical, verbal, spatial and word fluency abilities in dizygous twins is due to hereditary factors. While an estimate of the amount of change in the frequency of the genetic factors favouring high intelligence must await further elucidation of the exact genetic factors involved, it is possible to estimate the direction of change in relation to these factors. A positive relationship between intelligence and fertility would indicate that an increase in the frequency of the genetic factors favouring high intelligence is taking place, while a negative relationship would indicate that a decrease in the frequency of these factors is taking place.

The observed positive relationship between the IQ of an individual and his subsequent completed fertility ($r = +0.05$) would seem to indicate that a small but positive increase in the genetic factors favouring high intelligence has taken place in the population under study. However, the negative effect of generation length (see Table 16.6) tends to counterbalance the positive effect due to the number of offspring produced to a certain extent. When generation length is taken into account, it has been shown that there is little difference between the relative fitness of the IQ $\geqslant$ 120 group and that of the 80–94 group. This bimodal relationship between IQ and total reproductive performance complicates any estimation of the change in the frequency of the genetic factors favouring high intelligence.

The degree of positive assortative mating in relation to intelligence was not determined for the population under study. While the direction of natural selection in relation to human intelligence is not affected by assortative mating, the rate at which the frequency of the genetic factors favouring high intelligence change is a function of the degree of positive assortative mating.

In spite of the complications due to generation length, the bimodal nature of the relationship between IQ and fertility, and the lack of assortative mating data, it can be safely concluded that the population under study has been in a state of equilibrium, or, more likely, has actually experienced a very slight increase in the genetic factors favouring high intelligence during the one generation that the population was

studied. The equilibrium or slight increase in the frequency of the
genetic factors favouring high intelligence is due not to the reproductive
success of the average IQ group but to the counterbalancing effects of
the high reproductive rates of the high IQ group ($\geqslant$ 120) and of the
low-normal IQ group (80–94).

SUMMARY

This is a follow-up study of 979 native white individuals born in 1916
or 1917 and who took the Terman Group Intelligence test in the sixth
grade while attending the Kalamazoo Public School system. It is the
first study that has taken into account all of the variables that affect
population growth (fertility, mortality, and generation length) by means
of the intrinsic rate of natural increase when estimating the direction and
intensity of natural selection in relation to human intelligence.

A bimodal relationship between intelligence and fertility was observed
in this study. The high fertility of the IQ $\geqslant$ 120 group relative to the
other IQ groups is probably a quite recent development brought about
by changes in the cultural environment during the last thirty to forty
years.

The observation that the intelligence of an individual is positively
correlated with the number of offspring he produces but negatively
correlated with the size of the family from which the individual comes
was explained by the facts that (1) the bias inherent in the relationship
between the intelligence of an individual and the size of the family
from which he comes tends to produce a negative relationship by itself;
and that (2) the relationship between intelligence and fertility is a dynamic one. It is highly probable that fertility is more positively correlated
with intelligence now than at any time during the past seventy-five
years.

When all variables affecting population growth have been taken into
account, the population under study has probably been in equilibrium
with respect to the genetic factors favouring high intelligence or, more
likely, has experienced a slight increase in the frequency of the genetic
factors favouring high intelligence.

The intensity of natural selection in relation to human intelligence
(the phenotypic load due to the variability in human intelligence) was
found to be 0·13 in this study where the IQ $\geqslant$ 120 group was the
optimum phenotype.

The conclusions of this paper pertain only to the population under
study. Because of the small size and uniqueness of the sample it is

impossible to estimate accurately the direction and intensity of natural selection in relation to human intelligence for the general population. Such an estimation must await the results of future studies which take into account all the variables affecting population growth and which are based on larger and different types of samples.

17

N. Bayley (1968)

Behavioural correlates of mental growth: birth to thirty-six years

American Psychologist, 23, pp. 1-17

The accumulated records of the Berkeley Growth Study have much to offer for explorations into the processes of growth. Their value is in part a function of the unusually complete set of longitudinal records, which cover a thirty-six-year life span for fifty-four cases who were seen at the most recent round of tests and interviews. Thus it is possible to trace the mental and physical trends of development in individuals with data observed and recorded at up to fifty-six scheduled testing sessions. Although the records include a variety of mental, motor, physical and behavioural measures, this report is concerned with mental growth and the relation to it of expressed emotions, attitudes and characteristic tendencies.

This sample was purposely selected for homogeneity, as full-term, healthy, hospital-born babies of white, English-speaking parents. The full sample of seventy-four babies remained in the study through seven months, sixty-three remained through at least three years, and of these forty-eight were seen regularly throughout the first eighteen years (at least forty times). At the thirty-six-year round, sixty-one of the three-year-or-longer sample were located and fifty-four of them were tested.

Although the sample is not strictly representative of the Berkeley population, it has a wide socioeconomic distribution which has remained essentially unchanged.

Our well-documented thirty-six-year histories of this essentially healthy population, though for the most part limited to certain developmental aspects of their lives, have generated data of a very compelling nature. These data, from very early in the study, have indicated the need to make changes in many of our assumptions, theories and hypotheses. Hence, from time to time, we have made relevant changes

in the research design, both in the nature of the data which were collected at successive ages, and in the procedures used in organizing and
evaluating the data.

The first challenge to accepted theory which was suggested by the
data was reported in a 1933 monograph on mental growth during the
first three years (Bayley, 1933b). The scores on the mental tests had
not conformed to the assumption, at that time widely held, that 'the IQ
is constant'. The finding that in the first two or three years of life the
children's rates of mental growth, and hence their IQs, were unstable
led me to various analyses of the items and subgroups of the items, in an
effort to understand the nature of the early mental processes, and to
find a core of mental items in the First-Year scale (Bayley, 1933a) that
would predict later intelligence.

In one form or another I have been continually preoccupied with
this process of analysis of the mental test scores and their correlates
ever since. During the first twenty years, with the exception of two
studies on socioeconomic correlates, one of which included some
moderate correlations with optimal and attitude ratings (Bayley, 1940;
Bayley and Jones, 1937), our analyses were concerned primarily with
the nature of the intellective processes themselves. Reports have been
made on the consistencies, labilities and variabilities over time of scores
on different aspects of mental function (Bayley, 1949, 1955).

These early studies, as I look back on them now, appear to have
suffered from too much combining, both of population samples and of
test scores. That is, almost invariably statistical analyses were made
only on the total sample of approximately equal numbers of males and
females. Furthermore, the emotional and attitudinal variables were
selected and combined by armchair decisions as to which kinds of
behaviours might enhance or depress the scores. Over time, it has
become increasingly evident that the cognitive as well as the emotional
processes of males and females must be treated separately in all statistical analyses. Also, recently, with the able help of colleagues (with both
theoretical and statistical sophistication) and with the advantages
of modern computer techniques, it has been possible to reanalyse both
the test items and behaviour ratings and to combine them, on the basis
of their intercorrelations, into new meaningful clusters composed of
related variables. When these new 'factors' are used in correlational
analyses they have revealed many intriguing patterns of interrelations.

Some ten years ago Schaefer and Bell's development of a material
behaviour research instrument, from notes and descriptive materials in
the Berkeley Growth Study files (Schaefer, Bell and Bayley, 1959),

furnished a new tool and initiated a new approach to the analyses of the behavioural data. Out of the use of the maternal behaviour scale and subsequent similar treatments of child behaviours, there grew a series of reports by Bayley and Schaefer, covering the first eighteen years of records, and exploring the interrelations among maternal and child behaviours and their relations to intelligence (Bayley and Schaefer, 1964; Schaefer and Bayley, 1963).

It has now become possible to extend these studies of both behavioural and mental variables through thirty-six years, and to look into patterns of interrelations among various kinds of cognitive abilities as well as among a variety of behaviours expressing emotions and attitudes.

We can look at concurrent intercorrelations of behaviours and cognitive functions; we can select cognitive abilities at any one age level and note the manner in which they relate over time, forward or backward, to various behaviours, or we can start with certain behaviours at a given age and explore their relations to mental abilities over time. It will be possible here to explore only a sampling of these interrelations, and I have chosen to concentrate on a series of scores based on two sets of data, one at each end of the thirty-six-year span. These are the Precocity factor scores of the First-Year Mental scale and concurrent infant behaviour ratings at one end of the age span; and at the adult end, the Wechsler intelligence subscales and the circumplex-ordered personality variables of the Block Q set as rated from the thirty-six-year interviews.

FIRST-YEAR MENTAL FACTORS

First, let us review briefly the First-Year Mental precocity scores, which have, in part, been reported previously (Bayley, 1966; Cameron, Livson and Bayley, 1967). Because the children were tested at monthly intervals from 1 through 15 months, it was possible to derive an age-at-first-passing score for each of the 115 items in this scale. With this range of scores, we were able to compute product-moment correlations for each item with each of the other 114, even though they might be at widely different levels of ability. A factor derived from this correlation matrix could, therefore, contain items from the scale's entire 15-month span of difficulty. Actually, the six factors which were derived by the Tryon cluster analysis did not follow any neat set of concomitantly developing separate functions. Instead they tend to draw loadings from restricted age ranges. Thus the six factors can be arranged in a chronological sequence. They fall into order, from Visual Following at 2 to 3 months, through Social Responsiveness 3 to 7 months, Perceptual Interest at two levels, 1 to 2 and 15 to 17 months, Manual Dexterities 4 to 7 months, Vocalizations 5 to 14 months and Object Relations 10 to 17 months. Of the six, only one factor, which we have called 'Vocalizations', and whose items range, in their median age placement, from 5·6 to 13·5 months, shows any clear correlation with later intelligence. However, this relationship after 3 years of age is found only for the girls and not for the boys. There is a striking sex difference in the correlations, and for the girls a striking consistency of the correlations into the adult years.

THE THIRTY-SIX-YEAR INTERVIEW *Q* SORT

Before exploring further the various correlates of this infant Vocalization factor, let us now turn to the thirty-six-year interview material, to present a new set of adult behaviour variables for use in further comparisons.

For the most recent round of tests and measures on this sample, after each subject's customary mental and physical tests and measures, an appointment was made with him or her for an interview with a person who knew nothing of the early history or current status beyond a few items such as education, marital status, and possibly occupation. With two exceptions, the women were interviewed by an experienced woman (Katherine Thanas) with a master's degree in social welfare. Two women, of necessity, were interviewed in places far removed from California, one by D. Eichorn and one by N. Bayley. The men were interviewed by a clinical psychologist (William Smelser) who had previously interviewed for one of the other Institute studies. All interviews were tape recorded and transcribed. Each interview was *Q*-sorted by three persons, the interviewer (with the two exceptions noted above) and two clinical psychologists (drawn from a pool of ten sorters), on the 100-item Block *Q* set (Block, 1961). The sorters listened to short segments of the tapes and then rated from the typescripts.

For each sex, the seventy *Q*-set items with the highest interrater agreement have been arrayed in a Guttman circumplex (Guttman, 1954a), using the computer programme developed by Lingoes (1965). The resulting order of behaviours is indicated diagrammatically in Fig. 17.1. The circumplex for males follows, in a general way, the pattern of correlational 'neighbouring' that had been derived for their earlier behaviours in infancy, childhood and adolescence. That is, if we section the circle by two orthogonal vectors, the behaviours on the upper half tend to be expressive or extraverted, those on the lower half internalized, withdrawn or introverted. Behaviours in the upper right quadrant in this instance described men who are uncontrolled, impatient, tending towards maladjustment. Behaviours in the lower right quadrant are hostile, fearful and distant. The lower left quadrant describes men who are problem-orientated, philosophical, with cognitive concerns and

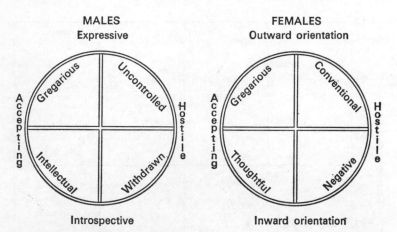

Fig. 17.1 General circumplex orientations of seventy Block *Q*-set items at 36 years.

wide interests. As they move along the circle towards 270° they grow increasingly well adjusted, and in the upper left quadrant, the behaviours include warmth, poise, social acceptance and gregariousness.

The circumplex for the women, shown here on the right, is somewhat different, primarily in the upper right quadrant. In this quadrant we find women's behaviours which are conventional, bland and more controlled; in the lower right quadrant are the negative, hostile and moody behaviours. The lower left quadrant, as for the males, contains behaviours which may be characterized as intellectual, insightful, thoughtful, with wide interests; while the upper left quadrant may be described in part by the adjectives cheerful, poised, gregarious.

THE RELATION OF THIRTY-SIX-YEAR *Q* SET TO MENTAL SCORES

In Fig. 17.2 we see, in their circumplex order, the pattern of correlations for the males of each of the seventy most reliable *Q*-set items, with the thirty-six-year WAIS Verbal and Performance IQs (Wechsler, 1958).

The twenty-five adult males for whom we have Q sorts from interviews at approximately thirty-six years show a clear pattern of correlations between IQs and these personality variables. The patterns of correlations are similar for both Verbal and Performance IQs but, at the extremes of both negative and positive relationships, the correlations are larger for the Verbal IQs.

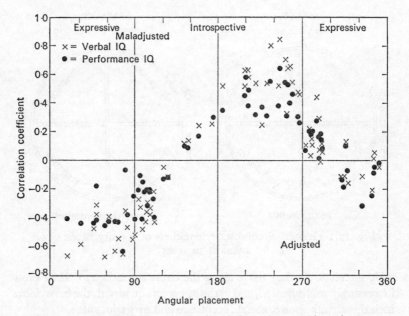

Fig. 17.2 Angular-placement-ordered Q set (seventy items): correlations with WAIS Verbal and Performance IQs at 36 years, males.

From this pattern of correlations we see that the impatient men who are lacking in inner controls have low IQs. The strongest correlation, of −0·68, is between Verbal IQ and the item, 'various needs tend toward relatively direct and uncontrolled expression; unable to delay gratification'. Other significant negative correlations are with more clearly maladjusted variables represented by the adjectives 'negativistic', 'self-pitying', 'moody' and 'hostile'. As we move along through fearful and withdrawn to increasingly controlled behaviours, the correlations change from zero with behaviours characterized as distant and avoiding. They then shift to correlations of positive sign with the attributes 'fantasy' and 'unusual thought processes'. The correlations become strongly positive with such Q-set variables as 'critical', at 185°, 'intro-

spective' and 'concern with philosophical problems', 'socially perceptive', 'intellectual value' and 'wide interests' (244°). The highest correlation with Verbal IQ, 0·84, is with the rating 'A high degree of intellectual capacity' (246°).

The correlations become much more modest in the extraverted,
adjusted quadrant, where we find rs below 0·20 with 'warm' (273°) and
the neighbouring items 'calm' and 'talkative', and a tendency towards
negative rs with 'gregarious' (333°) and 'conservative values' (351°).

In general, according to this circumplex order of behaviours, the

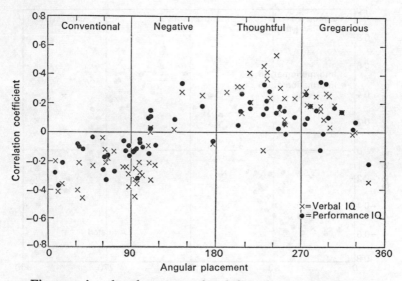

Fig. 17.3 Angular-placement-ordered Q set (seventy items): correlations with WAIS Verbal and Performance IQs at 36 years, females.

men in this sample with high intelligence are best characterized as
introspective, thoughtful, and concerned with problems, meanings and
values; they are men who are perceptive and have a wide range of
interests. The least intelligent are more often found to be impatient,
prone to vent their hostilities, and to project them on to others.

The women's correlations (for an N of 25) between behaviour and
intelligence test scores, shown in Fig. 17.3, are much smaller than the
men's. However, the pattern of positive and negative correlations is
very similar.

The women's IQs correlate negatively with the conventional, bland,
vulnerable and anxious; positively with the thoughtful and insightful

with wide interests; and very insignificantly with the cheerful, poised and gregarious attributes. Again, in the areas where the women's correlations tend towards significance, they are larger with the Verbal than the Performance IQs.

The foregoing patterns of relations are with the two main subdivisions of the WAIS (the Verbal and the Performance scales) and for the concurrent (thirty-six-year) data, both interview and mental test. We may extend the comparisons both by a look into selected subscales of the tests and by inquiry into the stabilities of these relations over time.

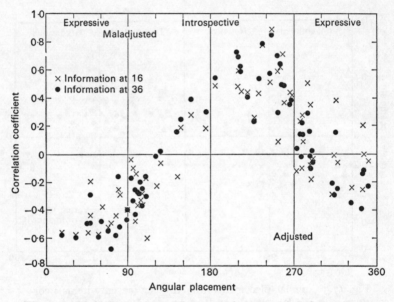

Fig. 17.4 Male *Q*-set circumplex: correlations with Information at 16 and 36 years.

A Tryon cluster analysis was made on this sample by James Cameron for the Wechsler scores on tests at five ages – the eleven scales of W–B at 16, 18, 21 and 26 years and the WAIS at 36 (Bayley, 1967, manuscript). I shall not at this time go into the details of this analysis. However, I have selected for comparisons on the *Q* sort, two scales which represent clearly different factors.

In Fig. 17.4 we see the males' circumplex-ordered thirty-six-year *Q*-set variables correlated with their scores on Information, at two ages, at 36 and at 16 years (Wechsler, 1944, 1958). The information test has the largest factor coefficients in the Information-Vocabulary dimension of the male cluster analysis. It is also, for these males, a highly stable test: The correlation between Information scores at 16 and 36 years is 0·79 (Bayley, 1966).

There is, here, marked stability in the patterns of behavioural-mental correlations over this twenty-year interval. In some instances, notably in the 'adjusted' half of the circumplex, the correlations with the 16-year Information scores are higher than with the 36-year scores. Again, the highest *r*s are with 'intellectual capacity' —0·84 at 36 years and 0·88 at 16 years.

By contrast, as seen in Fig. 17.5 the women's correlations between

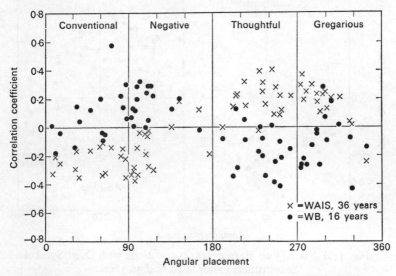

Fig. 17.5 Female *Q*-set circumplex: correlations with Information at 16 and 36 years.

personality variables and scores on Information are not only lower, but also unstable over time. Their 16-to-36-year retest correlation on the Information subscale is only 0·38. The pattern of the concurrent 36-year correlations tends to be in the same direction as for the males. However, at 16 years the correlations are reversed, with positive, though mostly low, correlations between scores and such attributes as 'weak ego' and 'thin skinned', and negative correlations with the traits 'ethically consistent' and 'candid'. The largest negative *r* (−0·43) is with 'interest in the opposite sex'.

Another subscale, Digit Symbol Substitution, is the most stable for the women over the 16-to-36-year interval (*r* = 0·64) and is also the identifying scale in an independent female factorial dimension. For the males this subtest is also strongly weighted in a factor which is also moderately stable (16×36 year r is 0·69) but it is less independent of the verbal factors. The male Q set circumplex-ordered correlations with Digit Symbol scores at 16 and at 36 years are shown in Fig. 17.6. Again, the pattern of correlations is clear and is even stronger for the 16-year than for the 36-year test. The pattern differs somewhat from that of the Information scale in showing significant positive correlations

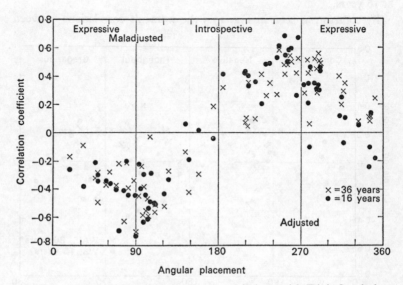

Fig. 17.6 Male Q-set circumplex: correlations with Digit Symbol Substitution scores at 16 and 36 years.

well into the extraverted adjusted quadrant of the behaviour circumplex.

For the females, however, (Fig. 17.7) it appears that scores on this Digit Symbol test are not only independent of other factors of the menral scale, but they are also independent of the behaviour variables, at both ages. This independence of both Digit Symbol scores and personality attributes raises the question whether for females the genetic determiners of intelligence may be relatively strong in this type of mental process.

One aspect of intelligence in which there is a well-known sex difference in ability is Arithmetic. What, then, are the sex differences in the correlates of Arithmetic scores?

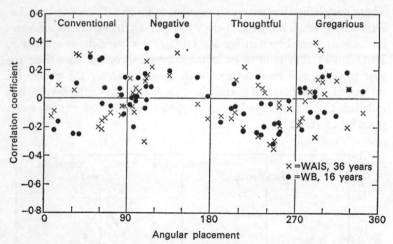

Fig. 17.7 Female Q-set circumplex: correlations with Digit Symbol
Substitution scores at 16 and 36 years.

We see in Fig. 17.8 the pattern of correlations for females between
16-year and 36-year Arithmetic scores and the circumplex-ordered
Q set. At 16 years, high scores in arithmetic are related to maladjusted
behaviours (the highest r of 0·64 is with the item 'subtly negativistic')
and low scores with 'personally charming' (the largest r is −0·62).

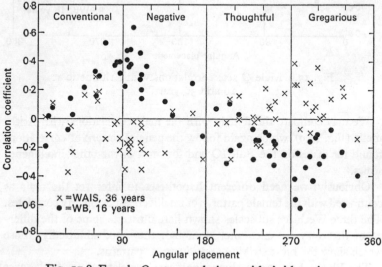

Fig. 17.8 Female Q set: correlations with Arithmetic at
16 and 36 years.

These correlational patterns are similar to those with the 16-year Information scale. This pattern does not persist, however. At 36 years (as indicated on the chart by the crosses) the correlations are lower. Furthermore, they tend to be in the opposite direction from their 16-year patterns, and more in line with those found for the males. An inspection of the tables of correlations for the 18-, 21- and 26-year tests indicates that the change has already, to a considerable extent, taken place by 18 years.

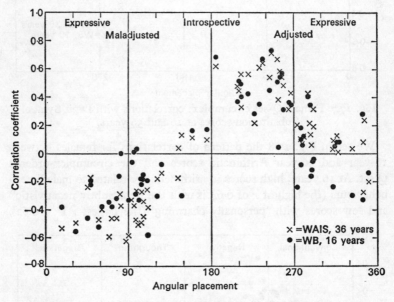

Fig. 17.9 Male Q set: correlations with Arithmetic at
16 and 36 years.

We may compare the female with the male correlations with Arithmetic (Fig. 17.9), which again follow the general pattern of correlations found for males on the Full IQ and for most of the other intelligence scales.

Obviously, we need different hypotheses to interpret the male as contrasted with the female patterns of intelligence-personality correlates. The three Wechsler subscales shown here illustrate some of the differences that may be encountered though they are, admittedly, those which show the most striking and divergent patterns.

The Block Q-set items show significant correlations for both sexes with 4-year-old precocity (i.e. age at first passing) factor scores on

'Verbal Knowledge'. The pattern of *r*s is similar to that for the 36-year IQs, and they range between plus and minus 0·60. The 1-year vocalization factor precocity scores, however, are entirely uncorrelated with the 36-year personality variables.

MENTAL SCORES AND BEHAVIOURS AT ADOLESCENCE

Possibly, we may find some clues to the sex differences in these correlations if we move further backward, down the age scale to an earlier set of behaviours.

The adolescent behaviour scores were developed by Schaefer (Schaefer and Bayley, 1963) from a set of notes written at the time of

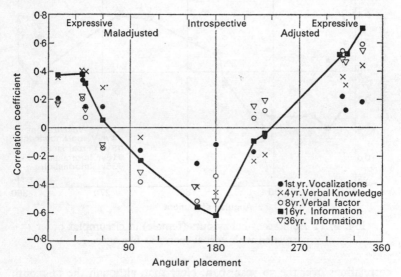

Fig. 17.10 Adolescent behaviours (male) in circumplex order correlated with verbal scores at five ages.

the tests for ages 13 to 18 years. Each child was rated on ninety-six adjectives which had been selected to represent Schaefer's theoretical personality circumplex. Cluster scores were then derived on the basis of intercorrelations of items; there are twelve behaviour clusters for the males and fourteen for the females. The ordinates of the circumplex-ordered variables have been called extraversion versus introversion and adjusted versus maladjusted. A set of correlations with mental scores on the twelve male behaviours, in their circumplex angular placements is shown in Fig. 17.10. The mental scores presented here are of verbal scores at five ages; the 11-month Vocalization Precocity Score, the 8-year Stanford Binet First Factor, which is primarily verbal (McNemar, 1942), and the Wechsler Information scale at 16 and at 36 years. Verbal scales were selected as most likely to show persistent relations. A line is drawn through the 16-year points, to show the trend at the age concurrent with the behaviour ratings. The solid dots represent the earliest test – the 11-month Vocalization factor, the open triangles, the 36-year *r*s. There is, for the males, a surprisingly consistent pattern of

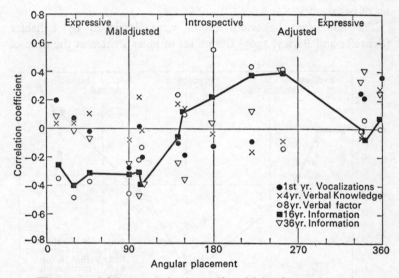

Fig. 17.11 Adolescent behaviours (female) in circumplex order correlated with verbal scores at five ages.

correlations over the 36-year span. Note that, although the 11-month Vocalization scales are not related to the boys' later IQs, they do relate in the same way to the personality variables.

Fig. 17.11 shows the correlations of the same mental tests with the female adolescent behaviours. The positive correlations occur in the introverted-adjusted quadrant for 8-year and older tests. There is little or no pattern or consistency in these correlations. Even the concurrent 16-year Information test shows only a mild directional pattern of correlations with the behaviours. The female Verbal intelligence scores, again, are seen to be relatively independent of their behaviours. It may be that the emotional turmoil of adolescence is more disruptive of the girls' than of the boys' cognitive processes. As we have already noted, for the 36-year Q sort the girls' correlations with the 16-year W-B scores are unlike those at later ages. However, at all of these ages their mental scores are correlated with 11-month Vocalization scores.

MENTAL SCORES AND BEHAVIOURS IN INFANCY

So far, we have been discussing the relations of intelligence to behaviours at midadulthood and at adolescence. Let us now look at behaviours in infancy, and their relations to later mental functioning.

For each of thirteen ages, 10 through 36 months, when the babies were given a variety of mental and physical measures and tests, they were rated (on a 7-point scale) on a number of behaviours. Some of these behaviours have been utilized in our studies of maternal and child interrelations. In their circumplex order, they may be identified by the names: Active, Rapid, Responsive to Persons, Calm, Positive Behaviour, Happy and Not Shy.

Bayley and Schaefer (1964) have shown that there are complex, but internally consistent patterns of correlations over the first eighteen years between these behaviours and Full Scale IQs. Briefly, boy babies who are active and rapid before 15 months earn high mental ability scores in infancy but low scores later; while if they are active and rapid at 18 to 36 months the reverse is true. Calm, happy and positively responding boys, particularly at 27 to 36 months, may earn low scores in infancy but are likely to have above-average IQs at 5 years and thereafter. In contrast, girl babies' scores were found to be correlated with concurrent measures, so that high scores were found for infant girls who tended to be responsive to persons, active, happy, positively responding, and calm, but after 3 years of age the correlations with IQ dropped to insignificant levels.

It has seemed possible, however, that there might be greater consistency in patterns of correlation between these behaviours and certain kinds of mental ability, that is, factor or subscale scores. To explore this possibility, again verbal scores have been selected because they seem to offer the greatest likelihood of long-term significant relations. Throughout our various comparisons with intelligence subscales, the verbal scores are most highly correlated with personality variables. Also, the verbal scores appear to be most stable. It is a Vocalization scale in the first year that, for the girls, shows significant correlations with their verbal scores over time; and in the twenty-year adult span the males' verbal scales are most stable.

We have, therefore, explored the correlations of verbal scores at all ages with each of the seven infant behaviours.

In Fig. 17.12 we see the correlations with Activity. There are four sets of curves, each of which covers the thirty-six-year span of the verbal subtests. In the upper left quadrant are the correlations with the average activity scores at 10, 11 and 12 months; at the upper right are the correlations with 13-, 14- and 15-month activity; at lower left with 18-, 21- and 24-month ratings; and at lower right with 27-, 30- and 36-month ratings. The solid line represents the correlations for boys; the broken line, for girls.

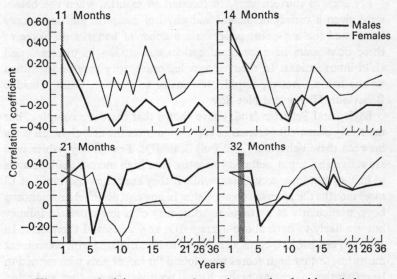

Fig. 17.12 Activity at 10 to 36 months correlated with verbal scores 1 to 36 years.

There is a tendency for boys who are active at 10 through 15 months (the two upper charts) to have low verbal scores (that is, the *rs* are of negative sign) from 4 through 36 years. However, there is an abrupt shift between 15 and 18 months. For the 18-to-36-month ages activity is correlated positively from 8 through 36 years. The correlations with the 18-to-24-month ratings are even higher, and at times approach statistical significance. The girls' verbal scores, after the first year, are unrelated to activity except for the 27-to-36-month ratings. Even though the correlations involved in this comparison are moderate there is a consistency over time in their trends which lends some credence to their representatives.

In Fig. 17.13 the verbal scores for ages 1 to 36 years are correlated with Rapidity (i.e. speed of movement) at the same four age levels in infancy. Again, starting at the 4-year verbal score, boys' Rapidity through 15 months is negatively correlated, and from 18 to 36 months it tends to be positively correlated with verbal scores. The girls' verbal scores show little or no correlation with early rapidity.

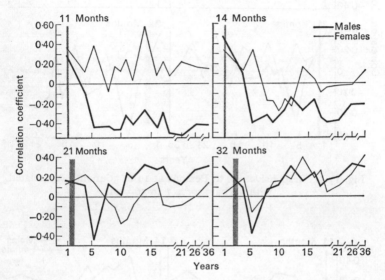

Fig. 17.13 Rapidity at 10 to 36 months correlated with verbal scores 1 to 36 years.

Responsiveness to Persons, in Fig. 17.14, shows no correlational trends for either sex. The girls in this sample tended to be more responsive to persons than were the boys, but this variable, as such, does relate to mental abilities.

In Fig. 17.15 ratings of Calmness (the reverse of Excitability) at all ages for boys, but not for girls, tend to be positively correlated with verbal scores, and most highly for the 27-to-36-month ratings. The girls' ratings early (10 to 15 months) are negatively correlated with their mental scores after about 12 years.

Positive Behaviour (as opposed to Negativism) in Fig. 17.16 shows no sex differences for the first two sets of ratings, but clear differences for the 18-to-36-month ratings. At this age level, the boys' correlations with verbal scores at all ages tend to be positive, and they increase in size through the 36-month ratings. For the girls, the correlations

K

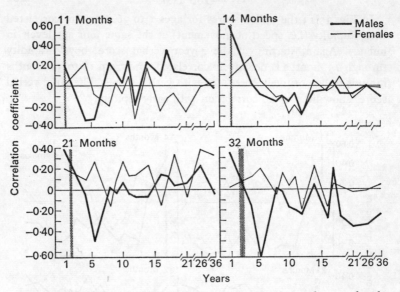

Fig. 17.14 Responsiveness to Persons at 10 to 36 months correlated with verbal scores 1 to 36 years.

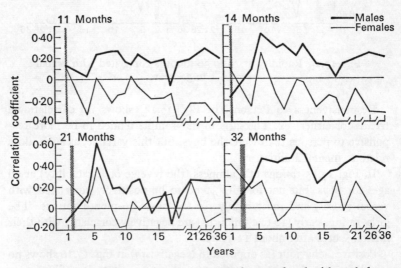

Fig. 17.15 Calmness at 10 to 36 months correlated with verbal scores 1 to 36 years.

are negligible, but with a tendency towards negative sign at the 18-to-24-month level.

Going on to Fig. 17.17, Happiness, we see that happy boy babies, especially as 2- and 3-year-olds, are likely to earn high verbal scores. By contrast, it appears that girl babies who are *un*happy around 1 year of age may have higher verbal scores later.

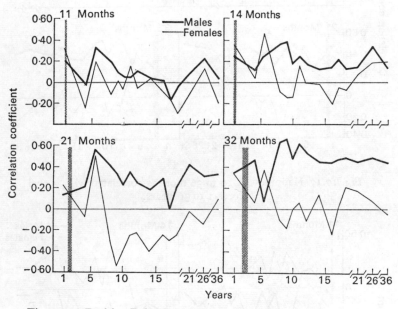

Fig. 17.16 Positive Behaviour at 10 to 36 months correlated with verbal scores 1 to 36 years.

In Fig. 17.18, Shyness, we find one other early behaviour which appears to correlate with the girls' later verbal scores. The girl babies who are shy with strangers in the first 2 years, tend to do well later, though their shyness in the third year is, like the boys' at all four age-levels, unrelated to verbal scores.

In summarizing the patterns of correlation between behaviours in the first three years and verbal scores over the thirty-six-year span, there are, for these samples, some persistent patterns of correlation. If we were to generalize from these patterns, we should expect high verbal scores for the boys who are calm, positively responding and happy, and who are active after 15 months. What is more, these scores should remain high through thirty-six years. However, if we were to try to predict the girls'

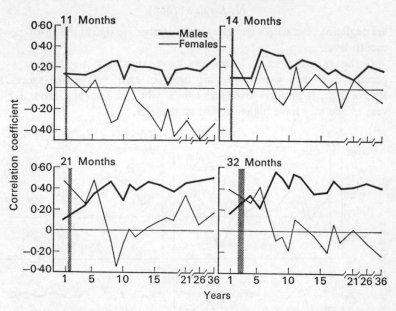

Fig. 17.17 Happiness at 10 to 36 months correlated with verbal
scores 1 to 36 years.

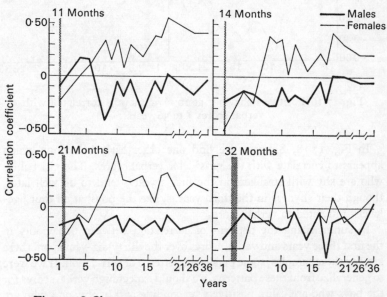

Fig. 17.18 Shyness at 10 to 36 months correlated with verbal
scores 1 to 36 years.

adult verbal scores from these behaviours, we could only make some tentative guesses that high scorers would have been shy between 10 and 24 months, and perhaps unhappy between 10 and 12 months.

MATERNAL BEHAVIOURS AND IQS

An aspect of the children's early environment which also plays a part in their mental abilities is the maternal behaviours which these children experienced. Ratings of maternal behaviours in the first 3 years were shown by Schaefer and Bayley (1963) to be correlated with their children's behaviours, and also (Bayley and Schaefer, 1964) with the children's intelligence through 18 years. The correlations were greater for the boys than for the girls. Furthermore, the boys' scores, of both behaviours and intelligence, correlated throughout the eighteen-year span with maternal behaviours in the first three years. The girls' scores, on the other hand, showed persistent correlations primarily with indicators of parental *ability*. These sex differences in patterns of correlations led us to the suggestion that there are genetically determined sex differences in the extent to which the effects of early experiences (such as maternal love and hostility) persist. The girls appeared to be more resilient in returning to their own characteristic inherent response tendencies. Boys, on the other hand, were more permanently affected by the emotional climate in infancy whether it was one of warmth and understanding or of punitive rejection.

To bring this aspect of the study up to date, we show in Fig. 17.19 the patterns of correlations between the early maternal behaviours and their children's IQs at thirty-six years. Although most of the correlations are small, again we find negative correlations as low as -0.60 with maternal hostility and positive correlations as high as 0.49 with maternal love and understanding, with the stronger relations for the boys.

In general, these findings extend through the entire thirty-six-year span the same patterns of correlations Bayley and Schaefer (1964) reported for the first eighteen years. They reflect stability in a number of both personality variables and mental abilities. We have noted elsewhere (Bayley, 1966) that in this study the females' mental abilities stabilize at an earlier age, while the males exhibit greater stability later.

When one general type of mental function is involved, in this instance vocal–verbal ability, then the girls' scores at as young as 1 year, on the Vocalization Precocity score, are persistently correlated with later verbal scores. The relation reaches a high point with W–B Verbal IQ at 26 years, when the r is 0.80 for the girls, but only 0.26 for the boys.

At thirty-six years, there is something of a drop, with correlations of 0·35 for the women and 0·06 for the men. A study of the personality correlates of these intelligence scores repeatedly reveals considerable independence of the girls' intelligence from their personality variables. The only early behaviour which shows even moderate relations with the females' later intelligence is shyness. Later, their correlations with both adolescent and adult attributes of personality are for the most part small and insignificant.

By contrast to the girls, the boys' test scores are far more bound to

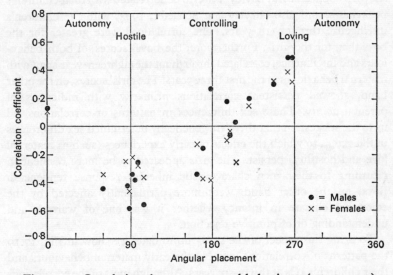

Fig. 17.19 Correlations between maternal behaviours (0 to 3 years) and WAIS IQs at 36 years.

behaviour variables which may be characterized as adjusted or introspective, versus maladjusted or hostile. Their close tie between intelligence and introspective adjusted behaviours becomes established at or near 3 to 4 years of age. Their verbal test scores become stable only with the 4-year Verbal Knowledge Precocity score. There is, before this age, short-term consistency in the boys' First-Year Vocalization scores. Their correlation with total mental scores, at three age levels for tests at months 13 through 36 are 0·51, and 0·53, but at the 48-month level the correlation drops suddenly to 0·20, and subsequent correlations remain low, varying between plus and minus 0·26 (see Fig. 17.2). When this abrupt change in the boys' retest correlations between intelligence test scores is compared with the increase at about the same age of correlations between their test scores and ratings of Positive Behaviour and Happiness, it seems possible that this is a 'critical period' for boys and that emotional factors operating at this time may serve permanently to depress or to enhance the abilities of many children, primarily boys.

SUMMARY

This paper has been a factual and objective report on some behavioural correlates of mental growth. The non-specialist, in reading it, may well suffer from data overload and understandably yearn for a good theory, or set of coherent theories, to explain the data and correlations presented. But on this occasion, at least, I must leave this needed theory construction to others. What I have tried to do, rather, is to give you an empirically warranted map which, though incomplete, has, I trust, helped to focus attention on some heretofore overlooked areas that appear to be well worth exploring. Much available information from other studies, using both similar and different research methods, is in accord with our findings (e.g. Drews, 1964; Honzik, 1967; Kagan and Moss, 1962; Terman and Oden, 1947). To this extent other researches tend to confirm the assumption that our Berkeley Growth Study sample is generally representative. When we have integrated, from this and other studies, the available information on the pattern of interrelations among cognitive processes and other behaviour variables, together with their relative stability over time, for each sex separately, we shall have gained useful knowledge about the processes of mental growth. We can then see more clearly what new researches will be most fruitful. More specifically, we shall be better prepared to undertake scientific inquiries into sex-linked processes of interaction between the genes and their various environments in the growth of intelligence.

18

J. McV. Hunt (1969)

Some implications of Piaget's observations and theoretical conceptions

D. Elkind and J. H. Flavell (eds.), *Studies in Cognitive Development*:
Essays in Honour of Jean Piaget (Oxford University Press), pp. 6–30

Piaget's observations and his theorizing provide a basis for a critical re-evaluation and assessment of various of the theoretical beliefs that many of us hold because we were taught them by Piaget's predecessors or by some of his contemporaries. Important among these is the contrast between the views of behavioural development formulated by Gesell and by Piaget.

PIAGET VERSUS GESELL

As I read the writings of contemporary students of developmental psychology, I glean that the depth of the dissonance between the outlooks and conceptions of Piaget and Gesell has hardly yet been fully appreciated. It is true that their methods and results show certain similarities. Both have employed the cross-sectional method of confronting children of various ages with situations and materials and then observing how these children behave. Both describe behaviours typical of children at successive ages. Both recognize an epigenetic system of change in the structure of behaviour as essentially predetermined. Piaget, however, views them as products of the sensorimotor interaction between the infant or child and his environmental circumstances. Moreover, in his observations of his own three children, Piaget employed a longitudinal method. He observed them repeatedly in similar situations and confronted them repeatedly with given objects and materials.

To be sure, Gesell and his collaborators occasionally discussed organism-environment interaction. Thus, Gesell (1928) wrote, 'The constitution and conditions of the organism are intimately inter-dependent. The organismic pattern of one moment, responsive to both internal and external environment, influences the pattern of succeeding moments. In a measure previous environmental effects are perpetuated by incorporation with constitution.' This statement, in itself, is an excellent expression of interactionism. Elsewhere, Gesell *et al.* (1940) noted,

> . . . this serve(s) to show how supremely important it is for society to achieve through education and family life an optimal culture to insure a maximum of growth to infants and children. Culture provides the milieu . . . the conditions of growth. It provides a vast complex of symbols, cues, and foci of interest, which are assimilated into the very texture of the growing personality. Culture operates most profoundly and projectively in the first five years of life.

In one of his still later publications, Gesell (1954, p. 335) wrote, 'Infancy is the period in which the individual realizes his racial inheritance . . . but infancy itself is a product of evolution. It was evolved not only to perpetuate a groundwork of racial inheritance, but also to add thereto a contingent margin of specific modifiability.'

In terms of the general impact of Gesell's contributions, however, these statements are little more than lip service. His work was basically normative in nature. He described the patterns of behaviour typical, or statistically modal, for each age. In the *First Five Years of Life*, Gesell described mental growth as, 'A progressive morphogenesis of patterns of behaviour . . .' (1940, p. 7). Moreover, in a majority of his statements about the causal basis for mental growth, he said, in one form or another, the following, 'The basic configurations, correlations, and successions of behaviour patterns are *determined by the innate process of growth called maturation*' (Gesell, 1945, italics are mine). In the introduction to his film, *Life Begins*, he emphasized the importance of 'intrinsic growth'. Elsewhere he defined intrinsic growth as, 'the unfolding of behaviour with anatomical maturation'.

In his theorizing, Gesell articulated several principles. All are essentially descriptive in character, and all but one reflect his emphasis on genetic predeterminism. In introducing his principles, Gesell (1954, p. 337) wrote, 'The growth of tissues, of organs, and of behaviour is obedient to identical laws of development morphology.' Gesell's (1954) principles numbered five: (1) developmental direction, (2) reciprocal interweaving, (3) functional asymmetry, (4) individuating maturation, (5) self-regulatory fluctuation. In the first three and the fifth Gesell explicitly put the causal basis for behavioural development on anatomical maturation. The developmental processes go on in time, to be sure, but Gesell's conception of them gave no indication that he considered them to be plastic, or subject to appreciable modification by the circumstances encountered. Only the fourth of these principles, that of 'individuating maturation', makes an explicit place for environmental influence. In opening his discussion of this principle, he made these statements (Gesell, 1954, p. 354):

> This principle may help us to recognize the mechanism by means of which the behavioural organism achieves its species characteristics and yet at the same time, makes specific adaptations within its environmental field. From the moment of fertilization, intrinsic and extrinsic factors cooperate in a unitary manner, but the original impulse of growth and the matrix of morphogenesis is endogenous rather than exogenous. The so-called environment, whether internal of external, does not generate the progressions of development. Environmental factors support, inflect, and specify; but they do not engender the basic forms and sequences of ontogenesis.

In the subsequent sections of this theoretical paper on growth and development, Gesell discusses 'self-regulatory fluctuation', 'the individuality of growth careers' and 'the stability of mental growth careers'. In each of these sections, as their headings imply, Gesell contended, and supported his contention with evidence of a sort, that the individual's behavioural development is essentially predetermined. Moreover, in his consideration of predeterminism, Gesell made no distinction between the rate of development and the order in which the patterns of behaviour appear.

In his theory of the causal basis for the epigenetic changes in behaviour and thought, Piaget (1936, 1937, 1950a) continually emphasizes accommodation, assimilation and the lack of equilibrium between aspects of the infant's behavioural repertoire and the circumstances encountered. These are his terms for the adaptive changes that organisms make in their encounters with environmental circumstances. Accommodation may be defined as that modification in a sensorimotor organization (or schema – to use Piaget's term), or in a conceptual operation or construction, that comes about in the course of encounters with new circumstances where the existing organization does not quite fit. Assimilation is the term given to the internalization of the accommodative change. One knows that assimilation has occurred when the infant or child employs the newly modified sensorimotor or conceptual organization in a novel situation. One might say that one recognizes assimilation when an accommodative change in behaviour or thought (as reflected in language) generalizes to a new situation.

The concept of equilibrium is more difficult to explain. Equilibrium is Piaget's (1950a, pp. 6–8) term for the stability of a behavioural organization. In the case of sensorimotor organizations, including all perceptions and motor habits, the equilibrium is limited to certain circumstances. Each such sensorimotor organization involves cognitive and affective regulation (which I would term its motivational aspect). On the inside of the organism, this regulation is based on interest, effort, and such. On the outside, it is based on the value of the objects concerned in this search and in the solutions sought. When the infant or child encounters circumstances beyond the limits of his sensorimotor systems the equilibrium is upset. This lack of equilibrium of sensorimotor and pre-conceptual systems leads continually to accommodative modifications in them until certain of them achieve either the limits set by the genotype or achieve structures that can generalize indefinitely to the circumstances encountered. If the circumstance is not too far beyond the limits of his sensorimotor systems, these systems become modified in the attempt to accommodate the new circumstances.

In the locomotor domain, the infant gyrates on his stomach and squirms towards objects desired; then he creeps or scoots towards them; then he gets up on his feet and cruises and toddles, until he can finally walk and run. The child's strides may increase in length with his skeletal growth, and he may obtain minor increases in force, duration and rate of strides with special training, if he aspires to be an athlete. Otherwise, these locomotor skills remain essentially stable as they are employed as means in an endless variety of goal-directed activities. They achieve their genotypic limits. Only as men supplement their locomotor abilities mechanically with bicycles, automobiles, aeroplanes and rockets can men alter these abilities appreciably.

In the intellectual domain, ready-made systems of information-processing become extended with use. Each becomes coordinated through accommodations with other such systems, until sensorimotor action systems become internalized as imaginal symbolic systems that are combined with vocal imitation in language. These preconceptual named-images are transformed through accommodative modifications, demanded perhaps largely by efforts at communication, into what Piaget calls intuitive regulations. These regulations are then further transformed into the concrete intellectual operations that permit classifying, serializing of asymmetrical comparisons and counting. These concrete intellectual operations acquire an equilibrium because classifying, serializing and counting can be generalized to new circumstances indefinitely. Yet, since they constitute thought processes directed entirely by encounters with circumstances, they are inadequate to provide a basis for an examination of those operations. The lack of equilibrium induced by examining these operations in linguistic propositions leads to the formation of those formal operations of thought that Piaget (1950a) and his collaborators (Inhelder and Piaget, 1955) find appearing during adolescence. At this stage, thought directs perception in investigation, and the imaginal standards of what life and society might be supply the standards that motivate the adolescent towards reforming the world that exists. Piaget (1950a, p. 27) contends that 'logic is the mirror of thought'. The classificatory logic of Aristotle reflected the thought of the Aristotelian era. The formal logic of Boole (1854) represents the thought that man, in his scientific efforts, has developed largely since the Renaissance. Piaget has contended further that man may yet invent new modes of thought in the process of coping with the new instruments of his own invention.

In sum, then, Gesell and Piaget propose radically different interpretations of behavioural development. Yet, their interpretations do not represent the opposite poles on a polarity of emphasis on heredity and environment. While Gesell has presented a picture of behavioural development as something based essentially on anatomical maturation that is predetermined by heredity, Piaget has presented a picture of behavioural development as a process of changes in the structure of behaviour and of thought that come with the infant's or child's interacting with his circumstances. Piaget's position is neither hereditarian nor environmentalistic; it is both. It is interactionist.

PIAGET VERSUS S–R BEHAVIOUR THEORY

Piaget's view of development is not the polar opposite of Gesell's. The opposite of Gesell's predeterminism is extreme environmentalism. Environmentalism has its conceptual roots in John Locke's (1690) famous *Essay Concerning Human Understanding*. In the first book of this essay, Locke took his epistemological stand against innate ideas and against the notion that anything need be true simply because it has the weight of traditional authority. The first sentence in the second paragraph of Book II may be paraphrased as follows: 'Let us then suppose the mind to be, as we say, white paper void of all characters without any ideas; how comes it to be furnished?' The answer given by Locke to this question came in the words: 'From EXPERIENCE'.

Taken from the domain of mind in general and applied to individual organisms, and especially infant human beings, this assumption of the organism as a *tabula rasa* implies that the organism is something statically passive and that the course of knowledge resides in receptor input from environmental circumstances. While no serious theory of behavioural development has ever accepted fully these assumptions about the nature of living organisms, and especially of human beings, several of the central conceptions of stimulus–response (S–R) behaviour theory have approached such extreme environmentalism.

S–R behaviour theory appears to derive its origin from revolts against three relatively unrelated views that were dominant in the latter half of the nineteenth century. Two of these views were part and parcel of post-Darwinian thought. First, Darwin was especially interested in the continuity of evolution between the infrahuman species of animals and man. He was interested in showing this continuity of evolution both in anatomy (Darwin, 1859) and in behaviour. Darwin's (1872) behavioural efforts are to be found in his studies of the expression of emotions in man and animals. The theory of psychological faculties prevailed in the nineteenth century. Emotion was one faculty, intelligence another. Darwin was interested equally in seeing a continuity of evolution demonstrated for the faculty of intelligence as for that of emotion. Romanes (1883a, 1883b) attempted to do for intelligence what Darwin had already done for the expressions of the emotional faculty. Moreover, Darwin's younger cousin, Francis Galton (1869, 1883, 1886), extended the notion of predeterminism in individuals into that of fixed faculties and abilities. These he proposed to measure with his anthropometric tests, and he hoped to develop human excellence in these tested traits through eugenics.

Second, both the biologists and psychologists of the post-Darwinian period tended to conceive not only of the sources of action but also of the patternings of action in terms of instincts predetermined by the heredity of the species or of the individual. Probably the most recent statement of instinct theory applied to human behaviour is to be found in William McDougall's (1908) *Social Psychology*.

Third, the human psychology of the late nineteenth century was largely concerned with consciousness and it took as its method introspection. This is true of the psychology of America (witness James, Hall and Ladd), of England (witness the mental chemistry of John Stuart Mill, the physiological psychology of Bain, and the evolutionary associationism of Herbert Spencer), of France (witness the psychopathologies of Charcot and Janet), and of Germany (witness the work of Fechner and Wundt).

S–R behaviour theory arose as a rejection of all three of these positions.

Its conceptual roots may be found in the mechanistic philosophy of the eighteenth century, in the theory of tropistic behaviour by Jacques Loeb (1890, 1912), in the critical extirpation of the intelligence faculty, imputed by Romanes (1883a, 1883b), from the causation of animal behaviour by C. Lloyd Morgan (1894) and in the experimental studies of problem solving in animals carried out by E. L. Thorndike (1898, 1911) in the basement of William James's home. S–R theory got a tremendous boost in popularity, moreover, in the polemics over the instinct theory. From the day of Thorndike onward, most of the S–R theorists were students of animal learning. Their studies of animal learning provided evidence against the instinct theory. In the polemics, Dunlap (1919) uttered the battle-cry, and John B. Watson (1924) and many others took up the cudgels shortly after World War I. Finally, behaviourism came into being as a reaction against the psychology of consciousness. Boring (1929) dates the beginning of the behaviouristic movement from Watson's (1913) first polemic entitled *Psychology as the Behaviorist Views It.* Shortly thereafter he published *Behavior, an Introduction to Comparative Psychology* (Watson, 1914). The behaviouristic movement adopted the objective methods of classical conditioning (Pavlov, 1927) and of trial-and-error learning (Thorndike, 1898, 1911).

In coming to an approximation of the Lockian *tabula rasa,* however, the revolt against the instinct theory is most important. In consequence of the evidence coming from the laboratories of animal psychology and the arguments made in the polemics over instinct theory, the S–R behaviour theories of such leading Americans as Thorndike (1911, 1935), Watson (1914, 1924), Weiss (1925), Hull (1943, 1952), and Skinner (1938, 1953) developed what became the dominant view in American psychology. While substantial differences existed among the theories of these men (Hilgard, 1956), they embraced in common not only something approaching the *tabula rasa* of original nature but also several other conceptions for which Piaget's observations and theorizing yield a relevant dissonance.

Original nature as an abundant repertoire of minute reflexes

The approximation of the *tabula rasa* in S–R behaviour theory derives from the assumption that the original nature of mammalian organisms including man consists in an abundant repertoire of minute reflexes. Instinct theory had held that even highly complex patterns of behaviour could have their organizations predetermined from the innate constitution of the species or the individual, and this made the problem of the criteria of innate behaviour important (Marquis, 1930). When the instinct theory was largely rejected (and it was never completely rejected by such behaviourists as Hunter (1920) and Thorndike (1935)), the alternative conception of original nature came to consist of a large number of minute, elementary, reflexes for which the knee-jerk was an approximate model. It was this conception that Dewey (1896) inveighed against in his famous paper on the reflex. Inasmuch as it was also conceived that any given reflex could be evoked through conditioning by any stimulus or combination of stimuli, and also that these minute reflexive actions could be combined without appreciable restraint into any sort of organization, this view constituted a near equivalent to the *tabula rasa* of John Locke. In this context John B. Watson (1928) claimed that, with the control of the circumstances to be encountered by any healthy infant from birth to 7 years, he could make of that infant anything desired. This has been the nature of environmentalism at its most extreme. It is a view that also emphasizes action in the process of learning and that minimizes the role of perception and of central processes. It is a view that has largely failed to take into account the developmental aspect of behaviour, for those embracing S–R behaviour theory have, in their investigations, employed as subjects chiefly nearly adult rats, often characterized as naïve because they have not participated in a preceding experiment, nearly adult dogs, nearly adult monkeys, and at the human level, chiefly college sophomores who were available because they were students in the first course in psychology.

Piaget's (1936, 1937) observations are highly dissonant with such a form of extreme environmentalism. In place of a repertoire of numerous minuscule reflexes, Piaget finds in the human neonate a very limited number of quite highly organized behavioural systems. These include: (*a*) sucking, (*b*) looking, (*c*) listening, (*d*) vocalizing, (*e*) grasping and (*f*) the various motor activities of the trunk and limbs. Piaget emphasizes that each of these is a ready-made sensorimotor organization at the human infant's birth. Unlike the investigators of the embryology of behaviour (Carmichael, 1954; Kuo, 1921, 1922, 1932a, 1932b, 1932c, 1932d, 1932e), Piaget has not concerned himself with how these ready-made organizations came into being before birth. It is interesting, however, that in his *Design for a Brain*, Ashby (1952) suggests precisely such component ready-made organizations. In his argument, Ashby suggests that if one were to design a complex electronic automaton to do what all mammals do, one would almost necessarily have to begin with a limited number of subsystems that the encounters with circumstances would then reorganize. Such a conception is, at once, a long way from the notion of instincts and a long way from the S–R behaviour theorists' notion of an innate repertoire consisting of a set of numerous simple reflexes. It is perhaps more important for the empirical validity of the notion, however, to note that the sensorimotor schemata that Piaget reports from his observations of his own three infants show a rather substantial degree of correspondence with the systems that neuro-anatomists have uncovered in their anatomical explorations of the brain as related to function (Papez, 1929). The neurologists find not only the visual system for looking and the auditory system for listening but also an olfactory system, a complex system for contact reception, and a vestibular system. While neurologists have never spoken of a grasping system or a vocalizing system, the motor portion of the brain has con-siderable differentiation, and there is a definite speech area. This prob-lem of defining units in behaviour is both old and difficult, but the correspondence here between Piaget's sensorimotor organizations and those systems traditional in neurology is sufficient to be impressive.

The existence of a few component organizations rather than a repertoire of numerous minuscule reflexes implies a theoretical con-ception of the nature of behavioural organization at birth intermediate between the predeterministic view on the one hand and the extreme environmentalism on the other. Piaget's (1936) observations tend to confirm such an intermediate view. These observations attest to an ample place for the effect of encounters with circumstances, but the infant organism is seen to be far from a blank page on which experience can write without constraint. Orderliness in the course of development derives not only from genetic preprogramming, but also from the nature of the manner in which these ready-made sensorimotor systems are capable of being coordinated and differentiated in the course of the infant's interaction with his environmental circumstances.

The ontogenesis of 'operants'

Piaget's observations and his theorizing provide evidence and con-ceptions dissonant with the conception prevalent among S–R behaviour theorists that organisms, including human beings, tend to be passive and inactive until driven into action by impelling stimulation. Among S–R behaviourists, Skinner (1938, 1953) is an exception to the rule that they are drive theorists, especially in the case of what he calls 'operant' activities. These are activities for which the instigating events in the environment cannot be specified, and they are to be contrasted with 'respondents' for which the instigating event can be specified.

In his aversion to theory, Skinner (1950) accepts the existence of 'operants' and 'respondents' as given. He is unconcerned with enlarging the nomological net to include either their ontogenetic origins or their physiological bases. Moreover, he avoids so completely conceptions based on the experimental subject's report that he eliminates consideration of such conceptions as expectations and intentions. The result is an almost endless list of empirical relationships with almost no principles (Ferster and Skinner, 1957).

Piaget's (1936) observations provide evidence of ontogenetic origins of actions that Skinner probably would call 'operants', and also of an epigenetic shift from 'respondent' status to 'operant' status. Immediately following birth, during the first sensorimotor stage, Piaget finds the human neonate with various ready-made systems – already named above – that are essentially responsive in character. At first, for instance, the sucking movements can be elicited only by contact of the lips with some external object, even under what Skinner calls the 'setting condition' of hunger from going several hours without food. In his observations of his son Laurent, Piaget (1936, pp. 343–8) noted that,

After the first feedings, one observes . . . sucking-like movements in which it is difficult not to see a sort of auto-excitation . . . [and] one is compelled to state that, in such a case, there is a tendency toward repetition, or, in objective terms, cumulative repetition . . . this need for repetition is only one aspect of a more general process which we can qualify as assimilation. The tendency of the reflex being to reproduce itself, it incorporates into itself every object capable of fulfilling the function of excitant . . . [this] assimilation belonging to the adaptive process appears in three forms: cumulative repetition, generalization of the activity with incorporation of new objects to it, and finally, motor recognition.[1] But, in the last analysis, these three forms are but one: the reflex must be conceived as an organized totality whose nature is to preserve itself in functioning and consequently to function sooner or later for its own sake (repetition) while incorporating into itself objects propitious to its functioning (generalizing assimilation) and discerning situations necessary to certain modes of its activity (motor recognition) . . . the progressive

[1] Piaget illustrates each of these with concrete observations of the behaviour of his children. Elsewhere, I have selected observations to illustrate the points Piaget makes. Here, there is no space to present them, and the reader is invited to examine Piaget's (1936, Chapter 1) own observations or my selection (Hunt, 1961, pp. 117 ff).

adaptation of reflexive schemata [such as sucking], therefore, presupposes their organization.

Thus, even in the case of such a reflexive motor schema as sucking,
successive encounters with the nipple and the breast and with other
objects that touch the lips are observed to lead from what, in Skinner's
(1953) language, would be the status of a 'respondent' to the status of
an 'operant'.

This progressive adaptation continues through the second sensorimotor stage during which reflexive looking, to use the language of
Piaget, incorporates things heard so that the things heard become
something to look at as the infant acquires what is commonly termed
'auditory localization'. This process exemplifies coordination between
looking and listening. In this process of the second stage of sensorimotor
development, it should be noted that Piaget's observations imply a redefinition of 'stimulus'. Instead of mere energy delivered at receptors,
the effective instigators of reflexive looking and reflexive listening appear
to be changes in the ongoing characteristics of the light or of the sound
impinging on the neonate's eyes or ears. The reflexive looking and the
reflexive listening appear to be special cases of what the Russian investigators, since Pavlov, have called the 'orienting reflex' (Berlyne,
1960; Razran, 1961). This being the case, assimilating things heard into
the looking schema appears to be a special case of stimulus to stimulus
conditioning for which the motivation consists in changes in the ongoing characteristics of the input.

Piaget observed that as his children exercised a schema such as
looking, and as the exercise brought them in perceptual contact with
objects seen or heard in the external environment, they exhibited 'new
behaviour relating to the objects which have disappeared' (1936, p. 155).
Piaget's observations seem to indicate that these new efforts brought on
by the escape of objects from perceptual contact occur only after the
child has had repeated perceptual contact with those objects. The
infant's efforts appear to be directed towards retaining or regaining the
perceptual contact with these recognitively familiar objects, persons
and places. Even in a very young infant, recognitive familiarity appears
to be the chief basis for what Piaget has termed 'spectacles of interest'.
Everyone who has jounced an infant on his knee is familiar with this
phenomenon, even though the example cited typically occurs some
months after infants manifest their first efforts to retain or regain
perceptual contact with objects becoming recognitively familiar. When
the adult jouncer stops his jouncing, the infant typically begins a

jouncing of his own. It is extremely difficult to escape the interpretation that the infant, when he starts a jouncing of his own, intends to renew his own perceptual contact with the jouncing event. It is hard to escape the interpretation that the infant anticipates the goal of his action, for when the adult jouncer resumes his jouncing, the infant quickly stops his own efforts, manifests a benign expression and appears to enjoy what he anticipated all along. In his long third chapter on the 'secondary circular reactions' that constitute sensorimotor stage three, Piaget (1936) cites many examples of such behaviour. At this point, the human infant clearly ceases to be a reactive responder and becomes an initiator of a great many different kinds of activities in which certain of his sensorimotor schemata are goals clearly anticipated, while others serve as means to the anticipated goals or ends.

One may, following Skinner (1938, 1953), call these self-instigated activities 'operants', if one wishes, but such mere naming of a category of non-respondents fails to consider their developmental origin. Such naming fails to consider that these activities emerge as a product of the infant's early encounters with his circumstances in the course of his development. Skinner's (1950) aversion to theorizing and to consideration of the developmental process leaves him with a pair of categories of activities, 'respondents' and 'operants', that are of little interest because they are tied neither to hypotheses of their origin nor to hypotheses of the physiological processes which mediate them. From the fact that, as Hebb (1949) has pointed out, central processes run off more rapidly than do events, one gains a hypothetical physiological basis for self-instigation growing out of encounters with circumstances. Combining Piaget's observations of the ontogenetic origins of self-instigated activities with such a hypothesis of their physiological basis yields, in turn, a foundation for 'expectations' and 'intentions' that is quite consonant with a mechanistic view of living beings.

The S–R conception of learning

Piaget's observations and theorizing are highly relevant to the S–R conception of learning. They imply a variety of kinds of learning to which attention is seldom given, and a variety differing greatly from that to which Gagné (1965, ch. 2) comes from reviewing the investigative work on learning and problem solving. In fact, Piaget's conceptions of accommodation and assimilation and his concept of the lack of equilibrium constitute a domain essentially equivalent to the concept of learning broadly defined. I shall return to this topic in my critique of these constructs below.

Piaget's observations and theorizing call into question also the traditional conception of what in an organism's encounters with circumstances induces modifications in behaviour. In our traditional formulations, modification of behaviour has been attributed to events that follow behavioural acts. Thus, in the theorizing of Thorndike (1911, 1935) it is a matter of whether the action or behaviour leads to annoyance or to satisfaction. Hull's (1943) position was somewhat similar. Actions that failed to reduce the drive that evoked them were gradually extinguished, others took their place at the top of the hierarchy. Only those actions that led to a reduction in drive survived. If I understand Skinner's (1958) formulation, it also depends upon reinforcement, where reinforcement is any event following the action of the organism that results in an increase in the readiness of the action or in a modification of the action to occur. As Skinner (1953, p. 73) put it, 'We observe the frequency of a selected response (operant level) then make an event contingent upon it and observe any change in frequency. If there is a change, we classify the event as reinforcing to the organism under the existing circumstances.' Such modification appears to be chiefly one of motivation. Yet in the case of shaping behaviour, about which we now hear so much in the work of Skinner and his collaborators, the modification is a genuine alteration in the structure of the activity. This shaping is cognitive in nature in the sense that it must involve a change in the organization in the central processes that mediate the change in behaviour. Although Piaget professes concern only with matters cognitive and epistemological, we have here in the S–R theory of reinforcement something closely related to Piaget's notion of 'lack of equilibrium' and its role in behavioural and conceptual development.

According to Skinner (1958) and to behaviour theorists generally, the modifications in behaviour that constitute the shaping occur because of the rewarding events that follow their occurrence. Piaget's observations, on the other hand, suggest strongly that the modifications in behaviour come at the point in time that the learner encounters circumstances that will not permit him to proceed as he anticipated. These are circumstances that upset the child's equilibrium and force him into accommodative modifications. Relevant observations include those concerned with modifications of sophisticated sucking, of sophisticated grasping, and of manual groping to solve various problems (Piaget, 1963, ch. 1, 3 and 5), modifications in the intuitive regulations leading to the concrete conceptual operations (Piaget and Inhelder, 1940; Piaget and Szeminska, 1939), and the modifications in thought that derive from encounters with problems for which concrete operations are inadequate and result in the development of formal conceptual operations (Inhelder and Piaget, 1955). Piaget views the child in all of these various situations as highly active. He holds that the child has an end in view, and it seems that the child does have an end in view because he ceases striving once he achieves that end. Moreover, one would expect ends-in-view from the fact that in familiar situations central processes run off faster than events. Thus, from a physiological standpoint, the child can be expected to anticipate what is coming and to have intentional ends in view. The modifications in the structure of behaviour or thought, then, can be viewed as an active, creative, coping operation. The modification becomes part of the child's standard repertoire only when it has achieved the child's anticipated goals repeatedly in a number of situations for which it was adequate. In the language of Piaget, then, reinforcement would consist in achieving the child's anticipated goals, would permit at least some degree of equilibrium and would aid the assimilation of the creative modification in the behavioural structure that came about with the encounter with circumstances novel but not beyond the child's accommodative limits. It is interesting to note that Piaget's view is highly consonant with the view of social psychologists that changes in attitude and belief come directly from encounters with new and dissonant information (Festinger, 1957; Hovland, Mandell *et al.* 1957). It is also interesting, in passing, to note that the studies of change in attitude and belief from encounters with dissonant information generally have not been considered to belong within the traditional domain of learning.

PIAGET VERSUS GESTALT PSYCHOLOGY

Piaget (1950a, p. 60) clearly accepts the essential, organized 'wholeness' of sensorimotor, perceptual and conceptual structures or schemata. His acceptance of their gestaltish nature is a major reason for his preference for the notion of accommodative groping in new circumstances over the notion of trial-and-error. According to the theory of trial-and-error, the subject is seen to emit by chance a series of discrete responses. Each one is a trial. Each one is also an error until by chance one occurs that achieves success. The one that repeatedly succeeds survives because it is somehow reinforced. Piaget admits the descriptive accuracy of such an account for instances in which 'the problem transcends the subject's intellectual level or knowledge' (1936, pp. 397–8). Under such circumstances, however, success brings little intellectual growth. When the subject grasps a problem, or sees it as akin to others he has already solved, the role of chance is greatly reduced. Instead, the subject brings to bear his ready-made perceptual organization of the situation and his prepared coping strategy. When the fit between this organization and the actual situation is such as to be relevant but inadequate, the subject typically modifies in creative fashion his organized perception and coping strategy to get a solution that consists of an elaboration of the previous organization and brings with it new understanding.

According to the central idea of gestalt theory, the sensorimotor, perceptual, or conceptual organizations never consist of an association of elements that exist in isolation before they come together. They exist rather in configurations or complex structures that are organized wholes from the outset. They obey such gestalt laws as simplicity, regularity, proximity, symmetry and *Prägnanz*. According to gestalt theory, these laws of organization are simply the principles of the equilibrium that governs the neuro-excitation released by perceptual contact with external objects combined in a field that embraces the organism and its immediate environment simultaneously. Köhler (1929) viewed this field as comparable to an electromagnetic field of forces and considered it to be governed by analogous principles, such for instance, as that of least action.

The notion that the psychological field is comparable to an electromagnetic field implied that the laws of organization must be universal and therefore common to all stages of both evolutionary and ontogenetic development. Gestalt psychologists (Köhler, 1929; Wertheimer, 1920), even those concerned explicitly with developmental psychology (see Koffka, 1924; Werner, 1948), have devoted themselves to accumulating an impressive series of illustrations of perceptual and conceptual structures that are the same in various mammals along the evolutionary scale, and the same in young children as in adults. Moreover, gestalt psychologists (Duncker, 1935; Wertheimer, 1920) have attempted to explain intelligent activity as a sudden restructuring of perception that comes with an 'aha' moment of insight. Gestalt students of intelligence also have attributed a minimal importance to past experience. From their point of view, both the basic perceptual organizations and these restructurings are essentially preformed in the sense that they arise inherently out of the nature of neural processes evoked by organism's perceptual encounter with its circumstances. In this sense, gestalt psychologists belong to the tradition of the nativists, and their theory remains as a psychological vestige of preformationism.

Piaget (1950a, pp. 60 ff.) has taken explicit issue with the hypothesis of universal 'physical Gestalten'. He points out that the dilemma of either organized wholes or the atomism of isolated sensations or reflexes is quite unnecessary. Instead of these two terms, he finds three. In his own words as translated, Piaget (1950a, pp. 63–4) states:

> A perception may be a synthesis of elements, or else it may con-
> stitute a single whole, or it may be a system of relations (each relation
> being itself a whole, but the complete whole becoming unanalysable
> and not relying at all on atomism). This being the case, there is no
> reason why complex structures should not be regarded as the
> product of a progressive construction which arises, not from 'syn-
> theses' [of atomistic elements], but from adaptive differentiations and
> combined assimilations, nor is there any reason why this construction
> should not be related to an intelligence capable of genuine activity as
> opposed to an interplay of pre-established structures.

To support his third alternative view, Piaget reviews work showing a progressive development of size constancy during the first year of life, other work showing that the 'systematic error of the standard' in paired-comparisons of heights at a distance is underestimated by children of 5 to 7 years of age but is overestimated by adults, and that the incidence of size constancy increases in children up to nearly 10 years of age.

These findings suggest that the phenomena of size constancy depend upon the solidity of representative central processes that derive their existence from repeated sensorimotor encounters with distances, sizes and objects.

In his observations of the early psychological development of his own three children, Piaget (1936) noted sensorimotor adaptations not unlike those observed by Köhler (1924) on the use of implements by chimpanzees. Köhler noted that a chimpanzee failed to use a stick in his efforts to obtain a banana beyond reach except when that stick was available to be perceived at the same time that the animal was looking at the out-of-reach banana. Paralleling this observation of Köhler's, Piaget noted repeatedly that, at ages ranging from 3 to 5 months, his children would grasp seen objects only when the hand and the object were simultaneously in view (1936, ch. 2). From such observations, Piaget argues that eye–hand coordination comes about only as the schemata of hand motion and grasping become incorporated in looking to constitute a new gestalt organization. He argues further (Piaget, 1963, p. 128) that,

Wherever we may speak of conditioned reflexes being stabilized as the result of experience, we always perceive that a scheme of the whole organizes the parts of the associations. If the nursling seeks the breast when he is in a position to nurse, follows moving objects with his eyes, tends to look at the people whose voice he hears, grasps objects he perceives, etc., it is because the schemata of sucking, vision, and prehension have assimilated increasingly numerous realities, through this very fact of endowing them with meaning. Accommodation and assimilation combined, peculiar to each schema, insure its usefulness and coordinate it to the others, and it is the global act of complementary assimilation and accommodation which explains why the relationships of the parts which presuppose the schema are confirmed by experience.

In similar fashion, Piaget explains the successive coordinations which, when combined with differentiation, provide the basis for the hierarchical nature of intelligence and intellectual functions. Following the six stages of the sensorimotor development, the sensorimotor systems of the infant become internalized as imitative imagery combines with the imitated vocal signs of early language. These are gradually modified in the accommodations demanded by communication into intuitive regulations that, in turn, are coalesced or grouped into the concrete operations of intelligence of which Piaget and his collaborators find evidence in the children of Geneva at about 7 to 8 years of age (Inhelder and Piaget, 1955). At this stage, the child becomes able to manipulate hierarchies of classes, to serialize asymmetrical relations and appreciate transpositions, and to employ additive compensations that enable him to conserve quantity, length and number. At each stage, after the first sensorimotor one, the child's anticipation of the end or goal of his action or thought serves to unify the system. Even though concrete thought continues to be directed by encounters with circumstances, the 'groupings' of regulatory expectations serve to organize conceptually the classes, asymmetrical relations and compensatory additive combinations.

Such coordination is then repeated when the concrete additive operations become recoordinated and reorganized into formal, multiplicative operations (Inhelder and Piaget, 1955). At this final stage, the thought of adolescents confronted with various kinds of problems begins to reflect various of Boole's (1854) logical structures. These logical structures include the proportionality which underlies the 'education of correlates' that Spearman (1923) considered to be one of the distinguishing characteristics of intelligent action or thought, 'the 16 binary operations of two-valued propositional logic', and the 'INRC group'. Piaget (1953) views each of these systems of formal operations as a gestaltish whole.

Thus, while Piaget can readily accept the gestalt principles of organization, the main burden of his life-work, in uncovering a progressive epigenesis of actional, imaginal, and intellectual structures and of epistemological constructions, is maximally dissonant with the notion that 'the laws of organization' are constant in the course of human development. Rather, the systems of behaviour and of thought are seen to develop into more complex hierarchical organizations in the course of the child's sensorimotor and informational interaction with his environmental circumstances.

PIAGET VERSUS PSYCHOANALYSIS AND DRIVE THEORY

Piaget (1952b) began his scientific career as a zoologist, but his first psychological concerns were psychoanalytic. His first publications concerned the anatomical variations in molluscs developing under various ecological conditions. These publications began appearing when he was but 15 years old. He earned his doctorate in zoology with a thesis on molluscs. Only then did he turn to psychology in Zurich. There he worked part-time in Bleuler's psychiatric clinic, and he attributes his initial concern with psychoanalysis to the personal factor of his mother's poor mental health (Piaget, 1952b). In Bleuler's clinic, he learned the interview method. He used this method in his early studies, first, at the Sorbonne where he was concerned with the reasons children failed on Burt's tests and, later, in the first group of studies at the Rousseau Institute in Geneva (Piaget, 1923, 1924, 1926, 1927, 1932).

Despite this background in psychoanalysis, Piaget's later work, beginning with his observations of the behaviour of his own infant children in their repeated encounters with everyday things, has been concerned almost entirely with the development of intelligence and with children's construction of the Kantian categories of reality. A concern with affectivity appears only incidentally in the role of a lack of equilibrium in accommodative modifications of intellectual and epistemological structures. It is undoubtedly in the difference between Piaget's concerns and the concerns of psychoanalytic observers, as well as in the differences between the two vantage points of observation, that one finds the origin of such a radical difference in concern and findings with respect to affectivity and motivation. While Freud and the other psycho-analysts were concerned with understanding the origins of neurotic and psychotic behaviour, Piaget concerned himself with the develop-ment of intelligent procedures for coping with environmental circum-stances and with the construction of the various Kantian categories of reality. Where Freud and the other analysts started with neurotically distressed, adult patients and attempted to reconstruct the basis for their distress from their reported memories or from their free associa-tions, Piaget observed the behaviour and talk of infants and young children, typically well fed and well cared for, when they were con-fronted repeatedly with various environmental situations. The resulting difference in findings – the tremendous importance of the affective aspect of life in psychoanalysis and the tremendous place of the cog-nitive aspect of life by Piaget – comes inevitably.

Freud's revolt against the rationalism of the conscious in the psy-chology of his day was made inevitable by the vantage point from which he observed life and attempted to reconstruct lives. The theory of drives (*Treiben*) as the springs of behaviour, Freud found almost ready-made in the thought of the German version of the romantic movement. Freud's drive theory can be found in part in Schopenhauer's notion that man finds his essence in will or desire, in part in Feuerbach's related notion of the wish coupled with his notion that happiness is founded upon the universal impulse of sexual love, in part in Bückner's psyiolo-gizing of will and wish as drive which von Hartmann also espoused. Freud's theory of the unconscious can also be found almost ready-made; it had been explicit in the psychological theory of Herbart, and it became popular with the widespread reading of von Hartmann's (1869) *The Philosophy of the Unconscious*. Freud combined these ideas of drives and of the unconscious with his observations made through his inter-views with his patients and through their free associations to create his theory of psychosexual development (Freud, 1905). What was originally the Freudian wish became explicitly tied to physiological stimulation in his paper, 'Instincts and their vicissitudes' (Freud, 1915).

The concept of drive got support in America from the physiological investigations of Walter B. Cannon (1915) concerned with the bodily changes in pain, hunger, fear and rage. It got further support from the psychological investigations of Curt Richter (1922, 1927), from the theorizing of Woodworth (1918), and finally, it got incorporated into the dominant motivational theories of psychology by such expositors as Dashiell (1925), Dollard and Miller (1950), Guthrie (1938), Hull (1943), Mowrer (1950) and Thorndike (1935); see also Hunt (1963a).

According to this drive theory, organisms are instigated to act only by strong and painful external stimuli, or by such internal needs as hunger, thirst, sex, or by innocuous stimuli that have been associated with (conditioned to emotional responses evoked by) either painful external or internal stimuli. When these conditions cease to operate, the drive ceases and the behaviour is supposed to stop. Freud (1915) made explicit that the 'aim' of all behaviour is to remove the stimuli that produce excitation and to minimize the excitation in the nervous system. Moreover, according to Freud's (1905) theory of psychosexual development, the individual's character, neurotic or healthy, is largely a function of the fate of these instinctual drives and the emotional conditions related to them. Certainly, in those patients who come for psychotherapy, distressing emotions do loom large in the impressions that the psychotherapist gets from his patients' talk.

In the children observed by Piaget, however, the emotions loomed far less large. Although Piaget (1936) has been avowedly unconcerned with emotion and motivation, his observations are an interesting source for hypotheses concerning the development of motivation (Hunt, 1963b). Piaget's own children were typically without pain, without hunger, without thirst and presumably without sexually strong excitement at the points at which he made the observations reported. Nevertheless, his children were highly active and highly interested from a motivational standpoint, and were not without affectivity – delight when they achieved their intentional ends and distress when they failed. Presumably they were active by virtue of motivation based on their sensori-motor interaction with their environmental circumstances, interaction based largely on input chiefly through the eyes and the ears but also from tactual contact with things and kinesthetic feedback from the muscles. If the other abundant evidence for motivation inherent in information processing and action (Hunt, 1963a) did not exist, Piaget's observations would strongly suggest that something in the infant's informational commerce with his environment through the eyes and ears contains a basis for motivation. Moreover, as I have said elsewhere (Hunt, 1963b, 1965a), Piaget's observations give us at least a first approximation of the nature of the epigenesis of this motivation intrinsic to the infant's informational interaction with his circumstances.

Piaget's observations suggest an epigenesis in which there are four phases. At birth, the human infant is essentially responsive from the motivational standpoint. During this phase, the effective instigator appears, as noted above, to be less a matter of energy delivered at the receptor than one of change in some characteristics of the light and sound delivered to the eyes and ears and, perhaps, change in the characteristics of contact with the receptors in the skin. The second stage begins with the appearance of intentional activities calculated to retain or regain perceptual contact with objects, persons and places made desirable through recognitive familiarity. As the infant shifts from efforts to gain mere perceptual contact with desired objects to efforts to grasp them, his intentional efforts gradually change to primitive plans in which one of his schemata serves as the goal while others serve as instrumental means. In the observations of Piaget (1936), few of the ends for which his infant children strove were even remotely concerned with relief from pain, with getting objects with which to gratify homeostatic needs, or with sex. Precisely what makes objects desirable during this second motivational phase remains problematical, but from considering the fact that Piaget's children appeared first to desire objects made recognitively familiar with repeated perceptual encounters in conjunction with the phenomenon of imprinting in birds and various mammals, as described by Lorenz (1937), I have been led to the hypothesis that recognitive familiarity is perhaps central. In the third stage, the infant becomes interested in what is new and novel within a complex of familiar circumstances (Hunt, 1963b, 1965b). Finally, as the child achieves language, he comes to the stage of informational interaction in which we all find ourselves. At this final fourth stage, there are two kinds of informational interaction, one through linguistic communication, the other through the perception of reality. The discrepancy between the constructions of reality deriving from these two sources of information provides a never-ending process of motivation and interest as Festinger (1957), Kelly (1955) and Rogers (1951) have recognized in their theoretical writings.

   In each of these stages, one can find a motivational basis for many of those infant activities that have long been considered predetermined in their appearance because they do have an autogenic basis (Hunt, 1965b, pp. 231 ff.). Although I have tended to emphasize information-processing, many correspondences exist between my concept of intrinsic motivation, which the observations of Piaget (1936) helped to justify, and Robert White's (1959) conception of 'competence motivation', which emphasizes the action side of sensorimotor organizations. I suspect that the perceptual and the active aspects of the sensorimotor organizations of the infant or child are but two sides of the same coin whose substance is their intentionality. Piaget's observations clearly imply that during a major share of his time, the human infant developing in a middle-class home is little concerned with his instinctual needs.

He is looking and listening, manipulating and locomoting, and he is continually increasing the complexity of his self-directed activities. I suspect that it is the fate of these, his own intentions, that control his psychological development rather than the fate of his instinctual needs – except where such needs intrude to become the basis for intentions (Hunt, 1965b).

Although Piaget has concerned himself centrally with intelligence and epistemological constructions, he has not denied the affective side of life. Rather, he regards the affective and the intellectual as inseparable because (Piaget, 1950a, p. 6) 'all interaction with the environment involves both a structuring and evaluation . . . we cannot reason, even in pure mathematics, without experiencing certain feelings, and conversely, no affect can exist without a minimum of understanding or of discrimination'. These propositions imply a basis for motivation inherent in information processing and action. As such, they constitute a view of motivation highly dissonant with that in psychoanalytic theory and also with the drive conception so widely accepted by S–R behaviour theorists.

19

*F. W. Warburton, T. F. Fitzpatrick, J. Ward
and M. Ritchie (1970)*

Some problems in the construction of individual intelligence tests

P. J. Mittler (ed.), *The Psychological Assessment of Mental and
Physical Handicaps* (Methuen), ch. 24, pp. 719–33

I INTRODUCTION

Since January 1965 a research team at Manchester University has been
engaged on the construction of a new individual test of intelligence
which, it is anticipated, will eventually replace such tests as the Stanford–Binet and the various Wechsler scales for clinical use with
children. The proposed form of this test has been described by Warburton (1966a, 1966b); its present stage of development is designed to
test the age range 5–12 (although some items are available from 2 to
15 years in order to accommodate dull 5-year-old and bright 12-year-
old children). It consists of twelve subscales organized round six hypothetical 'factors' or special abilities. The material has been subjected to
large-scale try-out and work on the preparation of a final version for
standardization is now in progress.

The research was established after several years of preparatory work
by a special committee of the British Psychological Society; for as long
ago as 1921 Sir Cyril Burt (1921) had written that to replace the Binet
scales would require a lifetime of researches; the considerable resources
necessary for the various revisions of the Binet and for the construction
of the Wechsler scales gave an indication of the magnitude of the task.
It was predictable, therefore, that a wide range of problems would be
encountered. These may be seen as concerned with two basic issues:
(1) the construction of a scale of general mental capacity or 'educability'
adapted to British culture and standardized on a British population, and
(2) the extension of the scale into a measure of special abilities.

It is obvious that the latter objective poses the main problem since
most of the requirements for the construction of a test of general ability

could be satisfied simply by the adaptation or restandardization of one of the tests in current use.

II ITEM WRITING

Choice of a rationale. Most acceptable accounts of psychological research attempt to give some justification of the procedure adopted in order to permit integration of the results into a systematic theory. In this respect the constructors of individual tests have been found seriously wanting, for, although the empirical value of their work is not seriously questioned, its place in a general theory of mental functioning has been difficult to assess owing to the lack of adequate rationales – cf. Littell (1960), Eysenck (1967b) and Guilford (1967). Traditionally individual testing has been associated with the measurement of general intelligence – a concept which has been under consistent attack on the grounds that it is too vague to merit scientific status. Admittedly much of this criticism has been indirect in the sense that it has been linked with Spearman's *g* and the methodological issues surrounding factor analysis, but the need for developed rationales has met with little response from test constructors. Thus Terman (1916) offered no satisfactory definition of what he was trying to measure except to stress the primacy of conceptual thinking largely mediated by language; Wechsler (1958) took a global view of intelligence, acknowledging the importance of *g* and pointing to significant 'performance' elements in test performance. It might be said that neither of these has gone much further than Binet's (Binet and Simon, 1905) original attempt to measure 'judgement' which he considered the most important among a hierarchy of diverse intelligences; and despite an early lead given by Burt (1921), reasoning items have been poorly represented in test content although their high *g* loading has been known for many years. The statement of an explicit rationale is thus an obvious step forward in the construction of a new test.

III THE PRINCIPAL SOURCES OF EVIDENCE

In arriving at such a rationale the constructors have had to consider three principal sources of evidence: (1) psychometric work on the structure of human ability, (2) the rapidly accumulating knowledge of the nature and sequence of cognitive structures obtained from developmental psychology and (3) the vast experience of individual testing gained by clinicians and research workers over the last sixty years.

1 *Psychometric factors*

A major criticism of established tests is that they fail to sample the more important group factors or mental abilities identified in factor analytical research by such workers as Thurstone (1938), Burt (1949) and Cattell (1957b). Almost all researchers in this field recognize the presence of such abilities; they differ, however, in the extent to which they regard them as related to one another, predictively useful, or indeed measurable at all. Of the many contemporary theorists, undoubtedly the most extreme position has been taken by Guilford (1967) whose 'Model of the Intellect' postulates no less than 120 abilities categorized by content process and product. It must be conceded that the model is very useful for the analysis of test content and, in focusing attention to neglected areas such as reasoning and fluency, he has performed a valuable service. However, despite the body of supportive evidence supplied, this is essentially an experimental approach, and Guilford's use of homogeneous populations together with an insistence on orthogonal factors rather restricts the generality of the model. McNemar (1964) called the model 'scatterbrained', and latterly Eysenck (1967b) has observed that if this is the best model currently available then something has gone very wrong indeed.

It must be emphasized that the nature of individual testing calls for a comparatively simple factorial model; the groups studied are usually heterogeneous and the constraints of time and presentation are against the achievement of complex factorial profiles. A cautious but more realistic approach is suggested by the evidence for stable and predictively useful factors of the 'Primary Mental Ability' type advanced by Thurstone (1938).

The model of the present scale is based upon the assumption that intelligence is a composite of related mental abilities, some of which are more closely associated with learning – and consequently the prediction of scholastic attainment – than others. The same factors are included at each age level, although the nature of the test material changes radically.

Table 19.1 is based on the distinction between (1) the *content* of an item and (2) the main mental *process* involved. For example, the subject may be presented with a list of words and be asked to memorize and later recognize them. The content of these two tasks is the same (viz. words), but the mental processes of memory and recognition are different. Analogously, if we are asked to classify separate series of words and shapes, the mental process of classification is the same in the two tasks, but the content (words and shapes) is different.

It is not difficult to draw up a list of types of content. The six categories below cover a very considerable proportion of the material in published tests:

(1) Shapes
(2) Symbols
(3) Numbers
(4) Objects (and pictures of objects)
(5) Words
(6) Sentences

It is, however, not easy to agree on a classification of types of mental process, partly because the number of categories included in the list depends on how detailed an examination is made of the nature of the mental processes involved. In Table 19.1 mental processes have been classified as follows:

(1) Perception
(2) Memorization
(3) Recognition
(4) Conceptualization
(5) Convergent reasoning (classification)
(6) Convergent reasoning (operational)
(7) Divergent reasoning (creativity)

These seven processes combined with the six types of content above yield $7 \times 6 = 42$ categories of test. Table 19.1 presents types of mental test which fall into each of these 42 categories. A comprehensive intelligence test could be designed to cover all these categories. For practical reasons this was not possible in the case of the British Intelligence Scale, but the material can be classified according to a reduced model comprising all the content categories and all the mental processes except Perception and Memory, i.e. $5 < 6 = 30$ types of test.

It would be possible by means of statistical techniques such as analysis of variance to separate out the influence of (1) different types of test content, (2) different types of mental process and, most importantly, (3) their conjoint effects and interactions.

The various classifications and cross-classifications of scores that would be afforded might prove valuable for diagnostic and predictive purpose in educational guidance and profiles of the children's performance might be drawn up according to some such scheme. This rationale would be heavily criticized by Gestalt theorists as too atomistic and it would no doubt have crippling limitations as an explanation of children's

L

TABLE 19.1. *Content × mental processes model*

Mental process	Shapes	Symbols	Numbers
Perception	Perceptual speed (shapes) Gottschaldt	Perceptual speed (symbols), letter cancellation	Perceptual speed (numbers), number cancellation
Memorization	Memory for designs	Memory for symbols	Memory for numbers
Recognition		Symbol recognition	Number recognition
Conceptualization	Meaning of shapes	Meaning of symbols	Notation
Convergent reasoning (classificatory)	Matching, classifying and resorting figures	Symbol matching (classification of symbols)	Handling relative quantities, sets and subsets, matching number groups
Convergent reasoning (operational)	Completion, temporal integration, block designs, mazes, figure series, formboard, rotation, reflection, figure fitting	Symbol series	Inductive and deductive problems (both arithmetical and mathematical) number series, seriation
Divergent reasoning (creativity)	Design construction, Rorschach	New symbols	Number series (original)

(7 processes × 6 types of content = 42 categories)

Objects	Words	Sentences
Perceptual speed (objects)	Clerical tests, perceptual speed	Perceptual speed (sentences)
Memory for objects	Memory for words	Memory for sentences
Recognition of objects	Word recognition	Sentence recognition
Object assembly, pictorial identification	Vocabulary, names	Sentence completion scrambled sentences, information
Similarities of pictures, differences of pictures, picture classification	Differences, similarities, opposites, controlled association, word classification	Classification of sentences
Bead chain, orientation, conservation, equivalence, seriation	Word series, word games, coding	True-false, comprehension, verbal induction, verbal deduction, syllogism, assumptions, relevance, logical tests
New uses for objects, hidden objects	Novel uses for words, word lists, free association, suffixes, prefixes, word fluency	Essay, story making, fluency of ideas, unusual consequences, new proverbs

thinking in every day life, but some such analysis of the data nevertheless seems well worth carrying out, as the present Scale has a range of
items that has rarely been obtained from a single (large) group of
subjects.

The general notion of distinguishing between content and process is,
of course, not new. Guilford's structure of the intellect (Guilford, 1967)
puts forward certain modes of classification, two of which – Contents
and Operations – closely resemble the contents and mental processes of
the present model, as follows:

Guilford's 1967 categories

Contents	Operations
Figural	Cognitive
Symbolic	Memory
Semantic	Divergent thinking
Behavioural	Convergent thinking
	Evaluation

(Guilford also puts forward a third category, viz. products, comprising units, classes, relations, systems, transformations, implications.)
Similarly Eysenck (1953) distinguishes between:

Test material	Mental process
Verbal	Perception
Numerical	Memory
Spatial	Reasoning

(Eysenck also puts forward a third category, viz. quality, comprising
speed and power.)

These two schemes are somewhat less detailed than the present
model. The only substantive difference appears to be our omission of
the content 'Behavioural' and the operation 'evaluation' put forward by
Guilford. 'Behavioural' content is concerned with the information,
essentially non-verbal, involved in human interactions, where awareness of the attitudes, moods, intentions, perceptions, thoughts, of other
persons and of ourselves is important. This category was not included
in the present model (although the Scale has a few items with behavioural content) since most of this type of material was considered to
be more apposite to tests of temperament and personality than to
intelligence scales. The other category excluded from the present
scheme is the operation of 'evaluation' which is concerned with reaching
decisions or making judgements concerning the goodness (correctness,
suitability, adequacy, desirability) of information in terms of criteria of

identity, consistency and goal satisfaction. It was not included as a separate mental process since the evaluative tests used by Guilford appear to rest mainly on other operations such as perception (perceptual speed, clerical aptitude), classification (similarity of proverbs), and convergent reasoning. Moreover, evaluation implies the use of non-cognitive criteria, e.g. notions of suitability, adequacy and desirability, which depend on cultural background rather than cognitive capacity.

Incidentally, Thurstone's classification of the 'primary mental abilities' into verbal ability (V), verbal fluency (W), numerical ability (N), spatial ability (S), perceptual ability (P), inductive reasoning (R) and memory (M) does not fit into the content/mental process model. For example, the distinction between numerical ability, spatial ability and verbal ability is drawn according to differences in content, i.e. between numbers, shapes and words and phrases, whereas the distinction between perceptual ability, inductive reasoning and memory is made between different types of mental process – each process involving the use of items of various content, i.e. words, symbols, numbers and shapes.

The same criticism may be made of the try-out form of the British Intelligence Scale, which is organized (at least for administration) into Thurstonian factors. Analysis of the results will show whether it is worth while to retain these categories, or whether it would be better to substitute other modes. The classification does not have to be vertical: alternative rationale might group the contents horizontally following the developmental stages suggested by Piaget (1950a), and the feasibility of this has been carefully considered.

2 Developmental scales

The traditional intelligence scale is used in two ways, diagnostic and prognostic: first, to examine the child's present level of intellectual functioning and to relate this to his educational and social background and, secondly, to assess his intellectual *potential* and make appropriate recommendations about his future education. Yet none of the existing scales are based on any recognized theory of intellectual development. In the construction of traditional scales the designers have relied, perhaps too heavily, on empirical evidence for their results. The placement of items at a given age level has depended on that item meeting statistical requirements rather than psychological criteria. This does not imply that the constructors of the present scale have questioned orthodox methods of item analysis and test construction, but rather

TABLE 19.2. *The main Piagetian stages of intellectual development and operational skills that characterize them*

Stage	Age range	Cognitive skill characteristics
1 *Sensorimotor*	(0–2 years)	Gradual integration of reflex activity to develop motor habits in response to objects in the immediate environment. This leads to a sense of *object permanence* and crude concepts of space, time, causality and intentionality. There is a tendency to fixate on individual objects rather than the relations between objects. The child can begin to imitate visual and auditory models.
2 *Pre-operational* (i) Preconceptual	(2–7 years) (2–4 years)	Verbal symbols begin to be substituted for objects (naming). Imitation of language models in immediate environment leads to 'deferred imitation'. Tendency to fixate on single objects persists. This period is characterized by the use of *transductive logic*.
(ii) Intuitive thought	(4–7 years)	Can successfully decentre from one object to another but such decentring is successive and discrete. Errors are corrected by alternative guessing. Cannot 'conserve' by relating variables, or classify, or ordinate successfully. The earliest classification operations of sorting, numbering and relating start towards the close of this period. At this stage the child's thinking is irreversible, bound by the immediate perceptual field, as in conservation problems. The main features are the representation of objects and the growth of language.
3 *Operational* (i) Concrete operational thought	(7–11 years)	Uses concrete materials to carry out operations which have the properties of combinativity, reversibility, associativity and identity in a logical or mathematical sense. Capable of 'situation directed' thought and requires the materials and objects to reach a solution. Conservation skills are available. Well-organized classificatory systems are available. The child can construct hierarchies.
(ii) Formal operational thought	(11–16 years)	Concrete reasoning skills become internalized. The child is capable of reflecting on operations, setting up hypotheses and testing them. He can begin to deal with logical relationships of identity, negation, reciprocity, and correlation. He readily uses the laws of logic or mathematics in dealing with implication, proportionality, permutations and combinations. The child can turn round on his schema and think about thought. The thought processes approximate more closely to formal logico-mathematical lattices.

that they have also considered the psychological suitability of the items that have been included in terms of children's thinking.

Workers concerned with children's thinking such as Hamley (1936), Piaget (1950a), Brunswik (1956), Dienes (1964) and Bruner *et al.* (1966) have outlined developmental structures and mechanisms which should be taken into account in the construction of any new scale of intelligence. These models are derived from logical or mathematical sources. Their fundamental idea is that the quality of a person's thinking must be assessed against qualitative criteria. Within certain areas of ability, Mathematics or Languages for example, conventional operations and logical sequences can be readily discerned, but it is extremely difficult to extend these concepts to all types of ability and to write adequate test items.

Several theories of intellectual development have been examined in a search for items which will enable psychologists to relate their assessments systematically to educational practice and opportunities. Among these theories, that outlined by Piaget (1950a) undoubtedly deserves the greatest attention. It has had an impact in a great variety of psychological and educational fields, and his experimental findings have been replicated in a wide range of circumstances. Piaget postulates the development of a structure which systematizes thinking in the child as he develops. This structure is, fundamentally, his knowledge of the world, developed by activity and changing with age and experience. It acts as a mediating link in the assimilation of, and subsequent accommodation to, new experiences. Assimilation is the incorporation of input into existing structures of knowledge. Accommodation, on the other hand, is the changing of existing structure to make it better adapted to the new condition. Thus the quality of adaptive behaviour is partly determined by the state of development of this scheme which stores organizations or 'strategies'. Considerable research work has already been carried out on the adaptive styles of children, in order to determine the quality of their cognitive skills at different ages. Table 19.2 outlines the principal Piagetian stages and states briefly the cognitive operations which appear to be available in the repertoire of the normally developing child.

An attempt has been made in the scale to test the child's understanding of concepts and operations by means of a series of questions which it is hoped will illustrate the Piagetian levels. Explanations are sought and scored differentially at two or three levels. Some of the items are, therefore, different from those found in the traditional scales. Earlier experiments have shown that the sequential ordering of the main Piagetian stages is the same for all children, but there is a considerable

TABLE 19.3. Test content classified by subscale and developmental level

Stage	Reasoning	Number	Verbal	Creativity	Memory	Spatial
2 (i) Pre-operational (conceptual)	Simple classification, Tactile testing, Pattern completion	Counting, Matching tasks	Picture vocabulary, Double description	Naming objects (fluency), Creative play with blocks	Recognition of toys, Imitation (digit span), Object memory	Imitation, Matching, Shapes
2 (ii) Pre-operational (intuitive)	Simple Matrices, Inclusion classes, Inductive problems, Sorting	Conservation, Various	Verbal classification, Differences, Similarities, General knowledge	Controlled word association, Pattern meaning, Unusual uses, Consequences	Recognition of designs, Recall designs, Object memory, Sentence M., Sense of a passage	Block designs, Matching involving reversals, Copying tasks
3 Concrete operational	Sorting (several attributes), Logical multiplication (Matrices), Inference problems (several variables)	Shapes	Definitions, Social reasoning, Similarities	As above, plus Number of synonyms, Number of meanings	As above	Block designs, Visualization of cubes, Reversal and rotation of shapes
4 Formal operational	Matrices (sets and operations), Hypothesis testing (induction), Inference problems, Propositional logic	Number bases, Practical calculations	Abstract definitions, Proverbs, Harder similarities	As above	As above	Block designs (three dimensional), Cube development three views of cube

overlap between one content area and another. Nor has it been clearly demonstrated that skills or strategies available in the earlier stages of development remain available at a later stage. However, it seems likely that there will be a fairly reliable step-wise development in at least two of the content areas we have selected, namely Number and Verbal ability. Because of their substantive nature, these areas of knowledge are built up systematically and develop more regularly in complexity as the body of knowledge increases.

A developmental scale would constitute an exciting departure from orthodox practice, but at present the evidence does not lead one to believe that such a model would possess sufficient stability to be used as the basis for a test of this nature. However, an obvious compromise exists since most factorists – cf. Burt (1954), Vernon (1960) and Guilford (1967) – would regard the work of the developmental psychologists, such as Piaget and Bruner, as complementary to a factorial model. A combined classification of test content is shown in Table 19.3 where, in addition to the factors, the areas of qualitative change in children's thinking are represented. Here Piaget's stages replace chronological age or, more relevantly, mental age on the vertical axis and form a second principle for the choice of items.

3 Clinical aspects

We also have to consider the clinical aspects of the test, and this introduces a fresh set of methodological problems. In the clinical situation everything has to justify itself not only in terms of discriminative power but also in terms of variety, clinical richness and ease of rapport. The main purpose of the test is to generate as many hypotheses as possible about the subject.

On the other hand, it would not be viable to categorize subscales according to types of clinical usefulness, since this would cut clean across the factorial structure and content of the tests. For instance, the division of the Memory subscale into auditory and visual memory tests has no obvious justification purely in terms of clinical practice.

Table 19.4 shows the main 'clinical dichotomies' for the six subscales – i.e. the crucial point that has to be borne in mind when evaluating the child's responses.

(a) Work with young children

Clinical aspects are particularly important at the lower end of the age scale. This arises largely from the need for clarification of the crucial stages through which the child passes. If successful tests for young children can be developed they will enable educational programmes to be evaluated more realistically and facilitate the early and accurate diagnosis of cases of mental or physical handicap. For these reasons, the construction of items for the younger children has been given particular attention in the construction of the present scale, despite the fact that building up cognitive profiles at these ages raises special difficulties.

Information from the previous literature which would aid in the construction of homogeneous scales is sparse. Despite the criticisms of multiple factorists such as Guilford (1967), the theory that ability in the young child is largely undifferentiated finds support among many psychologists – cf. Burt (1954). Moreover, non-cognitive influences such as Bayley's (1958) 'goal directed' factors must be borne in mind. There is, of course, a wealth of general observational data on the adaptive behaviour of young children in the work of Isaacs (1933), Gesell and Ilg (1946) and, particularly, Piaget (1950a) leading to distinctive theories of child development. From the point of view of the test constructor, however, Bayley's (1958) work is perhaps the most

TABLE 19.4. *Clinical dichotomies*

Subscale	Tests	Clinical dichotomies
Verbal	Vocabulary Comprehension Information	Definition versus Identification
Reasoning	Induction Operational thinking Matrices	Verbal versus Non-verbal Reasoning Induction versus Deduction
Creativity	Creativity	Verbal versus Pictorial Fluency versus Originality
Memory	Auditory Visual	Recognition versus Recall
Number	Number	Numerical versus Conceptual
Spatial	Visual Spatial Block designs	Visual versus Visuo-motor (manipulative)

relevant. She considers that three main factors operate constructively at the preschool level. These are:

(1) A sensorimotor factor in the first year of life.

(2) A factor related to persistence and goal directed behaviour which predominates in the second and third years.

(3) The factor she refers to as 'intelligence' which is not present until 8 months but eventually becomes dominant at 4 years. Bayley described it as the 'general basic and stable mental capacity that is found in children of school age and is characterized as the ability to learn and carry on abstract thinking'. These analyses have served as a basic rationale in the construction of items for young children in the present scale.

The linguistic aspects of testing are particularly important. Instructions must be very short in order to cater for the short span of attention and general distractability of young children, yet they should give all the information required by a child to give an adequate response; they must be capable of spontaneous and varied delivery so that a relaxed and informal atmosphere can be maintained. It is often found that the language used by young children in problem solving is idiosyncratic or culturally distinctive and that instructions entirely appropriate for adults do not necessarily evoke the correct response in children. It is desirable that concepts should be tested out in as many ways as possible, as children sometimes use original strategies; for example, it was found that a whole series of items on conservation and transitivity could be answered correctly simply by adopting a certain method of counting.

For young children the tester must have a wide variety of items at his disposal, almost all of which should be attractive to the subject, easily administered and readily scored; many items must be very easy, since the child's interest is sustained by success and continuous involvement in the task. These items facilitate clinical observation and enable the psychologist to base his judgements on actual behaviour.

The preschool years are a period of very rapid mental growth in which the feeling, exploring and manipulating of objects plays a large part in mental development. Thus, the Visual–Spatial and Operational Thinking scales are very important. The main difficulty is to find tasks and materials which are really attractive to the subject – no one can be more stubborn than a 3-year-old child who does not want to cooperate. Thus materials must be easy and pleasant to handle, attractive to the eye, robust enough to stand up to the rough treatment handed out to them by toddlers, and preferably washable. Whenever possible, toys have been made from gaily coloured plastic or perspex materials, which have the additional advantage of being reasonably light in weight.

As a general rule, toys and apparatus are more interesting to the child than pictures. Items based on pictures have caused an unforeseen number of difficulties. It is remarkable how often children interpret pictures of everyday objects in a completely new way, e.g. what to an adult is a perfectly obvious drawing of an eye is seen as a fish by some children. It is important to have uncluttered line-drawings with a minimum of detail. These experiences confirm Vernon's (1952) work on visual perception in children presented with simple outline drawings of animals and familiar household objects. Vernon found that these drawings were recognized correctly by 11 per cent of 2-year-olds, 67 per cent of 3-year-olds and 90 per cent of 4-year-olds. However, if the drawings were made more complicated and were coloured, they were not identified until much later. It was found that when children were presented with a detailed scene they could not give even a partial interpretation of it until they were 7 years old, and they could not interpret it as a whole until about 11 years of age. Young children do not concentrate easily and it is necessary to present them with a constant flow of materials and apparatus, interspersing manipulative items with verbal tasks in an attempt to balance the various types of activity.

It is also important that the psychologist's test administration work should be kept to a minimum. Whenever possible, the same piece of apparatus has been used in different items – e.g. certain sets of pictures are used in both the comprehension and classification items.

(b) Cooperation with Psychologists

The opinion of clinicians about a test designed specifically for their use is paramount, since they will probably be using it most of their professional careers. They will have to be satisfied with each step in the administration of the test and with the scoring system. Several discussions have been held, therefore, with educational psychologists who were collaborating in the project. This led to considerable modification in the form and content of many of the items and sometimes major alterations to whole subscales. 'Workshops' and residential courses have been held for these psychologists, first to enable them to try out the items with children and then to meet for discussion, criticism and consideration of new items. The procedure helped in spotting badly worded and administratively cumbersome items. However, experience shows that many difficulties become evident only after an item has been used extensively over a period of weeks or months; very often the test constructor is seduced by a brilliant idea and does not see serious deficiencies in the procedure until he has used it a great deal. Those who took part in the preliminary discussions were drawn from all the ten regions in which the try-out was to be made. This training of psychologists did much to overcome some of the difficulties of standardizing the testing procedure and scoring of items.

The try-out sampling, will, in the end, have been carried out by a hundred or so trained psychologists working with children at various age levels. It might have been more desirable if each psychologist worked on all sections of every scale, but some degree of specialization was found necessary for practical reasons.

The reader may question our policy in using so many testers at this stage, but it was thought that the advantages clearly outweigh the disadvantages. It means that at the constructional stage of the research most of the items had already been modified by consultation with practising psychologists. The overall effect was to spread the testing load which exceeded 5000 hours of testing time. The employment of a few full-time testers could have involved an undue waste of time in locating suitable subjects. L.E.A. psychologists, having a knowledge of local conditions, are more likely to find a more truly representative sample. Another disadvantage in using few testers, each working on large subsamples, is that they may have tended to take highly individual, efficient, but short cut methods to achieve their goals. It seems more likely that the method adopted led to testing being carried out under real-life conditions.

IV CONCLUSIONS

Ideally, therefore, the new test will permit the measurement of special abilities together with a qualitative assessment of the level of thinking achieved. It must be stressed, however, that this is a proposed rather than an attained factorial structure; if the factors are reproduced over most of the age range of the test then this will be a remarkable piece of test construction. On the other hand, if the test results do not follow the predicted pattern, then the heavy weight of reasoning items together with other items known to load high on *g* will nevertheless ensure a powerfully discriminative test. It is hoped, of course, that the subscales from which factors are derived will be long and strong enough to allow profile analysis, but even if this is not the case there should be sufficient representative items to give strong clinical hints as to the presence of special abilities.

20

J. McV. Hunt (1968)

Environment, development and scholastic achievement

M. Deutsch, I. Katz and A. R. Jensen (eds.), *Social Class, Race and Psychological Development* (Holt, Rinehart & Winston), pp. 293-330

It is very interesting, and very exciting for me, to encounter people who are generally considered sensible, planning to utilize preschool experiences as an antidote for what we are now calling cultural deprivation and social disadvantage. The group at the Child Welfare Research Station in Iowa, under George D. Stoddard (see Stoddard and Wellman, 1940), described effects of nursery school which they considered evidence that would justify just such a use of nursery schools. This was over twenty-five years ago. Their work, however, was picked to pieces by critics and in the process lost much of the suggestive value it was justified in having. Many of you will recall the ridicule that was heaped upon the 'wandering IQ' (Simpson, 1939) and the way in which such people as Florence Goodenough (1939) derided in print the idea of a group of thirteen 'feebleminded' infants being brought within the range of normal mentality through training by moron nursemaids in an institution for the feebleminded (referring to the work of Skeels and Dye, 1939, to which we shall return). The fact that just such a use of preschool experience is now being seriously planned by sensible people with widespread approval means that something has changed.

The change, of course, is not in the nature of man or in the nature of his development; it is rather in our conceptions of man's nature and of his development. Some of our most important beliefs about man and his development have changed or are in the process of changing. It is these changes in belief which have freed us to try as demonstrative experiments that only as recently as World War II would have been considered a stupid waste of effort and time. It is also these changes in theoretical belief about man and his development which provide my topic, namely, the psychological basis for using preschool enrichment as an antidote for cultural deprivation.

I number these changed or changing beliefs as six. Let me state them in their prechange form; in the form, in other words, that has so much hampered the sort of enterprise in which this group is about to engage:

(1) A belief in fixed intelligence.
(2) A belief in predetermined development.
(3) A belief in the fixed and static, telephone-switchboard nature of brain function.
(4) A belief that experience during the early years, and particularly before the development of speech, is unimportant.
(5) A belief that whatever experience does affect later development is a matter of emotional reactions based on the fate of instinctual needs.
(6) A belief that learning must be motivated by homeostatic need, by painful stimulation, or by acquired drives based on these.

Let me discuss the evidential and conceptual bases for the change which has been taking place since World War II in these hampering beliefs, one by one.

THE BELIEF IN FIXED INTELLIGENCE

Almost every idea has roots in a communicated conceptual history and in observed evidence. The notion of fixed intelligence has conceptual roots in Darwin's (1859) theory of evolution and in the intense emotional controversy that surrounded it. You will recall that Darwin believed that evolution took place, not by changes wrought through use or disuse as Lamarck (1809) had thought, but by changes resulting from variations in the progeny of every species or strain which are then selected by the conditions under which they live. Their selection is a matter of which variations survive to reproduce so that the variations are passed on into the successive generations. The change is conceived thus to be one that comes via the survival of a variation in a strain through reproduction. Implicit in this notion was the assumption that the characteristics of any organism are predetermined by the genetic constitution with which the organism comes into being as a fertilized ovum. Probably this implicit assumption would never have caught on with anywhere near the force it did, had it not been for two outstanding figures in the history of relatively recent thought. The first of these is Sir Francis Galton, Charles Darwin's younger cousin. You will remember that it was Galton who made the assumption of the hereditary determination of adult characteristics explicit. Galton reasoned, further-more, that if his cousin were correct it would mean that the hope of improving the lot of man does not lie in *euthenics*, or in trying to change him through education; rather, such hope lies in *eugenics*, or in the selection of those superior persons who should survive. Second, he saw that if decisions were to be made as to which human beings were to sur-vive and reproduce, it would be necessary to have some criteria for survival. So he founded his anthropometric laboratory for the measure-ment of man, with the hope that by means of tests he could determine those individuals who should survive. Note that he was not deciding merely who should be selected for jobs in a given industry, but who should survive to reproduce. This was his concern. Because of the ab-horrence which such a plan met, Galton talked and wrote relatively little about it. However, the combination of the context of his life's work with the few remarks he did make on the subject gives these re-marks convincing significance (see Hunt, 1961).

Galton had a pupil who was very influential in bringing such con-ceptions into the stream of American thought. This was J. McKeen Cattell, who brought Galton's tests to America and beginning in 1890 gave them to college students, first at the University of Pennsylvania and then at Columbia University. Because Cattell was also an influential teacher at both Penn and Columbia, his influence spread through the many students he had before World War I – when his sympathies with Germany led to a painful separation from Columbia.

A second psychologist who was almost equally influential in bringing the stream of thought supporting fixed intelligence into American thought is G. Stanley Hall. Hall did not personally know Galton; neither did he personally know Darwin, but he read about evolution while still a col-lege student, and, as he has written in his autobiography, 'it struck me like a light; this was the thing for me'. Hall's importance lies in that he communicated a strong attachment to the notion of fixed intelligence to his students at Clark University, of which he was the first President, and these students became leaders of the new psychology in America (see Boring, 1929, p. 534). Among them were three of the most illustrious leaders of the testing movement. One was Henry H. Goddard, who first translated the Binet tests into English for use at the Vineland Training School and also wrote the story of the Kallikak family (1912). Another was F. Kuhlmann, who was also an early translator and reviser of the Binet tests and who, with Rose G. Anderson, adapted them for use with preschool children. The third was Lewis Terman, who is the author of the Stanford–Binet revision, the most widely known version of the Binet tests in America. These three communicated their faith in fixed intelligence to a major share of those who spread the testing movement in America.

So much for the conceptual roots of the belief in fixed intelligence that come by way of communication in the history of thought.

The assumption of fixed intelligence also had an empirical basis. Not only did test–retest reliabilities show that the positions of individuals in a group remained fairly constant, but also the tests showed some capacity to predict such criterion performances as school success, success as officers in World War I, and so on. All such evidence concerned children of school age for whom the experience to which they are exposed is at least to some degree standardized (see Hunt, 1961). When investigators began to examine the constancy of the developmental quotient (DQ) or IQ in preschool children, the degree of constancy proved to be very much lower. You will recall some of the very interesting interpretations of this lack of constancy in the preschool DQ (see Hunt, 1961, pp. 311 ff.). Anderson argued that since the tests at successive ages involved different functions, constancy could not be expected. But an epigenesis of man's intellectual functions is inherent in the nature of his development, and the implications of this fact were apparently missed by these critics of the findings from the infant tests. While they knew that the basic structure of intelligence changes in its early phases of development just as the structures of the body change in the embryological phase of morphological development, they appear not to have noted that it is thus inevitable that the infant test must involve differing content and functions at successive ages.

It was Woodworth (1941) who argued, after examining the evidence from the studies of twins, that there might be some difference in IQ due to the environment but that which exists among individuals in our culture is largely due to the genes. In the context of cultural deprivation, I believe Woodworth asked the wrong question. He might better have asked: What would be the difference in the IQ of a pair of identical twins at age 6 if one were reared as Myrtle McGraw (1935) reared the trained twin, Johnny (so that he was swimming at four months, roller-skating at eleven months, and developing various such skills at about one half to one fourth the age that people usually develop them), and if the other twin were reared in an orphanage, like the one described by Wayne Dennis (1960) in Tehran, where 60 per cent of the infants 2 years of age are still not sitting up alone, and where 85 per cent of those 4 years of age are still not walking alone? While observations of this kind come from varied sources and lack the force of controlled experimentation, they suggest strongly that lack of constancy is the rule for either IQ or DQ during the preschool years and that the IQ is not at all fixed unless the culture or the school fixes the programme of environmental encounters. Cross-sectional validity may be substantial, with predictive validity being little above zero (see Hunt, 1961). In fact, trying to predict what the IQ of an individual child will be at age 18 from a DQ obtained during his first or second year is much like trying to predict how fast a feather might fall in a hurricane. The law of falling bodies holds only under the specified and controlled conditions of a vacuum. Similarly, any laws concerning the rate of intellectual growth must take into account the series of environmental encounters which constitute the conditions of that growth.

THE BELIEF IN PREDETERMINED DEVELOPMENT

The belief in predetermined development has been no less hampering, for a serious consideration of preschool enrichment as an antidote for cultural deprivation than that in fixed intelligence. This belief also has historical roots in Darwin's theory of evolution. It got communicated into the main stream of psychological thought about development by G. Stanley Hall (see Pruette, 1926). Hall gave special emphasis to the belief in predetermined development by making central in his version of the theory of evolution the conception of recapitulation. This is the notion that the development of an individual shows in summary form the development of the species. Hall managed to communicate many valuable points about psychological development by means of his parables based on the concept of biological recapitulation. One of the most famous of these is his parable of the tadpole's tail. To Hall also goes a very large share of the responsibility for the shape of investigation in child and developmental psychology during the first half of this century. This shape was the study of normative development, or the description of what is typical or average. It was, moreover, as you all know, Arnold Gesell (1945, 1954), another student of G. Stanley Hall, whose life's work concerned the normative description of children's behavioural development. Gesell took over Hall's faith in predetermined development in his own notion that development is governed by what he has termed 'intrinsic growth'. It should be noted that once one believes in intrinsic growth, the normative picture of development is not only a description of the process but an explanation of it as well. Thus, whenever little Johnny does something 'bad', the behaviour can be explained by noting that it is just a stage he is going through. Moreover, following Hall's parable of the tadpole's tail – in which the hind legs fail to develop if the tail is amputated – Johnny's unwanted behaviour must not be hampered else some desirable future characteristic will fail to appear.

This notion of predetermined development also has an empirical basis, for the evidence from various early studies of behavioural development in both lower animals and children was readily seen as consonant with it. Among these are Coghill's (1929) studies of behavioural development in amblystoma. These demonstrated that behavioural development, like anatomical development, starts at the head end and proceeds tailward, starts from the inside and proceeds outward and consists of a progressive differentiation of more specific units from general units. From such evidence Coghill and others inferred the special additional notion that behaviour unfolds automatically as the anatomical basis for behaviour matures. From such a background came the differentiation of the process of learning from the process of maturation.

Among the early studies of behavioural development are those of Carmichael (1926, 1927, 1928), also with amblystoma and frogs, which appeared to show that the circumstances in which development takes place are of little consequence. You will recall that Carmichael divided batches of amblystoma and frog eggs. One of these batches he chloretoned to inhibit their activity; another batch he kept in tap water on an ordinary table; and a third group he kept in tap water on a work bench, where they received extra stimulation. Those kept in tap water on an ordinary table swam as early as did those that got the extra stimulation from the work bench. Moreover, even though those that were chloretoned had been prevented from activity through five days, they appeared to be as adept at swimming within a half an hour after the chloretone was washed out as were either of the two batches reared in tap water. Although Carmichael himself was very careful in interpreting these results, they have commonly been interpreted to mean that development is almost entirely a function of maturation and that learning, as represented in practice, is of little consequence.

Such an interpretation got further support from early studies of the effects of practice. In one such study of a pair of identical twins by Gesell and Thompson (1929), the untrained twin became as adept at tower building and stair climbing after a week of practice as was the trained twin who had been given practice in tower building and stair climbing over many weeks. In another such study by Josephine Hilgard (1932), a group of ten preschool children were given practice cutting with scissors, climbing a ladder and buttoning over a period of twelve weeks; yet they retained their superiority over the control group, which had received no special practice, for only a very short time. One week of practice in those skills by the control group brought their performance up to a level which was no longer significantly inferior to that of the experimental group from a statistical standpoint. Later work by two other investigators appeared to lend further support. Dennis and Dennis (1940) found that the children of Hopi Indians raised on cradle-boards, which inhibited the movements of their legs and arms during waking hours, walked at the same age as did Hopi children reared freely, in the typical white man's manner. Moreover, Dennis and Dennis (1935, 1938, 1941) found the usual sequence of autogenic behaviour items in a pair of fraternal twins reared under conditions of 'restricted practice and minimal social stimulation'. Many such studies appeared to yield results which could be readily seen as consonant with the notion that practice has little effect on the rate of development, and that the amount of effect to be got from practice is a function of the level of maturation present when the practice occurs.

It was just such a notion and just such evidence that led Watson (1928) to argue in his book, *The Psychological Care of the Infant and Child*, that experience is unimportant during the preschool years because nothing useful can be learned until the child has matured sufficiently. Thus, he advised that the best thing possible is to leave the child alone to grow. Then, when the child has 'lain and grown', when the response repertoire has properly matured, those in charge of his care can introduce learning. He conceived that learning could 'get in its licks' tying these responses to proper stimuli, via the conditioning principle, and by linking them together in chains to produce complex skills. I suspect that the use of B. F. Skinner's baby box, with controlled temperature, humidity and so on, may be based upon just such assumptions of predetermined development and of an automatic unfolding of a basic behavioural repertoire with anatomical maturation.

It should be noted that the animal evidence cited here comes from amblystoma and frogs, which are well down the phylogenetic scale. They have brains in which the ratio of those portions concerned with association or intrinsic processes to the portions concerned directly with input and output is small; that is, the A/S ratio, as formulated by Hebb (1949), is small. When organisms with higher A/S ratios were studied, in somewhat the fashion in which Coghill and Carmichael studied the behavioural development of amblystoma and frogs, the evidence yielded was highly dissonant with the implications of predetermined development. When Cruze (1935, 1938) found that the number of pecking errors per twenty-five trials decreased through the first five days, even though the chicks were kept in the dark – a result consonant with the notion of predeterminism – he also found facts pointing in a contrary direction. For instance, chicks kept in the dark for twenty consecutive days, and given an opportunity to see light and have pecking experience only during the daily tests, *failed* to attain a high level of accuracy in pecking and exhibited almost no improvement in the striking–seizing–swallowing sequence.

Similarly, Kuo's (see Hunt, 1961) wonderful behavioural observations on the embryological development of chicks in the egg indicate that the responses comprising the pecking and locomotor patterns have been 'well practised' long before hatching. The 'practice' for pecking seems to start with head-bobbing, which is among the first embryonic movements to be observed. The practice for the locomotor patterns begins with vibratory motions of the wing buds and leg buds; these movements become flexion and extension as the limbs lengthen and joints appear. At about the eleventh day of incubation, the yolk sac characteristically moves over to the ventral side of the embryo. This movement of the yolk sac forces the legs to fold on the breast and to be held there. From this point on, the legs cannot be fully extended. They are forced henceforth to hatching to remain in this folded position with extensive thrusts only against the yolk sac. Kuo argues that this condition establishes a fixed resting posture for the legs, and prepares them for lifting of the chick's body in standing and locomotion. Moreover, his interpretation gets some support from 'an experiment of nature'. In the 7000 embryos that he observed, nearly 200 crippled chicks appeared. These crippled chicks could neither stand nor walk after hatching. Neither could they sit in the roosting position, because their legs were deformed. Over 80 per cent of those with deformed legs occurred in those instances in which the yolk sac failed for some reason, still unknown, to move over to the ventral side of the embryo.

Such observations suggest that the mammalian advent of increasingly long uterine control of embryological and fetal environment in phylogeny reflects the fact that environmental circumstances more and more become important for early development, as the central nervous system control becomes more predominant. It should be noted, moreover, that as central nervous system control becomes more predominant, capacity for regeneration decreases. Perhaps this implies a waning of the relative potency of the chemical predeterminers of development as one goes up the phylogenetic scale.

Perhaps even more exciting in this connection is the work of Austin Riesen (1958), Brattgård (1952) and others. Riesen undertook the rearing of chimpanzees in darkness in order to test some of Hebb's (1949) hypotheses of the importance of primary learning in the development of perception. What he appears to have discovered – along with Brattgård (1952), Liberman (1962), Rasch *et al.* (1961) and Weiskrantz (1958) – is that even certain anatomical structures of the retina require light stimulation for proper development. The chimpanzee babies who were kept in the dark for a year and a half have atypical retinas; and, even after they are brought into the light, the subsequent development of their retinas goes awry and they become permanently blind. The result of such prolonged stimulus deprivation during infancy appears to be an irreversible process that does not occur when the chimpanzee infant is kept in darkness for only something like seven months. Inasmuch as Weiskrantz (1958) has found a scarcity of Müller fibres in the retinas of kittens reared in the dark, and since other investigators (especially Brattgård, 1952) have found the retinal ganglion cells of animals reared in the dark to be deficient in the production of ribonucleic acid (RNA), these studies of rearing under conditions of sensory deprivation appear to be lending support to Hydén's (1959, 1960) hypothesis that the effects of experience may be stored as RNA within the glial component of retinal tissue, of Deiter's nucleus (Hydén and Pigon, 1960) and, perhaps, of brain tissue as well.

For our present purposes it is enough to note that such studies are bringing evidence that even the anatomical structures of the central nervous system are affected in their development by encounters with circumstances. This lends credence to Piaget's (1936) aphorism that 'use is the aliment of a schema'.

Consider another study of the effects of early experience. This is a study by Thompson and Heron (1954), comparing the adult problem solving ability of Scotty pups which were reared as pets in human homes from the time of weaning until they were 8 months of age with that of their litter-mates reared in isolation in laboratory cages for the same period. The adult tests were made when the animals were 18 months old, after they had been together in the dog pasture for a period of ten months. Adult problem solving was measured by means of the Hebb–Williams (1946) test of animal intelligence. In one of these tests, the dog is brought into a room while hungry. After being allowed to smell and see a bowl of food, the dog is permitted to watch as his food is removed and put behind a screen in one of the opposite corners of the room. Both pet-reared and cage-reared dogs go immediately to the spot

where the food disappeared. After the same procedure has been repeated several times, the food is then placed, while the animal watches,
behind a screen in another opposite corner of the room. In order to
see this clearly, think of the first screen being in the corner to the dog's
right, the second in the corner to the dog's left. Now, when the dog is
released, if he is pet-reared he goes immediately to the screen in the left
corner for food. But, if he was cage-reared, he is more likely to go to the
screen in the right corner where he had previously found food. In his
tests of object permanence, Piaget (1936) describes behaviour of children
about 9 months old resembling that of the cage-reared pups, and of
children about 14 months old resembling that of the pet-reared pups.

It is interesting to compare the results of this study by Thompson and
Heron (1954), in which dogs were the subjects, with the results of
various studies of the effects of early experiences on adult problem
solving in which rats were subjects (see Hebb, 1947; Gauron and
Becker, 1959; Wolf, 1943). Whereas the effects of early experience on
the problem solving of dogs appear to be both large and persistent, they
appear to be both less marked and less permanent in the rat. Such a
comparison lends further credence to the proposition that the importance of the effects of early experience increases as the associative or
intrinsic portions of the cerebrum increase in proportion, as reflected in
Hebb's notion of the A/S ratio.

But what about the fact that practice appears to have little or no effect
on the development of a skill in young children? How can one square
the absence of the effects of practice with the tremendous apathy and
retardation commonly to be found in children reared in orphanages?
In the case of the orphanage in Tehran reported on by Dennis (1960),
the retardation in locomotor function is so great, as I have already noted,
that 60 per cent of those in their second year fail to sit up alone, even
though nearly all children ordinarily sit up at 10 months of age; and 85
per cent of those in their fourth year still fail to walk alone even though
children typically walk at about 14 or 15 months of age. I believe the
two sets of results can be squared by taking into account the epigenesis
in the structure of behaviour that occurs during the earliest years. The
investigators of the effects of practice neglected this epigenesis. They
sought the effects of experience only in practice of the function of
schema to be observed and measured. The existence of an epigenesis of
intellectual function implies that the experiential roots of a given schema
will lie in antecedent activities quite different in structure from the
schema to be observed and measured. Thus, antecedent practice at
tower building and buttoning may be relatively unimportant for the

development of skill in these activities; but an unhampered antecedent opportunity to throw objects and to manipulate them in a variety of situations, and an even earlier opportunity to have seen a variety of sights and to have heard a variety of sounds, may be of tremendous importance in determining both the age at which tower building and buttoning will occur and the degree of skill that the child will manifest.

BRAIN FUNCTION CONCEIVED AS A STATIC SWITCHBOARD

One can not blame Darwin for the conception of brain function as static, like that in a telephone switchboard. The origin of the ferment leading to these conceptions, however, does derive from Darwin's (1872) shift of attention from the evolution of the body to the evolution of mind. This he began in his book, *The Expressions of the Emotions in Man and Animals*. It was thus Darwin who provided the stimulus for what was later to be called *comparative psychology*. The original purpose was to show that there is a gradual transition from the lower animals to man in the various faculties of mind. It was Romanes (1882, 1883) who took up this task in an attempt to show the manner in which intelligence has evolved. Romanes's method was to show through anecdotes that animals are capable of intelligent behaviour, albeit at a level of complexity inferior to man's. It was C. Lloyd Morgan (1894) who said that it was reasoning by very loose analogy to impute to dogs, cats, and the like, the same kind of conscious processes and faculties that man can report. It was Morgan who applied Occam's 'razor of parsimony' to the various mental faculties. Then, shortly, Thorndike and Woodworth (1901) knocked out such old-fashioned faculties as memory with their studies showing that such forms of practice as daily memorizing poetry does not improve a person's capacity to memorize other types of material, and that being taught mathematics and Latin does not improve performance on reasoning tests.

It was still obvious, however, that animals do learn and that they do solve problems. Morgan (1894) saw this occurring by a process of trial and error. According to this conception, as Hull (1943) later elaborated it, an organism comes to any given situation with a ready-made hierarchy of responses. When those at the top of the hierarchy fail to achieve satisfaction, they are supposed to be weakened (extinguished). Other responses lower in the hierarchy then take their places and become connected with stimuli from the situation. Or, as Thorndike (1913) put it earlier, new S–R bonds are established. Complex behaviour was explained by assuming that one response can be the stimulus for another, so that S–R chains could be formed. The role of the brain in such learning also needed explanation. Here the telephone was the dramatic new invention supplying a mechanical model for a conception of the brain's role. Inasmuch as the reflex arc was conceived to be both the anatomical and the functional unit of the nervous system, the role of the brain in learning could readily be conceived to be analogous to that of a telephone switchboard. Thus, the head was emptied of active functions, and the brain, which filled it, came to be viewed as the focus of a variety of static connections.

All this led to what I think is a basic confusion in psychological thought, one which has been prominent for at least the last thirty-five or forty years. This is a confusion between S–R methodology, on the one hand, and S–R theory on the other. We cannot escape S–R methodology. The best one can possibly do empirically is to note the situations in which organisms behave and to observe what they do there. But there is no reason why one should not relate the empirical relationships one can observe between stimulus and response to whatever the neurophysiologist can tell us about inner brain function and to whatever the endocrinologist can tell us. The broader one makes his nomological net, the better, in that the more nearly his resulting conceptions will approach those of the imaginary, all-seeing eye of Deity.

Stimulus–Response (S–R) methodology appeared at first to imply the notion of the empty organism. It is interesting to recall, however, that very shortly after the mental faculties had been removed by C. Lloyd Morgan with Occam's razor of parsimony, Walter Hunter (1912, 1918) discovered that various animals could delay their responses to stimuli and also learn double alternation. Both achievements implied that there must be some kind of representative or symbolic process intervening between stimulus and response. It was to explain just such behaviour, moreover, that Hull (1931) promulgated the notion of the pure-stimulus act. This became in turn the response-produced cues and the response-produced drives of Miller and Dollard. When Miller and Dollard (1941, p. 59) began conceiving of the responses which serve as stimuli occurring within the brain, traditional S–R theory with its implicit peripherality of both stimulus and response began to fade. The demise of peripheral S–R theory became nearly complete when Osgood (1952) turned these response-produced cues and drives into central mediating processes. It is interesting to note in this connection that it is precisely observations from S–R methodology which have undone traditional peripheral S–R theory, and it is these observations which are now demanding that brain function be conceived in terms of active processes.

The theoretical need for active brain processes, however, has been stimulated by and has got much of its form from cybernetics (Wiener, 1948). Such investigators as Newell *et al.* (1958), in the process of programming computers to solve problems, and especially logical problems, have been clarifying the general nature of what is required for solving such problems. They have described three major kinds of requirements: (1) memories or information stored somewhere, and presumably in the brain; (2) operations of a logical sort which are of the order of actions that deal with the information in the memories; and (3) hierarchical arrangements of these operations and memories in programmes. Thus, the electronic computer has been replacing the telephone switchboard as the mechanical model for brain function.

Such a notion of memories and, even more, the notion of operations of a logical sort as actions, and the notion of hierarchical arrangements of these operations – these notions differ markedly from the notion of reflexes being chained to each other. Moreover, ablation studies have been showing that it is not communication across the cortex from sensory-input regions to motor-output regions that is important for behaviour. The cortex can be diced into very small parts without serious damage to behavioural function; but if the fibres, composed of white matter, under an area of the grey matter cortex are cut, behaviour is damaged seriously. Thus, the notion of transcortical association gives way to communication back-and-forth from the centre to the periphery of the brain (see Pribram, 1960). With such changes in conception of brain function being dictated by their own observations, when neuropsychologists become familiar with what is required in programming computers to solve logical problems, it is not surprising that they ask themselves where one might find a locus for the various requirements of computer function – that is, for the memories, the operations and the hierarchical arrangements of them. Karl Pribram (1960) has reviewed the clinical and experimental findings concerning the functional consequences of injuring various portions of the brain, and he has come up with a provisional answer. The brain appears to be divided into intrinsic portions and extrinsic portions. This is the terminology of Rose and Woolsey (1949), and here the term *intrinsic* is used because this portion has no direct connections with either incoming sensory fibres or outgoing motor fibres. The extrinsic portion is so called because it does have such direct peripheral connections. What Pribram suggests is that these components of what is required for the various kinds of information processing and of decision making may well reside in these intrinsic portions of the brain.

There are two intrinsic portions: One is the frontal portion of the cortex, with its connections to the dorsal frontal nuclei of the thalamus; the other, the non-sensory portions of the parietal, occipital and temporal lobes with their connections with the pulvenar or the posterior dorsal nucleus of the thalamus. Injury to the frontal system disrupts executive functions and thereby suggests that it is the locus of the central, neural mechanism for plans. Injury to the posterior intrinsic system results in damage to recognitive functions, which suggests that it may be the locus of central, neural mechanisms for information-processing *per se*. The intrinsic portions of the cerebrum appear to become relatively larger and larger as one samples organisms up the phylogenetic scale. Perhaps what Hebb (1949) has called the A/S ratio might better be called the I/E ratio – for 'Intrinsic/Extrinsic'.

From such studies, one can readily conceive the function of early experience to be one of 'programming' these intrinsic portions of the cerebrum so that they can later function effectively in the forms of learning and problem solving traditionally investigated.

PREVERBAL EXPERIENCE UNIMPORTANT

Early experience, particularly preverbal experience, however, has historically been considered to be relatively unimportant. It has been argued that such experience can hardly have any effect on adult behaviour, because it is not remembered. There have been, of course, a few relatively isolated thinkers who have given at least lip-service to the importance of early experience in the development of the personality. Plato is one who thought that the rearing and education of children was too important a function to be carried out by mere amateur parents. But when he described the rearing that children should have in his *Republic*, he described only experiences for youngsters already talking. Rousseau (1762) gave somewhat more than lip-service in *Emile* to the importance of early experience. Moreover, at least implicitly, he attributed importance to preverbal experience with his prescription that the child, Emile, should very early be exposed to pain and cold in order that he might be toughened.

An even earlier example is to me somewhat embarrassing. I thought that I had invented the notion of split-litter technique for determining the effects of infant feeding-frustration in rats – but later I found, in reading Plutarch's *Lives*, that Lycurgus, the Law-Giver of the Spartans, took puppies from the same litter and reared them in diverse ways, so that some became greedy and mischievious curs while others became followers of the scent and hunters. He exhibited these pups before his contemporaries, saying, 'Men of Sparta, of a truth, habit and training and teaching and guidance in living are a great influence towards engendering excellence, and I will make this evident to you at once.' Thereupon he produced the dogs with diverse rearing. Perhaps it is from the stories of the Spartans that Rousseau got his notion that Emile should be toughened. Such followers of Rousseau as Pestalozzi and Froebel certainly saw childhood experience as important, but as educators they were concerned with the experiences of children who had already learned to verbalize. So far as I can tell, the notion that preverbal experience is seriously important for adult personal characteristics comes from Freud (1905) and his theory of psychosexual development.

According to Hebb's (1949) theory, firing systems, which he terms *cell assemblies* and *phase sequences*, must be built into the cerebrum through what he has termed *primary learning*. This may be seen as another way of expressing the idea that the intrinsic regions of the cerebrum must be properly programmed by preverbal experience if the mammalian organism is later to function effectively as a problem solver. Most of this primary learning Hebb (1949) presumed, moreover, to be based upon early perceptual experience. It is in this presumption that he broke most radically with the traditional emphasis on the response side in learning.

It was this conception which led Hebb (1947) early to compare the problem solving ability in adulthood of those rats which had their perceptual experience limited by cage-rearing, with that of rats which had had their perceptual experience enriched by pet-rearing. As I have already noted in connection with my comments on the notion of predetermined development, the problem solving ability of the cage-reared rats was inferior to that of the pet-reared rats. The theory, as encouraged by these exploratory results, led then to a series of studies in which various kinds of early perceptual experiences were provided for one sample of rats and not for an otherwise comparable sample. Thus, the difference between the groups in later problem solving or maze learning provided an index of both the presence and the degree of effect. Such studies have regularly yielded substantial effects for various kinds of early perceptual experience. These studies, moreover, appear to be clearly reproducible (Hunt and Luria, 1956). Furthermore, as I have already noted in connection with my remarks on predetermined development, these effects of early perceptual experience on adult problem solving appear to become more and more marked up the phylogenetic scale as the intrinsic portions come to constitute a higher and higher proportion of the cerebrum. It looks now as though early experience may be even more important for the perceptual, cognitive and intellective functions than it is for the emotional and temperamental functions. [. . .]

It also looks as if there may be two quite different kinds of effect of painful experience in early infancy. One is that in which the effect of painful experience is one of reducing the aversiveness of later painful or strange circumstances. Although the evidence is not clear yet, that from Salama's experiment indicates that such other kinds of early experience as mere picking up or petting do not have this effect. The other kind of effect is one increasing the capacity of an organism to learn. I have already mentioned that both the shocked rats and the handled rats in the study by Levine *et al.* (1956) learned to respond to a signal to avoid shock more rapidly than did the rats that remained unmolested in the maternal nest. This is adaptive. Denenberg (1962) has shown that even shocking animals once on the second day of life will decrease the number of trials they require to learn an avoidance response, as compared with those left unmolested in the maternal nest. This kind of effect appears to result not only from shock during the preweaning phase of development but also from handling and petting. It looks very much as if any increase in the variation of circumstances encountered during those first three weeks of life will facilitate later learning, not only in the avoidance situation but also in such problem solving situations as those to be found in the Hebb–Williams (1946) tests of animal intelligence.

Change in conception of the relative importance of the sensory and the motor

Yet another belief about what is important in early experience appears to need correction. G. Stanley Hall was fond of the aphorism that 'the mind of man is handmade' (Pruette, 1926). Watson (1919) and the other behaviourists have believed that it is the motor side, rather than the sensory side, that is important in learning. Dewey (1902) gave emphasis to the motor side also in his belief that the child learns chiefly by doing. Dewey went even further to emphasize that the things that the child should be encouraged to do are the things that he would later be called upon to do in taking his place in society. More recently, Osgood (1952) has conceived that the central processes which mediate meanings are the residues of past responses. I am simply trying to document my assertion that in the dominant theory of the origin of mind or of central mediating processes, these have been conceived to be based upon the residues from past responses.

Hebb's (1949) theorizing, as I have already noted, took sharp issue with this dominant theoretical position. He has conceived the basis for primary learning to be chiefly on the sensory side. Riesen (1958) began his experiments on the effects of rearing chimpanzees in darkness with what he called S–S, or Stimulus–Stimulus relations. Piaget (1936), although he has emphasized 'activity as the aliment of a schema', has conceived of *looking* and *listening*, both of which are typically viewed as sensory input channels, as existing among the schemata ready-made at birth. Moreover, it is looking and listening to which he attributes key importance during the first phases of intellectual development. This emphasis is registered in his aphorism that 'the more a child has seen and heard, the more he wants to see and hear' (Piaget, 1936, p. 276).

Evidence requiring this correction of belief comes from more than just the studies of the effects of early perceptual experience on the later problem solving capacity of animals. It also comes from comparing the effects of the cradling practice on the age of onset of walking in Hopi children, with the effects of the homogeneous auditory and visual stimulation on the age of onset of walking in the children in a Tehran orphanage. The cradling practice inhibits actions of an infant's legs and arms during his walking hours through most of the first year of his life. Yet, the mean and standard deviation of the age of walking for those cradled proved to be the same as that for those Hopi children reared with free use of their legs and arms (Dennis and Dennis, 1940). Contrariwise, 85 per cent of the children in the Tehran orphanage were still not walking alone in their fourth year – and here the factor in which the circumstances of these children most differ from those of most young infants was probably the continuous homogeneity of auditory and visual experience (Dennis, 1960). The children of the Tehran orphanage had full use of the motor function of their legs and arms. The Hopi children reared with the cradling practice did not have free use of their legs and arms – but they were exposed, by virtue of their being carried around on their mothers' backs, to a very rich variety of auditory and visual inputs.

Perhaps this emphasis on the motor side is erroneous only as another example of failure to take into account the epigenesis of behavioural and intellectual functions. While it may be true that education by doing is best for children of kindergarten and primary school age, it appears that having a variety of things to listen to and look at may be most important for development during the first year of life (see also Fiske and Maddi, 1961).

ALL BEHAVIOUR AND ALL LEARNING IS MOTIVATED
BY PAINFUL STIMULATION OR HOMEOSTATIC NEED

The fact that both apathy and retardation have been regularly noted in orphanage-reared children who typically live under conditions of homogeneous circumstances (especially marked of the children observed by Dennis in the Tehran orphanage) suggests that homogeneous stimulation somehow reduces motivation. This suggestion brings me to yet another major change of theoretical belief.

It is common to state that 'all behaviour is motivated'. But to make this statement specific, it must be completed with the complex phrase, 'by homeostatic need, painful stimulation, or by innocuous stimuli which have previously been associated with these'. This has been the dominant conception of motivation for most of the last half century – dominant because it has been held both by academic behaviour theorists (for example, Dashiell, 1928; Freeman, 1934; Guthrie, 1938; Holt, 1931; Hull, 1943; Melton, 1941; Miller and Dollard, 1941; Mowrer, 1960) and by psychoanalysts (for example, Fenichel, 1945; Freud, 1915).

This notion implies that organisms should become quiescent in the absence of painful stimulation, homeostatic need, or the acquired drives based upon them. Since World War II, evidence has accumulated to indicate quite clearly that neither animals nor children actually do become quiescent in the absence of such motivating conditions (see Hunt, 1963a). Bühler (1928) noted earlier that the playful activity of children is most evident in the absence of such motivating conditions, and Beach (1945) has reviewed evidence to show that animals are most likely to show playful activity when they are well fed, well watered and in comfortable circumstances. Harlow *et al.* (1950) have found that monkeys learn to disassemble puzzles with no other motivation than the privilege of disassembling them. Similarly, Harlow (1950) found that two monkeys worked repeatedly at disassembling a six-device puzzle for ten continuous hours even though they were quite free of painful stimulation and homeostatic need. Moreover, as he notes, at the tenth hour of testing they were still 'showing enthusiasm for their work'.

In an important series of studies beginning in 1950, Berlyne (see 1960) found that comfortable and satiated rats will explore areas new to them if only given an opportunity, and that the more varied the objects in the region to be explored, the more persistent are the rats' explorations. In a similar vein, Montgomery (1952) has found that the spontaneous tendency for rats to go alternately to the opposite goal-boxes in a T- or Y-maze is no matter of fatigue for the most recently given response, as Hull (1943) contended, but it is one of avoiding the place which the animals have most recently experienced. The choice of place is for the one of lesser familiarity (Montgomery, 1953), and rats learn merely in order to get an opportunity to explore an unfamiliar area (Montgomery, 1955; Montgomery and Segall, 1955). In this same vein, Butler (1953) has observed that monkeys will learn discriminations merely to obtain the privilege of peeking through a window in the walls of their cages, or (Butler, 1958) of listening to sounds from a tape recorder. All these activities appear to be most evident in the absence of painful stimulation, homeostatic need and cues which have previously been associated with such motivating stimuli. It is these findings which call for a change in the traditionally dominant theoretical conception of motivation.

Some of the directions of change in belief show in the modes of theoretical significance given to such evidence. One of these ways is drive-naming. Thus, in recent years, we have been hearing of a manipulatory drive, an exploratory drive, a curiosity drive and so on. This form of theoretical recognition, which is logically circular, appears to be revisiting McDougall's (1908) theory of instincts.

A second mode of theoretical recognition is naming what appears to be the telic significance of an activity. This is what Ives Hendrick (1943) has done in conceiving of the delight which children take in their newfound accomplishments as evidence of an 'urge to mastery'. This is also what White (1959) has done in his excellent review of such evidence by attributing the various activities observed to 'competence motivation'. Such terms of telic significance may be helpful as classificatory and mnemonic devices, but they provide few implications of antecedent-consequent relationships to be investigated.

A third mode of theoretical recognition has consisted in postulating *spontaneous activity*. I have been guilty of this (Hunt, 1960) and so also have Hebb (1949), Miller *et al.* (1960) and Taylor (1960). When my good colleague, Lawrence I. O'Kelly, pointed out that the notion of spontaneous activity may be just as malevolently circular as drive- and instinct-naming, however, I could readily see the force of his argument. But I could also see that I had begun to discern at least the outlines of a mechanism of what I have termed 'intrinsic motivation' or 'motivation inherent in information processing and action' (Hunt, 1963a). [. . .]

APPLICATIONS OF SUCH THEORIZING FOR THE DEVELOPMENT
OF AN ANTIDOTE FOR CULTURAL DEPRIVATION

It remains for me to examine some applications of the theoretical fabric
that I have been weaving to the development of a preschool enrichment
programme for the culturally deprived. First of all, cultural deprivation
may be seen as a failure to provide an opportunity for infants and young
children to have the experiences required for adequate development of
those semi-autonomous central processes demanded for acquiring skill
in the use of linguistic and mathematical symbols and for the analysis
of causal relationships. The difference between the culturally deprived
and the culturally privileged is, for children, analogous to the difference
between cage-reared and pet-reared rats and dogs. At the present time,
this notion of cultural deprivation or of social disadvantage is gross and
undifferentiated indeed. On the basis of the evidence and conceptions
I have summarized, however, I believe the concept points in a very
promising direction. It should be possible to arrange institutional settings where children now culturally deprived by the accident of the social
class of their parents can be supplied with a set of encounters with circumstances which will provide an antidote for what they may have
missed.

The important study of Skeels and Dye (1939), that met with such
a derisive reception when it first appeared, is highly relevant in this
context. You will recall that it was based on a 'clinical surprise'. Two
infants, one aged 13 months with a Kuhlman IQ of 46 and the other
aged 16 months with an IQ of 35, after residence in the relatively
homogeneous circumstances of a state orphanage, were committed to a
state institution for the feebleminded. Some six months later, a psychologist visiting the wards noted with surprise that these two infants had
shown a remarkable degree of development. No longer did they show
either the apathy or the locomotor retardation that had characterized
them when they were committed. When they were again tested with
the Kuhlman scale, moreover, the younger had an IQ of 77 and the
older an IQ of 87 – improvements of 31 and 52 points respectively, and
within half a year. You will also remember that in the experiment which
followed this clinical surprise, every one of a group of thirteen children
showed a substantial gain in IQ upon being transferred from the
orphanage to the institution for the feebleminded. These gains ranged
between 7 points and 58 points of IQ. On the other hand, twelve other
youngsters, within the same age range but with a somewhat higher mean
IQ, were left in the orphanage. When these children were retested after

M

periods varying between twenty-one and forty-three months, all had shown a substantial decrease in IQ, ranging between 8 and 45 points of IQ, with five of these decreases exceeding 35 points.

In recent years, Harold Skeels has been engaged in a following-up study of the individuals involved in these two groups. With about three-fourths of the individuals found, he has yet to find one of the group transferred from the orphanage to the institution for the feeble-minded who is not now maintaining himself effectively in society. Contrariwise, he has not yet found any one of the group remaining in the orphanage who is not now living with institutional support (1965). Although the question of the permanence of the effects of experiential deprivation during infancy is far from answered, such evidence as I have been able to find, and as I have summarized here, would indicate that if the experiential deprivation does not persist too long, it is reversible to a substantial degree. If this be true, the idea of enriching the cognitive fare in day-care centres and in nursery schools for the culturally deprived looks very promising.

Probable nature of the deficit from cultural deprivation

The fact that cultural deprivation is such a global and undifferentiated conception at present invites at least speculative attempts to construe the nature of the deficit and to see wherein and when the infant of the poor and lower-class parents is most likely to be experientially deprived.

One of the important features of lower-class life in poverty is crowding. Many persons live in little space. Crowding, however, may be no handicap for a human infant during most of his first year of life. Although there is no certainty of this, it is conceivable that being a young infant among a large number of people living within a room may actually serve to provide such wide variations of visual and auditory inputs that it will facilitate development more than will the conditions typical of the culturally privileged during most of the first year.

During the second year, on the other hand, living under the crowded conditions of poverty must almost inevitably be highly hampering. Under these conditions, the child encounters a markedly smaller variety of objects than does the middle-class child. As he begins to throw things and as he begins to develop his own methods of locomotion, he is likely to find himself getting in the way of adults already made ill-tempered by their own discomforts and by the frustrations of getting into each other's ways. Such considerations are dramatized by Lewis's (1961) *The Children of Sanchez*, an anthropological study of life in poverty. In such a crowded atmosphere, the activities in which the child must indulge for the development of his own interests and skills must almost inevitably be sharply curbed. 'Being good' comes to be defined as both doing nothing and getting nothing interesting. Moreover, adult utterances provide such poor models of the vocal side of language that it is no wonder that children of the poor lag in their language development and in the abilities which depend upon language for their development (Bernstein, 1960; Deutsch, 1964; Deutsch and Brown, 1964; John, 1963; John and Goldstein, 1964).

In the third year, moreover, when imitation of novel patterns of action and verbalization should presumably be well established and should provide a mechanism for learning vocal language, the models of vocal patterns are wrong for standards to be encountered later in school. When the toddler has achieved the 'learning sets' that 'things have names' and that 'things come in groups' and is prompted by these sets to ask such questions as 'what's that?' or 'is it a this or a that?' his questions are typically met with 'shut up!' Seldom do such parents, who are preoccupied with the problems associated with their poverty or who are chronically in a state of disorganization and apathy, ask the child questions that will force him to use language to identify prepositional relationships and to organize sequences of his experience in linguistic form. With things to play with and with room to play in highly limited, with opportunities to learn standard English – or any other standard language – markedly reduced, the youngster beyond his first year who is in the typical conditions of lower-class life has little opportunity to develop at an optimal rate in the direction demanded for later adaptation in schools and in our highly technological culture (see also Beilin and Gotkin, 1964; Bernstein, 1961; Keller, 1963).

If this armchair analysis has any validity, it suggests that the infant developing in the crowded circumstances of lower-class poverty may develop well through the first year; begin to show retardation during the second year; and show even more retardation during the third, fourth, and fifth years. Presumably, that retardation which occurs during the second year, and even that during the third year, can probably be reversed to a considerable degree by supplying proper circumstances in either a nursery school or a day-care centre for children of 4 and 5 – but I suspect it would be preferable to start with children at 3 years of age. The analysis made here, which is based largely upon what I have learned from Piaget (1936) and from my own observations of development during the preschool years, could be tested. Dr Ina Uzgiris and I have developed an instrument for assessing infant psychological development which consists of six series of situations, arranged according to their difficulty for a sample of eighty-four infants (Uzgiris and Hunt, 1966, 1967). These are situations designed to evoke the various early sensorimotor schemata that Piaget (1936) has described for the first two years. It should provide a tool with which to determine when and how the conditions of development within the crowded circumstances of poverty begin to result in retardation and/or apathy.

Preschool enrichment and the problem of the match

Our traditional emphasis in education upon arithmetic and language skills can well lead us astray in the attempt to develop a programme of preschool enrichment. If Piaget's (1945) observations are correct, spoken language – that is to say the motor side of the language skill – comes only after images, or the central processes representing objects and events, have been developed out of repeated encounters with those objects and events. The fact that chimpanzees show clearly the capacity to dissemble their own purposes even though they lack language (Hebb and Thompson, 1954) lends support from phylogenetic comparisons to this notion of Piaget's. You have most likely heard that O. K. Moore, of Yale, has been teaching preschool children to read with the aid of an electric typewriter hooked up to an electronic system of storing and retrieving information. The fact that, once children have learned to recognize letters by pressing the proper keys of a typewriter, they are enabled to discover spontaneously that they can draw these letters with chalk on a blackboard, lends further support to the image–primacy thesis. Moreover, Moore has observed that the muscular control of such 4-year-olds – who have presumably acquired solid imagery of the letters in the course of their experience with those letters at the electric typewriter – corresponds to that typical of 7- or 8-year-olds (personal communication).

What appears to be important for a preschool enrichment programme is an opportunity to encounter circumstances which will foster the development of these semi-autonomous central processes that can serve as imagery representative of objects and events and which can become the referents for the spoken symbols required in the phonemic combinations of spoken or written language. Moore's results also suggest to me that these semi-autonomous central processes, if adequately developed, can serve as the basis for motor control. Such considerations suggest that a proper preschool enrichment programme should provide children with an opportunity to encounter a wide variety of objects and circumstances. They suggest that the children should also have an opportunity to imitate a wide variety of models of action and of motor language. The danger of attempting to prescribe materials and models at this stage of knowledge, however, is that the prescriptions may well fail to provide a proper match with what the child already has in his storage. The fact that most teachers have their expectations based on experience with culturally privileged children makes this problem of the match especially dangerous and vexing in work with the culturally deprived.

Revisiting Montessori's contribution

In view of the dangers of attempting prescriptions of enrichments for preschool children, it may be well to re-examine the educational contributions of Maria Montessori. Her contributions have been largely forgotten in America. In fact, until as late as August 1962, I could have identified Maria Montessori only by saying that she had developed some kind of kindergarten and was an educational faddist who had made quite a splash about the turn of the century. I was, thus, really introduced to her work by Dr Jan Smedslund, a Norwegian psychologist, who remarked to me, during a conference at the University of Colorado, that Maria Montessori had provided a practical answer to what I have called 'the problem of the match' (Hunt, 1961, pp. 276 ff.).

When I examined the library for materials on Maria Montessori, I discovered that the novelist, Dorothy Canfield Fisher, had spent the winter of 1910–11 at the Casa de Bambini in Rome and that she had returned to write a book on Montessori's work. This book, entitled *A Montessori Mother* (1912), may still be the best initial introduction to Montessori's work. Books by E. M. Standing (1957) and Nancy Rambusch (1962) have brought the record up to date, and the book by Rambusch contains a bibliography of the materials in the English language concerning Montessori's work assembled by Gilbert E. Donahue.

Montessori's contribution is especially interesting to me because she based her methods of teaching upon the spontaneous interest of children in learning, that is, upon what I am calling 'intrinsic motivation'. Moreover, she put great stress upon teachers observing the children under their care to discover what kinds of things foster their individual interests and growth. Furthermore, she put great stress on the training of what she called sensory processes, but what we might more appropriately call information processes today. The fact that she placed strong emphasis upon the training of sensory processes may well be one of the major reasons why her work dropped out of the main stream of educational thought and practice in America before World War I. This emphasis was too dissonant with the dominant American emphasis in learning upon the motor response, rather than upon the sensory input or information processes. It was Montessori's concern to observe carefully what interested a child that led her to discover a wide variety of materials in which she found children showing strong spontaneous interest.

Second, Montessori broke the lock step in the education of young children. Her schools made no effort to keep all the children doing the same thing at the same time. Rather, each child was free to examine and to work with whatever happened to interest him. This meant that he was free to persist in a given concern as long as he cared to, and also free to change from one concern to another whenever a change appeared appropriate to him. In this connection, one of the very interesting observations made by Dorothy Canfield Fisher concerns the prolonged duration of children's interest in given activities under such circumstances. Whereas the lore about preschoolers holds that the nature of the activity in a nursery school must be changed every ten or fifteen minutes, Mrs Fisher described children typically remaining engrossed in such activities as the buttoning and unbuttoning of a row of buttons for two or more hours at a time.

Third, Montessori's method consisted in having children from 3 to 6 years old together. As I see it, from taking into account the epigenesis of intellectual development, such a scheme has the advantage of providing the younger children with a wide variety of models for imitation. Moreover, it supplies the older children with an opportunity to help and teach the younger. Helping and teaching contain many of their own rewards.

There may well be yet another advantage, one in which those financing preschool enrichment will be heartily concerned. Montessori's first teacher was a teenage girl, the superintendent's daughter in the apartment house in the Rome slums where the first Casa de Bambini was established in 1907. In that school, this one young woman successfully set the stage for the learning of fifty to sixty children from 3 to 7 years old. I say 'successfully' because, as Dorothy Canfield Fisher (1912) reported, some of the children had learned to read by the time they were 5 years old. On the other hand, current observations suggest that the Montessori approach may need supplementation to correct the linguistic deficit of children from culturally deprived backgrounds. It may be well to supplement the Montessori approach with the very recently developed approach of Bereiter et al. (1966). Their academically orientated preschool for culturally deprived children focuses directly on language and arithmetic; and their teaching method combines concrete experience with the modern method of teaching foreign languages. Starting with 4-year-olds one and one-half to two and one-half years below chronological age on the Illinois Test of Psycholinguistic Abilities (see McCarthy and Kirk, 1961), they increased the median psycholinguistic test age of these children by two years within six months in their programme – a programme consisting of merely three twenty-minute sessions for groups of five with a teacher on each of five days a week. This approach reverts to the lock step for short periods, and doctrinaire followers of Montessori may resist using such a supplement. Alternatively, one might consider adding to the Montessori apparatus something like O. K. Moore's 'talking typewriter' (1963), reported effective in correcting the language deficit. Before any confident assertions can be made about such matters, however, solid evaluative investigations are necessary.

SUMMARY

I began by saying that it was very exciting for me to encounter people – generally considered sensible – in the process of planning to utilize preschool experience as an antidote for the effects of cultural deprivation. I have tried to summarize the basis in psychological theory and in the evidence from psychological research for such a use of preschool enrichment. I have tried to summarize the evidence: (1) that the belief in fixed intelligence is no longer tenable; (2) that development is far from completely predetermined; (3) that what goes on 'between the ears' is much less like the static switchboard of the telephone than it is like the active information processes programmed into electronic computers to enable them to solve problems; (4) that experience is the programmer of the human brain-computer and, thus, that Freud was correct about the importance of the experience which comes before the advent of language; (5) that, none the less, Freud was wrong about the nature of the experience which is important, since an opportunity to see and hear a variety of things appears to be more important than the fate of instinctual needs and impulses; and, finally (6) that learning need not be motivated by painful stimulation, homeostatic need, or the acquired drives based upon these, for there is a kind of intrinsic motivation which is inherent in information processing and action.

In applying these various lines of evidence and these various changes in conception, I have viewed the effects of cultural deprivation as

analogous to the experimentally found effects of experiential deprivation in infancy. I have pointed out the importance of 'the problem of
the match' and the dangers of using our present knowledge to prescribe
programmes of circumstantial encounters to enrich the experience of
culturally deprived preschool children. In this connection, I have
suggested that we re-examine the work of Maria Montessori for suggestions. For she successfully based her teaching method on children's
spontaneous interest in learning; she found a solution to the 'problem
of the match' by carefully observing children's interests and then giving
them individual freedom to choose which circumstances they would
encounter.

21

P. E. Vernon (1969)

Intelligence and, cultural environment

P. E. Vernon, *Intelligence and Cultural Environment* (Methuen),
summary from end of book

Although the psychologist's tests are highly inadequate instruments
for bringing out the full strengths and weaknesses of different groups
or individuals, particularly when applied outside the cultural group
for which they were constructed, they nevertheless tend to confirm our
everyday observations. Each group certainly shows variations in patterns of abilities: members of an underdeveloped country may reach,
or surpass, western standards on some tests, and fall below what we
would regard as the borderline for mental deficiency on others. But
the average performance on quite a wide range of tests only too strikingly
fits in with the observed inequalities of mankind. Similarly, within
any one western country, there are obvious differences in the status,
vocational and educational achievements of subgroups such as the social
classes, the coloured immigrants in Britain, the Negroes and Indians of
North America; and, however open to criticism our tests of intelligence
and other abilities may be, they tend to reflect these differences.

No one would deny the importance of geographical and economic
handicaps, of disease and malnutrition in the production of such
differences. But to a very great extent man makes himself and fashions
his own environment, and it is he who must be changed if he is to
achieve a more prosperous and healthy existence. We suspect that his offspring fail to develop the high-level skills and mental abilities required
for adaptation and progress in the modern world because of the way
he brings them up in the home and community, and the schooling or
training he provides. It is not only the poor circumstances of the parents
but their backwardness and resistance to change which result in the
underdevelopment of their children's capacities. However, in every
group there are the more and the less able; and many of the former
do achieve good education and positions of leadership. They influence
their own societies, sometimes dramatically, usually more gradually,

and bring up their own children less disadvantageously. Changes are occurring, too, as groups and subgroups come in contact with and try to help one another, even if the influences they exert are often motivated by self-interest and political considerations.

These, however, are not matters for the scientific psychologist to dabble in. Yet he can make very real contributions by studying the present situation and trying to disentangle the main factors underlying the stimulation or retardation of intellectual growth, by clarifying the nature of the essential variables and developing and testing sound hypotheses, also by improving the diagnostic tools which he uses in his evaluations. He cannot, of course, claim to be wholly impartial or free from ethnocentrism and middle-class prejudice; inevitably he views other groups through the spectacles of the values and concepts of his own group. Indeed even these opening paragraphs sound as though the middle-class western way of life was being held up as the ideal to which all inferior groups aspire. True, there is a kind of universal scale of economic prosperity and technological advance; and psychologically there is a scale ranging from the relatively simple to the more complex and powerful types of mental process, and the two are interlinked. But the writer has been at pains to point out that the complex intelligence of the western middle-class is not the only one, and that its development is accompanied by serious drawbacks; that over and above variations in position on these scales there are, and doubtless always will be, countless variations which promote the adjustment and stability of different cultures. Also that although most tests, including those used in the writer's researches, do reflect western-type intelligence, there is no reason why psychological techniques should not be applied in studying the particular abilities and qualities of other groups, and the factor underlying their growth.

Much of the controversy regarding differences in abilities between ethnic groups and subgroups has arisen because the term 'intelligence' is ambiguous. It is used here to refer to the effective all-round cognitive abilities to comprehend, to grasp relations and reason (Intelligence B), which develops through the interaction between the genetic potential (Intelligence A) and stimulation provided by the environment. One must also distinguish constitutional equipment, that is, the potential as affected by pre-natal or other physiological conditions; and Intelligence C – the results obtained on various intelligence tests, which provide merely a limited sample of the Intelligence B displayed in behaviour and thinking at home, at school, at work. There is strong evidence that differences in Intelligence B and C between individuals within one culture are largely – certainly not wholly – genetically determined. But when environmental differences are more extreme, as between ethnic groups, their effects predominate. This does not mean that there are no innate racial differences in abilities, but they are probably small and we have no means of proving them. Differences between subgroups such as social classes are partly genetic, not wholly environmental.

Current conceptions of cognitive growth derive largely from the work of Piaget, Hebb and Bruner. From the initial sensorimotor reflexes of the newborn, a succession of more complex and adaptive schemata or skills are built up through the impact of environmental stimulation on the maturing nervous system and through the infant's active exploration and experiment. Thus a series of stages or successive reorganizations can be recognized in the child's perception, speech and thinking, through which different children progress at different rates (Bruner's enactive, iconic and symbolic modes of coding differ in important respects from Piaget's sensorimotor, preoperational, concrete and formal stages, but both are useful in describing intellectual development). Moreover, more backward groups typically fail to progress as far as others along this scale, and though they may develop lower-order skills which are highly effective for survival, their reasoning capacities remain similar in many ways to those of younger children, or even regress through lack of appropriate stimulation. That is they learn to be unintelligent, instead of acquiring the skills that constitute intelligence. An important implication is that man has by no means reached the limits of his mental powers; there is immense room for improvement at the lower end of the scale, and also the possibility of more effective 'techniques' at the top end.

General intelligence is merely the common element in a whole host of distinguishable, but overlapping, cognitive abilities. When dealing with homogeneous or highly selected populations, it is profitable to study different mental faculties and abilities along special lines, adopting the factorial models of Thurstone and Guilford. But with more heterogeneous populations, and particularly when considering different ethnic groups or subgroups, the common element or g factor tends to dominate. And there are advantages in following the hierarchical or group-factor model, which successively subdivides more specialized types of ability. This implies that, while we should certainly try to study a wide variety of mental functions in contrasted ethnic groups or subgroups, we are most likely to discover conditions that affect general or all-round ability; then those that favour or inhibit verbal and educational as contrasted with perceptual, spatial and practical abilities, and later the smaller (but still quite broad) group factors such as number, memorizing, fluency or creativity, etc. Intelligence B cannot be precisely defined since it refers to the totality of our schemata, but its essence lies in the more generalized thinking skills, which can be applied to a wide variety of problems.

What then do we mean by the potential ability of an underdeveloped group or individual? It is not Intelligence A or constitutional potential, since these cannot be assessed and are of use only in so far as previous environment has developed them. Equally the conventional expedient of contrasting achievement measures with intelligence test scores (verbal or non-verbal) is beset with fallacies. Abilities at different types of test often differ, and by surveying these patterns of abilities in the light of the individual's or group's physical and cultural background, education and motivation, the psychologist can often arrive at useful diagnoses and remedial proposals. If plausible reasons can be suggested either for general backwardness or for unevennesses in performance, and if the remedial measures at the disposal of the community can be shown to, or reasonably be expected to, work, then that person or group has potentiality.

Most studies consist of cross-sectional comparisons of groups or individuals who differ in respect of many interacting conditions, and these do not readily demonstrate the effects of any particular condition. The methodologically superior experimental approach, where one condition is changed and other factors are kept constant, and the longitudinal follow-up of a sample who undergo various conditions, have their own difficulties. Thus even in the case of relatively clear-cut conditions such as malnutrition during pregnancy or later, and debilitating diseases, our knowledge is scrappy and often indirect. The incidence of dietary deficiencies is worldwide, especially in the low-income countries, and it is found that they can cause permanent impairment to the brain at the formative stage of pregnancy and early infancy, and seriously reduce later intellectual capacity. After this stage, poor health and nutrition or endemic diseases, though often associated with poor performance, do not seem to affect mental growth as such.

Particular stress is laid by most psychologists on the sensory stimulation, opportunities for activity, and the emotional relationships of the first year or two of life, as basic to later psychological development. But the evidence, apart from that of animal experiments, is unconvincing. While it is clear that extreme social deprivation has traumatic effects on human infants, probably the ordinary range of social and physical environments (even among relatively primitive groups) provides adequate stimulation. In other words, conceptual and linguistic deprivation during the period from about one-and-a-half years and throughout childhood, when children should be building up their concepts of objects and their relations, labels and thinking skills, may be more important than so-called sensory or perceptual deprivation. And while the preschool and early school periods are crucial, the modifiability of intellectual capacities by changed conditions even in adolescence has been underestimated.

Certain types of visual discrimination are strengthened in environments where they are important for survival. But the evidence for the effects of ecological environment on susceptibility to illusions is conflicting. Perceptual development seems to depend to a greater extent on social norms, education and acculturation. Clearly 'however' many African peoples have difficulties with analytic perception of figures and pictures, and with three-demensional interpretation. This deficiency is not found among other quite backward groups such as Eskimos. Its origins are obscure, and it may be remediable by appropriate training, but the main explanation would seem to lie in lack of visual-kinaesthetic experience and of encouragement of play and exploration throughout childhood.

The interactions of language with thinking are highly complex and controversial. But a child's language, which is wholly shaped by his cultural group, must be intimately involved in his perceptions and conceptualizations of the world. Hence his intellectual development is highly vulnerable to poverty of linguistic stimulation, and to the inadequacies of the mother tongue – in many societies – as a medium for education. Bernstein's analysis of 'formal' and 'public' language codes describes the extremes of a continuum which is typical not only of the British socioeconomic classes, but applies in many respects to technological as against more primitive cultures. Bernstein brings out also the close connection between linguistic training and cultural values: the formal code is associated with internalized controls (Superego formation), high educational aspirations and planning for the future; the public code with externally imposed discipline and with less purposeful attitudes to life.

Infant rearing practices and maternal deprivation may cause temporary emotional traumata, and seem to be associated with certain cultural traits. But their long-term effects on personality and particularly on the development of abilities, are more dubious. A number of investigations indicate that socialization practices and the home 'climate' during the preschool and school years are more influential. The 'democratic' but demanding home climate makes for better intellectual progress than the over-protective, the autocratic or the 'unconcerned' homes. The work in this area of Witkin and his colleagues provides important evidence that the encouragement of resourcefulness and independence in growing children leads to greater clarity and differentiation of perceptions and concepts, while maternal over-protection tends to favour verbal abilities. It is not clear whether it is general intelligence or spatial abilities which are chiefly affected, nor what parts are played in causation by social class differences, by sex or temperament, or by masculine identification, etc. However Witkin's generalizations have fruitful applications to differences between cultural groups, e.g. Eskimos and certain African groups.

Turning then to intellectual progress at school: the major researches in the U.K. of E. Fraser, Wiseman and Warburton, and J. W. B. Douglas, show that, although the handicaps of poverty are much less marked than forty years ago, socioeconomic class and its associated conditions of child care, neighbourhood morale, and good or poor schooling, still make substantial differences to children's intelligence and achievement. Even between 8 and 11 years the differential between the middle-class and lower-working-class child becomes progressively greater. But the most important factor of all appears to be the cultural level of the home and the parents' interest in and aspirations for their children's education. Hence the further improvements that we would desire in material conditions, social welfare and schooling, will not of themselves eliminate the handicaps of the lower working and less educated classes.

Much the same factors are shown to be significant by research in the U.S.A., though the major differences there are not so much between socioeconomic classes as between ethnic and linguistic groups, i.e. between whites and Negroes or recent immigrants. American Negroes tend to score in the low 80s on tests of intelligence and achievement, though there are considerable geographic variations, and differences on different types of test. Moreover younger children perform better and show a cumulative deficit at later ages. Negroes are at least as handicapped in non-verbal or spatial tests as in verbal abilities, though relatively better in simple number and rote learning tests; and this may be attributable to familial factors such as the frequent absence of masculine identification models for boys. The interpretation and implications of observed differences in abilities have given rise to even more heated controversy in the U.S.A. At the same time there have been valuable positive efforts to reduce the handicaps of 'disadvantaged' children by compensatory or introductory schooling, or by integrating schools of different ethnic composition. It is too early to say how successful these measures are in improving general intellectual growth and scholastic performance, or whether the effects of home upbringing and of inter-group suspicions are too strong.

There is rather little evidence of the effects of different kinds of schooling, or of studying different subjects in different ways, on general mental growth. But it is clear that sheer amount of schooling, even – in backward countries – of low-quality education, helps to promote both school achievement and the kind of reasoning measured by non-verbal tests. Also if such schooling is unduly delayed, the possibilities of mental growth deteriorate. The acquisition of lower-order schemata opens up the way to higher-order thinking, but they can also become rigidified and block further progress. Likewise in western countries the level of adult intelligence depends on the kind and amount of intellectual stimulation provided by the adolescent's secondary schooling and occupation. The notion of optimal or critical periods for learning probably has less applicability to conceptual than to sensorimotor functions, and greater importance should be attached to motivational factors – to the maintenance or repression of curiosity, and to the child's or young adult's aspirations and prospects of advancement. In this sense growth depends on the future as well as on the past.

Cultural groups and subgroups are exceedingly varied, and so also must be their effects on the intellectual growth of their members. A number of attempted classifications or typologies exist, but it seems reasonable to regard the Puritan ethic of the western middle class as producing the greatest development of intelligence, in contrast both to western lower class and to the 'less civilized' cultures. The two latter differ in important respects, but the less civilized can be subdivided into hunting and agricultural types, which coincide rather closely with Witkin's field-independent and dependent; i.e. they are to some extent linked with the major group factors of spatial and verbal abilities.

The evidence that Intelligence B is built up in response to environmental stimulation and is therefore affected in many ways by cultural differences does not mean that tests constructed in western cultures are always worthless elsewhere. Despite the valuation of different skills in different ethnic groups, all groups have increasing need for complex, symbolic thinking. Researches in Africa and other countries in fact show that adaptations of western tests possess promising validity in assessing educational aptitudes and work effectiveness, though this may be partly because they are measuring language skills required for advanced schooling in the former situation, or acculturation and cooperativeness with white employers in the latter. Correlations with job efficiency assessments (which tend to be unreliable) are low, but this is true in western cultures also. However tests may often be inappropriate not so much because they do not measure useful abilities as because they are also greatly affected by unfamiliarity with the materials, or with the testing situation, or by other irrelevant 'extrinsic' factors.

Cross-cultural comparisons are unavoidable when members of different cultural groups or subgroups, who have very likely been reared under different conditions and are differently handicapped, are in competition for the same schooling or same jobs. Different regression equations, or different norms or cut-offs for acceptance, may be needed for such groups. Another legitimate cross-cultural application is for studying the effects of different background conditions on abilities.

Unsophisticated testees are handicapped in many ways by lack of relevant experience, failure to understand the instructions, and absence of the motivations and sets which sophisticated testees bring with them to the testing situation. However the distinction between these extrinsic factors, and intrinsic factors which affect the underlying ability, is only a relative one. Probably it is best defined in terms of how readily the handicap can be overcome, e.g. by better conditions of administration. A bimodal score distribution or the piling up of low scores among 'nonstarters' is another useful indication of extrinsic difficulties. Also differences in the order of item difficulty may show that a test is measuring different things in different groups. However a number of investigations of practice effects among Africans indicate that these are not so large as is sometimes supposed, particularly when the testees have received some schooling. The results are comparable to those obtained with unsophisticated testees in the U.K., and the same kind of measures used to familiarize British children with tests can be applied or extended. The suggestion that abilities should be judged from scores on several successive administrations, i.e. from learning curves, is technically unsound.

It is obviously far more difficult to transfer western-type tests to relatively unacculturated groups, with little or no schooling, and the psychologist may have to confine himself to individual testing with specially constructed materials, under informal conditions. However, Biesheuvel's work shows that it is possible to get across performance tests to groups of linguistically heterogeneous and illiterate adults; and Schwarz has formulated a series of useful principles for giving group tests, e.g. to applicants for technical training, which amount to teaching the testees beforehand precisely what they have to do. For most purposes it would be better to construct new tests based on materials and conditions appropriate to the culture concerned, than to adapt western ones, though this is difficult in view of the shortage of trained personnel. It is essential to validate old or new tests locally and to devise an appropriate system of norming.

In attempting to assess the educational potential of immigrant children, verbal tests are preferable to non-verbal or performance – either standard tests in English if they can communicate in it, or if not then similar tests in their own tongues. Alternatively a varied battery should be given and the results interpreted in the light of their educational, linguistic and social history, i.e. clinically. Objective tests of achievement are being produced in many developing countries and used on a large scale for secondary school selection. Less progress has been made with aptitude tests, e.g. for technical training, largely because, in the absence of suitable background experience, the skills needed for technical work are too underdeveloped to provide a basis for worthwhile tests.

In the present writer's investigations a battery of varied group and individual tests was applied to small groups of 10–12-year-old boys in England, Scotland (the Hebrides), Jamaica, Uganda and Canada (Indians and Eskimos). All the boys were being educated in the English medium. The chief aim was – not to show that some groups are more backward than others – but to link up patterns of scores on different types of tests with differences of background. No intelligence tests as such were used. The main categories were:

(a) Verbal and educational – arithmetic, silent reading and English, oral vocabulary, rote learning and learning of meaningful information.
(b) Induction – versions of the Shipley Abstraction and the Matrices test.
(c) Conceptual development – sorting and labelling, and a series of Piaget tasks dealing with conservation and other concepts.
(d) 'Creativity' tests of fluency and imagination.
(e) Perceptual and spatial tests, including Kohs Blocks, Embedded Figures, Bender-Gestalt, Porteus Mazes and Draw-a-Man.

In interpreting what the tests measure, reference is made to previous evidence of their validity, and to factorial analysis of the scores in several groups. The scores on each test were converted into Deviation

Quotients or Standard Scores (similar to IQs), on the basis of the distributions in the English group, so that relative performance of different tests could be compared. Each boy was also interviewed, usually by a local teacher, to obtain information on his background, home, schooling, interests and vocational aspirations.

Within the English group, the *g* factor, or general ability in all the tests, correlated highly with an assessment of Cultural Stimulus in the home, and to a lesser extent with Socioeconomic level and with Planfulness or Purposiveness of the home; but there was no correlation with Stable *v.* Broken homes. The educational, verbal, perceptual and practical group factors, measured by particular groups of tests, also gave small correlations with several background conditions, though [there was only limited support for the hypothesis that masculine dominance in the home and encouragement of initiative are associated with perceptual-spatial abilities.

Small groups of delinquent boys in an Approved School, and maladjusted children, gave unusual patterns of scores. The delinquents were very low in educational attainments, but also in the two Induction tests and certain perceptual tests. Their oral vocabulary, concept development and rote learning were rather better (quotients in the 80s); on some performance tests they scored in the 90s, and their performance on creativity tests was close to average. The maladjusted boys were specially backward in arithmetic, less so in verbal abilities; they were near average in concept development and in most spatial-perceptual tests and above average in creativity. The poor reasoning of the former, and the well-developed ability of the latter to deal with concrete notions of space, conservation, etc. – in contrast to their disturbed emotional and social relations – suggest that a wide-ranging battery of ability tests may be valuable diagnostically. In addition the Drawing and Creativity tests have projective possibilities. Socioeconomic level, Planfulness and Regular Schooling were found to correlate moderately with verbal and educational performance, but not Broken Home or Parental Tension. Patterns of family relationships, mother or father dominance and affection or rejection, together with neurotic, aggressive or other syndromes, seemed to be related to test scores, but in no clear-cut manner.

A group of Scottish Hebridean boys was tested in or near Stornoway, Isle of Lewis; half of them were from English-speaking, half from Gaelic-speaking, homes. Apart from the linguistic differences, both groups are of interest as growing up in a relatively isolated community, free from the rush of modern civilization. There are strong traditions of responsible and provident living, of rather rigid upbringing and respect for formal education. The Gaelic-background group was handicapped in oral vocabulary, the Sorting test and Piaget, but did not differ significantly from the English-background boys in other respects. Both were superior to English norms in scholastic achievement and learning tests, though there was some restriction in originality. The test correlations were unusual in showing no distinction between *g* and verbal abilities. This does not seem to be due so much to linguistic heterogeneity as to a strong contrast between the more culturally stimulating and sophisticated homes *v.* the more traditional and restricted.

Turning now to deprived groups – two of African and two of indigenous Canadian origin: we will first summarize the cultural and other characteristics most likely to affect their ability development, and then compare and discuss the test results. Jamaica is a country in transition from a primitive agricultural to a technological economy, and the population ranges from extremely poor, largely illiterate and superstitious rural communities – descendants of African slaves – to a well-educated middle class, often of mixed descent. The sample of boys for testing was drawn from schools representing all levels. The mother tongue of the majority is a kind of pidgin English which considerably impedes education, and primary schooling tends to be irregular, of poor quality and far too formal and repressive of initiative. Family life is apt to be unstable, female-dominated and likewise conformist and authoritarian.

Uganda is basically a rural subsistence economy, with a low standard of living and much malnutrition, though the writer's sample was derived mainly from urbanized east Africans living in or near to Kampala, i.e. a relatively acculturated group. As in many African countries there is a diversity of tribes with different dialects. Education is mainly conducted in English, though the language is seldom used by the children outside the classroom. Schooling is available only for about one third of this age group, but it is greatly prized. Because of the language difficulties (among teachers as well as pupils) and the strong motivation, and for historical reasons, education tends to be highly mechanical. But the major differences between African and western intelligences probably arise from the emphasis on conformity and social integration as against individual responsibility and internal controls; and from the acceptance of magical beliefs which inhibit analytic perception and rational thinking.

Canadian Indians and Eskimos are equally disadvantaged linguistically, though English has greater currency in transactions with the white culture, and is freely used by Eskimo boys in and outside school.

Readings in Human Intelligence

The quality of schooling is good also, especially in our Eskimo sample, though attendance may be delayed or irregular. The majority of families live at a low economic and cultural level, and show the traditional improvidence, or generous sharing now, rather than planning for the future. Vocational prospects for the boys are poor, partly because of geographical difficulties and partly because of the reputation of the indigenes for shiftlessness; also because of the apathy and demoralization consequent on the breakdown of the traditional hunting economies and, in the case of reservation Indians, their continued resentment and resistance to acculturation. At the same time, the traditional child-rearing practices and values mean that boys of 10–12 years are still trained for resourcefulness and show strong identification with hunting and other masculine pursuits. This was most marked among a sample of Eskimo boys boarding at a school hostel, whose families still tend to live on the land rather than in settlements.

Table 21.1 provides a crude summary of the main handicaps thought

TABLE 21.1. *Environmental conditions and test score patterns in nine groups*

Conditions	Maladjusted	Delin.	Hebr. Engl.	Hebr. Gael.	Jamaica	Ugandan	Indian	Esk. Town	Esk. Host.
Socioeconomic level		−			−			−	−
Providence–planfulness		−	+	+				−	−
Cultural stimulus		−	+					−	−
Language			−		−	−	−		
Adequacy of schooling			+	+	−	−			
Progressive *v.* formal	+		−	−	−	−			
Encouragement of initiative					−	−		+	+
Home security and stability	−	−			−	−			−
Perceptual–kinaesthetic stimulation			?−	?−		−			
Health, nutrition					−	−	−	−	−
Deficiencies in: All-round level	−	− −	−		−	−	−	−	−
Induction		−		−	−			−	+
School attainments	−	−	+	+				−	−
Oral English and comprehension					−	−	−	−	−
Conservation	+		−		+	−		−	−
Memorizing	−		+	+	+	+	−		
Fluency and originality	+	+					+	+	+
Practical–spatial	+		−	−	−		−	+	+
Perceptual			−	−		+			
Drawing	+				+	+		+	+

to operate in nine of the above groups or subgroups, together with the main features of their test score patterns. In the top half are listed assessments of environmental conditions, *relative to those of children in western cultures.* Inevitably these are somewhat subjective. Below, the groups are first graded on all-round ability, and then for *relatively* better or poorer performance on particular sets of tests, i.e. they are *compared with their own means* rather than with English standards. All-round ability is roughly graded, a single minus indicating a mean quotient of about 87–93, a double minus about 80–85. It should be pointed out that most of these groups are *not* representative samples. They are drawn from school attenders only; some groups are a little older than others; and the Ugandans, in particular, come mainly from urbanized families of above average socioeconomic level.

Nevertheless there is clearly a general correspondence between the numbers of adverse conditions and overall performance: the main exceptions, who score lower than might be expected from their backgrounds, are the three most socially maladjusted groups – Maladjusted, Delinquents and Indians. It may be seen that the assessment of Cultural Stimulus is most diagnostic of all-round ability; most other variables overlap but show greater discrepancies (for example, Ugandans are among the lowest scorers though relatively high socioeconomically). Had we had a considerably larger number of groups and more objective techniques of comparing their relative standing on these environmental conditions, it would have been interesting to correlate each condition with the group scores.

Several other fairly close correspondences are apparent. Thus the language rating, based on lack of English in the home, is naturally related to deficiency in Oral English and Comprehension, though not so closely to School Attainments or to Fluency. Formality of schooling always tends to produce superior performance in Memorizing (i.e. the Word Learning test + Spelling), but good School Attainments in English and arithmetic seems to be more related to the Providence or Planfulness rating of the average home. On the non-verbal side, the connections are less clear-cut, and give only limited support to the hypotheses that spatial ability is favoured by a hunting economy, or by cultures which train for initiative. Performance on the perceptual tests (mainly Embedded Figures, Design Reproduction and Mazes) does not correspond with any of the environmental variables. However practical–spatial ability (Kohs, Formboard and Picture Recognition) does tend to go with Encouragement of Initiative, and to some extent with Perceptual–Kinaesthetic Stimulation. Inductive ability also seems to be related to Initiative. What we can say is that there is a closer resemblance in test score patterns between Jamaicans (descended from west Africans) and east Africans, also between Indians and Eskimos, than across these two groups. Although our tests fail to pin down very clearly the essential ability factors in which they differ, Kohs Blocks – which mainly measures inductive + spatial ability – comes nearest to doing so. Thus 66 per cent of all the Jamaicans and (highly selected) Ugandans as against 22 per cent of Indians and Eskimos scored under 10 points on this test. In contrast the Jamaicans and Ugandans were much superior in Word Learning and arithmetic despite roughly equivalent linguistic handicap.

The results of our inquiries show that we cannot afford to ignore the factor of general retardation. On the whole these groups and those individuals who are most backward in, say, linguistic tests also tend to be below average on all other types of tests. Nevertheless there are considerable irregularities in score patterns, and we have made a little, though not very much, progress in explaining why particular groups do some things better than others.

Some of the main results in particular groups are as follows: the Jamaicans, in common with others, were noticeably more successful on standard classroom tests of English (including multiple-choice vocabulary) and arithmetic than on oral comprehension of language. Thus western tests of verbal intelligence and achievement are less unsuitable, e.g. for school selection purposes, than might be supposed, though naturally western norms are apt to be misleading. Much more striking is their deficiency on non-verbal materials such as Matrices, Kohs and Formboard (the latter test probably being additionally affected by conditions of health and nutrition), though relatively high on perceptual and drawing tests. They differ most markedly from Africans on the Piaget tasks, probably due to their greater sophistication, their many contacts with British and American cultures, the absence of tribalism and fewer magical beliefs. But there were big differences on most of the tests between the urban boys, who were within the normal English range (except in comprehension and induction) and the rural ones who are much less touched by modern civilization. Somewhat as in the Hebridean groups, there was a closer correlation between verbal and other abilities than in English groups, suggesting that schooling and acculturation are necessary to development on the perceptual-spatial side. This may arise when many of the homes provide little stimulus to any kind of intellectual development, or even repress such development.

The Ugandan group was the most handicapped of any in oral vocabulary, although they were supposed to have been taught in English for five years. This seemed to be due, at least partly, to their unfamiliarity in analysing words out of context. But the effects of their very formal schooling were manifest in high spelling and rote memorizing. A particular retardation was noted also in the conservation items of the Piaget tests, and in three-dimensional interpretation of pictures, both of which confirm previous observations of African abilities. On the other hand there was no general retardation on the spatial-perceptual side; Gottschaldt Figures, for example, Drawing and Mazes were within the normal range. The structuring of abilities differed markedly from that in other groups: instead of verbal abilities (in English) permeating intellectual development generally, they were relatively distinct from other types of ability – inductive, practical – perceptual and imaginative. There seems to be a clear need for greater integration of their learning of English with daily life, based on less mechanical, more active, methods; also for the introduction of greater opportunities for concrete, practical training to compensate for the inadequacies of psychomotor stimulation in the homes.

The interests of the majority of Eskimo and Indian boys still lie mainly in hunting, trapping, fishing or riding and ice hockey. But those who were tested were attending good schools, on the Canadian pattern, and had made some progress in classroom English, less in oral comprehension, in Piaget-type concepts or in arithmetic (where they are handicapped by 'the new' mathematics). In most other respects Eskimos who have had some exposure to schooling tend to score within the normal range, and are generally superior to the Indians, partly because of the greater apathy and uncooperativeness of most Indian families. Eskimo hostel boarders do better than those living in settlements on tests of induction and concept development, indicating that these abilities are promoted by the more resourceful and independent mode of existence. Indians are particularly restricted in imaginative ideas, i.e. they receive no encouragement to think 'divergently'. All groups are good at drawing, and their relatively high scores on spatial tests suggest mechanical potentialities. An unusual feature of the general factor in Eskimo test scores was that it does not correlate with cultural and economic characteristics of the homes, but does with amount of schooling. Probably therefore it is much less developed among the indigenous population who obtain less regular or no schooling. In the Indians, on the other hand, it correlated highly with an assessment of the initiative or morale v. apathy of the boy and his family.

IMPLICATIONS

In summing up, it is desirable to stress once again that surveys of this kind are not very effective in pinning down the factors that underly any particular deficiency, or superiority, in an ability. In other words, our attributions are often speculative, though the fact that they are mostly based on the results of several tests, and on comparisons of several samples, gives them more substance. On the other hand, it should also be admitted that tests may measure rather different abilities in different groups, or be affected in different ways by what we have called extrinsic factors. Particularly non-verbal, spatial and perceptual tests are apt to show varied factor loadings (though this is no doubt partly due to the small sizes of the samples). Verbal and educational tests are more likely to measure the same thing in different contexts, since all our samples are being taught a similar body of knowledge and skills in English-medium schools. Hence, while our results on the whole justify quite widespread use of western-type tests across cultures (provided these are not too widely dissimilar), they also indicate the need for more intensive studies of particular aspects of mental development with locally constructed tests within non-western cultures.

Many psychologists might be inclined to banish further studies of 'intelligence' in non-western cultures on the grounds that it has no precise meaning or uniform content. While admitting its difficulties, the writer would point out that the same objection applies to any other more specialized abilities, e.g. perceptual discrimination, ideational fluency, problem solving, etc., not to speak of the American psychometrist's factors; since the structure and content of these are likely to be equally variable. Even if an investigator talked only in terms of performance on particular tests, e.g. Progressive Matrices or Kohs Blocks, he would still not be measuring the same ability, since the tests have to be given in different ways to, and have different meanings to, North American whites and, say, Africans. 'Intelligence' is justifiable in so far as it has been shown that a general factor always emerges from a wide range of varied tests, though one must be aware that it is culturally-loaded. What is important is that, in concentrating on abilities recognized by western culture, psychologists should not neglect special talents that might be more highly developed in other cultures. For example, in the writer's researches, little opportunity was provided for Eskimos to demonstrate their artistic and mechanical abilities, and none at all for Ugandans to display their auditory and rhythmic skills.

In the light of our surveys of four seriously handicapped groups, what are the main factors underlying poor performance on tests either of general intelligence or of more specialized mental faculties and educational or other attainments? A summary list will be useful, not only in considering how to help underdeveloped nations, but also in trying to diagnose the underlying handicaps of disadvantaged children, particularly immigrants, in our own culture. They are classified below under three or four main headings to correspond to our distinction between Intelligences A, B and C:

C: Extrinsic handicaps

(1) Unfamiliarity of testees with any test situation, and lack of motivation.

(2) Difficulties due to particular form of items or materials (e.g. pictures), and conditions of testing (e.g. working at speed).

(3) Anxiety, excitement, suspicion of tester.

(4) Linguistic difficulties in understanding instructions or communicating responses.

B: Constitutional handicaps

(5) Brain damage due to pre- or post-natal malnutrition, maternal stress, or disease. Birth injury; later brain pathology and deterioration.

Positive environmental factors

(6) Reasonable satisfaction of biological and social needs, including exercise and curiosity.

(7) Perceptual and kinaesthetic experience; varied stimulation, encouragement of exploration, experiment and play.

(8) Linguistic stimulation encouraging a 'formal code' and clarity of concepts.

(9) 'Demanding' but 'democratic' family climate, emphasizing internal controls, responsibility and interest in education.

(10) Conceptual stimulation by varied environment, books, television, travel, etc.

(11) Absence of magical beliefs; tolerance of non-conformity in home and community.

(12) Reinforcement of Nos. 8 and 9 by school and peer group.

(13) Regular and prolonged schooling, also demanding-democratic; emphasizing discovery rather than rote learning only.

(14) Appropriate methods to overcome language problems.

(15) Positive self-concepts with realistic vocational aspirations.

(16) Broad and deep cultural and other leisure interests.

A: Genetic factors

(17) General plasticity.

(18) Genes relevant to special aptitudes.

Naturally many other classifications are possible, and some of the factors listed (e.g. B, 15 and 16) are less well attested than others. Note that socioeconomic status as such does not appear, though it is, of course, associated with Nos. 6–13; nor does emotional security or maternal warmth, except under No. 6. Ecological and climatic conditions might merit inclusion, but are probably covered by No. 7.

What can be done to improve these conditions? Economic progress within the developing nations, and technical assistance from abroad, will obviously impinge at some points, particularly in reducing malnutrition and disease, building up the educational system, and providing worthwhile occupational prospects for much larger numbers. Likewise reduction of unemployment and better housing among immigrants in Britain should open the way to advance in many or most of the categories.

We would naturally expect the education system to provide the chief mode of attack on the syndrome of negative factors in a backward culture or subculture. Schooling is given by fairly small numbers of the more intelligent members of the population, who should be open to new ideas and who can be trained to follow new methods and aims; and they influence the minds of a large proportion or even the whole of the population over the period when concepts, skills and values are being built up. However the school is by no means as powerful an instrument in practice as in theory. Teachers are themselves so strongly imbued with the traditions of the old culture that they do not readily absorb or communicate the new; and the younger, more progressive, individuals cannot easily stand up to the entrenched beliefs of older, more conservative colleagues or of the community in which they work. And when they have charge of thirty to sixty and over, it is only the exceptional personality whose influence is sufficient to outweigh that of the home and the peer group. They can get across 'peripheral' skills such as spelling and mechanical arithmetic fairly successfully, and therefore – in backward educational systems – tend to concentrate unduly on these. But it is far more difficult to develop logical reasoning, flexibility of mind, the use of 'formal' language, understanding of the world and society, initiative, responsibility and democratic attitudes. The effects of peripheral training are easily forgotten and, of course, have scarcely any transfer to the daily life of ex-pupils or to the bringing up of their children more intelligently. Nevertheless one should not be too pessimistic. When even a few in each school generation are helped to be more intelligent, they leaven the community.

The greatest promise of quick advance lies in the field of language-teaching, that is the spread of effective methods of aquiring a language which is suitable as a medium for advanced education, communication and thinking among children whose mother tongue is ineffective for these purposes. This applies equally to dialect-speaking Africans, to Jamaicans in Jamaica or Britain, and to lower-working-class or deprived children in any western nation whose natural speech is of the 'public' type. However it is not sufficient to teach the second language as a subject, i.e. peripherally. Our own results have shown that current techniques, not only in Jamaica and Uganda but even in Canada, produce some competence in written English tests but fail to develop English as a cental tool of comprehension and thought. But linguistic and psychological research, together with the experiments under way in American introductory schools, in Kenya and elsewhere, offer prospects of a considerable breakthrough.

Whether it is realistic to advocate the extension of such methods to the complete populations of developing countries is a moot point, since the mother tongues are adequate for the lives that the majority are going to live for generations to come, and much more useful types of education could be devised for them. But such a policy would involve a split between the minority educated in the foreign language and the rest; and even if this was not socially disastrous, how would the minority be chosen at a sufficiently early age?

Clearly the major barrier to the fuller realization of human intellectual potential lies in the realm of adult values and child-rearing practices, and we have scarcely any assured techniques of modifying these. Changes are occurring all the time, but seldom as planned by the administrators; and although anthropological and psychological studies have greatly increased our understanding of the dynamic forces of social change, we are hardly in a position yet to offer much practical advice (psychological theories of crime and delinquency, for example, do not seem to have done anything to reduce the amount of social deviancy). And yet it is not impossible to plan and to carry through radical changes – an outstanding example being supplied by Soviet Russia. There can be no doubt that over the past fifty years the average level of Intelligence B of the Russian population has been raised tremendously.

Ruthless techniques may indeed have been applied which other countries would be loath to adopt, and they have not always achieved their purpose. But to a large extent they have succeeded in transforming a country which was as economically weak, as educationally backward and as culturally and linguistically heterogeneous as many underdeveloped nations of today.

Among the more humane approaches are community development schemes where local or foreign teams persuade a backward community to cooperate in improved agricultural techniques, in an industrial or housing project, in health or child care measures, or in local government. Usually these are small-scale, trial and error ventures, and frequently they fail or have no lasting effects. But they can be conducted in the people's own language, be shown to have direct value to the community, and be integrated with, rather than destroying, the existent culture. Where they do take roots they are likely to spread geographically, and to affect many cultural elements beside the particular practices worked on.

More sure, perhaps, but slower is the traditional method of educating the upper strata of the population to a high level and encouraging their contacts with outside cultural groups. If they thereby acquire good intelligence and adopt some of the attitudes associated with it, they are better able to bridge the gulf between the old and the new. In so far as they achieve prestige positions, their influence tends to percolate and they make possible greater progress in subsequent generations. Admittedly this mode of attack does not always work; it seems to have broken down among Canadian indigenes, and it is clearly failing to meet the needs of American Negroes. The more able and acculturated members of the relatively backward group often meet with rejection, either from their own or from the more advanced groups.

We return finally to the point that changes in material conditions, which the more favoured nations and subcultures are in a position to facilitate, are important, but not the whole answer. Even more important and vastly more difficult are changes in people's attitudes and ways of life. Developing nations often seem to be trying to bring about in a matter of years developments which, in Europe, took place over centuries. There are far more resources of technology, of communication, of intelligent and trained people anxious to help, in the world of today than ever before. But our knowledge of human individuals and societies and our control over our own prejudices and emotions are still so rudimentary that progress can only be fragmentary and disappointing.

22

S. Wiseman (1966)

Environmental and innate factors and educational attainment

J. E. Meade and A. S. Parkes (eds.), *Genetic and Environmental Factors in Human Ability* (Oliver & Boyd), pp. 64–79

The relationship between social class and educational opportunity, the iniquities of eleven-plus selection, the comprehensive school – these form the talking points not only in school staff rooms and meetings of educationists, but also in the railway carriage and over the coffee table. There is now a general awareness that the educational system and the social system cannot be separated, that they interpenetrate and inter-act; a general suspicion that, though our overall objectives may be reasonably correct, there is a serious mis-match in the organizations of the two systems. The involvement of such matters with political thought and political belief is obvious, and inescapable. And this leads to the inevitably exaggerated attitudes on both wings, the overemphasis of some facts and factors and the playing down of others, the introjection of emotive description and propaganda techniques. All this makes it the more important – and the more difficult – to set out soberly and dis-passionately what we *know* about the educational–social interaction, rather than to proclaim what we *believe*.

And what we know is precious little. We have only just begun to tease out one or two of the significant strands in what is an enormously complex fabric: the time for certainty is still far away. Most work has been done on the connections between environmental factors – mainly social class – and educational opportunity rather than educational attainment. It is not my intention to consider this part of the field, but merely to note its importance in demonstrating the existence of a major problem, and in acting as a motivator for further work.

The first significant attack in this country on the school environment and its relation to attainment was that of Kemp in 1955. He studied fifty primary schools in London, identifying twenty-eight environmental

bles (subsequently pooled to make twelve) and two criteria of
nment: comprehension, and rote learning. His main conclusions
e: (1) that the main factors determining level of attainment in the
formal school subjects are, in decreasing order of importance, intelligence, socioeconomic status, and size of school; and (2) that progressive-
ness, new buildings and class size are little (though positively) related
to level of attainment. In 1956, Mollenkopf in the U.S.A. reported a
study of 18,000 ninth and twelfth grade pupils in 206 schools. He concluded:

> As was expected, the IQ of the students predicted the achievement
> test means considerably better (0·90) than did the best-weighted
> composite of school, parent and community characteristics (0·59).
> Yet some characteristics did add to the effectiveness of this prediction.
> Among these were the percentages of graduates going on to college,
> the size of the average instructional class, and the presence or absence
> of a community library.

The results of these two researches are hardly epoch-making, nor do
they throw much light on the school factors important for scholastic
success. It will be noted that intelligence comes out as the supreme
determinant of achievement in both inquiries. No doubt, you will say,
this is because of its well-known dependence on socioeconomic status.
Kemp, however, investigated this particular aspect of his results. His
comprehension variables correlated 0·73 with intelligence.

> However (he says), it must be noted that socioeconomic status
> is correlated very significantly with both intelligence (0·52) and this
> kind of attainment (0·56). When socioeconomic status is partialled
> out the correlation (of 0·73) drops to 0·62. If *intelligence* is held con-
> stant, the correlation between socioeconomic status and attainment
> drops (from 0·56) to 0·30. The influence of socioeconomic status on
> attainment appears thus to be much less powerful than that of
> intelligence.

A similar result was obtained with his measures of rote attainment.
During the past decade we have carried out four surveys in the
Manchester district, in which we have endeavoured to lay bare some of
the associations between environmental factors and educational attainment. Three of these have already been described in detail in *Education
and Environment* (Wiseman, 1964) and I do not propose to dwell on these,
except in so far as they bear on particular matters discussed later. The

fourth – an investigation of forty-four primary schools – has just been completed, and although the analyses are not yet finished, some interesting and suggestive results are already to hand. One feature of the Manchester surveys which differentiates them from other researches in this field is the use of measures of backwardness and brightness as well as of average score. All our surveys have used the school as a unit, and we have calculated the percentage of 'bright' and of 'backward' children in each school (using these terms as a shorthand for describing those scoring more than 1 SD above the mean on a particular test, and those scoring less than 1 SD below). All four surveys demonstrate conclusively that brightness and backwardness are not just simple opposites, that some social factors correlate significantly with one and not with the other, and vice versa. It is curious that other researchers have not shown more interest in investigating this aspect of the environment–attainment interaction. Burt in 1943 reported 'decidedly higher' correlations with environmental factors for brighter children than for duller; Fraser (1959) found a significant relationship between ability level and the effect of abnormal home background, with the brighter children being more affected; while Maxwell (1953) concluded from the results of the 1947 Scottish Mental Survey that 'high intellectual ability is more widely distributed over different social environments than is low intellectual ability'. Our own results fall into line with this general trend: brightness has higher correlations with environmental factors than does backwardness. We shall return to this point later.

Our sample of forty-four primary schools was a random one, stratified by school type (county, C. of E., R.C.) and by area of the city. We concentrated on the 10+ pupils, who had been longest in school. For these pupils we had standardized test results at four ages: 7+, 8+, 9+ and 10+, on tests of intelligence, English and Arithmetic, so that we were able to look at age-trends. There were twelve tests altogether (two at 7, three at 8, two at 9 and five at 10), and each test gave us three 'scores' for each school (mean score, per cent bright and per cent backward) so we had thirty-six criterion variables. In addition to this we had fifty-two environmental variables, eighteen relating to the home and the neighbourhood, thirty-four relating to the school itself – its buildings, its equipment, its teachers and its atmosphere. This gave us a total of eighty-eight variables and a matrix of 3828 correlations. The factor analysis of this is not yet completed, but I can report on the chief results from the intercorrelations.

Perhaps the easiest way of summarizing the data is to calculate the average correlation of each environmental variable with all the thirty-six test variables (making appropriate sign adjustments, since the signs for backwardness and brightness are in opposite directions). A stronger connection is found with the social factors in the home and neighbour-hood than with the school variables. This is shown if we average the correlations of all the eighteen social variables with the total tests. The result, 0·295, contrasts sharply with a similar average for the thirty-four school variables, 0·199. It seems as if the forces operating outside the school walls are more pervasive and more powerful than those within. The highest correlations underline the factors of *poverty* and *maternal care* that we found in our previous surveys with secondary school children:

Per cent verminous children	0·48
Cleanliness of home	0·48
Per cent free meals	0·47
Material needs inadequate	0·44
Parental occupation	0·42
Family crime	0·38

The highest 'school' correlations are:

Appearance and sociability of children	0·42
Attendance	0·41
Streaming	0·39

The first of these three measures is probably wrongly placed, and ought to be included among the 'home' variables; no doubt the school may have some effect here, but the home is almost certainly the major influence. The second on the list – attendance – is a logical result, though many might have expected a higher correlation. The third variable, streaming, is one of particular topical interest. Our results show that streamed schools have *better* records of attainment. As might be expected, the highest individual correlations are with our measures of brightness: brightness, 10+ Composition, 0·66; brightness, 10+ Arithmetic I, 0·60; brightness, 9+ English, 0·60. But there is no sug-gestion that streaming has an adverse effect on the children of low ability: streamed schools tend to have fewer backward children at all ages and in all tests. It is possible, however, that the association between streaming and attainment is an artefact, since many of our unstreamed schools were one-form entry, and therefore perforce unstreamed. And the smaller schools tend to be found in the poorest areas. We therefore calculated the partial correlation between streaming and attainment holding size of school constant. This reduces the correlation – but only from 0·46 to 0·33: it is still significant.

BACKWARDNESS AND BRIGHTNESS

Let us now take a closer look at the average correlations with our measures of backwardness and brightness. As I have already mentioned, we find higher correlations with brightness, and this is true for both 'school' variables and 'social' variables: for the thirty-four school variables the average correlations with brightness and backwardness are 0·21 and 0·16 respectively; for the home and neighbourhood variables 0·29 and 0·26. When we look at the individual variables, we find only four having mean correlations greater than 0·4 with backwardness (cleanliness of home, 0·44; appearance and sociability, 0·42; verminous children, 0·42; and free meals, 0·42) while there are ten such with brightness. The four school variables having the strongest associa- tion with high scorers on the tests are: streaming, 0·47; attendance, 0·42; school size, 0·41; and percentage of children qualified for special schools, 0·41. The social variables over 0·4 emphasize again the *maternal care* factors that we have previously identified: verminous children, 0·50; mother working, 0·48; material needs inadequate, 0·48; free meals, 0·48; cleanliness of home, 0·46; and free clothing, 0·41.

It must be emphasized that these results have been obtained from an investigation of *schools* and not of individual children. We have found a correlation of 0·50, for example, between the percentage of verminous children in a school, and the percentage of high scorers on the tests given at four ages. Such results must be supported by parallel studies of individual children before one can begin to hazard a guess as to the underlying forces, and how they operate. Such studies are in hand, but I have as yet no results to report. Nevertheless, this association between brightness and environmental factors is a particularly im- portant one. The potential profit if we can discover how to counteract such effects is very considerable. The evidence from the Manchester surveys, together with the work of Burt and Fraser, points to the virtual certainty that an adverse environment has its greatest educational effects on children of above average ability.

INTELLIGENCE

Let us now turn to a comparison of the results from the tests of Intelli- gence with those from our tests of English and Arithmetic. The gross

N

average correlations of all environmental variables with the three types of test show English and Intelligence (0·24 and 0·23) as slightly higher than Arithmetic (0·21). When we separate the social variables and the school variables, however, we find an interesting difference. For the home and neighbourhood variables the average r is 0·314 for Intelligence, 0·299 for English and 0·262 for Arithmetic. The school variables put English clearly at the top (0·215) as against Intelligence, 0·190, and Arithmetic, 0·182. These differences may seem relatively small, but it must be remembered that these are average correlations, and are based on a considerable number of single correlations. The least stable of these (IQ *v.* social) is derived from 162 separate coefficients, while English *v.* school variables is based on no fewer than 408.

We are now confronted with an interesting problem. Of the three kinds of test, why should IQ have the strongest association with the social variables? And why should the pattern be different for the school variables? I suggest that the crucial difference between the school variables and the home and neighbourhood variables lies in the fact that the latter are affected by, and affect, the *parents* of the children, while school variables are those which affect children only. In other words, I am emphasizing the heavier *genetic* element in the results of the intelligence tests. This is, at present, rather an unfashionable line to take, but in my view the evidence is inescapable. I do not intend to embark on a review of this evidence, but I may perhaps refer you to a recent survey by Erlenmeyer-Kimling and Jarvik (1964) which summarizes fifty-two studies involving some 30,000 correlations. Fig. 22.1 shows graphically the results of their analysis, which shows, as they point out, that

the *median* of the empirical correlations closely approaches the theoretical value predicted on the basis of genetic relationship alone. The average correlation between parent and child, as well as that between siblings (including dizygotic twins) is 0·50 . . . At the other end of the relationship scale, where monozygotic twins theoretically have 100 per cent genetic correlation, medians of the observed correlations in intellectual functioning are 0·87 for the twins brought up together, 0·75 for those brought up apart.

The authors go on: 'We do not imply that environment is without effect upon intellectual function; the intellectual level is *not* unalterably fixed by the genetic constitution. Rather, its expression in the phenotype results from the patterns laid down by the genotype under given environmental conditions.'

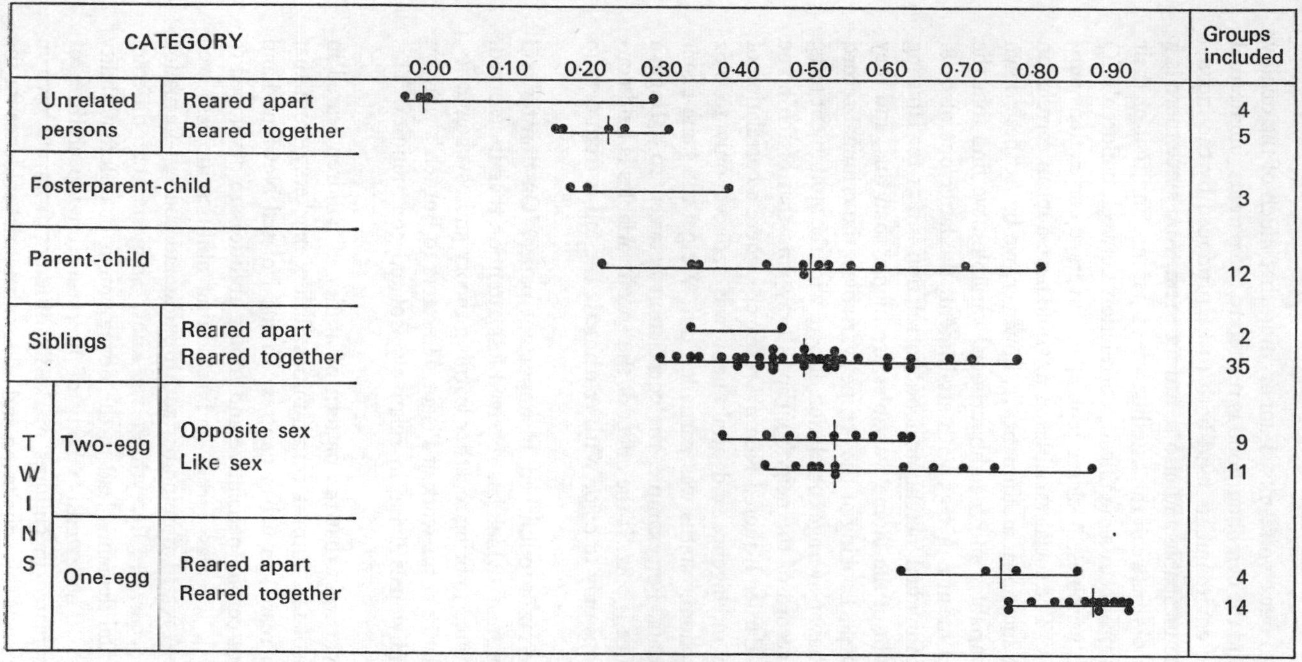

Fig. 22.1 Correlation coefficients for 'intelligence' test scores from fifty-two studies.

Some studies reported data for more than one relationship category; some included more than one sample per category, giving a total of ninety-nine groups. Over two-thirds of the correlation coefficients were derived from IQs, the remainder from special tests (for example, Primary Mental Abilities). Midparent–child correlation was used when available, otherwise mother–child correlation. Correlation coefficients obtained in each study are indicated by dark circles; medians are shown by vertical lines intersecting the horizontal lines which represent the ranges.

To return to our own results, I am arguing that much of the quality of the home and the neighbourhood is related to the parents' intellectual level. Adverse environments tend both to be produced by the incompetent and the incapable and also to attract them. And since there is a correlation of 0·5 between the intelligence of parents and that of their children, this produces a significant correlation between children's IQ and the social variables. A closer look at our average correlations supports this view. The social variables as a whole have a mean correlation of 0·28 with educational attainment. If, however, we break these down into 'home' variables and 'neighbourhood' variables, we find that the former have a mean r of 0·33 with attainment, the latter one of 0·18. The highest individual 'neighbourhood' correlation is 0·31 for Housing Standard. Eight of the 'home' variables are higher than this, and they range up to 0·48. Looking at the 'crime' variables, the criminal record of the family has an average correlation of 0·36 with the attainment tests, the criminal record of the neighbourhood 0·27, and that of the home address 0·05. Earlier I quoted Kemp's research, where a correlation of 0·73 between intelligence and attainment was reduced only to 0·62 when socioeconomic status was partialled out. We get the same result on our own data. For example, the correlation between 10+ English and Intelligence is 0·82. If the effect of the social variables is held constant, this drops only to 0·80. With Arithmetic the fall is from 0·77 to 0·74.

In 1956 Ferguson published an important paper, 'On transfer and the abilities of man', which has received less attention than it deserved. In it he attempted to bring together learning theory and psychometrics, with a side-glance at the work of Piaget. He refers to Burnett's work on abilities of individuals living in relatively isolated communities. This

shows conclusively that the pattern of ability of children reared in relatively isolated outpost communities differs markedly from that of children reared in urban centres. In the isolated Newfoundland environment certain perceptive and motor abilities are developed to a high level, whereas verbal and reasoning abilities are less well developed. A retardation in abstract thinking and concept-formation seems to occur. . . . Everything we know suggests that different environmental demands lead to the development of different ability patterns. . . . The extensive body of literature on the abilities of individuals reared in cultures markedly different from our own in general supports this conclusion and adds substantial evidence for the role of learning in the formation of abilities. (p. 129)

Ferguson suggests that differences in ability pattern resulting from differing environmental demands will show themselves not only in comparisons between individuals reared in markedly different environments, but also in the same individual at different stages of growth, since environmental demands change radically as the child grows up. In other words, his hypothesis postulates different factor-patterns of ability at different ages. There is certainly some evidence of the truth of this. Fig. 22.2 is based on the results from the Californian Growth Study,

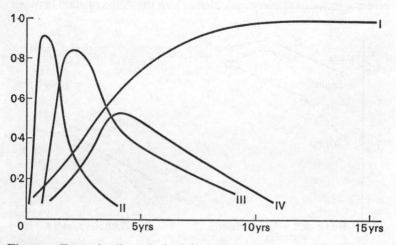

Fig. 22.2 Factor loadings devised from age-level. Intercorrelations from the Californian Growth Study (Bayley, N., 1933b, 1943, 1949 and 1951).

first reported by Bayley in 1933, with additional data up to 1951. Bayley started testing the development and intelligence of a group of sixty-one infants within three days of birth, and continued testing them at stages up to the age of eighteen years. She provides a matrix of intercorrelation of the scores of the same individuals at ages ranging from 2 months to 210 months. In 1954 Hofstaetter reported a factor analysis of this matrix, but since his centroid analysis was followed by rotation by hand, it was thought worth while to perform a new principle components analysis followed by a varimax rotation. Four major factors, as opposed to Hofstaetter's three, were found, and the loadings of these are plotted against age in the diagram. No clearer indication could be given of the change in factor pattern with age. Factor I is clearly the one usually labelled 'intelligence', but from birth up to at least the middle of the primary school this is supplemented by three other factors. I do not propose to embark on an attempt to 'label' these factors, except to comment that, by inspection of the items of the Californian scale, Factor II (which finds its peak during the first year of life) is most probably a sensorimotor factor.

Our own survey provides test results at four different ages, and it is worth while seeing whether there is any variation in the pattern of correlation over the four years. Fig. 22.3 shows average correlations of the three types of test for the home and neighbourhood variables and for the school variables separately (it will be seen that all three tests were not included at every age). Notice how the differentiation between

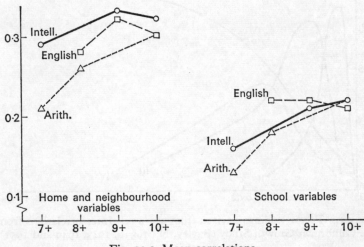

Fig. 22.3 Mean correlations.

the tests is greatest at 7+, and gets progressively less as the children get older. If we were able to extrapolate back into the infant school, no doubt the gaps would widen even more. And notice, too, the commanding position of the intelligence test for the home and neighbourhood variables.

I have some doubt as to whether the general upward trend of each single line on these graphs is really significant. It must be remembered that these correlations are between the test results of children who were 10 years of age when the environmental variables were measured, so that the 10+ results and other variables are coincident in time. But the 7+ results are those of these same children three years ago, the 8+ two years ago, and so on. It would not be surprising therefore, if these correlations have been subject to some degree of shrinkage. If so, the possibility exists that the level of correlation may *fall* with age. A comparison of our primary school results with those from secondary schools in 1957, using pupils of 14+, certainly suggests that this is so. The correlations of attainment with environmental variables all tend to be higher at 10+ than at 14+. Two of the social variables were identical in the two surveys: percentage of verminous children, and percentage in receipt of free shoes and clothing. The average correlations of the former with attainment were 0·483 at 10+ and 0·383 at 14+; for the latter the figures are 0·237 and 0·173. The fall from 10+ to 14+ is apparent for all three types of test, with the change for Arithmetic being rather greater than for English, the smallest change being with the intelligence test.

It seems, then, that not only do we find different patterns of ability at different age-levels, but also that the impact of environmental factors on attainment gets progressively weaker as we go up the age-range. There are other pieces of evidence which support this age trend. Furneaux, in his book *The Chosen Few* (1961), comments on the fact that 'occupational group membership acts as a very important determinant of academic history throughout the stages of education up to that of entry to the sixth form', but then goes on: 'The proportion of those wishing to have a university education who are actually able to apply is much the same for pupils in all occupational groups', and again: 'Among pupils who have already reached the upper-sixth form, differences of home background are associated only to a very small degree with the strength of the desire for a university education.' This analysis of sixth formers receives strong support from the evidence provided by the Robbins Committee, who comment (App. I, p. 46): 'The proportion of working-class children who stay on to the age when A-level is normally attempted is smaller than the proportion of middle-class children who actually achieve two passes. But these working-class children who do stay on are on average as successful as their counterparts in other social groups.' The Committee present data connecting 11+ results with A-level performance, classifying pupils into top, middle and bottom thirds on 11+ results. They find: 'Within each ability group at 11+, there is no significant difference in performance between children from the different classes who stay on.' Table 22.1 presents the Robbins data from the relevant table of the Report, and from this it is clear that differences of social class have ceased to be effective determinants of achievement at this level and at this age (Ministry of Education, 1963).

From the evidence so far discussed, it seems to be likely: *first*, that the influence of environmental factors on educational attainment is greatest at the youngest ages, and gets progressively less influential as the children get older; *second*, that as far as social class is concerned – a very crude measure of environmental differences – its effect seems to disappear by the age of seventeen or eighteen; *third*, that factors in the home and neighbourhood, and particularly those associated with maternal care and material needs, are much more powerful determinants of educational achievement than are factors within the walls of the school itself; *fourth*, that the stronger association between the intelligence test results and the 'home' variables suggest that their primacy of effect might be due largely to genetic factors; and *fifth*, that adverse forces in the environment have their greatest effect on the more able children.

The question now arises, what can we do to counteract the effects of poor environment? The prognosis is bleak, since it seems more than likely that the greatest harm to the child occurs before ever he reaches school at five years of age, and that any efforts the school might make are rather in the nature of shutting the stable door after the horse has bolted. But this may be too pessimistic a view, and it would certainly

TABLE 22.1. *Percentage of school leavers aged 18 or more who have at least two A-levels*
(from Table 7, p. 45, Appendix I, of the Robbins Report)

	11+ Grading		
Father's occupation	Upper third	Middle third	Lower third
Professional and managerial	79	63	43
Clerical	74	56	58
Skilled manual	77	59	51
Semi- and unskilled	81	58	53

be premature to conclude that ameliorative action on the part of teachers and local authorities is unlikely to have much effect. What such action should be, however, and what chances it has of success, cannot be decided until we know something about causality. So far we have been dealing with correlations, with measures of association. The leap from these to causal factors is a hazardous and difficult one. Piaget has charted certain stages in the intellectual development of the child and has demonstrated the interaction between the child's abilities and the environment's opportunities. As he says: 'Life is a continuous creation of increasingly complex forms and a progressive adaptation of these forms to the environment' (Piaget, 1936, p. 3). There is much evidence both from animals and from children that environmental deprivation not only slows down development, but may permanently lower the level of later performance. These intellectual and logical schemata of Piaget may have their counterpart in the effective and creative life of children, and particularly of preschool children. The years before 5 are notoriously crucial for the development of mental health: they may be equally so for educational health. It is perhaps unnecessary to see the required causal links through Freudian spectacles. For my part I would prefer to go back to McDougall and suggest that at least part of the system of causality lies in the emergence of the self-regarding sentiment in the preschool child. This, nourished in the home, is the architect of the child's attitude to authority, and structures his decisions as to which environmental opportunities he accepts and which he rejects. I have no time to do more than to indicate a possible line of approach here, but it is one which, in my view, demands further exploration. Psychologists and sociologists have often interested themselves in the suburban phenomenon of keeping up with the Joneses: it is time they took a more intensive look at the parallel phenomenon in the lower socioeconomic echelons, that of keeping down with the Smiths.

If part of the system of causality is revealed along such lines, then it follows that the best hope of ameliorative action lies not so much in improvements in the physical environment of the child's home, his neighbourhood and his school – necessary though these are from other points of view – not in organizational changes within the school itself, but rather in a reorientation of our training of teachers. They must not only be made aware of the nature of the adverse forces with which they are faced, but they must be expected to engage in positive action with parents as well as children. It would be wildly unrealistic to suggest that all teachers, and primary school teachers in particular, should be trained as social workers as well as educators, but the careful selection of a proportion of teachers for specialist training for general liaison work between school and home is a perfectly feasible proposition. Movement in this direction has already begun, but it needs rapid acceleration if any sensible impact is to be made on the problem, and if we hope to rescue at least a proportion of the large number of potentially able children who, at present, sink down under the weight of so many adverse conditions.

References

ADAMSON, R. E. and TAYLOR, D. W. (1954) Functional fixedness as related to elapsed time and set. *J. Exp. Psychol.*, **47**, 122–6.

AGNEW, M. (1922) A comparison of the auditory images of musicians, psychologists and children. *Psychol. Monogr.*, **31**, 279–87.

AKUTAGAWA, D. and BENOIT, E. P. (1959) The effect of age and relative brightness on associative learning in children. *Child Develpm.*, **30**, 229–38.

ANASTASI, A. (1956) Intelligence and family size. *Psychol. Bull.*, **53**, 187–209.

ANDERSEN, D. H. (1949) Effect of diet during pregnancy upon the incidence of congenital hereditary diaphragmatic hernia in the rat. *Amer. J. Path.*, **25**, 163–84.

ANDERSON, J. E. (1939) The limitations of infant and preschool tests in the measurement of intelligence. *J. Psychol.*, **8**, 351–79.

ANDERSON, J. E. (1940) The prediction of terminal intelligence from infant and preschool tests. *39th Yearbook of National Society for Studies in Education*, **1**, 385–403.

ANDERSON, W. J. R., BAIRD, D. and THOMSON, A. M. (1958) Epidemiology of still births and infant deaths due to congenital malformation. *Lancet*, **172** (1), 1304.

ARNHEIM, R., AUDEN, W. H. and SHAPIRO, K. (1948) *Poets at Work*. New York: Harcourt, Brace & World.

ARNOLD, J. E. (1962) Education for innovation. In PARNES, S. J. and HARDING, H. F. (eds.) *A Source Book for Creative Thinking*. New York: Scribner. pp. 127–38 (a), 252–68 (b).

ASHBY, W. R. (1952) *Design for a Brain*. New York: Wiley.

ATKINSON, J. W. (1958) *Motives in Fantasy Action and Society*. New York: Van Nostrand.

BADDELEY, A. D. and DALE, H. C. A. (1966) The effects of semantic similarity on retroactive interference in long- and short-term memory. *J. Verbal Learn. Verbal Behav.*, **5**, 417–20.

BAGGALEY, A. R. (1955) Concept formation and its relation to cognitive variables. *J. Genet. Psychol.*, **52**, 297–306.

BARNETT, C. D., ELLIS, N. R. and PRYER, M. W. (1960) Serial position effects in superior and retarded subjects. *Psychol. Rep.*, 7, III–13.

BARRON, F. (1953) Complexity–simplicity as a personality dimension. *J. Abnorm. Soc. Psychol.*, 48, 163–72.

BARRON, F. (1958) The psychology of imagination. *Scient. Amer.*, September.

BARRON, F. (1963) *Creativity and Psychological Health.* New York: Van Nostrand.

BAUMEISTER, A. A., BEEDLE, R. and HAWKINS, W. F. (1964) Transposition in normals and retardates under varying conditions of training and tests. *Amer. J. Ment. Defic.*, 69, 432–7.

BAUMEISTER, A. A., BEEDLE, R. and URQUHART, D. (1964) GSR conditioning in normals and retardates. *Amer. J. Ment. Defic.*, 69, 114–20.

BAYLEY, N. (1933a) *The California First-Year Mental Scale.* Berkeley: University of California Press.

BAYLEY, N. (1933b) Mental growth, the first three years: a developmental study of 61 children by repeated tests. *Genet. Psychol. Monogr.*, 14, 1.

BAYLEY, N. (1940) Factors influencing the growth of intelligence in young children. In WHIPPLE, G. M. (ed.) *Intelligence: its Nature and Nurture*, Part 2. *39th Yearbook of the National Society for the Study of Education.* Bloomington, Ill.: Public School Publishing. pp. 49–79.

BAYLEY, N. (1943) Mental growth during the first three years. In BARKER, R. G., KOUNIN, J. S. and WRIGHT, H. F. (eds.) *Child Behaviour and Development.* New York: McGraw-Hill.

BAYLEY, N. (1949) Consistency and variability in the growth of intelligence from birth to eighteen years. *J. Genet. Psychol.*, 75, 165–9.

BAYLEY, N. (1951) Development and maturation. In HELSON, H. (ed.) *Theoretical Foundations of Psychology.* New York: Van Nostrand.

BAYLEY, N. (1955) On the growth of intelligence. *Amer. Psychologist*, 10, 805–18.

BAYLEY, N. (1958) Value and limitations of infant testing. *Children*, July–August.

BAYLEY, N. (1965) Comparison of mental and motor test scores for ages 1–15 months by sex, birth order, race, geographical location and education of parents. *Child Develpm.*, 36, 379–411.

BAYLEY, N. (1966) Learning in adulthood: The role of intelligence.

In KLAUSMEIER, H. J. and HARRIS, C. W. (eds.) *Analyses of Concept Learning*. New York: Academic Press. pp. 117–38.

BAYLEY, N. (1967) *Cognition*. Paper presented at the West Virginia Conference on Theory and Methods of Research on Ageing. Morgantown.

BAYLEY, N. and JONES, H. E. (1937) Environmental correlates of mental and motor development: a cumulative study from infancy to six years. *Child Develpm.*, 8, 329–41.

BAYLEY, N. and SCHAEFER, E. S. (1964) Correlations of maternal and child behaviors with the development of mental abilities: data from the Berkeley Growth Study. *Monogr. Soc. Res. Child Developm.*, 29 (6) (Whole No. 97).

BEACH, F. A. (1945) Current concepts of play in animals. *Amer. Naturalist*, 79, 523–41.

BEHRENS, R. and ELLIS, N. R. (1960–2) Simultaneous and trace eyelid conditioning in normals and defectives. *Abstracts of Peabody Studies in Mental Retardation*, 2 (20).

BEIER, E. G. (1951) The effect of induced anxiety on flexibility of intellectual functioning. *Psychol. Monogr.*, 65 (9) (Whole No. 326).

BEILIN, H. and GOTKIN, L. (1964) *Psychological Issues in the Development of Mathematics Curricula for Socially Disadvantaged Children*. Paper presented to the Invitational Conference on Mathematics Education, Chicago.

BENDIG, A. W. (1958) Extraversion, neuroticism and verbal ability measures. *J. Consult. Psychol.*, 22, 464.

BENDIG, A. W. (1960) Extraversion, neuroticism and student achievement in introductory psychology. *J. Educ. Res.*, 53, 263–7.

BENNETT, G. K., SEASHORE, H. G. and WESMAN, A. G. (1952) *Differential Aptitude Tests, Manual* (2nd ed.). New York: Psychological Corporation.

BEREITER, C. S., ENGELMANN, J. O. and REDFORD, P. A. (1966) An academically orientated pre-school for culturally deprived children. In HECHINGER, F. M. (ed.) *Pre-school Education Today*. New York: Doubleday. Ch. 6.

BERKSON, G. and CANTOR, G. N. (1960) A study of mediation in mentally retarded and normal school children. *J. Educ. Psychol.*, 51, 82–6.

BERLYNE, D. E. (1960) *Conflict, Arousal and Curiosity*. New York: McGraw-Hill.

BERLYNE, D. E. (1962) Uncertainty and epistemic curiosity. *Brit. J. Psychol.*, 53, 27–34.

BERNSTEIN, B. (1960) Language and social class. *Brit. J. Sociol.*, 11, 271–6.

BERNSTEIN, B. (1961) Social class and linguistic development: a theory of social learning. In HALSEY, A. H., FLOUD, J. and ANDERSON, C. A. (eds.) *Education, Economy and Society.* New York: Free Press. pp. 288–314.

BEVERIDGE, W. J. E. (1950) *The Art of Scientific Investigation.* New York: Norton.

BEXTON, W. H., HERON, W. and SCOTT, T. H. (1954) Effects of decreased variation in the sensory environment. *Canad. J. Psychol.*, 8, 70–6.

BINET, A. and SIMON, T. (1905) Méthodes nouvelles pour le diagnostic du niveau intellectuel des anormaux. *L'Année Psychol.*, 11, 191–244.

BIRCH, H. G. (1945a) The relation of previous experience to insightful problem solving. *J. Comp. Physiol. Psychol.*, 38, 367–83.

BIRCH, H. G. (1945b) The role of motivational factors in insightful problem solving. *J. Comp. Physiol. Psychol.*, 38, 295–317.

BIRCH, H. G. and DEMB, H. (1959) The formation and extinction of conditioned reflexes in 'brain-damaged' and normal children. *J. Nerv. Ment. Dis.*, 129, 162–70.

BIRCH, H. G. and RABINOWITZ, H. S. (1951) The negative effect of previous experience on productive thinking. *J. Exp. Psychol.*, 41, 121–3.

BLEWETT, D. B. (1954) An experimental study of the inheritance of intelligence. *J. Ment. Sci.*, 100, 922–33.

BLOCK, J. (1961) *The Q-Sort Method in Personality Assessment and Psychiatric Research.* Springfield, Ill.: Charles C. Thomas.

BLUE, MILTON C. (1963) Performance of normal and retarded subjects on a paired-associate task. *Amer. J. Ment. Defic.*, 68, 228–34.

BOND, N. (1955) *An Experimental Study of Transfer Effects in Human problem Solving.* Unpublished doctoral dissertation, University of Southern California.

BOOLE, G. (1953) *An Investigation of the Laws of Thought.* New York: Dover (originally published 1854).

BORING, E. G. (1929) *A History of Experimental Psychology.* New York: Appleton-Century-Crofts.

BOTZUM, W. (1951) A factorial study of reasoning and closure factors. *Psychometrika*, 16, 361–86.

BOUSFIELD, W. A. and COHEN, B. H. (1953) The effects of

reinforcement on the occurrence of clustering in the recall of randomly arranged associates. *J. Psychol.*, **36**, 67–81.

BRAIN, W. R. (1948) Some reflections on genius. *Eugen. Rev.*, **40**, 12–20.

BRANDON, M. W. G. (1957) Intellectual and social status of children of mental defectives. *J. Ment. Sci.*, **103** (433), 710.

BRATTGÅRD, S. O. (1952) The importance of adequate stimulation for the chemical composition of retinal ganglion cells during early post-natal development. *Acta Radiologica* (Stockholm), Suppl. 96.

BRAZIER, M. A. B. (1950) Neural nets and integration of behaviour. In RICHTER, D. (ed.) *Perspectives in Neuropsychiatry*. London.

BROADBENT, D. E. (1952) Listening to one of two synchronous messages. *J. Exp. Psychol.*, **44**, 51–5.

BROADBENT, D. E. (1954) The role of auditory localisation in attention and memory span. *J. Exp. Psychol.*, **47**, 191–6.

BROADBENT, D. E. (1958) *Perception and Communication*. Oxford: Pergamon Press.

BROADBENT, D. E. and GREGORY, M. (1961) On the recall of stimuli presented alternately to two sense organs. *Quart. J. Exp. Psychol.*, **13**, 103–9.

BROADBENT, D. E. and GREGORY, M. (1964) Stimulus set and response set: the alternation of attention. *Quart. J. Exp. Psychol.*, **16**, 309–17.

BRUNER, J. S. and OLVER, R. R. (1963) Development of equivalence transformations in children. In WRIGHT, J. C. and KAGAN, J. (eds.) Basic cognitive process in children. *Monogr. Soc. Res. Child Develpm.*, **28** (2) (Serial No. 86), 125–41.

BRUNER, J. S., GOODNOW, J. J. and AUSTIN, G. A. (1956) *A Study of Thinking*. New York: Wiley.

BRUNER, J. S., OLVER, R. R. and GREENFIELD, P. M. (1966) *Studies in Cognitive Growth*. New York: Wiley.

BRUNSWIK, F. (1956) *Perception and the Representative Design of Psychological Experiments*. Berkeley: University of California Press.

BRYDEN, M. P. (1964) The manipulation of strategies of report in dichotic listening. *Canad. J. Psychol.*, **18**, 126–38.

BÜHLER, K. (1928) Displeasure and pleasure in relation to activity. In REYMERT, M. L. (ed.) *Feelings and Emotions: The Wittenberg Symposium*. Worcester, Mass.: Clark University Press. Ch. 14.

BURGMEISTER, B. B., BLUM, L. H. and LORGE, I. (1959) *Columbia Mental Maturity Scale* (rev. ed.). New York: Harcourt, Brace & World.

BURKHART, R. C. (1962) *Spontaneous and Deliberate Ways of Learning*. Scranton, Pa.: International Textbooks.

BURKS, B. S. (1928) The relative influence of nature and nurture upon mental development. *27th Yearbook of the National Society for the Study of Education*. Chicago: University of Chicago Press (1940). Bloomington, Ill.: Public School Publishing Co. pp. 219–316.

BURT, C. (1912) The inheritance of mental characteristics. *Eugen. Rev.*, 4, 168–204.

BURT, C. (1921) *Mental and Scholastic Tests* (4th ed., 1962) London: P. S. King, Staples Press.

BURT, C. (1933) *Handbook of Tests for Use in Schools*. London: Staples Press.

BURT, C. (1943) Ability and income. *Brit. J. Educ. Psychol.*, 13, 83–98.

BURT, C. (1949a) Group factor analysis. *Brit. J. Psychol.* (Stat. Sec.), 3, 40–75.

BURT, C. (1949b) Subdivided factors. *Brit. J. Statist. Psychol.*, 19, 176–99.

BURT, C. (1954) Differentiation of intellectual ability. *Brit. J. Educ. Psychol.*, 24, 76–90.

BURT, C. (1955) The evidence for the concept of intelligence. *Brit. J. Educ. Psychol.*, 25, 158–77.

BURT, C. (1958) The inheritance of mental ability. *Amer. Psychologist*, 13, 1–15.

BURT, C. and HOWARD, M. (1956) The multifactorial theory of inheritance and its application to intelligence. *Brit. J. Statist. Psychol.*, 9, 95–131.

BURT, C. and HOWARD, M. (1957) Heredity and intelligence: a reply to criticism. *Brit. J. Statist. Psychol.*, 10, 33–63.

BUTCHER, H. J. (1968) *Human Intelligence: Its Nature and Assessment*. London: Methuen.

BUTLER, R. A. (1953) Discrimination learning by rhesus monkeys to visual exploration motivation. *J. Comp. Physiol. Psychol.*, 46, 95–8.

BUTLER, R. A. (1958) The differential effect of visual and auditory incentives on the performance of monkeys. *Amer. J. Psychol.*, 71, 591–3.

CAMERON, J., LIVSON, N. and BAYLEY, N. (1967) Infant vocalization and its relationship to mature intelligence. *Science*, 157, 331–3.

CAMPBELL, D. T. and FISKE, D. W. (1959) Convergent and discriminant validation by the multitrait-multimethod matrix. *Psychol. Bull.*, 56, 81–105.

CANTOR, G. N. and RYAN, T. J. (1962) Retention of verbal paired-associates in normals and retardates. *Amer. J. Ment. Defic.*, **66**, 861–5.

CARMICHAEL, L. (1926) The development of behavior in vertebrates experimentally removed from influence of external stimulation. *Psychol. Rev.*, **33**, 51–8.

CARMICHAEL, L. (1927) A further study of the development of behavior in vertebrates experimentally removed from the influence of external stimulation. *Psychol. Rev.*, **34**, 34–47.

CARMICHAEL, L. (1928) A further study of the development of behavior. *Psychol. Rev.*, **35**, 253–60.

CARMICHAEL, L. (1954) The onset and early development of behavior. In CARMICHAEL, L. (ed.) *Manual of Child Psychology*. New York: Wiley. Ch. 2.

CARR-SAUNDERS, A. M. and JONES, D. C. (1937) *A Survey of the Social Structure of England and Wales*. Oxford: Clarendon Press.

CASE, D. and COLLINSON, J. M. (1962) The development of formal thinking in verbal comprehension. *Brit. J. Educ. Psychol.*, **32**, 103–11.

CASSELL, R. H. (1957) Serial verbal learning and retroactive inhibition in aments and children. *J. Clin. Psychol.*, **13**, 369–72.

CATTELL, J. MCK. (1890) Mental tests and measurements. *Mind*, **15**, 373–80.

CATTELL, R. B. (1936) *A Guide to Mental Testing*. London: University of London Press.

CATTELL, R. B. (1941) Some theoretical issues in adult intelligence testing. *Psychol. Bull.*, **38**, 592 (Abstract).

CATTELL, R. B. (1952) *Factor Analysis: An Introduction and Manual for the Psychologist and Social Scientist*. New York: Harper.

CATTELL, R. B. (1957a) *Personality and Motivation Structure and Measurement*. Yonkers-on-Hudson, New York: World Book. pp. 1–20, 871–80.

CATTELL, R. B. (1957b) A universal index for psychological factors. *Psychologia*, **1**, 74–85.

CATTELL, R. B. (1963) Theory of fluid and crystallized intelligence: a critical experiment. *J. Educ. Psychol.*, **54**, 1–22.

CATTELL, R. B. (1964) Fluid and crystallized abilities. In CATTELL, R. B., *Personality and Social Psychology*. San Diego: Knapp.

CATTELL, R. B. (1967) The theory of fluid and crystallized general intelligence checked at the 5–6 year old level. *Brit. J. Educ. Psychol.*, **37**, 209–24.

CATTELL, R. B. and HORN, J. L. (1963) An integrative study of the factor structure of adult attitude-interests. *Genet. Psychol. Monogr.*, **67**, 89–149.

CATTELL, R. B. and HORN, J. L. (1964) *The Handbook for the MAT.* Champaign, Ill.: Institute for Personality and Ability Testing.

CATTELL, R. B. and STICE, G. F. (1960) *The Dimensions of Groups and Their Relations to the Behaviour of Members.* Champaign, Ill.: Institute for Personality and Ability Testing.

CATTELL, R. B., BLEWETT, D. B. and BELOFF, J. R. (1955) The inheritance of personality: a multiple variance analysis determination of approximate nature–nurture ratios for primary personality factors in *Q*-data. *Amer. J. Hum. Genet.*, **7**, 122–46.

CATTELL, R. B., HORN, J. L. and BUTCHER, H. J. (1962) The dynamic structure of attitudes in adults. *Brit. J. Psychol.*, **53**, 57–69.

CHAMBERS, J. A. (1964) Relating personality and biographical factors to scientific creativity. *Psychol. Monogr.*, **78**, 584.

CHILD, D. (1964) The relationships between introversion-extraversion, neuroticism and performance in school examinations. *Brit. J. Educ. Psychol.*, **34**, 187–96.

CHORNESS, M. H. and NOTTELMANN, D. H. (1957) The prediction of creativity among Air Force civilian employees. *Res. Bull.*, AFPTRC-TN-57-36. Lackland Air Force Base, Texas: Air Force Personnel and Training Research Center.

CHRISTENSEN, P. R. and GUILFORD, J. P. (1963) An experimental study of verbal fluency factors. *Brit. J. Math. Statist. Psychol.*, **16**, 1–26.

CHRISTENSEN, P. R. et al. (1957) Relations of creative responses to working time and instruction. *J. Exp. Psychol.*, **53**, 82–8.

CLARKE, A. D. B. and CLARKE, A. M. (1958) *Mental Deficiency: The Changing Outlook.* London: Methuen.

CLINE, V. B., RICHARDS, J. M., JR, and ABE, C. (1962) The validity of a battery of creativity tests in a high school sample. *Educ. Psychol. Measmt*, **22**, 781–4.

CLINE, V. B., RICHARDS, J. M., JR, and NEEDHAM, W. E. (1963) Creativity tests and achievement in high school science. *J. Appl. Psychol.*, **47**, 184–9.

COGHILL, G. E. (1929) *Anatomy and the Problem of Behavior.* Cambridge University Press; New York: Macmillan.

COLE, L. C. (1954) The population consequences of life history phenomena. *Quart. Rev. Biol.*, **29**, 103–37.

CONRAD, H. S. and JONES, H. E. (1932) A field of the differential birth rate. *J. Amer. Statist. Ass.*, **27**, 153–9.

CONRAD, R. and HULL, A. J. (1964) Information, acoustic confusion, and memory span. *Brit. J. Psychol.*, **55**, 429–32.

CONWAY, J. (1958) The inheritance of intelligence and its implications. *Brit. J. Statist. Psychol.* **11**, 171–90.

CONWAY, J. (1959) Class differences in general intelligence. *Brit. J. Statist. Psychol.*, **12**, 5–14.

COOPERATIVE TEST DIVISION (1957a) *Cooperative School and College Ability Tests: Technical report.* Princeton, N.J.: Educational Testing Service.

COOPERATIVE TEST DIVISION (1957b) *SCAT: Directions for Administering and Scoring.* Princeton, N.J.: Educational Testing Service.

COOPERATIVE TEST DIVISION (1957c) *Cooperative Sequential Tests of Educational Progress: Technical Report.* Princeton, N.J.: Educational Testing Service.

COOPERATIVE TEST DIVISION (1957d) *STEP: Directions for Administering and Scoring.* Princeton, N.J.: Educational Testing Service.

COOPERATIVE TEST DIVISION (1959) *Cooperative Sequential Tests of Educational Progress: Teacher's Guide.* Princeton, N.J.: Educational Testing Service.

COWELL, H. (1926) The process of musical creation. *Amer. J. Psychol.*, **37**, 233–6.

CRAWFORD, A. B. (1929) *Incentives to Study.* New Haven, Conn.: Yale University Press.

CROMWELL, R. L., PALK, B. E. and FOSHEE, J. G. (1961) Studies in activity level, V: The relationships among eyelid conditioning, intelligence, activity level and age. *Amer. J. Ment. Defic.*, **65**, 744–8.

CRONBACH, L. J. (1957) The two disciplines of scientific psychology. *Amer. Psychologist,* **12**, 671–84.

CROSS, P., CATTELL, R. B. and BUTCHER, H. J. (1967) The personality pattern of creative artists. *Brit. J. Educ. Psychol.*, **37**, 292–9.

CROW, J. (1962) Population genetics: selection. In BURDETTE, W. J. (ed.) *Methodology in Human Genetics.* San Francisco: Holden-Day. pp. 53–75.

CRUTCHFIELD, R. S. (1959) Personal and situational factors in conformity to group pressure. Proceedings, XVth International Congress of Psychology. *Acta Psychol.*, **15**, 386–8.

CRUZE, W. W. (1935) Maturation and learning in chicks. *J. Comp. Psychol.*, **19**, 371–409.

CRUZE, W. W. (1938) Maturation and learning ability. *Psychol. Monogr.*, **50** (5).

DARLINGTON, C. D. (1963) Psychology, genetics and the process of history. *Brit. J. Psychol.*, 54, 292–9.

DARLINGTON, C. D. and MATHER, K. (1949) *The Elements of Genetics*. London: Allen & Unwin.

DARWIN, C. (1859) *On the Origin of the Species*. London: Murray.

DARWIN, C. (1873) *The Expression of the Emotions in Man and Animals*. New York: Appleton-Century-Crofts (originally published: London: Murray, 1872).

DASHIELL, J. F. (1925) A quantitative demonstration of animal drive. *J. Comp. Psychol.*, 5, 205–8.

DASHIELL, J. F. (1928) *Fundamentals of Objective Psychology*. Boston: Houghton Mifflin.

DAVIES, W. A. (1948) *Social-Class Influences upon Learning*. Cambridge, Mass.: Harvard University Press.

DAVIES, W. A. and HAVIGHURST, R. J. (1946) Social-class and color differences in childrearing. *Amer. Soc. Rev.*, 11, 698–710.

DAVIS, D. R. and SINHA, D. (1950a) The effect of one experience upon the recall of another. *Quart. J. Exp. Psychol.*, 2, 43–52.

DAVIS, D. R. and SINHA, D. (1950b) The influence of interpolated experience upon recognition. *Quart. J. Exp. Psychol.*, 2, 132–7.

DEMBER, W. N., EARL, R. W. and PARADISE, N. (1957) Response by rates to differential stimulus complexity. *J. Comp. Physiol. Psychol.*, 50, 514–18.

DENENBERG, V. H. (1962) The effects of early experience. In HAFEZ, E. S. E. (ed.) *The Behavior of Domestic Animals*. London: Bailliere.

DENNIS, W. (1958) The age decrement in outstanding scientific contributors: fact or artifact. *Amer. Psychologist*, 13, 457–60.

DENNIS, W. (1960) Causes of retardation among institutional children. *J. Genet. Psychol.*, 96, 47–59.

DENNIS, W. and DENNIS, M. G. (1935) The effect of restricted practice upon the reaching, sitting and standing of two infants. *J. Genet. Psychol.*, 47, 21–9.

DENNIS, W. and DENNIS, M. G. (1938) Infant development under conditions of restricted practice and minimum social stimulation: a preliminary report. *J. Genet. Psychol.*, 53, 151–6.

DENNIS, W. and DENNIS, M. G. (1940) The effect of cradling practice upon the onset of walking in Hopi children. *J. Genet. Psychol.*, 56, 77–86.

DENNIS, W. and DENNIS, M. G. (1941) Infant development under conditions of restricted practice and minimum social stimulation. *Genet. Psychol. Monogr.*, 23, 149–55.

DENNY, M. R. (1963) Learning. In HEBER, R. and STEVENS, H. (eds.) *Review of Research in Mental Retardation.* Chicago: University of Chicago Press.

DEUTSCH, C. (1964) Auditory discrimination and learning: social factors. *Merrill-Palmer Quart.*, **10**, 277–96.

DEUTSCH, M. and BROWN, B. (1964) Social influences in Negro–white intelligence differences. *J. Soc. Issues*, **20**, 24–35.

DEWEY, J. (1896) The reflex arc concept in psychology. *Psychol. Rev.*, **3**, 357–70.

DEWEY, J. (1960a) *The School and Society.* Chicago: University of Chicago Press, Phoenix Books, 3 (first published 1900).

DEWEY, J. (1960b) *The Child and the Curriculum.* Chicago: University of Chicago Press, Phoenix Books. 3 (first published 1902).

DIENES, Z. P. (1964) *Mathematics in the Primary School.* Melbourne: Hutchinson.

DOBZHANSKY, T. and ALLEN (1956) Does natural selection continue to operate in mankind? *Amer. Anthrop.*, **58**, 591–604.

DOLLARD, J. and MILLER, N. E. (1950) *Personality and Psychotherapy: An Analysis in Terms of Learning, Thinking and Culture.* New York: McGraw-Hill.

DOMINOWSKI, R. L. (1965) Role of memory in concept learning. *Psychol. Bull.*, **63**, 271–80.

DREVDAHL, J. E. (1956) *An Exploratory Study of Creativity.* Unpublished doctoral dissertation, University of Nebraska.

DREVDAHL, J. E. and CATTELL, R. B. (1958) Personality and creativity in artists and writers. *J. Clin. Psychol.*, **14**, 107–11.

DREWS, E. M. (1964) *The Creative Intelligence Style in Gifted Adolescents, I: Motivation to Learn.* East Lansing: Michigan State University Press.

DUNCAN, D. B. (1955) Multiple range and multiple F tests. *Biometrics*, **11**, 1–41.

DUNCANSON, J. P. (1964) *Intelligence and the Ability to Learn.* Princeton, N.J.: Educational Testing Service.

DUNCKER, K. (1945) On problem-solving (trans. Lynne S. Lees). *Psychol. Monogr.*, **58** (270), 113 (originally published 1935).

DUNLAP, K. (1919) Are there any instincts? *J. Abnorm. Soc. Psychol.*, **14**, 307–11.

EINDHOVEN, J. E. and VINACKE, W. E. (1952) Creative process in painting. *J. Genet. Psychol.*, **47**, 139–64.

EISMAN, B. S. (1958) Paired associate learning, generalization and retention as a function of intelligence. *Amer. J. Ment. Defic.*, **63**, 481–9.

ELLIS, N. R., HAWKINS, W. F., PRYER, M. W. and JONES, R. W. (1963) Distraction effects in oddity learning by normal and mentally defective humans. *Amer. J. Ment. Defic.*, 67, 576–83.

ELLIS, N. R., PRYER, M. W., DISTEFANO, M. K., JR, and PRYER, R. S. (1960) Learning in mentally defective, normal and superior subjects. *Amer. J. Ment. Defic.*, 64, 725–34.

ELLIS, N. R. and SLOAN, W. (1959) Oddity learning as a function of mental age. *J. Comp. Physiol. Psychol.*, 52, 228–30.

EMMERICH, D. S. et al. (1965) Meaningfulness as a variable in dichotic hearing. *J. Exp. Psychol.*, 69, 433–6.

ERLENMEYER-KIMLING, L. and JARVIK, L. F. (1964) Genetics and intelligence: a review. *Science*, 142, No. 3598.

ESSEN-MÖLLER, E. (1941) Empirische Ähnlichkeitsdiagnose bei Zwillingen. *Hereditas*, 17, 1–23.

EYSENCK, H. J. (1939) Primary mental abilities. *Brit. J. Educ. Psychol.*, 9, 270–5.

EYSENCK, H. J. (1944) The effect of incentives on neurotics, and the variability of neurotics as compared with normals. *Brit. J. Med. Psychol.*, 20, 100–3.

EYSENCK, H. J. (1947) *Dimensions of Personality*. London: Routledge & Kegan Paul.

EYSENCK, H. J. (1953) *Uses and Abuses of Psychology*. Harmondsworth: Penguin Books.

EYSENCK, H. J. (1957) *The Dynamics of Anxiety and Hysteria*. London: Routledge & Kegan Paul.

EYSENCK, H. J. (1959) Personality and problem solving. *Psychol. Rep.*, 5, 592.

EYSENCK, H. J. (1960) *The Structure of Human Personality*. London: Methuen.

EYSENCK, H. J. (1963) The biological basis of personality. *Nature*, 199, 1031–4.

EYSENCK, H. J. (1966) Personality and experimental psychology. *Bull Brit. Psychol. Soc.*, 62, 1–28.

EYSENCK, H. J. (1967a) *The Biological Basis of Personality*. New York: C. C. Thomas.

EYSENCK, H. J. (1967b) Intelligence assessment: a theoretical and experimental approach. *Brit. J. Educ. Psychol.*, 37, 81–98.

EYSENCK, H. J. and HALSTEAD, H. (1945) The memory function. *Amer. J. Psychiat.*, 102, 174–80.

EYSENCK, H. J. and PRELL, D. B. (1951) The inheritance of neuroticism: an experimental study. *J. Ment. Sci.*, 102, 517–29.

EYSENCK, H. J. and WHITE, P. O. (1964) Personality and the measurement of intelligence. *Brit. J. Educ. Psychol.*, **34**, 197–202.

FARBER, I. E. (1948) Response fixation under anxiety and non-anxiety conditions. *J. Exp. Psychol.*, **38**, 111–31.

FARLEY, F. H. (1966) Individual differences in solution time in error-free problem solving. *Brit. J. Soc. Clin. Psychol.*, **5**.

FENICHEL, O. (1945) *The Psychoanalytic Theory of Neurosis*. New York: Norton.

FERGUSON, G. A. (1954) On learning and human ability. *Canad. J. Psychol.*, **8**, 95–112.

FERGUSON, G. A. (1956) On transfer and the abilities of man. *Canad. J. Psychol.*, **8**, 121–31.

FERSTER, C. B. and SKINNER, B. F. (1957) *Schedules of Reinforcement*. New York: Appleton-Century-Crofts.

FESTINGER, L. (1957) *A Theory of Cognitive Dissonance*. Evanston, Ill.: Row, Peterson.

FISHER, D. C. (1912) *A Montessori Mother*. New York: Holt, Rinehart & Winston.

FISHER, R. A. (1918) The correlation between relatives on the supposition of Mendelian inheritance. *Trans. Roy. Soc. Edin.*, **52**, 399–433.

FISHER, R. A. (1958) *The Genetical Theory of Natural Selections* (2nd rev. ed.). New York: Dover Publications.

FISKE, D. W. and MADDI, S. R. (1961) *Functions of Varied Experience*. Homewood, Ill.: Dorsey Press.

FLAVELL, J. H., COOPER, A. and LOISELLE, R. H. (1958) Effect of the number of pre-utilization functions on functional fixedness in problem solving. *Psychol. Rep.*, **4**, 343–50.

FLEISHMAN, E. A. and HEMPEL, W. E. (1954) Changes in factor structure of complex psychomotor tests as a function of practice. *Psychometrika*, **19**, 239–52.

FLEISHMAN, E. A. and HEMPEL, W. E. (1955) The relation between abilities and improvement with practice in a visual discrimination reaction task. *J. Exp. Psychol.*, **49**, 301–10.

FLESCHER, I. (1963) Anxiety and achievement of intellectually gifted and creatively gifted children. *J. Psychol.*, **56**, 251–68.

FRANK, H. (1963) Informations psychologie und nachrichtentechnik. In WEINER, N. and SCHADE, J. P., *Progress in Brain Research, Vol. 2: Nerve, Brain and Memory Models*. Amsterdam: Elsevier Publishing Co. pp. 79–96.

FRANKS, V. and FRANKS, C. M. (1962) Conditionability in defectives and in normals as related to intelligence and organic deficit: the application of a learning theory model to a study of the learning process in the mental defective. In RICHARDS, B. W. (ed.) *Proceedings of the London Conference on the Scientific Study of Mental Deficiency*. Dagenham: May & Baker. pp. 577–83.

FRASER, E. D. (1959) *Home Environment and the School*. London: University of London Press.

FRASER, F. C. and FAINSTAT, T. D. (1951) Production of congenital malformation in the offspring of pregnant mice treated with cortisone. *Pediatrics*, 8, 527.

FRASER, F. C. *et al.* (1954) Experimental production of cleft palate with cortisone and hormones. *J. Cell. Comp. Physiol.*, 43, Suppl. 1, 237.

FREEDMAN, A. (1957) *Drive Conditioning in Water Deprivation*. Unpublished doctoral dissertation, University of Illinois.

FREEMAN, F. N., HOLZINGER, K. F. and MITCHELL, B. C. (1928) The influence of environment on the intelligence, achievement and conduct of foster children. *27th Yearbook of the National Society for the Study of Education*. Chicago: University of Chicago Press (1940). Bloomington, Ill.: Public School Publishing Company. Ch. 9.

FREEMAN, G. L. (1934) *Introduction to Physiological Psychology*. New York: Ronald Press.

FRENCH, J. W. (1951) The description of aptitude and achievement tests in terms of rotated factors. *Psychometric Monographs*, No. 5.

FRENCH, J. W., EKSTROM, R. B. and PRICE, I. A. (1963) *Manual for Kit of Reference Tests for Cognitive Factors*. Princeton: Educational Testing Service.

FREUD, S. (1927) Instincts and their vicissitudes. *Collected Papers*, 4, 60–83. London: Hogarth (originally published 1915).

FREUD, S. (1936) *The Problem of Anxiety* (trans. H. A. Bunker). New York: Norton.

FREUD, S. (1938a) The interpretation of dreams. In BRILL, A. A. (trans. and ed.) *The Basic Writings of Sigmund Freud*. New York: Modern Library (originally published 1900).

FREUD, S. (1938b) The psychopathology of everyday life. In BRILL, A. A. (trans. and ed.) *The Basic Writings of Sigmund Freud*. New York: Modern Library (originally published 1905).

FREUD, S. (1938c) Three contributions to the theory of sex. In BRILL, A. A. (trans. and ed.) *The Basic Writings of Sigmund Freud*. New York: Modern Library (originally published 1905).

FRICK, J. W. *et al.* (1959) A factor-analytic study of flexibility in thinking. *Educ. Psychol. Measmt*, **19**, 469–96.

FROEBEL, F. (1896) *The Education of Man* (trans. W. N. Hailmann). New York: Appleton-Century-Crofts (*Die Menschenerziehung*, originally published 1826).

FRUCHTER, B. (1948) The nature of verbal fluency. *Educ. Psychol. Measmt*, **8**, 35–47.

FRUCHTER, B. (1950) Error scores as a measure of carefulness. *J. Educ. Psychol.*, **41**, 279–91.

FRUCHTER, B. (1953) Differences in factor content of rights and wrongs scores. *Psychometrika*, **18**, 257–65.

FURNEAUX, W. D. (1956) *The Nufferno Manual of Speed and Level Tests.* Slough: National Foundation for Educational Research.

FURNEAUX, W. D. (1960) Intellectual abilities and problem solving behaviour. In EYSENCK, H. J. (ed.) *Handbook of Abnormal Psychology.* London: Pitman.

FURNEAUX, W. D. (1961) *The Chosen Few.* London: Oxford University Press.

FURNEAUX, W. D. (1962) The psychologist and the university. *Univ. Quart.*, **17**, 33–47.

GAGNÉ, R. M. (1965) *The Conditions of Learning.* New York: Holt, Rinehart & Winston.

GALTON, F. (1869) *Hereditary Genius: An Inquiry into its Laws and Consequences.* London: Macmillan.

GALTON, F. (1883) *Inquiries into Human Faculty and Its Development.* London: Macmillan.

GALTON, F. (1886) Regression towards mediocrity in hereditary stature. *J. Anthrop. Inst.*, **15**, 246–63.

GARDNER, I. C. and NEWMAN, H. H. (1940) Mental and physical traits of identical twins reared apart. *J. Hered.*, **31**, 119–26.

GARDNER, L. P. (1945) Responses of idiots and imbeciles in a conditioning experiment. *Amer. J. Ment. Defic.*, **50**, 59–80.

GAURON, E. F. and BECKER, W. C. (1959) The effects of early sensory deprivation on adult rat behavior under competition stress: an attempt at replication of a study by Alexander Wolf. *J. Comp. Physiol. Psychol.*, **52**, 689–93.

GAW, F. (1925) *Performance Tests of Intelligence.* M.R.C. Report No. xxi. London: H.M.S.O.

GESELL, A. (1928) *Infancy and Human Growth.* New York: Macmillan.

GESELL, A. (1945) *The Embryology of Human Behavior: The Beginnings of the Human Mind.* New York: Harper & Row.

GESELL, A. (1954) The ontogenesis of infant behavior. In CAR-MICHAEL, L. (ed.) *Manual of Child Psychology*. New York: Wiley. Ch. 6.

GESELL, A. and ILG, F. L. (1946) *The Child from Five to Ten*. New York: Harper.

GESELL, A. and THOMPSON, H. (1929) Learning and growth in identical twin infants. *Genet. Psychol. Monogr.*, 6, 1–124.

GESELL, A. (1940) *The First Five Years of Life*. New York: Harper.

GESENIUS, H. (1952) Genwirkungen und Umwelteinflüsse. *Anat. Anz.*, 98, 272.

GETZELS, J. W. and JACKSON, P. W. (1962) *Creativity and Intelligence*. New York: Wiley.

GHISELLI, E. E. (1963) Managerial talent. *Amer. Psychologist*, 18, 631–42.

GIRARDEAU, F. L. (1959) The formation of discrimination learning sets in mongoloid and normal children. *J. Comp. Physiol. Psychol.*, 52, 566–70.

GIRARDEAU, F. L. and ELLIS, N. (1964) Rote verbal learning by normal and mentally retarded children. *Amer. J. Ment. Defic.*, 68, 525–32.

GIROUD, A. (1954) Malformations embryonnaires d'origine carientelle. *Biol. Rev.*, 29, 220.

GODDARD, H. H. (1912) *The Kallikak Family: A Study in the Heredity of Feeblemindedness*. New York: Macmillan.

GOLANN, S. E. (1962) The creativity motive. *J. Pers.*, 30, 588–600.

GOLDMAN, J. R. (1964) The effects of handling and shocking in infancy upon adult behavior in the albino rat. *J. Genet. Psychol.*, 104 (2), 301–10.

GOLDSCHMIDT, L. (1937) Vergleichende Darstellung dreier Intelligenzprufungssyteme (Comparative presentation of three systems of intelligence-testing). *Deutsch Zondenschule*, 4, 846.

GOODENOUGH, F. (1939) A critique of experiments on raising the IQ. *Educ. Methods*, 19, 73, 79.

GORDON, W. J. J. (1961) *Synectics*. New York: Harper & Row.

GOTTESMAN, I. I. (1963) Heritability of personality: a demonstration. *Psychol. Monogr.*, 77, 1–22.

GRABILL, W. H. (1959) Fertility and Reproduction. In BOGUE, D. J., *The Population of the United States*. Glencoe, Ill.: The Free Press, 288–324.

GRAY, J. A. and WEDDERBURN, A. I. (1960) Grouping strategies with simultaneous stimuli. *Quart. J. Exp. Psychol.*, **12**, 180–4.

GREBE, H. (1953) Zur Atiologie letaler Missbildungen. *Verh. dtsch. Ges. Path.*, 395–403.

GREBE, H. and WINDORFER, A. (1953) Beitrag zur erblichen und nichterblichen Missbildungsätiologie. *Dtsch. Med. Wschr.*, **78**, 149–51.

GREGG, N. MCA. (1941) Congenital cataract following German measles in the mother. *Trans. Ophthal. Soc. Austral.*, **3**, 35.

GRINGS, W. W., LOCKHART, R. A. and DAMERON, L. E. (1962) Conditioning autonomic responses of mentally subnormal individuals. *Psychol. Monogr.*, **76** (Whole No. 39).

GRISWOLD, F. H. (1939) *Creative Power, the Phenomena of Inspiration: an inquiry into the practical methods used by men of genius in devloping original ideas.* New York: McKay.

GUILFORD, J. P. (1950) Creativity. *Amer. Psychologist*, **5**, 444–54.

GUILFORD, J. P. (1954) *Psychometric methods* (2nd ed.). New York: McGraw-Hill.

GUILFORD, J. P. (1956) The structure of intellect. *Psychol. Bull.*, **53**, 267–93.

GUILFORD, J. P. (1961) Factorial angles to psychology. *Psychol. Rev.*, **68**, 1–20.

GUILFORD, J. P. (1962) Creativity: its measurement and development. In PARNES, S. and HARDING, H. (eds.) *A Source Book for Creativity Thinking.* New York: Scribner.

GUILFORD, J. P. (1966) Intelligence: 1965 model. *Amer. Psychologist*, **21**, 20–6.

GUILFORD, J. P. (1967) *The Nature of Human Intelligence.* New York: McGraw-Hill.

GUILFORD, J. P. and CHRISTENSEN, P. R. (1956) A factor-analytic study of verbal fluency. *Rep. Psychol. Lab.*, No. 17. Univ. Southern California.

GUTHRIE, E. R. (1938) *The Psychology of Human Conflict: The Clash of Motives within the Individual.* New York: Harper & Row.

GUTTMAN, L. (1944) A basis for scaling qualitative data. *Amer. Sociol. Rev.*, **9**, 139–50.

GUTTMAN, L. (1954a). A new approach to factor analysis: the radex. In LAZARSFELD, P. E. (ed.) *Mathematic Thinking in the Social Sciences.* Glencoe, Ill.: Free Press. pp. 258–348.

GUTTMAN, L. (1954b). *An Outline of some New Methodology for Social Research.* Paper read at World Association for Public Opinion

Research and American Association for Public Opinion Research, Ashbury Park, New Jersey.

HADAMARD, J. S. (1945) *An essay on the Psychology of Invention in the Mathematical Field.* Princeton, N.J.: Princeton University Press.

HALDANE, J. B. S. (1954) The measurement of natural selection. *Carylogia*, **6**, 480–7.

HALL, C. S. (1934) Emotional behavior in the rat, I: defecation and urination as measures of individual differences in emotionality. *J. Comp. Psychol.*, **18**, 385–403.

HALL, M. (1843) *New Memorie on the Nervous System.* London: Proc. Royal Academy.

HALSEY, A. H. (1959) Class differences in intelligence. *Brit. J. Statist. Psychol.*, **12**, 1–4.

HAMLEY, H. R. (1936) Formal training: a critical survey of experimental work. *Brit. J. Educ. Psychol.*, **6**, 233–41.

HARLOW, H. F. (1950) Learning and satiation of response in intrinsically motivated complex puzzle performance by monkeys. *J. Comp. Physiol. Psychol.*, **43**, 289–94.

HARLOW, H. F. (1958) The nature of love. *Amer. Psychologist*, **13**, 673–85.

HARLOW, H. F., HARLOW, M. K. and MEYER, D. R. (1950) Learning motivated by a manipulation drive. *J. Exp. Psychol.*, **40**, 228–34.

HARRELL, T. H. (1961) *Managers' Performance and Personality.* Cincinnati: South Western.

HARTER, H. (1960) Criminal values for Duncan's New Multiple Range Test. *Biometrics*, **16**, 671–85.

HARTER, S. (1965) Discrimination learning set in children as a function of MA and IQ. *J. Exp. Child. Psychol.*, **2**, 31–43.

HARTMANN, K. R. E. VON (1931) *The Philosophy of the Unconscious* (trans. W. C. Coupland). New York: Harcourt Brace (originally published 1869).

HARVEY, O. J., HUNT, D. E. and SCHROEDER, H. M. (1961) *Conceptual Systems and Personality Organization.* New York: Wiley.

HAVELKA, J. (1956) Problem-seeking behavior in rats. *Canad. J. Psychol.*, **10**, 91–7.

HAYAKAWA, S. I. (1949) *Language in Thought and Action.* New York: Harcourt Brace.

HAYES, K. J. (1962) Genes, drives and intellect. *Psychol. Rep.*, **10**, 299, 342.

HEBB, D. O. (1941) Clinical evidence concerning the nature of normal adult test performance. *Psychol. Bull.*, **38**, 593 (Abstract).

HEBB, D. O. (1946) On the nature of fear. *Psychol. Rev.*, **53**, 259–76.

HEBB, D. O. (1947) The effects of early experience on problem-solving at maturity. *Amer. Psychologist*, **2**, 306–7.

HEBB, D. O. (1949) *The Organization of Behavior*. New York: Wiley.

HEBB, D. O. and RIESEN, A. H. (1943) The genesis of irrational fears. *Bull. Canad. Psychol. Ass.*, **3**, 49–50.

HEBB, D. O. and THOMPSON, W. R. (1954) The social significance of animal studies. In LINDZEY, G. (ed.) *Handbook of Social Psychology*. Reading, Mass.: Addison-Wesley. Ch. 15.

HEBB, D. O. and WILLIAMS, K. (1946) A method of rating animal intelligence. *J. Genet. Psychol.*, **34**, 59–65.

HEIM, A. W. (1954) *The Appraisal of Intelligence*. London: Methuen.

HELSON, H. and HELSON, H. B. (1946) Some common features of concrete and abstract thinking. *Amer. J. Psychol.*, **59**, 458–72.

HENDRICK, I. (1943) The discussion of the 'instinct to master'. *Psychoanalyt. Quart.*, **12**, 561–5.

HERNÀNDEZ-PÉON, R., SCHERER, H. and JOUVET, M. (1956) Modification of electric activity in cochlear nucleus during 'attention' in unanesthetized cats. *Science*, **123**, 331–2.

HETHERINGTON, E. M. and BANTA, T. J. (1962) Incidental and intentional learning in normal and mentally retarded children. *J. Comp. Physiol. Psychol.*, **55**, 402–4.

HETHERINGTON, E. M., ROSS, L. E. and PICK, H. L., JR (1964) Delay of reward and learning in mentally retarded and normal children. *Child Develpm.*, **35**, 653–9.

HICK, W. (1952) On the rate of gain of information. *Quart. J. Exp. Psychol.*, **4**, 11–26.

HIGGINS, J., REED, E. and REED, S. (1962) Intelligence and family size: a paradox resolved. *Eugen. Quart.*, **9**, 84–90.

HILGARD, E. R. (1956) *Theories of Learning*. New York: Appleton-Century-Crofts (first pub. 1948).

HILGARD, J. R. (1932) Learning and maturation in pre-school children. *J. Genet. Psychol.*, **41**, 36–56.

HINDLEY, C. B. (1971) *Individual Differences in the Development of Intelligence Related to Social Class and Family Background*. Paper read at the Annual Conference of the British Psychological Society.

HOFFMAN, D. T., HOUSE, B. J. and ZEAMAN, D. (1963) Miniature experiments in the discrimination learning of retardates. In LIPSITT, L. P. and SPIKER, C. C. (eds.) *Advances in Child Development and Behavior*, vol. I. New York: Academic Press.

HOFSTAETTER, P. R. (1954) The changing composition of 'intelligence': a study in T-technique. *J. Genet. Psychol.*, **85**, 159–64.

HOFSTAETTER, P. R. and O'CONNOR, G. P. (1956) Anderson's overlap hypothesis and the discontinuities of growth. *J. Genet. Psychol.*, **88**, 95–106.

HOLLAND, J. L. (1961) Creative and academic performance among talent adolescents. *J. Educ. Psychol.*, **52**, 136–47.

HOLMES, F. B. (1935) An experimental study of children's fears. In JERSILD, A. T. and HOLMES, F. B. (eds.) *Children's Fears.* New York: Teachers College, Columbia University, *Child Develpm. Monogr.*, 20.

HOLMES, J. A. and SINGER, H. (1966) *Speed and Power of Reading in High School.* Washington, D.C.: United States Government Printing Office.

HOLT, E. B. (1931) *Animal Drive and the Learning Process.* New York: Holt, Rinehart & Winston.

HONZIK, M. P. (1967) Prediction of differential abilities at age 18 from the early family environment. In *Proceedings 75th Annual Convention American Psychological Association: 1967*, vol. 2. Washington, D.C.: American Psychological Association. pp. 151–2.

HORN, J. L. (1963) The discovery of personality traits. *J. Exp. Res.*, **56**, 460–5.

HORN, J. L. (1965) *Fluid and Crystallized Intelligence: A Factor Analytic and Developmental Study of Structure among Primary Mental Abilities.* Unpublished doctoral dissertation, University of Illinois.

HORN, J. L. (1966) *Short-Period Changes in Human Abilities.* National Aeronautics and Space Administration Report 618. Denver, Colorado: Denver Research Institute.

HORN, J. L. (1967) Intelligence – why it grows, why it declines. *Transaction*, **4**, 23–31.

HORN, J. L. and BRAMBLE, W. L. (1967) Second order ability structure revealed in rights and wrongs scores. *J. Educ. Psychol.*, **58**, 115–22.

HORN, J. L. and CATTELL, R. B. (1965) Vehicles, ipsatization and the multiple-method measurement of motivation. *Canad. J. Psychol.*, **19**, 265–79.

HORN, J. L. and CATTELL, R. B. (1966a) Age differences in primary mental abilities. *J. Gerontol.*, **21**, 210–20.

HORN, J. L. and CATTELL, R. B. (1966b) Refinement and test of the theory of fluid and crystallized intelligences. *J. Educ. Psychol.*, 57 253–70.

HORN, J. L. and CATTELL, R. B. (1967) Age differences in fluid and crystallized intelligence. *Acta Psychol.*, 26, 1–23.

HORN, J. L. and LITTLE, K. B. (1965) Methods for isolating changes and invariance in patterns of behavior. *Multivariate Behav. Res.*, 1, 219–29.

HOUSE, B. J. (1963) Recalls versus trials as factors in serial verbal learning of retardates. *Psychol. Rep.*, 12, 931–41.

HOUSE, B. J. and ZEAMAN, D. (1958) A comparison of discrimination learning in normal and mentally defective children. *Child Develpm.*, 29, 411–16.

HOUSE, B. J. and ZEAMAN, D. (1960) Visual discrimination learning and intelligence in defectives of low mental age. *Amer. J. Ment. Defic.*, 65, 51–8.

HOUSE, B. J. and ZEAMAN, D. (1963) Miniature experiments in the discrimination learning of retardates. In LIPSITT, L. P. and SPIKER, C. C. (eds.) *Advances in Child Development and Behavior*, vol. 1. New York: Academic Press.

HOUSTON, J. P. and MEDNICK, S. A. (1963) Creativity and the need for novelty. *J. Abnorm. Soc. Psychol.*, 66, 137–44.

HOVLAND, C. I., MANDELL, W., CAMPBELL, E. H., BROCK, T., LUCHINS, A. S., COHEN, A. R., MCGUIRE, W. J., JANIS, I. L., FEIERABEND, R. L. and ANDERSON, N. H. (1957) *The Order of Presentation in Persuasion*. New Haven, Conn.: Yale University Press.

HUDSON, L. (1965) A curious dispute: inheritance versus environment. *The Listener*, 73, 929–32.

HUDSON, L. (1966) *Contrary Imaginations*. London: Methuen.

HULL, C. L. (1920) Quantitative aspects of the evolution of concepts. *Psychol. Monogr.*, 28 (1) (Whole No. 123).

HULL, C. L. (1931) Goal attraction and directing ideas conceived as habit phenomena. *Psychological Rev.*, 38, 487–506.

HULL, C. L. (1943) *Principles of Behavior*. New York: Appleton-Century-Crofts.

HULL, C. L. (1952) *A Behavior System*. New Haven, Conn.: Yale University Press.

HUMPHREYS, L. G. (1952) Individual differences. *Annu. Rev. Psychol.*, 3, 131–50.

HUMPHREYS, L. G. (1960) Investigations of the simplex. *Psychometrika*, 25, 313–23.

HUMPHREYS, L. G. (1962) The organization of human abilities. *Amer. Psychologist*, **17**, 475–83.

HUMPHREYS, L. G. (1967) Critique of Cattell's theory of fluid and crystallized intelligence: a critical experiment. *J. Educ. Psychol.*, **58**, 120–36.

HUNT, J. MCV. (1941) The effects of infant feeding-frustration upon adult hoarding in the albino rat. *J. Abnorm. Soc. Psychol.*, **36**, 338–60.

HUNT, J. MCV. (1945) Experimental psychoanalysis. In HARRIMAN, P. L. (ed.) *Encyclopedia of Psychology*. New York: Philosophical Library.

HUNT, J. MCV. (1956) *Psychosexual Development: The Infant Disciplines*. Urbana: Psychological Development Laboratory, University of Illinois (mimeographed paper).

HUNT, J. MCV. (1960) Experience and the development of motivation: some reinterpretations. *Child Develpm.*, **31**, 489–504.

HUNT, J. MCV. (1961) *Intelligence and Experience*. New York: Ronald Press.

HUNT, J. MCV. (1963a) Motivation inherent in information processing and action. In HARVEY, O. J. (ed.) *Motivation and Social Interaction*. New York: Ronald Press. Ch. 3.

HUNT, J. MCV. (1963b) Piaget's observations as a source of hypotheses concerning motivation. *Merrill-Palmer Quart.*, **9**, 263–75.

HUNT, J. MCV. (1965a) Intrinsic motivation and its role in psychological development. In LEVINE, D. (ed.) *Nebraska Symposium on Motivation*, **13**, 189–282. Lincoln: University of Nebraska Press.

HUNT, J. MCV. (1965b) Traditional personality theory in the light of recent evidence. *Amer. Sci.*, **53**, 80–96.

HUNT, J. MCV. and LURIA, Z. (1956) *Investigations of the Effects of Early Experience in Sub-human Animals*. Urbana, Ill.: Psychological Development Laboratory, University of Illinois (mimeo).

HUNTER, W. S. (1912) The delayed reaction in animals and children. *Behav. Monogr.*, **2** (1), 1–85.

HUNTER, W. S. (1918) The temporal maze and kinesthetic sensory processes in the white rat. *Psychology*, **2**, 339–51.

HUNTER, W. S. (1920) Modification of instinct from the standpoint of social psychology. *Psychol. Rev.*, **27**, 247–69.

HUSÉN, T. (1959) *Psychological Twin Research*. Stockholm: Almquist & Wiksell.

HYDÉN, H. (1959) Biochemical changes in glial cells and nerve cells at varying activity. In BRUCKE, F. (ed.) *Proceedings of the 4th*

International Congress of Biochemistry, III: Biochemistry of the Central Nervous System. London: Pergamon Press.

HYDÉN, H. (1960) The neuron. In BRACHET, J. and MIRSKY, A. E. (eds.), *The Cell: Biochemistry, Physiology, IV: Specialized Cells.* New York: Academic Press. pp. 215–323.

HYDÉN, H. and PIGON, A. (1960) A cytophysiological study of the functional relationship between oligodendroglial cells and nerve cells of Deiter's nucleus. *J. Neurochemistry*, **6**, 57–72.

HYMAN, R. (1953) Stimulus information as a determinant of reaction time. *J. Exp. Psychol.*, **45**, 188–96.

HYMAN, R. (1964) Knowledge and creativity. In TAYLOR, C. W. (ed.) *Widening Horizons in Creativity.* New York: Wiley.

INGALLS, T. H. (1947) Etiology of mongolism. *Amer. J. Dis. Children*, **74**, 147.

INGALLS, T. H. (1956) Causes and prevention of developmental defects. *J. Amer. Med. Ass.*, **151**, 1047.

INHELDER, B. and PIAGET, J. (1958) *The Growth of Logical Thinking from Childhood to Adolescence: an essay on the construction of formal operational structures* (trans. A. Parsons and S. Milgram). New York: Basic Books (originally published 1955).

Intelligence and its measurement: a symposium, (1921a). *J. Educ. Psychol.*, **12**, 123–47.

Intelligence and its measurement: a symposium, (1921b). *J. Educ. Psychol.*, **12**, 195–216.

ISAACS, S. (1933) *Social Development in Young Children.* London: Routledge.

ISCOE, I. and SEMLER, I. F. (1964) Paired-associate learning in normal and mentally retarded children as a function of four experimental conditions. *J. Comp. Physiol. Psychol.*, **57**, 387–92.

JENSEN, A. R. (1964) *Individual Differences in Learning: Interference Factors.* U. S. Department of Health, Education and Welfare. Co-op Project No. 1867.

JENSEN, A. R. (1965) Rote learning in retarded adults and normal children. *Amer. J. Ment. Defic.*, **69**, 828–54.

JOHN, V. P. (1963) The intellectual development of slum children: some preliminary findings. *Amer. J. Orthopsychiat.*, **33**, 813–22.

JOHN, V. P. and GOLDSTEIN, L. S. (1964) The social context of language acquisition. *Merrill-Palmer Quart.*, **10**, 266–75.

JOHNSON, D. M. (1962) Problem solving processes. *Amer. Psychologist*, **17**, 327 (Abstract).

JOHNSON, G. O. and BLAKE, K. A. (1960) *Learning Performance of Retarded and Normal Children*. New York: Syracuse University Press.

JONES, F. E. and CATTELL, R. B. (1965) *Weighting of the 16 P.F. Questionnaire Factors in Predicting Industrial Creativity*. Private circular.

JONES, L. V. and WEPMAN, J. M. (1961) Dimensions of language performance in aphasia. *J. Speech. Hear. Res.*, 4, 220–32.

JUDSON, A. J., COFER, C. N. and GELFAND, S. (1956) Reasoning as an associative process, II: 'Direction' in problem solving as a function of prior reinforcement of relevant responses. *Psychol. Rep.*, 2, 501–7.

JUEL-NIELSEN, N. and MOGENSEN, A. (1957) Uniovular twins brought up apart. *Acta Genet.*, 7, 430–3.

KAGAN, J. and MOSS, H. A. (1962) *Birth to Maturity: A Study in Psychological Development*. New York: Wiley.

KAGAN, J., MOSS, H. A. and SIGEL, I. E. (1960) Conceptual style and the use of affect labels. *Merrill-Palmer Quart.*, 6, 261–78.

KAGAN, J., MOSS, H. A. and SIGEL, I. E. (1963) Psychological significance of styles of conceptualization. In WRIGHT, J. C. and KAGAN, J. (eds.) Basic cognitive processes in children. *Monogr. Soc. Res. Child Develpm.*, 28 (2) (Serial No. 86, 73–112).

KASS, N. and STEVENSON, H. W. (1961) The effect of pretraining reinforcement conditions on learning by normal and retarded children. *Amer. J. Ment. Defic.*, 66, 76–80.

KELLER, S. (1963) The social world of the urban slum child: some early findings. *Amer. J. Orthopsychiat.*, 33, 813–22.

KELLY, G. A. (1955) *The Psychology of Personal Constructs*. New York: Norton. 2 vols.

KEMP, L. C. D. (1955) Environmental and other characteristics determining attainments in primary schools. *Brit. J. Educ. Psychol.*, 25, 67–77.

KENDLER, H. H. and KENDLER, T. S. (1962) Vertical and horizontal processes in problem solving. *Psychol. Rev.*, 69, 1–16.

KINCAID, C. E. (1961) The determination and description of various creative attributes of children. *Stud. Art. Educ.*, 2, 43–53.

KLEINSMITH, L. J. and KAPLAN, S. (1963) Paired-associate learning as function and interpolated interval. *J. Exp. Psychol.*, 65, 190–3.

KLOTZ, R. (1952) Das Psychische Trauma in der Genese der Missgeburt. *Z. Gynack.*, 74, 906.

KNAPP, R. H. (1963) Demographic cultural and personality attributes
O

of scientists. In BARRON, F. and TAYLOR, C. W. (eds.) *Scientific Creativity: Its Recognition and Development*. New York: Wiley.

KNOBLOCH, H. and PASAMANICK, B. (1956) *Distribution of Intellectual Potential in an Infant Population*. Paper presented to conference, Epidemiology of Mental Disorder, New York.

KOFFKA, K. (1959) *The Growth of the Mind* (rev. ed.). Paterson, N.J.: Littlefield, Adams (originally published 1924).

KÖHLER, W. (1959) *The Mentality of Apes* (trans. E. Winter). New York: Vintage Books (originally published 1925).

KÖHLER, W. (1962) *Gestalt Psychology*. New York: Mentor Books (originally published 1929).

KUHN, T. S. (1963) The essential tension: tradition and innovation. In BARRON, F. and TAYLOR, C. W. (eds.) *Scientific Creativity: Its Recognition and Development*. New York: Wiley.

KUO, Z. Y. (1921) Give up instincts in psychology. *J. Phil.*, **18**, 645–64.

KUO, Z. Y. (1922) How are instincts acquired? *Psychol. Rev.*, **29**, 334–65.

KUO, Z. Y. (1932a) Ontogeny of embryonic behavior in aves: I, The chronology and general nature of the behavior in the chick embryo. *J. Exp. Zool.*, **61**, 395–430.

KUO, Z. Y. (1932b) Ontogeny of embryonic behavior in aves: II, The mechanical factors in the various stages leading to hatching. *J. Exp. Zool.*, **62**, 453–87.

KUO, Z. Y. (1932c) Ontogeny of embryonic behavior in aves: III, The structural and environmental factors in embryonic behavior. *J. Comp. Psychol.*, **13**, 245–71.

KUO, Z. Y. (1932d) Ontogeny of embryonic behavior in aves: IV, The influence of embryonic movements upon the behavior after hatching. *J. Comp. Psychol.*, **14**, 109–22.

KUO, Z. Y. (1932e) Ontogeny of embryonic behavior in aves: V, The reflex concept in the light of embryonic behavior in birds. *Psychol. Rev.*, **39**, 499–515.

KUSMIN, A. (1964) *Verbal Learning and Retention of Retardates at Varying IQ, MA and CA Levels*. Unpublished Doctoral Dissertation, University of Connecticut.

LAMARCK, J., CHEVALIER DE (1914) *Zoological Philosophy* (trans. of *Philosophie zoologique*, by ELLIOT, H.). London: Macmillan (originally published 1809).

LASHLEY, K. S. (1935) Studies of cerebral function, XI: the behavior of the rat in match-box situations. *Comp. Psychol. Monogr.*, **11** (2).

LEHMAN, H. C. (1953) *Age and Achievement*. Princeton, N.J.: Princeton University Press.

LEVINE, S., CHEVALIER, J. A. and KORCHIN, S. J. (1956) The effects of early shock and handling on later avoidance learning. *J. Pers.*, **24**, 475–93.

LEWIS, D. G. (1957) The normal distribution of intelligence: a critique. *Brit. J. Psychol.*, **48**, 98–104.

LEWIS, O. (1961) *The Children of Sanchez*. New York: Random House.

LIBERMAN, R. (1962) Retinal cholinesterase and glycolysis in rats raised in darkness. *Science*, **135**, 372–3.

LIENERT, A. A. (1963) Die Faktorenstrukter der intelligenz als Function des Neurotizismus. *Zhstr. F. Exp. Angew. Psychol.*, **10**, 140–59.

LILIENFELD, A. M. and PARKHURST, E. (1951) Association of factors of pregnancy and parturition with the development of cerebral palsy. *Amer. J. Hyg.*, **53**, 262.

LINGOES, J. C. (1965) An IBM-7090 program for Guttman-Lingoes smallest space analysis, I. *Behav. Sciences*, **10**, 183–4.

LIPMAN, R. S. (1963) Learning: verbal, perceptual-motor and classical conditioning. In ELLIS, N. R. (ed.) *Handbook of Mental Deficiency*. New York: McGraw-Hill.

LITTELL, W. M. (1960) The Wechsler Intelligence Test for Children: review of a decade of research. *Psychol. Bull.*, **57**, 149–60.

LOCKE, J. (1939) An essay concerning the true original extent and end of civil government. In BURTT, E. A. (ed.) *The English Philosophers from Bacon to Mill*. New York: Modern Library (originally published 1690). pp. 403–503.

LOEB, J. (1890) *Der Heliotropismus der Thiere und Seine Uebereinstimmung mit dem Heliotropismus der Pflanzen*. Wurzberg: Herts.

LOEB, J. (1912) *The Mechanistic Conception of Life*. Chicago: University of Chicago Press.

LORENZ, K. (1937) The companion in the bird's world. *Auk*, **54**, 245–73.

LOTKA, A. J. (1907a) Relation between birth rates and death rates. *Science*, **26**, 21–2.

LOTKA, A. J. (1907b) Studies on the mode of growth of material aggregates. *Amer. J. Science*, **24**, 199–216.

LOTKA, A. J. (1922) The stability of the normal age distribution. *Proc. National Acad. Sciences*, **8**, 339–45.

LOTKA, A. J. (1925) *Elements of Physical Biology*. Baltimore: Williams and Wilkins.

LOTKA, A. J. and SHARPE, F. (1911) A problem in age-distribution. *Philosophical Magazine*, **21**, 435–8.

LUCHINS, A. S. (1942) Mechanization in problem-solving behaviour. *Psychol. Monogr.*, **54** (6) (Whole No. 248).

LYNN, R. and GORDON, I. E. (1961) The relation of neuroticism and extraversion to intelligence and education attainment. *Brit. J. Educ. Psychol.*, **31**, 194–203.

MCCLELLAND, D. C. (1950) *Personality*. New York: McGraw-Hill.

MCCLELLAND, D. C. (1953) *The Achievement Motive*. New York: Appleton-Century-Crofts.

MCDOUGALL, W. (1908) *An Introduction to Social Psychology*. Boston: Luce.

MCGEOCH, J. A. and IRION, A. L. (1952) *The Psychology of Human Learning*. New York: McKay.

MCGRAW, M. B. (1935) *Growth: A study of Johnny and Jimmy*. New York: Appleton-Century-Crofts.

MCKEOWN, T. and RECORD, R. G. (1951) Seasonal incidence of congenital malformation of the central nervous system. *Lancet*, January, **27**, 192.

MACKINNON, D. W. (1962) The nature and nurture of creative talent. *Amer. Psychologist*, **17**, 484–95.

MCCARTHY, J. J. and KIRK, S. A. (1961) *The Illinois Test of Psycholinguistic Abilities* (experimental ed.). Urbana, Ill.: Institute for Research in Exceptional Children.

MCLEISH, J. (1963) *The Science of Behaviour*. London: Barrie & Rockliff.

MCKELLAR, P. (1957) *Imagination and Thinking*. New York: Basic Books.

MACMAHON, B. and MCKEOWN, T. (1953) Incidence of harelip and cleft palate related to birth rank and maternal age. *Amer. J. Hum. Genet.*, **5** (2).

MCNEMAR, Q. (1942) *The Revision of the Stanford–Binet Scale: An Analysis of the Standardization Data*. Boston: Houghton Mifflin.

MCNEMAR, Q. (1964) Lost: our intelligence? Why? *Amer. J. Psychol.*, **19**, 871–82.

MADDOX, H. (1957) Nature–nurture balance sheets. *Brit. J. Educ. Psychol.*, **27**, 166–75.

MAIER, N. F. R. (1931) Reasoning in humans: the solution of a problem and its appearance in consciousness. *J. Comp. Physiol. Psychol.*, 11, 181–94.

MAIER, N. F. R. (1940) The behaviour mechanisms concerned with problem solving. *Psychol. Rev.*, 47, 43–58.

MALTZMAN, I., BROOKS, L. O., BOGARTZ, W. and SUMMERS, S. S. (1958) The facilitation of problem-solving by prior exposure to uncommon responses. *J. Exp. Psychol.*, 56, 399–406.

MARQUIS, D. G. (1930) The criterion of innate behavior. *Psychol. Rev.*, 37, 334–49.

MARTIN, L. and ADKINS, D. S. (1954) A second order analysis of reasoning abilities. *Psychometrika*, 19, 71–8.

MARTIN, W. E. and BLUM, A. (1961) Interest generalization and learning in mentally normal and subnormal children. *J. Comp. Physiol. Psychol.*, 54, 28–32.

MATEER, F. (1918) *Child Behavior*. Bostock: Gorham Press.

MAXWELL, J. (1953) *Social Implications of the 1947 Scottish Mental Survey*. London: University of London Press.

MEADOW, A., PARNES, S. J. and REESE, H. (1959) Influence of brainstorming instructions and problem sequences on a creative problem-solving test. *J. Appl. Psychol.*, 43, 413–16.

MEDNICK, S. A. (1962) The associative basis of the creative process. *Psychol. Rev.*, 69, 220–32.

MEIER, N. C. (1939) Factors in artistic aptitude: a final summary of a ten-year study of special ability. *Psychol. Monogr.*, 51 (231).

MELTON, A. W. (1941) Learning. In MUNROE, W. S. (ed.) *Encyclopedia of Educational Research*. New York: Macmillan.

MERKER, J. (1885) Die zeitlichen Verhältnisse der Willenstätigkeit. *Philos. Studien*, 2, 73–127.

MERRIFIELD, P. R., GUILFORD, J. P., CHRISTENSEN, P. R. and FRICK, J. W. (1961) Interrelationships between certain abilities and certain traits of motivation and temperament. *J. Genet. Psychol.*, 65, 57–74.

MILES, T. R. (1957) On defining intelligence. *Brit. J. Educ. Psychol.*, 27, 153–65.

MILGRAM, N. A. and FURTH, H. G. (1964) Position reversal v. dimension reversal in normal and retarded children. *Child Develpm.*, 35, 701–8.

MILLER, G. A., GALANTER, E. E. and PRIBRAM, K. H. (1960) *Plans and the Structure of Behavior*. New York: Holt, Rinehart and Winston.

MILLER, N. E. and DOLLARD, J. (1941) *Social Learning and Imitation*. New Haven, Conn.: Yale University Press.

MINISTRY OF EDUCATION (1963) *Higher Education* (*The Robbins Report*). App. I. London: H.M.S.O.

MOLLENKOPF, W. G. (1956) A study of secondary school characteristics determining attainment. *Educ. Test. Service Res. Bull.*, **56** (6).

MONTGOMERY, K. C. (1952) A test of two explanations of spontaneous alteration. *J. Comp. Physiol. Psychol.*, **45**, 287–93.

MONTGOMERY, K. C. (1953) Exploratory behavior as a function of 'similarity' of stimulus situations. *J. Comp. Physiol. Psychol.*, **46**, 129–33.

MONTGOMERY, K. C. (1955) The relation between fear induced by novel stimulation and exploratory behavior. *J. Comp. Physiol. Psychol.*, **48**, 254–60.

MONTGOMERY, K. C. and SEGALL, M. (1955) Discrimination learning based upon the exploratory drive. *J. Comp. Physiol. Psychol.*, **48**, 225–8.

MOORE, O. K. (1963) *Autotelic Responsive Environments and Exceptional Children*. Hamden, Conn.: Responsive Environments Foundation.

MORAY, NEVILLE (1960) Broadbent's filter theory: Postulate H and the problem of switching time. *Quart. J. Exp. Psychol.*, **12**, 214–20.

MORGAN, C. L. (1909) *An Introduction to Comparative Psychology* (2nd ed.). London: Scott (original date of publication 1894).

MORRIS, D. (1962) The biology of art. *Portfolio Art News Annu.*, No. 6, 52–63, 122–4.

MORRISON, J. R. (1960) *Effects of Time Limits on the Efficiency and Factorial Composition of Reasoning Measures*. Unpublished doctoral dissertation, University of Illinois.

MOURSEY, E. N. (1952) The hierarchical organization of cognitive levels. *Brit. J. Statist. Psychol.*, **3**, 151.

MOWRER, O. H. (1950) On the psychology of 'talking birds' – a contribution to language and personality theory. In MOWRER, O. H. (ed.) *Learning Theory and Personality Dynamics*. New York: Ronald Press. Ch. 24.

MOWRER, O. H. (1960) *Learning and Behavior*. New York: Wiley.

MULLER, H. J. (1925) Mental traits and heredity. *J. Hered.*, **16**, 433–48.

MURPHY, D. P. (1947) *Congenital Malformations*. Philadelphia.

NEWELL, A., SHAW, J. C. and SIMON, H. A. (1958) Elements of a theory of human problem solving. *Psychol. Rev.*, **65**, 151–66.

NEWMAN, H. H., FREEMAN, F. N. and HOLZINGER, K. J. (1937) *Twins: A Study of Heredity and Environment*. Chicago University Press.

NICHOLS, R. C. (1965) The inheritance of general and special ability. *National Merit Scholarship Corporation Research Report I*, 1.

NISSEN, H. W. (1930) A study of exploratory behavior in the white rat by means of the obstruction method. *J. Genet. Psychol.*, **37**, 361–76.

O'CONNOR, N. and HERMELIN, B. (1959) Discrimination and reversal learning in imbeciles. *J. Abn. Soc. Psychol.*, **59**, 409–13.

ORLANSKY, H. (1949) Infant care and personality. *Psychol. Bull.*, **46**, 1–48.

OSBORN, A. F. (1963) *Applied Imagination* (rev. ed.). New York: Scribner.

OSGOOD, C. E. (1952) The nature and measurement of meaning. *Psychol. Bull.*, **49**, 192–237.

OSLER, S. F. and FIVEL, M. W. (1961) Concept attainment, I: The role of age and intelligence in concept attainment by induction. *J. Exp. Psychol.*, **62**, 1–8.

OSLER, S. F. and TRAUTMAN, G. E. (1961) Concept attainment, II: Effect of stimulus complexity upon concept attainment at two levels of intelligence. *J. Exp. Psychol.*, **62**, 9–13.

OTTO, W. (1965) Inhibition potential in good and poor achievers. *J. Educ. Psychol.*, **56**, 200–7.

OTTO, W. and FREDRICKS, R. C. (1963) Relationship of reactive inhibition to reading skill achievement. *Educ. Psychol.*, **54**, 227, 230.

PAPEZ, J. W. (1929) *Comparative Neurology*. New York: Crowell.

PASAMANICK, B. and LILIENFELD, A. M. (1955) Association of material and fetal factors with development of mental deficiency. *J. Amer. Med. Ass.*, **159**, 155.

PATRICK, C. (1935) Creative thought in poets. *Arch. Psychol., N.Y.*, **26**, 1–74.

PATRICK, C. (1937) Creative thought in artists. *J. Psychol.*, **5**, 35–73.

PATRICK, C. (1938) Scientific thought. *J. Psychol.*, **5**, 55–83.

PATRICK, C. (1941) Whole and part relationship in creative thought. *Amer. J. Psychol.*, **54**, 128–31.

PAVLOV, I. P. (1927) *Conditioned Reflexes* (trans. G. V. Anrep). London: Oxford University Press.

PAYNE, R. W. (1961) Cognitive abnormalities. In EYSENCK, H. J. (ed.) *Handbook of Abnormal Psychology*. London: Pitman.

PENROSE, L. S. (1948) The supposed threat of declining intelligence. *Amer. J. Ment. Defic.*, **58**, 114–18.

PENROSE, L. S. (1949) *The Biology of Mental Defect*. London: Sidgwick & Jackson.

PENROSE, L. S. (1950a) Genetical influences on the intelligence level of the population. *Brit. J. Psychol.*, **40**, 128–36.

PENROSE, L. S. (1950b) Propagation of the unfit. *Lancet*, **2**, 425–7.

PENROSE, L. S. (1951) Heredity and environment in the causation of foetal malformations. *Practitioner*, **166**, 429.

PENROSE, L. S. and SMITH, S. M. (1955) Monozygotic and dizygotic twin diagnosis. *Ann. Hum. Genet.*, **19**, 273–89.

PIAGET, J. (1926) *The Language and Thought of the Child* (trans. M. Worden). New York: Harcourt, Brace (first published 1923).

PIAGET, J. (1928) *Judgment and Reasoning in the Child* (trans. M. Worden). New York: Harcourt, Brace (first published 1924).

PIAGET, J. (1929) *The Child's Conception of the World* (trans. J. and A. Tomlinson). New York: Harcourt, Brace (first published 1926).

PIAGET, J. (1930) *The Child's Conception of Physical Causality* (trans. M. Worden). New York: Harcourt, Brace (first published 1927).

PIAGET, J. (1932) *The Moral Judgment of the Child* (trans. M. Worden). New York: Harcourt, Brace.

PIAGET, J. (1941) Le méchanism du développement mental et les lois du 'groupement' des opérations. *Arch. Psychol., Geneve*, **28**, 215–85.

PIAGET, J. (1942a) *Classes, relations et nombres: Essai sur les 'groupements' de la logistique et la reversibilité de la pensée*. Paris: Vrin.

PIAGET, J. (1942b) Les trois structures fondamentales de la vie psychique: rythme, régulation, et groupement. *Schweiz. Z. Psychol. Anwend.*, **I**, 9–21.

PIAGET, J. (1946) *Les notions de mouvement et de vitesse chez l'enfant*. Paris: Presses Universitaires de France.

PIAGET, J. (1950a) *The Psychology of Intelligence*. London: Routledge & Kegan Paul.

PIAGET, J. (1950b) Une expérience sur la psychologie du hasard chez l'enfant: le tirage au sort des couples. *Acta Psychol.*, **7**, 323–36.

PIAGET, J. (1951) *Play, Dreams and Imitations in Childhood* (trans. C. Gattegno and F. M. Hodgson). New York: Norton (originally published as *La formation du symbole chez l'enfant*, 1945).

PIAGET, J. (1952a) *The Origins of Intelligence in Children* (trans. M. Cook). New York: International Universities Press (originally published 1936).

PIAGET, J. (1952b) Jean Piaget. In BORING, E. G., LANGFELD, H. S., WERNER, H. and YERKES, R. M. (eds.) *A History of Psychology in Autobiography*. Worcester, Mass.: Clark University Press.

PIAGET, J. (1953) *Logic and Psychology* (trans. W. Mays and T. White-head). Manchester: Manchester University Press; New York: Basic Books.

PIAGET, J. (1954) *The Construction of Reality in the Child* (trans. M. Cook). New York: Basic Books (first published 1937).

PIAGET, J. (1955a) The development of time concepts in the child. In HOCH, R. H. and ZUBIN, J. (eds.) *Psychopathology of Childhood*. New York: Grune & Stratton.

PIAGET, J. (1955b) Essai d'une nouvelle interpretation probabiliste des effets de centration de la loi de Weber et celle des centrations relatives. *Arch. Psychol., Genève*, **35**, 1–24.

PIAGET, J., ALBERTINI, B. VON and ROSSI, M. (1944) Essai d'interpretation probabiliste de la loi de Weber et celles des centrations relatives. *Arch. Psychol., Genève*, **30**, 95–138.

PIAGET, J. and INHELDER, B. (1940) *Le developpement des quantites chez l'enfant. Conservation et atomisme*. Neuchâtel: Delachaux et Niestlé.

PIAGET, J. and INHELDER, B. (1947) Diagnosis of mental operations and theory of intelligence. *Am. J. Ment. Defic.*, **51**, 401–6.

PIAGET, J. and INHELDER, B. (1956) *The Child's Conception of Space* (trans. F. J. Langdon and E. A. Lunzer). London: Routledge & Kegan Paul (first published 1948).

PIAGET, J., INHELDER, B. and SZEMINSKA, A. (1960) *The Child's Conception of Geometry* (trans. E. A. Lunzer). New York: Basic Books (first published 1948).

PIAGET, J. and LAMBERCIER, M. (1943a) La comparaison visuelle des hauteurs à distances variables dans le plan fronto-parallèle. *Arch. Psychol., Genève*, **29**, 175–253.

PIAGET, J. and LAMBERCIER, M. (1943b) Le problème de comparaison visuelle en profondeur et l'erreur systématique de l'ètalon. *Arch. Psychol., Genève*, **29**, 255–308.

PIAGET, J. and LAMBERCIER, M. (1944) Essai sur un effet d'Einstellung survenant au cours de perceptions visuelles successives (effet Usnadze). *Arch. Psychol., Genève*, **30**, 140–96.

PIAGET, J. and LAMBERCIER, M. (1946) Transpositions perceptives et transitivité opératoire dans les comparaisons en profondeur. *Arch. Psychol., Genève*, **31**, 325–68.

PIAGET, J. and LAMBERCIER, M. (1953) La comparaison des différences de hauteur dans le plan fronto-parallèle. *Arch. Psychol.,* *Genève,* **34,** 73–107.

PIAGET, J., LAMBERCIER, M., BOESCH, E. and ALBERTINI, B. VON (1942) Introduction à l'étude des perceptions chez l'enfant et analyse d'une illusion relative à la perception visuelle de cercles concentriques (Delboeuf). *Arch. Psychol., Genève,* **29** (113), 1–107.

PIAGET, J. and SZEMINSKA, A. (1939) Quelques expériences sur la conservation des quantités continués chez l'enfant. *J. Psychol. Norm. Path.,* **36,** 36–65.

PIAGET, J. and SZEMINSKA, A. (1952) *The Child's Conception of Number* (trans. C. Gattegno and F. M. Hodgson). New York: Humanities Press (first published 1941).

PLENDERLEITH, M. (1956) Discrimination learning and discrimination reversal learning in normal and feeble-minded children. *J. Genet Psychol.,* **88,** 108–12.

POINCARÉ, H. (1913) *The Foundations of Science.* New York: Science Press.

POPENOE, P. (1922) Twins reared apart. *J. Hered.,* **5,** 142–4.

PRIBRAM, K. H. (1960) A review of theory in physiological psychology. *Annu. Rev. Psychol.,* **11,** 1–40.

PRUETTE, L. (1926) *G. Stanley Hall: A Biography of a Mind.* New York: Appleton-Century-Crofts.

PRYSIAZNIUK, A. W. and WICIJOWSKI, P. J. (1964) Learning sets in mongoloid children: a replication. *Amer. J. Ment. Defic.,* **69,** 76–8.

RAMBUSCH, N. M. (1962) *Learning How to Learn: An American Approach to Montessori.* Baltimore: Helicon Press.

RANKING, G. F. (1963a) *Reading Test Performance of Introverts and Extraverts.* 12th Yearbook of Nat. Reading. Conf., Milwaukee.

RANKING, G. F. (1963b) Reading test reliability and validity as function of introversion: extraversion. *J. Devel. Reading,* **6,** 106–17.

RASCH, E., SWIFT, H., RIESEN, A. H. and CHOS, K. L. (1961) Altered structure and composition of retinal cells in dark-reared mammals. *Experimental Cellular Research,* **25,** 348–63.

RAZRAN, G. H. S. (1933) Conditioned responses in children: a behavioral and quantitative critical review of experimental studies. *Arch. Psychol.,* No. 148, 1–120.

RAZRAN, G. H. S. (1961) The observable unconscious and the inferable conscious in current Soviet psychophysiology: interoceptive conditioning, semantic conditioning, and the orienting reflex. *Psychol. Rev.,* **68,** 81–147.

RECORD, R. G. (1956) Observations related to the aetiology of placenta praevia with special reference to the influence of age and parity. *Brit. J. Prev. Soc. Med.*, **10** (1).

REESE, H. W. (1963) Discrimination learning set in children. In LIPPSITT, L. P. and SPIKER, C. C. (eds.) *Advances in Child Development and Behavior*, vol. 1. New York: Academic Press.

RICHTER, C. P. (1922) A behavioristic study of the activity of the rat. *Comp. Psychol. Monogr.*, **1** (2).

RICHTER, C. P. (1927) Animal behavior and internal drives. *Quart. Rev. Biol.*, **2**, 307–43.

RIEBER, M. (1964) Verbal mediation in normal and retarded children. *Amer. J. Ment. Defic.*, **68**, 634–41.

RIESEN, A. H. (1947) The development of visual perception in man and chimpanzee. *Science*, **106**, 107–8.

RIESEN, A. H. (1951) Post-partum development of behavior. *Medical School Quart.*, **13**, 17–24.

RIESEN, A. H. (1958) Plasticity of behavior: psychological aspects. In HARLOW, H. F. and WOOLSEY, C. N. (eds.) *Biological and Biochemical Bases of Behavior*. Madison: University of Wisconsin Press. pp. 425–50.

RIMOLDI, H. J. (1948) Study of some factors related to intelligence. *Psychometrika*, **13**, 27–46.

RING, E. M. and PALERMO, D. S. (1961) Paired-associate learning of retarded and normal children. *Amer. J. Ment. Defic.*, **66**, 100–7.

ROE, A. (1952) *The Making of a Scientist*. New York: Dodd, Mead.

ROFF, M. A. (1941) Statistical study of the development of intelligence test performance. *J. Psychol.*, **11**, 371–86.

ROGERS, C. R. (1951) *Client-centered Therapy*. Boston: Houghton Mifflin.

ROGERS, C. R. (1962) Toward a theory of creativity. In PARNES, S. J. and HARDING, H. F. (eds.) *A Source Book for Creative Thinking*. New York: Scribner. pp. 64–72.

ROMANES, G. J. (1883a) *Animal Intelligence*. New York: Appleton-Century-Crofts.

ROMANES, G. J. (1883b) *Mental Evolution in Animals*. New York: Appleton-Century-Crofts.

ROSE, J. E. and WOOLSEY, C. N. (1949) The relations of thalamic connections, cellular structure and evocable electric activity in the auditory region of the cat. *J. Comp. Neurol.*, **91**, 441–66.

ROSS, L. E., HETHERINGTON, M. and WRAY, N. P. (1965) Delay of reward and the learning of a size problem by normal and retarded children. *Child Develpm.*, **36**, 509–17.

ROSSMAN, J. (1931) *The Psychology of the Inventor*. Washington, D.C.: Inventors Publishing Co.

ROTH, E. (1964) Die Geschwindigkeit der Verarbeitung von Information und ihr Zusammenhang mit intelligenz. *Atschr. F. Exp. Angew. Psychol.*, **11**, 616–22.

ROUSSEAU, J. J. (1916) *Emile* (trans. B. Foxley). New York: Everyman's Library (original date of publication 1762).

RUCH, F. L. (1936) The methods of common points of mastery as a technique in human learning experimentation. *Psychol. Rev.*, **43**, 229–34.

RUCH, F. L. (1961) Measuring gain from a common point of mastery. *Psychol. Rep.*, **9**, 234.

RUDEL, R. G. (1959) The absolute response in tests of generalization in normal and retarded children. *Amer. J. Psychol.*, **72**, 401–8.

RUGG, H. (1963) *Imagination*. New York: Harper and Row.

SALAMA, A. A. and HUNT, J. MCV. (1964) Fixation in the rat as a function of infantile shocking, handling and gentling. *J. Genet. Psychol.*, **105** (1), 131–62.

SANDERS, B., ROSS, L. E. and HEAL, L. W. (1965) Reversal and non-reversal shifts learning in normal children and retardates of comparable mental age. *J. Comp. Physiol. Psychol.*, **1**, 84–8.

SANDON, F. (1957) Relative numbers and abilities of some ten-year-old twins. *J. Roy. Stat. Soc.*, **120** (IV), 440.

SANDON, F. (1959) Twins in the school population. *Brit. J. Statist. Psychol.*, **12**, 133–8.

SARASON, S. B., DAVIDSON, K. S., LIGHTHALL, F. F., WAITE, R. R. and RUEBUSH, B. K. (1960) *Anxiety in the Elementary School Children*. New York: Wiley.

SAUGSTAD, P. and RAAHEIM, K. (1957) Problem solving and availability of functions. *Acta Psychol.*, **13**, 263–78.

SAUGSTAD, P. and RAAHEIM, K. (1959) Problem solving and availability of functions. *Acta Psychol.*, **16**, 45–58.

SAVAGE, R. D. (1962) Personality factors and academic performance. *Brit. J. Educ. Psychol.*, **32**, 251–2.

SCHAEFER, E. S. and BAYLEY, N. (1963) Maternal behavior, child behavior and their intercorrelations from infancy through adolescence. *Monogr. Soc. Res. Child Develpm.*, **28** (3) (Whole No. 87).

SCHAEFER, E. S., BELL, R. O. and BAYLEY, N. (1959) Development of a maternal behavior research instrument. *J. Genet. Psychol.*, **95**, 83–104.

SCHMID, J. and LEIMAN, J. (1957) The development of hierarchical factor solutions. *Psychometrika*, **22**, 53–61.

SCHMIDTKE, H. (1961) Zur Frage der informationstheoretischen Analyse von Wahlreaktionsexperimenten. *Psychol. Forschung*, **26**, 157–78.

SCHNEIRLA, T. C. (1959) An evolutionary and developmental theory of biphasic processes underlying approach and withdrawal. In JONES, M. R. (ed.) *Nebraska Symposium on Motivation*. Lincoln: University of Nebraska Press, pp. 1–43.

SCHONFIELD, D. (1965) Memory changes with age. *Nature*, **208**, 918.

SCHUSTERMAN, R. J. (1964) Strategies of normal and mentally retarded children under conditions of uncertain outcome. *Amer. J. Ment. Defic.*, **69**, 66–75.

SEGEL, D. (1957) The multiple aptitude tests. *Personnel Guid J.*, **35**, 424–32.

SHAYCOFT, M. F., DAILEY, J. T., ORR, D. B., NEYMAN, C. A., JR and SHERMAN, S. E. (1963) *Project Talent: Studies of a Complete Age Group – Age 15*. Pittsburgh: University of Pittsburgh (mimeo).

SHERRINGTON, C. S. (1906) *The Integrative Action of the Nervous System*. New York: Scribner.

SHIELDS, J. (1962) *Monozygotic Twins*. London: Oxford University Press.

SHURE, G. H. and ROGERS, M. S. (1963) Personality factor stability for three ability levels. *J. Psychol.*, **55**, 445–56.

SIGEL, I. E. (1963) How intelligence tests restrict our concept of intelligence. *Merrill–Palmer Quart.*, **9**, 39–56.

SIMPSON, B. R. (1939) The wandering I.Q. *J. Psychol.*, **7**, 351–67.

SKEELS, H. M. (1965) Some preliminary findings of three follow-up studies on the effects of adoption on children from institutions. *Children*, **12** (1).

SKEELS, H. M. and DYE, II. B. (1939) A study of the effects of differential stimulation on mentally retarded children. *Proc. Amer. Ass. Ment. Defic.*, **44**, 114–36.

SKINNER, B. F. (1938) *The Behavior of Organisms: an Experimental Analysis*. New York: Appleton-Century-Crofts.

SKINNER, B. F. (1950) Are theories of learning necessary? *Psychol. Rev.*, **57**, 193–216.

SKINNER, B. F. (1953) *Science and Human Behavior*. New York: Macmillan.

SKINNER, B. F. (1958) Reinforcement today. *Amer. Psychologist*, **13**, 94–9.

SMITH, A. (1955) A note on mongolism in twins. *Brit. J. Prev. Soc. Med.*, **9**, 212.

SMITH, A. and RECORD, R. G. (1955) Maternal age and birth rank in the aetiology of mongolism. *Brit. J. Prev. Soc. Med.*, **9**, 51.

SMITH, I. M. (1965) *Spatial Ability: Its Educational and Social Significance*. San Diego: Knapp.

SNEDECOR, G. (1956) *Statistical Methods* (5th ed.). Ames, Iowa: Iowa State College Press.

SPEARMAN, C. (1904) 'General intelligence' objectively determined and measured. *Amer. J. Psychol.*, **15**, 201–93.

SPEARMAN, C. (1923) *The Nature of 'Intelligence' and the Principles of Cognition*. London: Macmillan.

SPEARMAN, C. (1927) *The Abilities of Man*. New York: Macmillan.

SPENCE, K. W. (1964) Anxiety (drive) level and performance in eyelid conditioning. *Psychol. Bull.*, **61**, 129–39.

SPIEGELMAN, S. (1946) Nuclear and cytoplasmic factors controlling enzymatic constitution. *Lond. Sch. Hyg. Symp. Quant. Biol.*, **11**, 256–77.

SPIESS, E. B. (ed.) (1962) *Papers on Animal Genetics*. Boston, Mass.: Little Brown and Co.

SPITZ, R. A. (1946) The smiling response: a contribution to the ontogenesis of social relations. *Genet. Psychol. Monogr.*, **34**, 67–125.

STANDING, E. M. (1957) *Maria Montessori: Her Life and Work*. Fresno, Calif.: Academy Library Guild.

STAKE, R. E. (1961) Learning parameters, aptitudes and achievements. *Psychometric Monographs*, No. 9.

STEVENSON, H. W. (1960) Learning of complex problems by normal and retarded. *SS. Amer. J. Ment. Defic.*, **64**, 1021–6.

STEVENSON, H. W. (1965) Interrelationships in children's learning. *Child Develpm.*, **36**, 7–19.

STEVENSON, H. W. and ISCOE, I. (1955) Transposition in the feeble-minded. *J. Exp. Psychol.*, **49**, 11–15.

STEVENSON, H. W. and ZIGLER, E. F. (1957) Discrimination learning and rigidity in normal and feeble-minded individuals. *J. Pers.*, **25**, 699–711.

STODDARD, G. D. and WELLMAN, B. L. (1940) Environment and the I.Q. *Yearbook of National Social Studies Education*, **39** (1), 405–42.

STOTT, D. H. (1956) *Unsettled Children and their Families*. London: University of London Press.

STOTT, D. H. (1957) Mental and physical handicaps in the child following a disturbed pregnancy. *Lancet,* **171** (1), 1006.

STOTT, D. H. (1958) Some psychosomatic aspects of causality in reproduction. *J. Psychosomat. Res.,* **3**, 42.

STOTT, D. H. (1959) Evidence for pre-natal impairment of temperament in mentally retarded children. *Vita Humana,* **2**, 125–48.

TAYLOR, C. W. (ed.) (1955) *The 1955 University of Utah Research Conference on the Identification of Creative Scientific Talent.* Salt Lake City: University of Utah Press.

TAYLOR, C. W. (1964) *Creativity: Progress and Potential.* New York: McGraw-Hill.

TAYLOR, C. W. and BARRON, F. (eds.) (1963) *Scientific Creativity.* London: Wiley.

TAYLOR, C. W., SMITH, W. R., GHISELIN, B. and ELLISON, R. (1961) Explorations in the measurement and predictions of contributions of one sample of scientists. *USAF ASD Tech. Rep.* No. 61-96.

TAYLOR, D. W. (1960) Toward an information processing theory of motivation. In JONES, M. R. (ed.) *Nebraska Symposium on Motivation.* Lincoln: University of Nebraska Press. pp. 51–79.

TAYLOR, D. W. (1961) Variables related to creativity and productivity among men in two research laboratories. In TAYLOR, C. W. and BARRON, F. (eds.) *Scientific Creativity: Its Recognition and Development.* New York: Wiley.

TERMAN, L. M. (1916) *The Measurement of Intelligence.* Boston: Houghton Mifflin.

TERMAN, L. M. and ODEN, M. H. (1947) *Genetic Studies of Genius,* vol. 4: *The Gifted Child Grows Up.* Stanford: Stanford University Press.

THISTLETHWAITE, D. L. (1963) The college environment as a determinant of research potentiality. In TAYLOR, C. W. and BARRON, F. (eds.) *Scientific Creativity: Its Recognition and Development.* New York: Wiley.

THOMPSON, W. R. and HERON, W. (1954) The effects of restricting early experience on the problem-solving capacity of dogs. *Canad. J. Psychol.,* **8**, 17–31.

THORNDIKE, E. L. (1898) Animal intelligence. *Psychol. Rev. Monogr. Suppl.,* **2** (8), 1–109.

THORNDIKE, E. L. (1911) *Animal Intelligence: Experimental Studies.* New York: Macmillan.

THORNDIKE, E. L. (1913) *Educational Psychology,* vol. II: *The Psychology of Learning.* New York: Columbia University Press.

THORNDIKE, E. L. (1926) *The Measurement of Intelligence.* New York: Teachers College Press.

THORNDIKE, E. L. (1931) *Human Learning.* New York: Appleton-Century-Crofts.

THORNDIKE, E. L. (1935) *The Psychology of Wants, Interests and Attitudes.* New York: Appleton-Century-Crofts.

THORNDIKE, E. L. and WOODWORTH, R. S. (1901) The influence of improvement in one mental function upon the efficiency of other functions. *Psychol. Rev.,* 8, 247–61, 384–95, 553–64.

THORNDIKE, R. L. (1963) Some methodological issues in the study of creativity. In *Proceedings of the 1926 Invitational Conference on Testing Problems.* Princeton, N.J.: Educational Testing Service. pp. 40–54.

THURSTONE, L. L. (1962) *The Nature of Intelligence.* New York: Harcourt, Brace & World.

THURSTONE, L. L. (1938) *Primary Mental Abilities.* Chicago: University of Chicago Press.

THURSTONE, L. L. (1947) *Multiple-factor Analysis.* Chicago: University of Chicago Press.

THURSTONE, L. L. and THURSTONE, T. G. (1941) *Factorial Studies of Intelligence.* Chicago: University of Chicago Press.

TILTON, J. W. (1949) Intelligence test scores as indicative of ability to learn. *Educ. Psychol. Measmt,* 9, 291–6.

TOLLEFSON, D. (1961) *Response to Humor in Relation to Other Measures of Personality.* Unpublished doctoral dissertation, University of Illinois.

TORRANCE, E. P. (1960) Educational achievement of the highly intelligent and the highly creative: eight partial replications of the Getzels–Jackson study (Research Memorandum BER-60-18). Minneapolis: Bureau of Educational Research, University of Minnesota.

TORRANCE, E. P. (1962) *Guiding Creative Talent.* Englewood Cliffs, N.J.: Prentice-Hall.

TORRANCE, E. P. (1963) *Education and the Creative Potential.* Minneapolis: University of Minnesota Press.

TORRANCE, E. P. (1965) *Rewarding Creative Behaviour.* Englewood Cliffs, N.J.: Prentice-Hall.

TORRANCE, E. P. and GOWAN, J. C. (1963) The reliability of the Minnesota tests of creative thinking (Research Memorandum

BER-63-4). Minneapolis: Bureau of Educational Research, University of Minnesota.

UNDERWOOD, B. J. (1952) An orientation for research on thinking. *Psychol. Rev.*, **59**, 209–20.

UZGIRIS, I. C. and HUNT, J. MCV. (1966) *An Instrument for Assessing Infant Psychological Development*. Urbana: Psychological Development Laboratory, University of Illinois (mimeographed progress report to be revised and published as *Ordinal Scales of Infant Psychological Development*).

UZGIRIS, I. C. and HUNT, MCV. (1967) *Ordinal Scales of Infant Psychological Development*. Sound cinemas depicting scales of (1) object permanence, (2) development of means, (3) imitation: gestural and vocal, (4) operational causality, (5) object relations in space, (6) development of schemas. Urbana: University of Illinois Motion Picture Service.

VAN ZELST, R. H. and KERR, W. A. (1954) Personality self-assessment of scientific and technical personnel. *J. Appl. Psychol.*, **38**, 145–7.

VANDENBERG, S. G. (1956) The hereditary abilities study. *Eugen. Quart.*, **3**, 94–9.

VANDENBERG, S. G. (1962a) Innate abilities. *Louisville Twin Study Research Report* No. 3. University of Louisville.

VANDENBERG, S. G. (1962b) The heredity abilities study: hereditary components in a psychological test battery. *Am J. Hum. Gen.*, **14**, 220–37.

VERGASON, G. A. (1964) Retention in retarded and normal subjects as a function of amount of original training. *Amer. J. Ment. Defic.*, **68**, 623–9.

VERNON, M. D. (1952) *A Further Study of Visual Perception*. Cambridge: Cambridge University Press.

VERNON, P. E. (1950) *The Structure of Human Abilities*. New York: Wiley.

VERNON, P. E. (1960) *Intelligence and Attainment Tests*. London: University of London Press.

VERNON, P. E. (1961) *The Structure of Human Abilities* (2nd ed.). London: Methuen.

VERNON, P. E. (1965a). Environmental handicaps and intellectual development, Parts I and II. *Brit. J. Educ. Psychol.*, **35**, 1–22.

VERNON, P. E. (1965b) Ability factors and environmental influences. *Amer. Psychol.*, **20**, 273–733.

VICKERY, B. C. (1965) *On Retrieval System Theory* (2nd ed.). London: Butterworth. pp. 39–40.

WALKER, A. E. and WEAVER, T. A., JR (1940) Ocular movements from the occipital lobe in the monkey. *J. Neurophysiol.*, 3, 353–7.

WALLACH, M. A. and KOGAN, N. (1965) *Modes of Thinking in Young Children: A Study of the Creativity-Intelligence Distinction.* New York: Holt, Rinehart & Winston.

WARBURTON, F. W. (1958) Review of *Social Class and Educational Opportunity* by Floud, Halsey and Martin. *Brit. J. Educ. Psychol.*, 28, 89.

WARBURTON, F. W. (1966a) The construction of the new British Intelligence Scale. *Bull. Brit. Psychol. Soc.*, 19, 59.

WARBURTON, F. W. (1966b) The construction of the new British Intelligence Scale: progress report. *Bull. Brit. Psychol. Soc.*, 19, 68–70.

WARBURTON, F. W. (1970) The British Intelligence Scale. In DOCKRELL, W. B. (ed.) *On Intelligence*, Chapter 4. London: Methuen.

WARD, J. and FITZPATRICK, T. F. (1970) New British Intelligence Scale: construction of logic items. *Research in Education*, 4, 10–23.

WARKANY, J. (1947) Etiology of congenital malformations. *Advanc. Paediat.*, 2, 1.

WATSON, J. B. (1913) Psychology as the behaviorist views it. *Psychol. Rev.*, 20, 158–77.

WATSON, J. B. (1914) *Behavior: An Introduction to Comparative Psychology.* New York: Holt, Rinehart & Winston.

WATSON, J. B. (1919) *Psychology from the Standpoint of a Behaviorist.* Philadelphia: Lippincott.

WATSON, J. B. (1924) *Behaviorism.* New York: Norton.

WATSON, J. B. (1928) *The Psychological Care of the Infant and Child.* York: Norton.

WATSON, J. B. and RAYNER, R. (1920) Conditioned emotional reactions. *J. Exp. Psychol.*, 3, 1–14.

WEAVER, H. E. and MADDEN, E. H. (1949) 'Direction' in problem solving. *J. Psychol.*, 27, 331–45.

WECHSLER, D. (1944) *The Measurement of Adult Intelligence.* Baltimore: Williams & Wilkins.

WECHSLER, D. (1949) *Wechsler Intelligence Scale for Children: Manual.* New York: Psychological Corp.

WECHSLER, D. (1958) *The Measurement and Appraisal of Adult Intelligence* (4th ed.). Baltimore: Williams and Wilkins.

WEINER, B. (1966) Effect of motivation on the availability and retrieval of memory traces. *Psychol. Bull.*, **65**, 24–37.

WEIR, M. W. and STEVENSON, H. W. (1959) The effect of verbalization in children's learning as a function of chronological age. *Child Develpm.*, **30**, 143–9.

WEISKRANZ, L. (1958) Sensory deprivation and the cat's optic nervous system. *Nature*, **181** (3), 47–105.

WEISS, A. P. (1925) *A Theoretical Basis of Human Behavior*. Columbus, Ohio: Adams.

WEISSKOPF-JOELSON, E. and ELISEO, T. S. (1961) An experimental study of the effectiveness of brainstorming. *J. Appl. Psychol.*, **45**, 45–9.

WELCH, L. (1945) Recombination of ideas in creative thinking. *J. Appl. Psychol.*, **30**, 638–43.

WERNER, H. (1961) *Comparative Psychology of Mental Development*. New York: Science Editions (originally published 1948).

WERTHEIMER, M. (1945) *Productive Thinking*. New York: Harper & Row.

WESLEY, E. L. (1953) Perseverative behavior in a concept-formation task as a function of manifest anxiety and rigidity. *J. Abnorm. Soc. Psychol.*, **48**, 129–34.

WESTCOTT, M. R. (1961) On the measurement of intuitive leaps. *Psychol. Rep.*, **9**, 267–74.

WESTCOTT, M. R. (1964) Empirical studies of intuition. In TAYLOR, C. W. (ed.) *Widening Horizons in Creativity*. New York: Wiley. pp. 34–53.

WHERRY, R. J. (1959) Hierarchical solution without rotation. *Psychometrika*, **24**, 45–51.

WHITE, R. W. (1959) Motivation reconsidered: the concept of competence. *Psychol. Rev.*, **66**, 297–333.

WICKELGREN, W. A. (1965) Acoustic similarity and intrusion errors in short-term memory. *J. Exp. Psychol.*, **70**, 102–8.

WIENER, N. (1948) *Cybernetics*. New York: Wiley.

WILSON, R. C., GUILFORD, J. P., CHRISTENSEN, P. R. and LEWIS, D. J. (1954) A factor-analytic study of creative-thinking abilities. *Psychometrika*, **19**, 297–311.

WIMPERIS, V. (1960) *The Unmarried Mother and her Child*. London: Allen & Unwin.

WISCHNER, G. J., BRAUN, H. W. and PATTON, R. A. (1962) Acquisitions and long-term retention of an object quality learning set by retarded children. *J. Comp. Physiol. Psychol.*, **55**, 518–23.

WISCHNER, G. J. and O'DONNELL, J. P. (1962) Concurrent learning set formation in normal and retarded children. *J. Comp. Physiol. Psychol.*, 55, 524–7.

WISEMAN, S. (1964) *Education and Environment.* Manchester: Manchester University Press.

WOLF, A. (1943) The dynamics of the selective inhibition of specific functions in neuroses. *Psychosomatic Medicine*, 5, 27–38.

WOODROW, H. (1946) The ability to learn. *Psychol. Rev.*, 53, 147–58.

WOODWORTH, R. S. (1918) *Dynamic Psychology.* New York: Columbia University Press.

WOODWORTH, R. S. (1938) *Experimental Psychology.* New York: Holt.

WOODWORTH, R. S. (1941) Heredity and environment: a critical survey of recently published material on twins and foster children. *Soc. Sci. Res. Council Bull.*, No. 47.

WOOLF, B. (1952) Appendix to REEVE, E. C. R. and WADDINGTON, C. H. (eds.) *Quantitative Inheritance.* London: H.M.S.O.

WYCKOFF, L. B., JR (1952) The role of observing responses in discrimination learning, Part I. *Psychol. Rev.*, 59, 431–42.

YAMAMOTO, K. (1964) Role of creative thinking and intelligence in high school achievement. *Psychol. Rec.*, 14, 783–9.

YNTEMA, D. B. and TRASK, F. P. (1963) Recall as a search process. *J. Verbal Learn. Verbal Behav.*, 2, 65–74.

YOUTZ, R. P. (1948) The relation between number of confirmations of one hypothesis and the speed of accepting a new and incompatible hypothesis. *Amer. Psychologist*, 3, 248–9.

ZEAMAN, D. and KAUFMAN, H. (1955) Individual differences and theory in a motor learning task. *Psychol. Monogr.*, 69.

Name Index

Subject Index